This book was donated
to honor
the birthday of

Katherine Lynn Schifani

by

David, Marian, Chris
and Rocky
February 21, 1997

DATE

MASTERING THE SKY

MASTERING THE SKY

A History of Aviation from Ancient Times to the Present

By

JAMES P. HARRISON

SARPEDON
New York

Published by
SARPEDON
166 Fifth Avenue
New York, NY 10010

ISBN 1-885119-23-2

Cataloging-in-Publication data available from the
Library of Congress.

10 9 8 7 6 5 4 3 2

MANUFACTURED IN THE UNITED STATES OF AMERICA

To all those who
love to fly.

Contents

Preface

A subject as vast as human flight is obviously impossible to cover thoroughly in one book. Any one of its many aspects, whether a comprehensive or specific history, or attempt to understand major engineering or aeronautical developments, would require many volumes and experts. My idea is to try to give some general knowledge of the history and principles of human flight in one volume by concentrating on the "wonder" of it, for surely the lifting and transporting through the air of enormous weights and numbers of people to distant places at previously unimaginable speeds and altitudes is one of the great miracles of our times. Some of the innumerable good stories and literature accompanying aviation's progress over the centuries can help to capture the astonishment of what has been achieved.

This is not a comprehensive history of aviation, therefore, but an inducement to appreciate its achievements in historical perspective. Only the most remarkable episodes can be mentioned, and many important developments will not be covered adequately, especially for later topics, including engineering and technological breakthroughs, the commercial revolution in the air, and the jet and space ages. In addition, the now-extensive history of air combat, which combines the most primal elements of human behavior with our subject, has not been covered here nearly in full. Still, the greatest stories and accomplishments should give some basic history of aviation, as well as of the times during which it evolved. In the process, I hope to capture some of the wonder of the achievement of flight, defining that simply as the conveyance of humans, and at times other bodies, through the air.

My own fascination with flight began with the common patterns of gaping at birds, flying kites, airport visits, and wartime model building. It was firmly fixed by brief experience as an Air Force pilot, with the accumulation of barely a thousand hours of flying, mostly in World War II vintage T-6s and B-25s. But that experience, a generation later, ultimately has returned me from the writing of politico-social history about distant places to my first adult enthusiasm.

The book will use American pilots' terminology most of the time for the statistics used. The problem is that centuries of transportation in diverse areas of the world have left widely different systems. Thus, U.S. pilots use knots or nautical miles passed for speeds, but miles for distances and pounds for weight, whereas most others use the metric system of kilometers for distances and kilograms for weights. There are at least three different measurements of the ton: that of the U.S. (short ton, 2000 lbs.), Britain's (long ton, 2240 lbs.), and the metric (1000 kilos, or 2204.6 lbs.). Except for Russia and the former Communist bloc, which use meters, all other countries measure altitude in feet, and measure time according to that of Greenwich mean (GMC) or Universal (UTC) time, coordinated, after 1972, with International Atomic Time (IAT).

Aviation vocabulary deserves some additional, initial reference. "Knots," for example, originated with the 17th-century practice of measuring ship speed by the rapidity with which "log lines," using knots tied at regular intervals, passed a given point. The word "cockpit" to designate the forward part of the airplane housing the pilot and flight instruments came into use at the beginning of World War I, presumably to highlight the vicious fighting then beginning. Shakespeare opened his play *King Henry the Fifth* (1599) with the query ". . . Can this cockpit hold the vasty fields of France?"—as if the popular sport could satirize the earlier fighting there. Later, several London theaters were termed "cockpits," but after 1914 the term was used almost exclusively in aviation. The distress call "Mayday," from the French (*venez*) *m'aider* (help me) came into widespread use everywhere after it was adopted by the International Radio and Telegraph Convention of 1927. The *Oxford English Dictionary* (Clarendon Press, 1989) does not supply as much information as it does for the above terms for the origins of calling the control column "joy stick." Perhaps, its location in older planes in front of the pilot precluded further explanation. As speeds and acceleration increased, the greater gravity forces exerted on pilots and passengers in turns and pull-ups, became known as "G" forces if constant, or "g" forces if accelerating. "Over" is used for message given and reply expected, and "out" to signify the end of a conversation. The word "roger," for "message received and understood," became standard aviation slang for "affirmative" by the postwar period, but its provenance when first used in 1927 is unknown to me.

A book as ambitious as this naturally owes gratitude to many people, as well as to the many great names of aviation mentioned in it. My first thanks go to my Air Force instructors, especially for the class of 56 J, Fred Kitts and W.S. Burgess, who nurtured the love of flying so well, and to my fellow students and aviators who have continued to manifest that love. I thank also among 56 J classmates, Milford "Dusty" Davis, who rose to general's rank, ultimately piloting F-111s, and John Hoek, who became an American Airlines captain, flying modern airliners. Other informants include former Marine F-4 pilot John M. Daly, former Air Force F-111 pilot Mitch Bowman, Air National Guard F-100 pilot Charles Jenkins, and F-16 pilot Steve Hicks.

Thanks are due the many airline people with whom I have flown, especially my informants among them. The latter include Air France Captain Jean Marie Van Deinse, who, with engineers Jean Roche and Paul Vitrich, introduced me to many flight aspects of the Boeing 747, as did Commandants Pierre Chanoine and Jacques Mims for the Concorde. My American informants with the airlines and elsewhere are too numerous to mention here, but I am sure they understand my appreciation.

Many thanks are also due librarians in diverse places, especially at Hunter College, City University of New York. Numerous colleagues and students there have also given needed support. Although I retired before the book's completion, much of *Mastering the Sky* was written while I was still teaching, and on two leaves of absence. Sarpedon publisher Steven Smith, editors Dunn Teal and Sam Southworth, and designer Elizabeth Van Itallie deserve full credit for the final shape of the book.

Personally, all the generations important to me have helped in ways they could not know: my father, with his desire to have flown in World War I, his poetry and tales of business in distant places; my mother, for her spirit, art work and stories of many voyages; my daughters, Constance, Claire, Eve, Olivia, Alicia, and their mothers, Joy and Chantal, for their strong support; and friends, Frances Gallagher, Andrew Blane, Michael Gasster, Joan Pfitzenmaier, Pat Falk, Vicki Ericson, Pierre Oberling, and many others, for their continuing interest.

All the above and more have supported innumerable errancies due in part to my obsession with the subject of aviation, but naturally, I bear all responsibility for its product.

MASTERING THE SKY

1

The Take-off of a 747 and Other Miracles

Here we go! The roar of the Boeing 747's four engines presses you back against your seat. You observe with increasing wonder the ever more rapidly passing scene. Weeds, trees, trucks, telephone poles, distant houses flash by.

Still faster, and in about thirty or so seconds, the pilots note the speed passing 120 knots and you're at the point of no return. There's no stopping now!

No problem. All is in order, and past 154 knots, close to a mile or so down the runway and less than a minute from starting to roll, the pilot tilts the nose skyward some seven degrees, and as the tail clears the ground at near 167 knots, more steeply to ten or more degrees. The sixteen main and two front wheels are retracted and the beautiful craft vaults upward at 2000 or more feet a minute!

How is that possible?

The giant machine, close to sixty-four feet high, tall as a five-story building, and almost as big as a football field, close to 232 feet long and 196 feet wide. It routinely lifts 400 or 500 passengers, with a capacity for the latest 400 model of 420 to 569.

It weighs up to 435 U.S. tons!

Yes, tons! That's 870,000 pounds or 394,557 kilos, if you prefer. Have you recently tried to lift your few pounds—relatively speaking, of course—even a few feet up a steep incline? Moreover, one would think there is nothing out there where the airplane is climbing. A recent thirty-minute effort on the ground by the author, for example, involved a climb of only about 800 feet from Talloires, 447 meters high in French Savoy, to St. Germain Abbey at 695 meters. It left me panting and soaked in sweat, and made all the more impressive the next day's "sprint" of 12,365 feet up Mont Blanc (4807 meters) by a Swiss alpinist from Chamonix

(1037 meters) in three hours and thirty-eight minutes. But how much more impressive still is the 747's pushing 250 or more tons that high in a few minutes!

That is the most astonishing aspect of the wonder of flight, the seemingly effortless lifting and soaring of vast weights at great speeds. To repeat the question: how is it possible? This book will try to give some explanation of that and other miracles of contemporary flight as it explores the long history of arriving at those answers.

Not unnaturally, since the dawn of life, most people did not believe in human flight, reasoning, "if God had meant humans to fly, He would have given them wings." But not all have thought that way. For fly man has, and from ancient times—at least in spirit.

Legendary dreamers and visionaries, from Daedalus and Icarus to an emperor of China and an English king, to Africans fleeing slavery, to imaginary Peter Pans—countless souls, even if a tiny minority at any one time—have sought to realize the wish of the psalmist (55:6): "Oh that I had wings like a dove, for then I would fly away and be at rest." Why could not one soar like Shelley's skylark, "Hail to thee blithe spirit . . . higher still and higher from the earth thou springest." And Wordsworth's lark cried: "Up with me! Up with me into the sky."

Of course, it took the scientific and industrial revolutions to produce the knowledge, structures, and sources of power capable of mastering the mysteries and stresses of flight. And by then, the same human will which drove those revolutionary advances in information and technique was being turned to the problems of flying. After all, the December 17, 1903 flights of the Wright brothers seemed the perfect expression of the prevailing idea before World War I: "Every day, in every way, things are getting better and better." Many aviators even believed the airplane would make war too horrible to undertake.

Unfortunately, in the terrible but wondrous twentieth century, all too often the miraculous breakthroughs that made aviation take off so brilliantly have been used to the end of destroying designated "enemies." Already in reaction to the carnage of World War I, Orville Wright could declare, "What a dream it was, what a nightmare it has become."

And clearly, the very development of the wondrous soaring technologies was greatly accelerated by the two great and numerous lesser wars of the century. The horrific role of airpower in those wars is well known, and it remains to be seen whether man's use of aviation and space technology will lead him, like Icarus, to a last fatal flight, or like Daedalus, to the shores of more promising lands.

Since World War II, and especially since the end of the cold war, the promise and the dream have seemed uppermost for the majority of the world's peoples, although to be sure, that offers no consolation to the literally millions of wartime victims of airborne weapons, in Korea, Vietnam, Africa, Afghanistan, Iraq, Lebanon, Bosnia, Chechnya, and elsewhere.

But far greater numbers—some 1.116 billion a year by 1992, of whom more than a third, over 528 million in 1994, were Americans—have taken to the air on trips of a rapidity and distance never imagined in earlier years, creating a far-reaching revolution in the lives of hundreds of millions of travelers.

Aviation, defined here very generally as any sustained conveyance of humans into the air, also has seemed to symbolize other great human events—from the first persons to rise in balloons over France in 1783, which preceded by six years history's largest revolutionary rising of the masses to that time, to the first engine-powered airplane flights preceding World War I, to the intercontinental, speed, and altitude records set before World War II, to the world-spanning flights and rocket-powered space launches, demonstrating the establishment of the global communications and economies as well as the state-of-the art technologies of contemporary times.

Most of all, and it is the theme of this book, there has been the wonder of it all— whether of observing from the ground the great soaring arcs of the new winged creatures, or of being awed as pilot or passenger by the power of exploding jets of air pushing vast weights of machine, people, and matériel high in the air at breathtaking speeds.

And once into the air, flying machines stun us with beauty. The big jets seem all the more like "flying cathedrals" than earlier planes of that name. Like great works of art floating through the sky, their contrails at times seem like gossamer tapestries high in the sky. There are few more thrilling sights than watching the launching of space ships, or more dramatic ones than seeing the banks and turns of aerial acrobatics, or high-speed runs at low altitude, or through mountain canyons. Watched from cockpit or window, the whisking by of wisps of vapor and cloud gives the same hypnotic effect as looking at waterfalls or pounding surf.

Long before the jets, men rhapsodized over "sailing through the air with the greatest of ease." Over a year before the Wright brothers "took off," but over a century after the first balloon flights, Georges Besançon, the founder and editor of the first successful aviation journal *L'Aérophile*, wrote in February 1902:

> aeronautics confers beauty and grandeur, combining art and science for those who devote themselves to it. . . . The aeronaut, free in space, sailing in the infinite, loses himself in the immense undulations of nature. He climbs, he rises, he soars, he reigns, he hurtles the proud vault of the azure sky . . .

Another balloonist, the English pioneer Gertrude Bacon had thrilled in November, 1899:

> No one but we three, in all the world saw that wonderful scene that morning . . . that silent ocean of filmy, tossing billows, all silvered in the moonlight, stretching wave after snowy wave, in dark blue shadows, in their depths, to the limitless horizon— gleaming, ghostly pure—of heaven itself.

A 1911 ad for a training school for powered fixed-wing flight proclaimed:

> To become a companion of the birds; to search the skies and from great heights to look down upon the flattened earth while his monoplane bears him where his whim directs; to realize, to the throbbing of the motor and song of the propeller, the dream of men throughout the centuries; all of these and more are what flying means. And there are none, except the mentally or the physically unfit, who may not taste its delights.

In 1936, the British poet and World War I pilot Cecil Day Lewis enthused: "I sailed on for a time, alone in the wonderful skies, as happy as I have ever been or ever shall be, I suppose in this life . . ." Just before his death in 1944, French writer and aviator, Antoine de Saint-Exupéry, wrote from his height of 2,150 feet in a P-38 over German-occupied France:

> beneath my cloud bank the world is not black . . . it is blue.

Marvelously blue. Twilight has come and all the plain is blue . . .
On the left I see great slabs of light among the showers. They are
like panes in a cathedral window. Almost within reach . . .

He compared himself to the fairy-tale knight, who rides "in the blue of
evening toward my castle of flame."

Then, in a 1941 poem, not long before his death also in World II,
American fighter pilot John Gillispie Magee spoke of slipping "the surly
bonds of earth" to enter "the high untrespassed sanctity of space," where
"[I] put out my hand and touched the face of God." The full poem,
"High Flight," read:

> Oh! I have slipped the surly bonds of earth
>   and danced the skies on laughter-silvered wings.
> Sunward I've climbed, and joined the tumbling mirth
>   of sun-split clouds—and done a hundred things
> You have not dreamed of—wheeled and soared and swung
>   high in the sunlit silence. Hov'ring there
> I've chased the shouting wind along and flung
>   my eager craft through footless halls of air.
> Up, up the long, delirious burning blue
>   I've topped the wing-swept heights with easy grace
> Where never lark, or even eagle flew—
>   and, while with silent lifting mind I've tried
> The high untrespassed sanctity of space,
>   put out my hand and touched the face of God.

It is perhaps appropriate that one of the best descriptions of "hope"
as the essence of the wonder of flight was given by a Vietnamese, the people, including herself, who suffered more from air weapons than any other
in history. More than seven million tons of bombs, or over three times the
tonnage of all World War II, were dropped on that relatively small country and parts of neighboring Cambodia and Laos—or on far less than one
tenth of the territory of the United States. Describing her first flight as a
young woman from Danang to Saigon at the height of the war in the
1960s, Le Ly Hayslip wrote:

For me, however, the flight was much more than a thrilling ride.
When we left the ground and banked gently over the ocean, it

was as if I were seeing my homeland for the very first time—taking it all in at a glance like God in heaven—and I felt my first true sense of peace. The pale sky seemed infinite and I was climbing toward it like a celestial spirit. The shiny blue ocean with its ribbons of surf, the patchwork of paddies and dusty lots and lumpy green hills all grew smaller. . . . In those few moments I soared above and beyond all the tragedies I had known. That wonderful sense of climbing above and leaving things behind would come to me again and again in my life and I would train myself to listen for its secrets. Although I did not realize it at the time, that flight and those feelings brought with them something else, something I had never experienced in [my ancestral village of] Ky La, something even my wonderful parents—who knew everything about life and duty—could not, for their own heavy burdens, give me: the simple feeling of hope.

The wonder of aviation has inspired countless other observations, from humorist Dave Barry's jest, "Nah . . . nothing that heavy can fly . . . It's probably going to crash and you're going to die," to a 1927 poem's opposite point, commemorating Lindbergh's memorable flight of that year from New York to Paris:

I cannot die
Who have flown as eagles fly
Into the blue unknown.
I have throttled oblivion.
I have fathomed the myths
Of space and time . . .
I am one with immensity.
I cannot die.

Lindbergh himself later spoke of "what freedom lies in flying, what Godlike power it gives to men. . . . I lose all consciousness in this strong unmortal space crowded with beauty, pierced with danger." In 1953, he put it a bit more cynically:

I began to feel that I lived on a higher plane than the skeptics of the ground; one that was richer because of its very association with the element of danger they dreaded, because I was freer of the earth to which they were bound. In flying, I tasted a wine of the gods, of which they could know nothing.

Perhaps more than any other activity also, aviation inspires thoughts about the relativity of things. There are no more stupefying images than those of astronauts circling the earth in less than two hours, at over 17,000 miles an hour! Yet as veteran astronaut Michael Collins observed, "the ground goes by the window at about the same rate as in an airliner" because of being normally 150 to 200 or so miles up in "a fairyland, far above the squalor of the world below." He cited another astronaut, Joe Allen, stating, "It's more like being aboard a ship than in an aircraft—just floating along at 17,000 miles an hour." The first American to go into space, on February 20, 1962, future Senator John H. Glenn, Jr., told Congress six days later: "There seemed to be little sensation of speed although the craft was traveling at about 5 miles per second—a speed that I, too, find difficult to comprehend . . ."

According to a recent book on the Concorde, in that aircraft ten or eleven miles up, flying at Mach 2,* or twice the speed of sound (about 1172 knots or 1350 mph), "faster than a rifle bullet leaving its barrel . . . there is no sense of movement. No rushing of air . . . We seem to be stopped, fixed in the stratosphere . . ." Still, any passenger wishing proof of his plane's velocity can fix a dot on the window against the ground far below, or against a nearby cloud. He might see a big field or road that would take ten or twenty minutes to walk, but which is traced by his dot in several seconds.

For observers on earth, too, the seemingly motionless paths of distant airplanes is a disconcerting demonstration of relativity. To the child, or for that matter the drinker in a rooftop bar, the toy or person moving across the room in several seconds seems to be going faster than the image of an airplane taking several minutes to disappear from view because of its angle and distance, even though in fact it may be moving four or so miles a minute.

*Ernst Mach (1838–1916) was an Austrian physicist who determined the speed of sound. His name is now universally used for aircraft speeds approaching or passing the speed of sound, about 661.7 knots (762 mph, 1223 kph) at sea level on a normal day of 59 Fahrenheit (15 Celsius). The mach number falls with the temperature, and is therefore lower at altitude; for example, about 576.6 knots (664 mph, 1068 kph) at and above 35,000 feet, where a normal temperature is –65.8 Fahrenheit (–54.3 Celsius).

But the greatest excitement, of course, is in the air.

Imagine a scene like the one written by U.S. Air Force pilot Jack Broughton, describing a near miss he had on a 1951 mission in Korea, flying a Republic F-84 Thunderjet:

> The turbulence was really bad. . . . I kept bouncing around, over-controlling my machine, and despite the fact that I knew I should have aborted the mission I didn't. Instead I pressed in a lot closer than I should have. . . . The ground was coming up like crazy. Despite having bottomed out in the dive with my nose coming up, the aircraft was still sinking. I was way too close to the ground. But all you can do when it gets like that is pull back on the stick a little harder, but not too hard [or it would have stalled]. It all went by sort of like a slow-motion fight scene. There was no sense of panic as the terrifying panorama filled my eyes. . . . I eased in that little extra pull that makes so much dif-ference when you're sinking at 450 miles per hour . . . earth, rocks, and rocket debris hits my canopy and wings. Next came a spray of mud and rice paddy slop over my left wing and left canopy. I had flown through my own rocket blast. The nose struggled up and I had not only missed my target, I had only avoided auguring in by a few feet . . .

That literally would have been what is called "buying the farm" in lingo derived from pilots plowing into some out-of-the-way field. That kind of "terrifying panorama" is far more likely to occur in military aviation or in aerobatics.

But even the now "normal" flight, certainly in jet aircraft like the mil-itary fighters, or the huge Boeing 747 and 777, or the supersonic Concorde, not to speak of the hypersonic and other future airplanes, is filled with wonders. To return to our opening query: How can one explain the seemingly effortless lifting of the great jets weighing hundreds of tons to altitudes higher than Mount Everest at great speeds in a matter of minutes?

When the over 250 tons of a fully loaded 747-400 rises into the air a mile or so down the runway, about forty five or fifty seconds from beginning to roll at a speed of some 170 knots per hour, its four engines—most commonly the Pratt-Whitney JT9 or General Electric

CF6, are producing close to 58,000 pounds of thrust each, or 232,000 pounds of thrust at full power. Once the sixteen enormous (1.1 meters high, 90 kilos each, in four groups of four) main wheels and two smaller front wheels are retracted, the ship is soaring upward at over 2000 feet a minute. On reaching 1500 feet of altitude, the flaps are raised and the speed increased to 250 knots, and above 10,000 feet over populous areas, or over water, to 300 or more knots per hour. The rate of climb reduces to about 1000 feet a minute with declining air pressures. But the cruising altitude of about 35,000 feet is reached in about half an hour, and there, fuel consumption is reduced to ten or twelve tons an hour.

Thus, the trick of such incredible uplifts of people and machine is accomplished by a formidable combination of high motor power and aerodynamic structures capable of great lift. The engines, providing thrust equal to at least a fourth of the plane's weight, produce the speed and rush of air necessary to reduce the pressure on the tops of the wings and other surfaces sufficiently to create the necessary lift, by in effect pushing the onrushing air downward. Since "to every action there is a reaction," the air pushed down lifts the plane while that driven backward by jet or propellor drives the aircraft forward. And voilà! The plane, enormous as it is, rises "effortlessly" into the air.

The forces of lift, thrust, and drag created by speeding aircraft can be appreciated in comparison to the force of storm winds, which if over about 100 mph can not only blow you over, but peel walls off buildings and send cars flying. That is because air, seemingly empty, in fact is filled with literally billions of atoms, half of them below 18,000 feet. At sea level, it weighs on average 14.7 pounds per square inch, the equivalent weight of 29.92 inches, or 760 millimeters (hg) or 1013.25 millibars (hectopascals, hpa) of mercury, which are used for barometric indications.

For smaller advanced aircraft, the engines operate virtually as rockets, accelerating some contemporary fighters straight up! A recent record saw two engines of 23,930 pounds thrust each carry the twenty-ton McDonnell-Douglas F-15 to 65,616 feet (20,000 meters), or over twice the height of Mount Everest, in two minutes, three seconds. An advanced Air Force trainer, the Northrop T-38, already in production by the 1960s, reached 39,272 feet (12,000 meters) in a minute and a half, and the Mirage 2000 reaches Mach 2 at 49,215 feet (15,000 meters) in less than five minutes. New navy jets, like the McDonnell Douglas F-18, are catapulted to over 150 mph and take off from a carrier in under two seconds.

They then climb initially at 50,000 feet a minute! The General Dynamics F-16 also is able to go into vertical climb, as can the Mirage 2000, the MIG-29, and others.

Comparable figures for the Mach 2 Concorde (maximum weight 185 tons, normally about 150) are some 152,200 pounds of thrust at full power, generated by four Rolls-Royce/SNECMA Olympus 593 "simple flux" engines, which in about thirty seconds push the plane to take-off and initial climb (V-2) at 222 knots, 1500 or so meters (4921.5 feet) down the runway. The engines were pioneered by Bristol Siddeley, a firm bought by Rolls-Royce in 1966. The point of no return (V-1) at 154 knots, and nose-up (V-R) at 196 knots, long passed, the incredible machine reaches 255 knots at 2400 feet of altitude only one minute and twelve seconds after lift-off. By then it has consumed more than one of its ninety six tons (95,680 kgs, or 26,400 gallons) of fuel, stored for the transatlantic crossing. Cutting its afterburners and holding to 280 knots for noise control to six or seven, or ten thousand feet, depending on the locale, the aircraft then accelerates to 400 knots at an angle of attack of twenty degrees with a 3000-feet-a-minute climb (or 7000 if empty, even 10,000 with afterburners).

Once over the ocean, the beautiful craft accelerates past Mach 1 and reaches 53,000 feet and Mach 2 (2150 kph, 1335 mph; maximum speed Mach 2.02) in twenty minutes, usually climbing to 57,000 or 59,000 feet, 10,000 or 20,000 feet higher than subsonic planes for still less air resistance and maximum engine efficiency. Several hours later, close to a hundred (maximum 128) passengers have reached their destination, a world and many time zones away!

Other astonishing aspects of a Concorde flight include the fact that it shifts close to a third of its fuel to the rear as it passes supersonic speed in order to keep the nose up, as the aerodynamic pressures in the trans-sonic zone force the nose down without a shift in the center of gravity. The temperature differences at such speeds and altitudes are also most impressive. Temperatures fall with altitude about three degrees Fahrenheit every thousand feet, most dramatically in equatorial zones, and reach about minus 65 Fahrenheit (54 Celsius) in the stratosphere by 36,500 feet before rising slightly after that. Yet the friction caused by the high-speed air flow heats leading surfaces of the Concorde to 302 Fahrenheit (150 Celsius), and other surfaces to some 200 Fahrenheit (120 Celsius). In other words, it is over 130 Fahrenheit colder outside than inside and over

300 degrees hotter on the leading surfaces of the aircraft facing the greatest air friction. For still faster aircraft, including planned new supersonic airliners, more heat-resistant metals such as stainless steel and titanium rather than the mostly aluminum alloys of the Concorde are required for the over 600-degree temperatures at Mach 3. On the Concorde, multiple layers reduce the already great temperatures at Mach 2 to the warmth passengers can feel on the side windows. As the engines require steady air flows and temperatures, a system of valves and flaps keeps those constant.

Another remarkable feature of the plane is the shifting of the nose downward, below about 260 knots airspeed, some five degrees for takeoff and up to thirteen (normally eleven) degrees for landing, allowing the pilots to see their glide path adequately despite the steep ascents and descents. The recommended glide angle for most other jets is three degrees (the instrument landing or ILS glide slope), which gives speeds of one third over stall, and descents of 500–700 feet a minute. Yet, despite all these remarkably complicated features, the Concorde, which passed 193,300 hours of flight by 1996, has had no fatal accidents to date.

The Concorde touches down at 162 or so knots, and the 747 at about 145 knots. With the Boeing 747's lower cruising speed at 0.84 mach, the temperature differences between outside air and surfaces are some seventy degrees Celsius, or about two thirds those of the Concorde. An impressive feature of the 747 is that its 195-foot, 8-inch-wide wings are designed to move up and down some twenty nine feet at the tips to give the flexibility to deal with the effects of air turbulence on its giant lifting surfaces.

Aircraft such as the Boeing 747 and Concorde understandably burn enormous quantities of fuel. The 747, for example, consumes some 70 or 80 tons of its 143-ton, even 160-ton (according to model) capacity between New York and London, depending mostly on the direction and force of the wind. Qantas Air's 747s burn up to 156 tons of fuel on flights of 14 hours, 40 minutes between Sydney and Los Angeles. At take-off power, the 747 is burning fuel at a rate of up to 32 tons an hour, which is reduced to about 11 tons or less an hour, or some 3000 gallons an hour, at cruise using 20 percent or so of the available thrust. That is almost six gallons a mile! The Concorde burns 26 tons an hour on take-off, and 18 tons an hour of fuel at cruise. A typical flight of a DC-9 from Washington, D.C. to St. Louis burned 10,500 of its 21,000-pound capacity of fuel, or about 100 pounds a minute. Fuel costs make up about a third of airlines' operational costs.

By contrast, Lindbergh's famous May 20, 1927 flight from New York to Paris burned less than 400 gallons, or about a ton, and in May 1919 the first transatlantic flight of a two-engined craft burned about 870 gallons, or almost three tons (5829 pounds). In 1913, the first crossing of the Mediterranean from France to Africa left pilot Roland Garros with only one gallon of the fifty-five he started with. At the other extreme, the NASA shuttle consumes up to 800 tons of liquid oxygen and hydrogen fuel per flight, achieving some 2.5 million pounds of thrust at lift-off. The Saturn V rockets, after 1968, consumed 3000 gallons of fuel, or some 15 tons, per second at lift-off, producing up to 7.6 million pounds of thrust for the Apollo space ships that went to the moon!

Such dry facts. But what a miracle!

How could such astonishing flights, experienced every day by countless travelers, have come about? It is the aim of this book to explore that and other questions, stressing always the wonder of it all, through the history of aviation, primarily in the twentieth century.

2

The Age-Old Dream

The ancient myths and the great religions reveal to us over and over again man's dream to escape the bonds of earth, whether to flee the enemy or to demonstrate power or saintliness. But as we near the twenty-first century, it is astonishing to recall that the first realization of those dreams in a powered, fixed-wing aircraft under the pilot's control took place less than a century ago.

There were many predecessors to the Wright brothers, however. There were those who attempted to glide from towers or float in balloons, or by a mad beating of artificial wings to rise into the air by ornithopter flight. They attempted to emulate the dreamers and artists whose "images of ascension permeate the whole of Western culture," following the Genesis account of God's creation on the fifth day, of "fowl that may fly above the earth in the open firmament of Heaven."

Therefore, before exploring in more detail the extraordinary aerial phenomena of the twentieth century, let us briefly turn to some of the aviation forerunners of previous times. They too had that "right stuff," but they lacked the knowledge, equipment, and resources to accomplish their dreams.

The ancient peoples commonly used images of flying beasts, or half-bird, half-animal, such as the flying horse, Pegasus; or centaurs with humans on winged horses; or eagle-headed women, winged dogs, and birds with human heads. Or they depicted images of half-bird, half-person such as the Hindu god Garuda, or griffins and dragons, uniting air (eagle and hawk) and earth (lion and snake). A legend of the Babylonian king Nimrod told of using flying vessels drawn by cranes and herons, and some 5000 years ago tablets inscribed at Nineveh relate how a certain shepherd named Etana flew to the heavens. The tomb of Rameses II (d. 1224 B.C.) shows the Pharaoh of the Exodus standing on a tower with two wings outspread, as if about to fly. Another myth described how, also about 1200 B.C., a king of Persia was said to be borne by four eagles to the sky. The Persian god, Ahura Mazda, came to be represented as a "winged deity," and a striking winged sphinx was produced by the Urartu empire in what became Armenia about 700 B.C.

The Hindu epic *Rig Veda* dramatically states a common ancient belief: "He who knows, has wings." The other great ancient Indian classic, the *Ramayana*, relates stories of the monkey king Hanoman sailing through the air, as would other texts in later Asian literature, notably the great sixteenth-century Chinese novel, *Record of a Journey to the West*. It relates the astonishing derring-do of the magic monkey who assisted the famous seventh-century Buddhist Hsuan-tsang on his sixteen years of travel and study between China and India. As will be discussed in greater detail below, Taoist myths of that time commonly spoke of "immortals" riding "cloud chariots drawn by white deer," and the great T'ang Dynasty poet Li Po spoke of going "in a chariot born aloft swifter than wind or lightning by the phoenix and dragon." Indian Yogis and gurus have practiced "yogic flying" and "astral trips" from ancient times, and worship the "great solar bird" that carries the Hindu God Vishnu, often depicted as half-elephant, half-human. In Africa, a great warrior, Kibaga, flew over his enemies to bomb them, prior to being shot down himself. In South America, ancient statues depict human flyers—inspiring speculation, as by Erich Von Däniken in *Chariots of the Gods*, that the earth had been visited in earliest times by space ships from other planets.

The great religions not unnaturally placed their divinities in the heavens, Christian angels, winged Greek gods, and Asian flying guardians linking man with the great beyond. And the myths spoke of heroes being carried into the sky by flying beast or bird, or like Peter Pan, they rose into the air by their own magical powers.

The story of the flight of Daedalus and Icarus best describes that vision in the Western tradition. It tells how Daedalus and his son, Icarus, escaped through the air after being imprisoned by the legendary King Minos on the island of Crete. Daedalus, a master craftsman, made wings of wax and feathers, and flew with his son out of captivity into the freedom of the Greek skies. But Icarus, after passing the smaller islands of Samos and Delos, disobeyed his father's orders and climbed too close to the sun, which melted the wax fastenings and caused his plunge to become the world's first noted pilot fatality.

On April 23, 1988, the Greek cycling champion Kanellos Kanellopoulos, pedaling an American-built, human-powered plane, the "Daedalus," succeeded in traversing the record seventy-four miles from Crete to just off the island of Santorini in three hours and fifty-four minutes, to emulate a good part of the successful section of that 3500-year-old story. It had become the classic myth of the air, and poetically illustrated what Plato called "'the natural function of the wing . . . to soar upwards and carry that which is heavy up to the place where dwells the race of gods." The ancient Greeks made images of wings and flight central to their civilization, giving their gods the power of flight. As Clive Hart stated:

> By classical times, the Greeks had naturalized a large number of gods, demigods, and mythological creatures that were clearly and even assertively winged. The first wings of importance appear in the animal friezes on early Corinthian vases and on their Athenian progeny.

Neptune, the god of the sea, was later cited as a "winged personification of the spirit of flight" in the seaplane races after 1913, as, more frequently, was the winged horse Pegasus. The splendid "Victory of Samothrace," celebrating a 306 B.C. naval victory over an Egyptian fleet, is one of the most famous of all statues, its wings rising majestically skyward. In the second century A.D., Lucian of Samosata (Syria) wrote of a sailing ship being carried to the moon by a whirlwind. Passages in the Bible spoke also spoke of flight. For example, Isaiah 6:1–8 states: "In the year that King Uzziah died I saw the Lord sitting upon a throne, high and lifted up. . . . Above him stood the seraphim. Each had six wings . . . and with two He flew . . ." Apparently, therefore, the wing closely followed the wheel in the ancient imagination of locomotion.

There were stories that the people of legendary Atlantis had mastered flight, and others of Asians who could travel by "smoke," leading to speculation about hot-air balloons. In the midst of the Peloponnesian War in 414 B.C., Aristophanes wrote *The Birds*, imagining the growing of wings to master the Spartans and other enemies. In the fourth century B.C., the Greek Archytas of Tarentum, in the south of Italy, is said to have flown a steam-propelled wooden model of a pigeon; and a little later there were projects to use magnets and other devices to fly model birds. A century

later, Archimedes wrote a treatise entitled "On Floating Bodies," prefig-
uring by 2000 years the first known ascent of man in balloons. After
observing his body's buoyancy in a public bath, he wrote that if an object
is put into a fluid, it is buoyed upward by a force equal to the difference
between its weight and the weight it displaces. In addition to propound-
ing this basic principle of balloon flight, he is also said to have spoken of
a type of propulsion described as the first jet.

   The great conquests of Alexander, before his death in 323 B.C., were
explained in medieval prints as facilitated by airborne chariots pulled by
griffins or by fabulous creatures with eagle's heads and wings and bodies
of lions. In Roman times, there were numerous reports of men "simulat-
ing the flights of birds and rising from the ground," of prisoners being
equipped with wings to try to escape wild beasts released at circuses, and
of others being thrown to their fates to appease the gods and avert evil.
Suetonius spoke of the fatal fall of a person trying to fly before the emper-
or Nero about 60 A.D. More famously, six years later, Simon the Magician
attempted a flight before the same emperor and a large crowd said to
include Saint Peter. As Simon had been accused of Christian heresy, Peter
was said to interpret the attempt as the work of the devil, and to have led
prayers for its failure. Another story reported Simon's death trying to
emulate Christ by burying himself, expecting resurrection in three days.
The outcome of the attempted flight can only be imagined, but the effort
has been immortalized in art works such as the sculptures in the
Cathedral of Autun in Burgundy, France.

   By the third century A.D., the Romans employed a sort of wind-sock
banner, or "draco," that resembled a flying dragon. When billowed in the
wind, it was supposed to inspire troops and frighten the enemy. The
famous Arthurian magician, Merlin, and other medieval people are also
said to have placed lighted torches in a dragon's mouth to cause it to "emit
fire and smoke." Whatever their military effectiveness, the dragons apparently played a significant role in fostering an awareness of air currents and
their effects. Northern legends imagined Valkyries zooming about with
"swan plumage," one story describing how a certain "Wayland, the smith"
learned the skill to defeat his enemy and fly away to safety. To the south,
the winged lion of Venice came to symbolize the first post-Roman
Mediterranean empire. Chinese records speak of human attempts to sail
through the air long before the first millennium B.C. when they began to
practice the flying of kites, their greatest contribution to the history of

aeronautics. Two accounts before our era describe the supposedly successful escape of the legendary emperor Shun in 2254 B.C. from a granary
tower that had been set aflame in an attempt on his life. Having been
instructed in the art of "flying like a bird," he devised parachute-like
wings made out of large conical hats, or, according to the second account,
umbrellas, and descended safely to the ground to escape the assassination
plot. Another account describes the construction of a flying chariot for
the founder of the first proven Chinese dynasty in the eighteenth century
B.C.

A well-known myth, still celebrated at the time of the Chinese
Harvest festival in mid-August (the fifteenth day of the seventh moon of
the lunar calendar), speaks of the symbol of femininity, the beautiful
Chang-O, stealing a drug of immortality about 4000 years ago and soar
ing to the moon, where she was condemned to stay as punishment for her
theft.

Later but still very early Chinese accounts speak of "aerial carriages,
which with a fair wind traveled great distances." The Taoists claimed to
develop elixirs which would enable Ch'in and Han dynasty notables to fly
to eternal life on the "isles of the blest." About the time of Christ, there
was even a proposal for using aerial intelligence on the Hunnish enemies
of the short-lived Wang Mang Dynasty. The history reported:

> . . . one man said that he could fly a thousand li [about 333
> miles] in a day and spy out [movements of the] Huns. [Wang]
> Mang tested him without delay. . . . He flew a distance of sev-
> eral hundred paces, and then fell to the ground . . . [and the]
> methods could not be used.

About three centuries later another account cited a Taoist master who
stated:

> . . . some have made flying cars with wood from the inner part
> of the jujube tree, using ox leather [straps] fastened to returning
> blades so as to set the machine in motion. Others have had the
> idea of making five snakes, six dragons, and three oxen to meet
> the "hard wind" and ride on it, not stopping until they have
> risen to a height of forty li . . . As the teacher [Chuang Tzu] says,
> "the kite . . . flies higher and higher spirally, and then only needs

to stretch its two wings, beating the air no more, in order to go forward by itself." This is because it starts gliding [literally, riding] on the hard wind.

Buddhist worthies (*arhats*), like ancient Indian seers (*rishis*), were said to enjoy the power of flight. But Chinese alchemy especially featured flying by its heroes, the "immortals," who were termed "feathered scholars." After years of yoga and the discovery of various elixirs, they supposedly could "pass instantly from one place to another," to the spiritual world or the underworld.

The invention of gunpowder by the ninth century A.D., and the rocket two centuries later, also became fundamental Chinese contributions to aerodynamic knowledge. Black powder-propelled "fire arrows" were used in battle against the Mongols in 1232, and the Mongols quickly mastered the new weapons, demonstrating them as far west as Hungary in 1241. There were stories such as that of a certain fifteenth-century official who designed a first rocket flight, hooking forty-seven rockets to two large kites with a saddle linking them. Mounting it, he caused the rockets to be lit, and predictably blasted off to "his ancestors." Birds were already used to symbolize the prestigious civil officials—in contrast to the lion, bear, and other animal insignia used by the military. There was also the legend that the Chinese invented the balloon around 1300.

But the most important Chinese aerial invention was the kite. Aviation historian Charles Gibbs-Smith called it "the archetypal aeroplane wing, as well as the world's first aerial vehicle." The philosopher Mo Tzu (fifth century B.C.) reportedly constructed a wooden kite which "could indeed fly, but after one day's trial it was wrecked." An early report of a kite was given by a general in 206 B.C., shortly after the fall of the first Ch'in Dynasty. He described getting intelligence on a city under siege by flying a kite over it and then measuring the length of its string. Kite flying continued to be a popular pastime, and there were innumerable kite stories, as well as reports of the first bombs hooked to kites.

By the eighth and ninth centuries, Islamic peoples were flying the kite, and kites arrived in Europe by the 14th century; an illustration of one from 1326 shows a tethered kite carrying a fire bomb over a fortified city. *The Arabian Nights Entertainments* (10th to 15th centuries), on one of the thousand and one nights, recounts the destruction of the ship of Sinbad the sailor by a rock-carrying bird, perhaps the earliest speculation about aerial bombardment. Other *Nights'* tales describe magic carpets that carried passengers like some hovercrafts, as well as frequent ascents on flying horses. The Moslems also repeated stories of the biblical ladder to Heaven and of Mohammed's flight from Mecca to Jerusalem on a magic beast.

Medieval Western travelers brought word back of these Asian aerial tales. The 14th-century *Travels of Sir John Mandeville* spoke of griffins carrying a cavalier and his horse. The slightly earlier Marco Polo had far more readers in later centuries about the marvels of Cathay. At one point he described the lifting of a wicker frame in a gale, by

> some fool or someone who is drunk—for no one in his right sense would expose himself to so much risk. . . . The wind lifts it and carries it aloft, while the men hold it by hanging on to the cable . . .

A more reliable account may have been given by the French ambassador to Siam in 1688. He described an acrobat, who "leap'd from the hoop, supporting himself only by two umbrellas . . . the wind carry'd him accidentally sometimes to the ground, sometimes on trees or houses, and sometimes into the river." In neighboring Cambodia, paper hot-air balloons and flying lanterns attracted increasing attention, while kite-flying celebrations and contests became dominant expressions of Japanese and Indian social life.

In west Asia in the mid-third century, a Persian architect was said to escape Daedalus-style from his prison tower by constructing wings and jumping. "Driven by the wind, he rose into the air and landed unscathed at a safe place . . ." In 1010, the Persian poet Firdusi spoke of a throne being pulled to the moon by eagles.

There were similar Moslem efforts in Europe. About 852, an Arab attempted a leaping flight at Córdoba, Spain, with enough cloth in his cloak to balloon and break his fall, preventing serious injury. Then, about 875 A.D. in Andalucia, a Moorish doctor attached wings and feathers. He "flew to a considerable distance, as if he had been a bird, but in alighting again on the place where he had started, his back was very much hurt." Still another account made no claims for success at all. It described the leap of a Turkish lexicographer from the mosque roof at Nisabur shortly after 1000:

Perhaps in a fit of madness, he stood on the roof of the mosque and addressed the people, claiming that he would astonish posterity with a deed never before performed. Having attached two large wooden wings to his body, he then threw himself into the air only to fall immediately to the ground where he died instantly.

Undiscouraged, a Moslem Turkish birdman attempted another jump in the leading city of the medieval West, Constantinople, before the Emperor, Comnenus, on the occasion of a Sultan's visit in 1162. He met a similar fate, as, in the words of Peter Haining in *The Compleat Birdman*, "this foolish Icarus came tumbling down with such violence that he broke his neck, his arms, his legs, with almost all the bones of his body."

A century earlier, a monk of Malmesbury, England, fared somewhat better. He attached artificial wings to make what has been called the "first substantial glide in the history of flight," jumping from the top of his abbey about 1010 A.D. He broke both legs, but greatly improved upon the legend he was trying to better. This was the story of the supposed ninth king of England, Bladud, immortalized by Shakespeare as the father of King Lear. About 850 B.C., it was said, he attempted to overfly London on artificial wings, but crashed to his death. Another English monk was said to fly a furlong (220 yards) from a Spanish town, sometime before the Norman conquest of 1066.

Clearly, the tower jumpers, east and west, were indeed lucky to escape with broken bones. A list of over fourteen tower jumpers, from about 1000 A.D. to the eve of proven balloon flight in 1783, cataloged four deaths, seven injuries, and three partial successes.

But they kept trying—not always voluntarily, as tyrants not uncommonly used prisoners of war as guinea pigs for aerial experiments. Thus the Emperor Gao Yang, who reigned in a northern Chinese dynasty from 550 to 559 A.D.

caused many prisoners condemned to death be brought forward, had them harnessed with great bamboo mats as wings, and ordered them to fly down to the ground [from the top of a tower]. This was called a "liberation of living creatures." All the prisoners died, but the emperor contemplated the spectacle with enjoyment and much laughter.

At least the Chinese monarch, perverse Buddhist as he must have been, reportedly had experiments in mind.

In southern France, a feudal lord who was a vassal of the Avignon Pope in the fourteenth century was described as "laughing to tears" at the sight of some of his prisoners being thrown from the cliffs of the Château des Baux. He became known as the "scourge of Provence." In sixteenth-century Russia, the infamous Ivan the Terrible sentenced to death a man who tried to use wings of wood and cloth to soar into the skies, stating that "attempting to quit the confines of the earth was a gross and unnatural act."

Yet the jumps continued, voluntary or not, even as the worst of the craze of witch-hunting developed, some information on which begins our next chapter.

3

Tower Jumpers and Flying Witches

One of the great ironies of our chronology is that the acceleration of the development of scientific method, including the beginnings of modern aeronautics, came in the very same sixteenth and seventeenth centuries that saw the peaks of tower jumping and witch hunting. No doubt all three phenomena stemmed from similar drives for greater knowledge, even if their results were so very different.

The first references to witchcraft date to the ninth century, and concern over it developed in succeeding centuries, apparently out of the belief that Satan had carried Christ to a mountaintop on one of his trials and thus would certainly do the same with lesser mortals. It seemed convincing that the devil would use "wicked" women, especially, to advance his aims. He would supply them with broomsticks, the symbol of womanhood and domesticity, and "flying ointments"—probably hallucinants—that would enable them to fly about and work their evil.

A northern French account of 1460 reported five women describing how the devil "had given them a salve which they rubbed on their hands and on a small wooden rod, and with this between their legs they 'flew above good towns and woods and waters to their meeting place.'" A seventeenth-century Swedish manuscript related the confession of witches who reported:

> Then he [the devil] asked us whether we would serve him with soul and body. If we were content to do so, he set us upon a beast which he had there ready, and carried us over churches and high walls . . .

Although skepticism was being reported by the sixteenth century, the hysteria reached its peak about the same time. By 1750, Europeans had executed over 60,000 of some 110,000 accused witches.

Yet despite these extremes, the long progress toward scientific method and modernity was in fact accelerating during those very centuries. The church, the only dominant institution of medieval Europe, also greatly stimulated the dream of flight, not only by at times supporting charges of witchcraft, but still more by its patronage of artists and writers depicting angels and the Holy Mother ascending and devils descending. Birds, too, were very numerous in medieval art, the dove coming to symbolize the Holy Ghost.

Numerous theorists had begun to create the beginnings of what would become the science of aerodynamics. Already in 1260, the English Franciscan monk Roger Bacon spoke of ". . . engines for flying, a man sitting in the midst whereof . . . much after the fashion of bird's flight." The German theologian Albertus Magnus made references to flight about the same time, and toward 1300 the great poet Dante declared: "O human race, born to fly upward, wherefore at a little wind, dost thou so fall?" In 1532, the Italian poem *Orlando Furioso* spoke of the aerial journey of a knight.

By the fourteenth century, according to historian Charles Gibbs-Smith, Europe knew of "the two inventions which were to form the core, so to speak, of the powered airplane—the rigid inclined wing of the kite, and the active propulsive airscrew." They had been invented centuries earlier in China, but were greatly improved upon in Europe—as about the same time were the seminal inventions of the compass, gunpowder, and printing. Wings and airscrews came to be used in windmills, while toy helicopters, appearing in the twelfth century, became "the first type of powered aircraft in the western world."

In the fifteenth century, Giovanni de Fontana, who took a degree in medicine at Padova, gave a version of the popular medieval story of Alexander's travels:

> . . . when Alexander wished to preside over the air, he had the rather good idea of seating himself, so as to be carried up, on strong, flying griffins, holding roasted meats aloft on his sword. The griffins, smelling the food above their heads, pressed upwards . . . very high . . .

Fontana also may have tested a "rocket-powered bird," and stated:

> I indeed have no doubt that it is possible to attach to a man

wings which may be artificially moved, by means of which he
will be able to raise himself into the air and move from place to
place and climb towers and cross water . . .

His writings and sketches influenced many Renaissance thinkers,
including the great Leonardo da Vinci (1452–1519), who was also known
to have admired the flying angels of Giotto and other masters.

Leonardo began to study the problems of flight after 1485, while in
the service of Lodovico Sforza, the duke of Milan. In all, he did 160 pages
of notes and sketches, with some 400 references to 150 different flying
machines, to create what has been called "the birth of aeronautics."
Returning to his native Florence after 1499, he wrote the treatise "On the
Flight of Birds."

In that work of 1505, he prophesied: ". . . the famous bird will take
its flight, which will fill the world with its great renown." He thought that
one could use arms and legs, assisted by bowstring motors, airscrews, and
other devices to power wings and fly. In addition to sketches and speculations about such ornithopter flight, Leonardo envisaged an astonishing
number of ways to move through water and air, including the submarine,
the helicopter, the parachute, and the hang glider. He invented the word
"helicopter," and in 1485 made the first workable parachute design. He
provided, undoubtedly, the greatest demonstration of the "Renaissance
man," who, in the words of Pico della Mirandola (d. 1494), could ". . .
have whatever he chooses . . . be whatever he wills."

Because he sought to use his ideas and inventions to enhance the
power of his ruling prince, another famous name, Sigmund Freud, interpreted Leonardo's aeronautical work as an illustration of subconscious primal drives. The use of the word *uccello*, or bird, for his flying machines
gave, as a contemporary writer put it, "an expression of infantile erotic
desires for surface control over the external world," since it was a well-
known slang term for penis. Others have criticized such an interpretation,
but still others have pointed out that the popular images of witches flying
on broomsticks were suggestive of similar fantasies.

In any case, Leonardo da Vinci can claim not only to have been one
of the greatest artists and students of anatomy and other subjects who ever
lived, but to have been the first dreamer to have written and drawn extensively on key problems of aeronautics, including action and reaction; the
structure of wings, carrying surfaces, and landing gear; and even devices

for directional control.

Yet his work was misplaced and remained unknown until 1797, when, after Napoleon had his manuscripts brought to Paris, a French scholar published an essay on Leonardo's scientific works. Subsequently there has been speculation as to whether the first powered flight might have materialized much earlier had the work of Leonardo been known.

Almost certainly not, since in addition to the problem of a power plant, Leonardo made basic errors in falsely assuming that birds accomplished flight by moving their wings from front to back like a swimmer, where in fact they move more vertically to provide lift. And he greatly overestimated the power of human muscles to propel human ornithopter flight. By contrast, the flying muscles make up a third or more of a bird's weight. Though he envisaged a parachute already in 1485 and a helicopter a little later, he apparently never tested his flying machines, although there were hints of glides from the hills of Fiesole, above Florence, and elsewhere after 1496. Later he may have flown kites, and in the four years before his death in 1519 at Amboise, France, he greatly impressed King François I and other contemporaries with his many-sided genius. They frequently visited him in the beautiful chateau, now a museum, where he was housed.

It was just as well the great genius did not try to fly, since numerous contemporaries sustained serious injuries from tower jumps. About 1500, the "Daedalus of Perugia," a mathematician named Giovanni Battista Danti, crashed onto the roof of a church where a large wedding was taking place, after he had first paraded through the town square sporting his huge pair of wings. Previously, he was said to have made several glides over a nearby lake.

In 1507 another Italian, living in Scotland and called John Damian, broke a leg after astonishing a crowd by jumping from Stirling Castle. He had announced he would fly to Paris to welcome the new Scottish ambassador, who was arriving far more slowly by coach and boat. Still another Italian, a clockmaker known as Bolori, crashed to his death in 1536 from the cathedral tower of Troyes, east of Paris. Then, about 1580, according to Peter Haining, a "dolt of an Italian," otherwise unnamed, attempted to fly "like a turtle dove" between two towers before a huge crowd in Paris. But "he dropped like a pig . . . and broke his neck." At about the same time, another birdman was reported, probably apocryphally, to leap from the famous tower of St. Mark's, Venice; he "circled and swooped above the heads of the amazed population who felt certain that he was an angel of God . . ."

If 1500 is commonly taken as the round date dividing the Middle Ages from early modern times, the artist who in many ways best spanned the two epochs was Hieronymous Bosch (d. 1516). His pictures included a "fantastic flying beast" of that very date, rigged with harness and passenger seat, very much in medieval style. Shortly afterward, Peter Brueghel the Elder (d. 1569) painted a famous representation of the Daedalus myth, *Landscape with the Fall of Icarus*, as did Rubens in about 1636.

The great Habsburg emperor, Charles V, was said to have witnessed the flying of kites and model birds at Vienna in 1530 and again just before his death in 1556. Sixteenth-century Europe apparently was full of tower jumpers and tight-rope walkers who fitted wings to better manage their glides and balancing acts. Shakespeare's contemporary, Edmund Spenser, gave poetic expression to the dream in a famous poem of 1595:

> Oft when my spirit cloth spred her bolder winges,
> In mind to mount up to the purest sky;
> it down is weighd with thoght of earthly things
> and clogd with burden of mortality,
> Where when that soverayne beauty it doth spy,
> resembling heaven's glory in her light:
> drawne with sweet pleasures bayt, it back doth fly,
> and unto Heaven forgets her former flight.
> There my fraile fancy fed with full delight . . .

The seventeenth century saw the peak of tower jumping with a "veritable flurry of birdmen." At the turn of the century, an Italian painter, Paolo Guidotti, jumped from a tower at Lucca, falling through a roof into a room below with a broken leg. In Germany in 1614, a theologian with a doctorate from Rome, Kaspar Mohr, constructed goose-feather wings to jump from the top of his Schussenried monastery, but superiors confiscated his wings to prevent the attempt. An unconfirmed story states that he tried again and flew for two hours! About the same time, at Nürnberg, there were reports of a cantor, Senecio, breaking his arms and legs after "having risen into the air by the help of wings, or by means of some beating arrangement . . ." In 1630, there were two other attempts, one fatal, as was another at Frankfurt in 1673. In Moscow and southern Russia there were at least three reports of attempts at winged flight.

In 1627, *The Art of Flying* (*De arte volandi*) was actually the title of a book published by the German, Friedrich Hermann Flayder, though this was to be accomplished by the flapping of wings. So was the device of the English scientist, Robert Hooke, given description in mid-century.

Two English bishops in the 1630s even spoke of flights to the moon, possibly inspired by speculation earlier in the century by the great astronomer, Johannes Kepler (d. 1630). Others speculated about the use of kites to lift passengers. The first, Francis Godwin, Bishop of Hereford, wrote *The Man in the Moone, or a Discourse of a Voyage Thither by Domingo Gonsales the Speedy Messenger,* published as arranged three years after his death in 1635. It related how the imaginary Spanish adventurer used over ten wild birds to pull his trapeze bar and sail to the moon with twelve days of travel. The other bishop, John Wilkins, in his *Discovery of a New World* in 1638 and in subsequent works, envisaged other travels to the moon and elsewhere. He proposed four ways to fly like Daedalus, "with the spirits of angels, with the help of fowls, with wings fastened to the body and with a flying chariot." A friend claimed to fly in 1665, but gave no proof, as was the case with a German at Frankfurt in 1673.

In mid-century, another Italian, Tito Livio Burattini, working in Warsaw, was said to have been the first to create actual lift, using four pairs of wings attached to an elaborate "dragon." The device lifted a cat in 1648, but failed to successfully lift its inventor. About the same time, in Turkey, a certain Hezarfen Celebi even claimed to fly "several kilometers" along the shores of the Bosporus, landing safely in the marketplace of Scutari. Later in the century, the famous architect Christopher Wren, designer of London's St. Paul's Cathedral, expressed interest in a machine which could enable flight.

The English also began to use "knots" for the speed of ships during the 17th century. It was measured by timing the passage of a rope with knots tied at regular intervals as the boat moved away from the anchor to which the rope was tied.

Most astonishingly, also in that century, a Capuchin monk, Joseph, born in Copertino in southern Italy in 1603, supposedly made some 100 levitations there, as well as in Assisi, Naples, and Rome—to become the "most aerial of saints." A description of one of his flights described how

On Christmas Eve, Joseph, who had heard some shepherds play-
ing flutes . . . first began to dance about . . . and then having
breathed out a great sigh, flew like a bird through the air from
the middle of the church to the top of the high altar, a distance
of . . . [about 40 ft.], where he calmly remained embracing the
tabernacle of the Holy Sacrament for about a quarter of an hour.
. . . The shepherds were astonished beyond measure.

Not surprisingly, following his death in 1663, Joseph became "the patron
saint of flyers."

Without divine help, however, most came to agree with the mathematician Giovanni Alfonzo Borelli, who in 1660 published a study on the
musculature of animals, showing that birds possessed many times more
power for their weight than humans, and that therefore men could never
power ornithopter or wing-beating flight, the myth of Daedalus to the
contrary.

The mathematician-philosopher René Descartes in 1640 expressed
doubt whether man could ever fly by flapping wings, but Cyrano de
Bergerac, a writer in his own right before being made famous by the 1897
play of Edmond Rostand, spoke of five ways of becoming airborne,
including the use of rockets as well as the principle of rising dew. Like
Kepler and the English bishops, he also speculated about moon flight in
the "Voyage dans la Lune" in his *Histoire Comique* of 1650.

The famous Sun King, Louis XIV, just after assuming his duties in
1661, witnessed an unsuccessful attempt by a gymnast, Allard, to fly from
a terrace at St. Germain, and there were other attempts at Rosay Abbey
and Péronne, near Paris. Then in 1678, Besnier, a French locksmith, was
said to have accomplished several gliding flights at Sablé, between Le
Mans and Nantes, without injury. He attached four small wings to his
ankles and hands, and inspired what must have been the first news arti-
cle on flight, in *Le Journal des Scavans* on December 12 of that year. It
reported:

The inventor first flew down from a stool, then from a table,
afterwards from a window, and finally from a garret, from which
he passed above the houses in the neighborhood, and then,
moderating the working of his machine, he descended slowly to
earth.

Those reports in turn produced "one of the most widely illustrated 'aircraft' in history," which was of a nude man with four small wings gliding through the air.

In 1670, an Italian Jesuit, Francesco de Lana de Terzi of Brescia, designed a "flying ship" to be raised by vacuum and balloons. He also was the first Westerner to elaborate on the military uses of aerial attack. Presciently, he wrote:

> . . . God would surely never allow such a machine to be successful, since it would cause much disturbance among the civil and political governments of mankind . . . no city would be proof against surprise . . . or ships that sail the sea. . . . Houses, fortresses, and cities could thus be destroyed, with the certainty that the airship would come to no harm, as the missiles could be thrown from a great height.

As Charles Gibbs-Smith has stated, Lana's work formed "a major milestone in aeronautical history. It fired the imagination of many, including the great philosopher Leibnitz, and produced one of the most widely reproduced of aerial designs." It also gave "the first logical formulation of the balloon problem," since a 1684 Rome publication showed his craft hoisted by four hydrogen balloons. A decade later the great Polish leader Jan Sobieski placed wings on a part of his army, apparently not to fly, but to frighten the Turkish army trying unsuccessfully to advance on Vienna.

In 1708-1709, a Brazilian Jesuit at Lisbon, Bartolomeu Lourenço de Gusmão, became famous for designing a boat-like "great bird," or Passarola. He may have tested models and a hot-air balloon, but could offer little proof, and came to be widely satirized. The Swedish mystic Swedenborg, about 1714, and a Russian, Kriakoutnoi, in 1731, also claimed without proof to have devised craft that would fly. In 1754, a better-known scientist, Michael Vasilyevitch Lomonosov, was said to have succeeded in flying a helicopter design with twin contra-rotating rotors. Then, in 1768, the French mathematician Paucton made the "first specific suggestion for horizontal aerial propulsion by an airscrew."[15]

In 1742, at the age of 62, inspired by Besnier's attempt of 1678, the Marquis de Bacqueville announced his intention to cause a man (his valet) to fly from the top of what is now the Paris hotel Le Quai Voltaire, on the Seine River. His quick-witted valet declined to precede his master, however, and so Bacqueville himself felt obliged to jump to satisfy the sizeable crowd that had assembled. He supposedly glided almost 300 meters with elaborate wings attached to his arms and legs, only to break his legs crashing into a barge at the edge of the river. Although he became perhaps the most famous of "tower jumpers" because of the exploit, he considered he had been mocked, and did not repeat the experiment. In 1760, he died in a fire which also destroyed whatever records he had kept.

In mid-century, a Brother Cyprian supposedly "glided from a mountain in eastern Europe," as did a Bohemian called Fucik. An Englishman, Cadman, apparently crashed to his death from a spire in Shrewsbury, while the supposed flights of a certain John Childs, first in England, then in Boston, have been shown to have been faked. Other efforts achieved little, but made no false claims. In 1764, Melchior Bauer designed a device in Thuringia, central Germany, to be powered by rocking a system of flappers. It also came to nothing.

In 1772, Canon Desforges of Etampes, south of Paris, designed and tested a sort of gondola, made of willow, while a decade later the future balloonist Jean Pierre Blanchard, created an amphibious "flying boat," and later a helicopter. Also in 1781, a Baden architect, Karl Friedrich Meerwein, apparently made several brief glides, but without tail surfaces or controls of any kind. In 1784, Launoy and Bienvenu demonstrated a model helicopter before the French Academy of Sciences. The same year at Embrun, near Avignon, a Monsieur Ariés was said to have glided with fixed wings before many witnesses. About the same time, A. J. Renaux designed an elaborate ornithopter and an M. Gérard, a flying machine to be powered by exploding gunpowder. The new century opened with another tower jump, when a retired seventy-two-year-old general, Resnier de Goué, descended some sixty-eight meters from the fortifications of Angoulême into the Charente River, where a boat picked him up.

Debates about the possibility of flight had been continuous, and the minister of foreign affairs of Louis XV, about 1750, even proposed a secretary of state for air forces—surely the first proposed government aviation ministry. The eighteenth century also saw the greatest outpouring yet of literature and art on "travelers in imagination." Daniel Defoe imagined a flying machine called "the consolidator," and gave an account of travel to the moon in 1705. Then, writing in *The Guardian* in 1713, Joseph Addison even satirized the sexual dangers posed by the freedom of flight:

It would fill the world with innumerable immoralities, and give such occasions for intrigues as people cannot meet with who have nothing but legs to carry them. You should have a couple of lovers make a midnight assignation upon the top of the monument, and see the cupola of St. Paul's covered with both sexes like the outside of a pigeon house. Nothing would be more frequent than to see a beau flying in at a garret window, or a gallant giving chase to his mistress, like a hawk after a lark.

Addison himself proposed "to mount in the air, fly over Fleet Street and pitch upon the May Pole in the Strand." He also predicted of the air age:

I need not enumerate to you the benefits which will accrue to the public . . . as how the roads of England will be saved when we travel through these new highways. . . . When mankind are in possession of this art, they will be able to do more business in three score and ten years than they could do in a thousand by the methods now in use.

The famous *Gulliver's Travels* of Jonathan Swift, in 1726, narrated how a "Flying Island," four and a half miles wide and three hundred yards thick, powered by a huge magnet, housed

a ruler who could punish the territory below by hovering over it and thus excluding the sunlight and rain, by flinging great stones down or even by descending and flattening the area.

Dr. Samuel Johnson and the poet William Cowper, however, worried about aerial bombardments and other dangers of flying, such as being burned up like Icarus by "the fire of the sun" if one ventured into the upper atmosphere. In 1759, Johnson included a chapter, "A Dissertation on the Art of Flying," in his novel *Rasselas*, and described vain attempts to fly.

Over forty other works in England and France in the eighteenth century portrayed, in writing or art, flying wings and carriages transporting people through the air. In 1727, an Englishman known as Captain Samuel Brunt, in *A Voyage to Cacklogallinia*, envisaged the mining of gold from the moon. Jean-Jacques Rousseau, in his 1742 *Le Nouveau Dédale,* made references to the achieving of flight "by a new hero who will arrive to carry us all on wings into the heavens."

In mid-century, the writings and illustrations of Restif de la Bretonne have been described as the "climax of the romantic conception of flight by artificial wings." In 1755, another Frenchman, L.G. de la Follie, even imagined an interplanetary flying machine powered by electricity, which has been called the "scientific climax" of pre-modern writings about aviation. His machine would carry a scientist living on the planet Mercury to other planets, including Earth. A 1751 English poem discusses aerial warfare, and the same year a popular novel, *The Life and Adventures of Peter Wilkins* by Robert Paltock, related how winged people flew nearly to the South Pole and back.

There were also speculations after mid-century about the use of heat or gas to raise ships into the air. In 1755, a Dominican friar, Joseph Galien, published *L'Art de Navigation dans les Airs* at Avignon, describing a giant airship using the thin air of the upper atmosphere to float the ship, ten times the size of Noah's Ark, capable of carrying an army to Africa. In 1766, the English chemist Henry Cavendish described an "inflammable air," which was baptized "hydrogen" and shown by his colleague Dr. Joseph Black and others to be lighter than air and therefore capable of rising if enclosed. In 1781 and the next year, an Englishman and a Swiss proposed raising bladders of various sorts by filling them with hydrogen. In 1785, an Italian living in England, Tiberius Cavallo, wrote *The History and Practice of Aerostation,* and a popular play in Paris after 1789 had its peasant hero, Nicodemus, travel to the moon to proclaim the glory of the revolution.

Such works undoubtedly influenced the launching of the first manned balloon flights in 1783. Those flights in turn provided the fundamental divide between the dreamers and the 19th-century predecessors of the Wright brothers and contemporary aviation. For it was in 1783 that large numbers of people, including notables like Ben Franklin, first witnessed the safe rising into the air of man-carrying balloons.

From that point on, advanced thinkers knew that flight was possible without grave risk of life, and that therefore other ways of flying safely and faster would surely be developed. Before, as we have seen, dreamers also believed, but usually unrealistically, and they were very isolated. But from 1783, doubters could be silenced with the proof that people had indeed flown. If that was, so far, only suspended from balloons, now the knowledge was there, and people knew that man could mount into the air and begin to travel there with some degree of safety. The first phase of actual aviation was about to begin.

4

The Balloonists

As the phase of powered fixed-wing flight was initiated by the Wright brothers in 1903, another pair of brothers launched the first witnessed ascents into the air in 1783. They were Joseph and Etienne Montgolfier, and their name is still used for the large hot-air balloons which they pioneered. They were descendants of a paper-making family in the southeast of France.

It is not known if they had heard of the supposed hot-air balloon devised by Father Gusmão at Lisbon in 1709, but they undoubtedly knew of their countryman Joseph Galien's 1755 book, *The Art of Aerial Navigation,* which speculated about an ascending "aerostat," as lighter-than-air craft were first called. They learned of English scientist Henry Cavendish's 1766 description of hydrogen as being fourteen times as light as air, and hence capable of lifting bodies into space if a shape could be devised to contain the hydrogen. But finding that impossible, they began to experiment in late 1782 with the use of smoke and steam to raise various types of balloons, some rising to several hundred meters. While they did not understand that it was the heat rather than the smoke which caused the lift, they did succeed in containing the hot air that made the flights possible. Then on June 4, 1783, from the marketplace of their home town of Annonay, south of Lyon, they demonstrated the flight of a large aerostat, 110 feet in circumference, before an enthusiastic crowd.

Word of these achievements rapidly spread, and within two months the Academy of Sciences in Paris and the last pre-revolutionary Bourbon king, Louis XVI, decided to support further flights. A young physics professor, Jacques Alexandre César Charles, was the first to achieve that patronage, and with the help of the brothers Jean and Noël Robert, was able to construct a thirteen-foot-wide rubber-coated, silk aerostat, which, unlike the balloons of the Montgolfier brothers, could contain hydrogen.

It became the first hydrogen balloon to fly, tethered, some 100 feet on August 24.

Three days later, the tether was removed, and it flew from the Champ de Mars—where the Eiffel tower would later stand—before a crowd including the 77-year-old new American Ambassador, Benjamin Franklin. It sailed some fifteen miles (18 kms) to the northeast where it came down in the town of Gonesse (today 20,000 inhabitants). Local peasants promptly attacked the air-borne monster, declaring it "inhuman" and destroying it with stones and knives. Thereafter, the custom of rewarding a successful balloon flight with a glass of champagne or wine was said to originate with this incident. Wine, like music, can "soften customs."

Earlier, a Parisian witness expressed skepticism at its lift-off, asking "What good is it?" A century and a half before the classic response "Because it is there" to the query, "Why did you try to climb Mt. Everest," Benjamin Franklin gave the equally incisive answer to the Parisian's question: "What good is a new-borne baby?" After all, in 1752, Franklin had made perhaps the most famous aerial experiment yet, to prove the existence of electrical discharges in thunderstorms.

The ill-fated last government of France's ancien régime, at the urging of the Academy of Sciences, proceeded to announce further flights to satisfy what was now a veritable "balloon craze." Louis XVI and Queen Marie-Antoinette summoned the Montgolfier brothers to demonstrate their flights in Paris. They did so with a flair.

On September 19, 1783, before the king and queen, they launched "an animal ascent" in a brilliantly colored balloon over twenty meters high and some fifteen wide. It carried a cock, a duck, and a sheep an estimated 1700 feet up, and soared some two miles in eight minutes to Vaucresson Forest outside Paris. After animals, the first men and women rapidly took to the air. Another science professor, a twenty-six-year-old member of the Academy of Sciences, Jean-François Pilâtre de Rozier, volunteered to replace the criminals who, as in the past, had been first nominated for such experiments. While the very first human ascents on October 15 and 17, 1783, were controlled by a tether, two days later De Rozier ascended to 340 feet, and remained in the air four minutes and 25 seconds.

The first free, untethered human flight in history came on November 21, 1783. Feeding a small fire beneath their raised carriage to inflate the

Montgolfier, the biggest yet, Pilâtre de Rozier, now joined by the Marquis d'Arlandes, rose from the edge of the Bois de Boulogne to 3000 feet and flew in full view of Parisians some five miles to near the present Place d'Italie. The *Journal de Paris* of that day described how the balloon climbed

> in a most majestic fashion and when it reached about twenty five feet above the ground, the intrepid travelers, taking off their hats, bowed to the spectators. At that moment one experienced a feeling of fear mingled with admiration . . . the machine, floating on the horizon and displaying a most beautiful shape, climbed to at least 3000 feet . . . crossed the Seine . . . to a position where it could be seen by all Paris. . . . They . . . continued . . . until they had passed over the outskirts of Paris. They made a gentle descent into a field. . . .Their voyage had taken them 20 to 25 minutes over a distance of 4000–5000 fathoms.

Just over a week later came a still more impressive flight. The physics professor Charles and the elder of the two Robert brothers, Noël, on December 1 took off in the first manned hydrogen-filled balloon, 26 feet in diameter, before a crowd of 400,000. It rose from the garden of the Tuilleries in the center of Paris, and sailed over twenty miles north to Nesles.

Benjamin Franklin, among those observing the lift-off, remarked, "We think of nothing here at present but of flying. The balloons engross all attention." Charles ascended again that day on the first solo flight ever, climbing to almost 10,000 feet. He reported, "I passed in ten minutes from the temperature of spring to that of winter." Although stricken with sharp head pains, possibly caused by the fall in air pressure, he later described the flights as an unequaled "moment of joyous excitement which filled my whole being when I felt myself flying away from earth. . . . we gave ourselves up to the views which the immense stretch of country beneath us presented."

On June 4, 1784, balloon pioneer Joseph Montgolfier made his first and only flight over Lyon, in the company of De Rozier and four others, including the first woman to make a free flight, a Madame Thible. They traveled in the largest vehicle yet built, over 100 feet in diameter, containing 700,000 square feet (23,000 sq. meters) of hot air. After 18 minutes, a leak forced a precipitate descent from 3000 feet, but later in the year another French crew traveled 150 miles across France in a balloon.

In that first full year of true human flight, balloons took to the air with passengers in England, Italy, Sweden, and the brand-new United States. The first American to rise aloft, on June 24, 1784, was all of thirteen years old, chosen because of his size for the ascent at Bladensburg, ten miles northeast of Washington, D.C. A better-known American, the royalist physician Dr. John Jeffries, who had settled in England, shared in the first crossing of the English Channel in a hydrogen-filled balloon on January 7, 1785. The pilot was Jean Pierre Blanchard, who had begun his efforts to rise by balloon even before the Montgolfiers, and he was the first to attempt, though without success, to attach a motor and propeller to his craft. Not wanting to share the spotlight of the first Channel crossing, he tried to bump the American. But Jeffries had financed the venture in return for a historic ride, and persisted to become also the first to record scientific readings of pressure and temperatures at altitude. He noted the fall from 29.7 to 27.3 inches of mercury as they passed the coast, and of the temperature from 51 to 29 degrees Fahrenheit at 9000 feet. More poetically, Jeffries, who later returned to a successful medical practice in Boston, described views of ". . . a most enchanting prospect of the distant country back of Dover . . . the venerable city of Canterbury . . . [then] an extensive view of the coast of France."

Tragically, the death of the first man to ascend into the skies, Jean François Pilâtre de Rozier, came six months later when that "first test pilot" tried to cross—against the wind—from France to England. The year before, he had set an altitude record of 11,700 feet, but now his hydrogen-filled balloon exploded at 5000 feet, perhaps caused by static electricity from the rubbing of a valve cord against the balloon. The explosion also killed his co-pilot, Pierre Romain.

After the Montgolfiers, the greatest improvements in balloon making were worked out by the French military engineer, Jean-Baptiste Meusnier. In 1785, he designed the elongated shape and other improvements of later dirigibles. He also proposed aerial propellers, after their related use the year before on a river boat by M. Vallet, and put one on the passenger compartment of a balloon designed by Blanchard. In the decade after 1783, the fever continued and there were 76 balloon ascensions before the revolution. Then, understandably, given the subsequent turmoil, a sharp drop-off to only 6 between 1790 and 1800.

The other most famous French balloonist, after the Montgolfiers, Jean-Pierre Blanchard, prefigured the twentieth-century barnstormers after his Channel crossing with Jeffries in 1785. He made some eighty-one ascents in nine countries, including the first adult balloon trip in America. That was on January 9, 1793, from Philadelphia before a crowd including George Washington and four other future U.S. presidents, John Adams, Jefferson, Madison, and Monroe. The flight lasted forty-six minutes and descended in Deptford Township, New Jersey. Ironically, Blanchard suffered a heart attack on his last flight in 1809. He landed safely but could not be resuscitated.

The first humans to use parachutes safely also appeared during this revolutionary period. The Montgolfiers as early as 1779 dropped a sheep suspended from a two-meter-wide parachute, and Joseph later jumped with one from a housetop in Annonay. They and others improved on the medieval riggings and wrappings used to slow falling bodies to create the first successful parachutes, suspending first animals and then humans from their balloons. It proved one of the greatest contributions of ballooning to aviation.

In the fateful aviation year of 1783, a French physician, Sébastien Lenormand, made short jumps using two parasols and then a 14-foot conical parachute at Montpellier in the south of France. A more impressive demonstration came on October 22, 1797, when before a large crowd, André-Jacques Garnerin descended from a balloon floating almost 3000 feet over Paris. Standing in a gondola suspended from a forty-foot-wide "parasol," he descended to land safely in the Parc de Monceaux. Because for unknown reasons the launching balloon exploded above him, his descent was described a century later by the balloonist historian Charles Dolfuss as "one of the great acts of heroism in human history."

With his brother, Jean-Baptiste, an opening was made at the top of the parachute to prevent the wild swinging which plagued earlier descents and, in 1802, Garnerin jumped safely from almost 10,000 feet over London. But he felt disgraced two years later when his huge balloon, launched to mark the Paris coronation of Napoleon on December 16, 1804, drifted uncontrollably all the way to Rome. His wife also became a parachutist, while the wife of Pilâtre de Rozier became a famous balloonist before crashing to her death in 1819. Nevertheless, incredibly, there were only eight fatalities in the first 1000 balloon flights.

With such adventures, more and more people became convinced that human flight indeed had arrived and, as the German writer E.T.A. Hoffman, put it, "Every man has an innate inclination to fly." In about 1790, a group of Spanish villagers went further and thought a 25-year-old Italian balloonist, Vincent Lunnardi, was "a saint descended from heaven." By the turn of the century, balloons of the type still used today, inflated either with hot air or hydrogen or combinations of the two, were taking to the air everywhere. The first completely "scientific flight" came in 1804, when Joseph Gay-Lussac and Jean-Baptiste Biot collected at 19,000 feet samples of air, which they later analyzed. They reported increases in pulse and breathing rates, but people ascending in balloons must have experienced the thrill described by François Peyrey, a century later but a year and a half before the first Wright brothers' flights, when he reported in June 1902 as follows:

> I received the baptism of air . . . at 4,300 meters of altitude, above . . . a fabulous sea of clouds, in the fleeting and huge cathedrals of the air. . . . Thus, the first minutes of my life as an aeronaut were fixed forever in me.

After 1821, "coal gas," a mixture of hydrogen and methane, became a more effective and hence dominant means of inflating balloons. Then in the 20th century, non-flammable helium became the increasingly preferred gas for its greater safety, despite its higher density and cost. As they climbed higher, the balloonists found increasing problems of lack of oxygen, and yet they made important new observations of temperature and pressures at higher and higher altitudes, to 20,000 feet by 1804, to 30,000 feet by 1862, to 35,400 feet in 1901, and then with pressure suits and oxygen masks, to 50,135 feet in 1931, 72,395 feet in 1935, and to the all-time record of over 113,600 feet (34,668 meters), achieved in the United States in 1961.

They also traveled farther and farther. In 1859, Americans flew a record distance of some 809 miles from St. Louis, to Henderson, New York. In 1863, the biggest balloon yet lifted off before a Parisian crowd of a half-million people, including Napoleon the Third, and sailed 400 miles over France and the Low Countries before landing in the soon-to-be-united Germany. Appropriately called "Le Géant," it was 196 feet tall. As will be seen in the next chapter, the first of the later more common, longer-shaped dirigibles had been flown a decade before, but such were not yet in widespread use. Another vertical balloon, taller than the Arc de Triomphe, caused a sensation at the 1878 Paris World's Fair by carrying fifty-two passengers in its suspended car. A later children's best-seller by William Pene du Bois imagined a balloon flight from San Francisco to New York, on the centenary of the first ascent, in 1883.

Kites also played key roles in stimulating interest in flying and in its practical uses. For example, in the 1840s an American succeeded in flying one from his side to the Canadian side of Niagara Falls. That enabled the passing of the cables necessary for the construction of the first trans-Niagara bridge.

As the passion continued, dreamers considered flights across the Atlantic and even to the moon. In 1830, an American aeronaut, Charles Ferson Durant, poetized as he rose above New York: "Perhaps I may touch at the moon"; and in August, 1835, the *New York Sun* published "moon hoax" stories of a British astronomer sighting winged humanoid creatures walking on the moon through his telescope. On November 7, 1836, the Irishman Thomas Monck Mason, crossing from London to the continent by balloon, described the wonder of his flight at dusk: "Behind us, the whole of the English coast, its white cliffs melting into obscurity, appeared sparkling with scattered lights." With the flight's English organizer, Charles Green, and member of parliament, Robert Holland, Mason on that flight established a balloon distance record of some 400 miles, reaching Weilburg, in western Germany. His account of the flight was apparently used by the soon-to-be-famous writer Edgar Allan Poe to perpetrate another hoax in the *New York Sun*, on April 13, 1844. It reported a flight from North Wales to near Charleston, South Carolina! Two days later the paper was forced to admit that their story was "erroneous." But then, in 1869, American writer Edward Everett Hale even wrote of a manned space station with commercial uses. In 1872, an Austrian equipped a tethered balloon with the first-ever internal combustion engine used in the air, and in 1883 a Frenchman achieved a first aerial use of an electric motor. The Atlantic was not crossed without stop by balloon until August 1978, or the Pacific until November 1981. There are hopes for the first non-stop circling of the world by the end of the century.

But balloons also played a part in the first aerial warfare. The world's first air force was the Compagnie d'Aéronautiers, created on April 2, 1794, during the war of the first coalition against the French Revolution. In June, two French aeronauts spied on Dutch and Austrian troops from above Mauberge, twenty kilometers from Mons near the future Belgian border. Subsequent balloon observations contributed to his victories, but Napoleon scorned their use in his many wars from 1797 on. The first aerial bombing came when Austrians dropped them to suppress Venetian rebels in 1849. Fortunately for the city of Venice and those who love it, a reversal of wind sent the balloons back over the Austrian troops.

The first extended use of balloons in heavy combat came during the U.S. Civil War, when balloonists John Wise, John LaMountain, and especially Thaddeus Lowe, contributed to Union successes in 1862. Lowe had given a demonstration flight before President Lincoln on June 18, 1861, making the first telegraph message from air to ground as he did so. However, there was continuous squabbling among the balloonists, which, together with the lack of funds, limited their use and grounded them before the war's end.

Their next use was in the Franco-Prussian War of 1870, when up to 102 people used some sixty-six balloons to escape the siege of Paris and to deliver mail as far as Tours, 125 miles to the southwest. On one flight, two aeronauts, becoming lost, drifted 800 miles to Norway. Before being equipped with motors at the end of the century, balloons, even though coming to be called dirigibles, could not be well controlled, despite efforts to do so with wings and even rows of paddles. Improved versions, however, were used for bombing in various colonial military campaigns, as in the French capture of Dien Bien Phu near the Vietnam–Laos border in 1884, 70 years before the victory there of Ho Chi Minh's forces. Then, the Japanese used balloons against Russian forces in Manchuria in 1904–1905, as did the Italians in Tripoli, 1911–1912. The Japanese and Italians were in violation of the 1899 Hague Peace Conference ban on the ". . . discharge of any . . . explosive from balloons . . ." Far worse violations were to come after the partial renewal of that ban at the next 1907 Conference, along with an equally futile ban on poison gas. As we shall see, German zeppelin airships, first flown in July 1900, inaugurated commercial aviation with passenger flights after March 1911, but also committed the worst violations of the Hague prohibitions against their use in warfare. American dirigibles, called "blimps," came to be filled with the safer helium gas by and after 1923.

The taking of man to the air after 1783 marked a fundamental dividing line in the history of aviation. Before and after, there were dreamers. But now there were aviators. One can only wonder whether the "astonishing year," as 1783 was called, which included the American colonies winning their independence, followed by the first ascent of Europe's highest mountain, Mont Blanc, on August 2, 1787, did not somehow symbolize the greatest rising of the masses in history two years afterward with the outbreak of the great French Revolution.

For the history of aviation, the greatest contributions of ballooning were: stimulating the great popular interest that began to change man's perspective from the traditionally horizontal to the vertical, and hence the conviction that man would fly; the accumulation of knowledge about the upper air, especially regarding the fall of temperatures and pressures; and not least the development of devices like the parachute to protect against the better understood dangers of flight. The balloonists continue to fly and to contribute to such knowledge. But the powered aircraft which took off shortly after the turn of the twentieth century of course have completely superseded simply "floating in the air," however far or high. Therefore, it is to the nineteenth century fixed-wing predecessors of the Wright brothers that we now turn.

The Precursors of
Powered Flight

If, after 1783, it was known that humans could take to the air, the techniques of developing the power and controls for lifting heavier-than-air structures remained to be devised,

The person who did most to advance those techniques in the next stage of mastering aviation was Sir George Cayley. Born in Yorkshire in 1773, he turned out some fifty-five studies and projects between 1796 and his death in 1857. He thereby became, according to Charles Gibbs-Smith, the "greatest of all the early aeronautical pioneers; he invented the basic principles of the modern aeroplane, and is rightly called 'the father of aerial navigation.'" He "truly foretold 'a new era in society.'"

In 1804, he built what was arguably the first genuine "airplane," a kite-winged model glider with a wing-span of 154 square inches. He correctly saw the problem of mechanical flight as "to make a surface support a given weight by the application of power to the resistance of air." Then his 1809 treatise, "On Aerial Navigation," laid the "foundations of modern aerodynamics" as one of the seminal early works on aviation. By stressing careful analysis of problems and the need for testing models, Cayley "introduced the scientific method to the development of flight technology." In his writings, he made the first accurate descriptions of how birds fly—by "the propeller action of their outer primary feathers" serving as airscrews—of how lift is produced—by "low pressure above a cambered wing," caused by air passing faster over the curved top than over the flatter bottom—of the need for V-shaped, dihedral wings for lateral stability—and of tail surfaces for longitudinal stability and control of direction. In 1809 he predicted:

> . . . a new era in society will commence from the moment that aerial navigation is familiarly realized. . . . I feel perfectly confi-

dent . . . that this noble art will soon be brought home to man's convenience and that we shall be able to transport ourselves and families, goods and chattels more securely by air than by water, and with a velocity of 20 to 100 miles per hour.

A 1799 medallion, designed by Cayley, showed an early model airplane and the forces working on it; and an 1804 model produced "the first ever aeroplane of what can be termed classic configuration," with forward wings and aft tail. Already in 1809 he had envisaged the use of propellers rather than the futile attempt to flap wings, and in 1816–1817, he wrote of navigable balloons. By then, he also specified the need for semi-rigid, streamlined airships, while by 1843 he had come to realize the necessity of something like steam-powered motors to provide the power to produce the speed necessary for lift, control, and speed. In 1849, a full-scale aircraft designed by Cayley lifted a ten-year-old boy on a downhill descent, which may have been "the first ever recognized manned flight." Moreover, refining the earlier work of French scientists Launoy and Bienvenu, he influenced "directly the whole of modern helicopter development."

It was surely no accident that Cayley's life marked the take-off of the industrial revolution in the place of its birth. For that in turn accompanied important inventions, especially of the steam engine about 1700, and the later application of improved motors to various forms of locomotion, notably for boats after Hudson's on the Hudson River in 1807, and for trains after the first trip in 1829 between Manchester and Liverpool, England.

The great romantic poets also fully appreciated the significance of these advances for the age-old dream of flight. John Keats' 1819 "Ode to a Nightingale" is considered the greatest poem ever written about a bird, and the next year's "To a Skylark" (". . . bird thou never wert") by Percy Shelley "haunts" later literature and "offers us an image of the longing for the totality of experience symbolized by the upper air." In 1822, Lord Byron wrote: "I suppose we shall soon travel by air vessels; make air instead of sea-voyages; and at length find our way to the moon, in spite of the want of atmosphere." If Byron and still earlier writers foretold the moon flights, in 1842 Alfred Lord Tennyson predicted the two most striking features of twentieth-century aviation, in commerce and war:

For I dipt into the future, far as human eye could see,
Saw the Vision of the world, and all the wonder that would be.
Saw the heavens fill with commerce, argosies of magic sails.
Pilots of the purple twilight, dropping down with costly bales
Heard the heavens fill with shouting, and there rain'd a ghastly dew...
from the nations' airy navies grappling in the central blue.

With more authority, if less literary brilliance, the great Cayley described the flight of one of his models as "a noble bird" gliding "majestically from the summit of a hill" to the plain below, at an angle of eighteen degrees with the horizon.

From 1809 to 1817, a Swiss clockmaker, Jacob Degen, aroused much attention with repeated balloon ascents and glides from them at Vienna and elsewhere. In 1810, an English inventor, George Walker, wrote *A Treatise on the Art of Flying by Mechanical Means*, containing an amazing picture of a bird-like craft with a man seated in the middle. Then, twenty years later, in 1831, Walker designed a fixed tandem-wing airplane, which though never built, greatly influenced later designs. By then, there was great popularity for the "flying chariots" (*chur-volants*), or horseless carriages, of George Pocock, which were pulled by two huge kites. If there was sufficient wind, the vehicles carried four people at speeds approaching twenty mph. One overtook the London Mail coach near Bristol in 1827.

With the proof of the ability of humans to sustain themselves in the air after 1783, and with the acceleration of the industrial revolution well under way, the dream of flight increasingly turned to ways to harness the new sources of machine power and to new materials for lighter and stronger construction. By the 1840s, more specific designs appeared for fixed-wing and propeller-driven aircraft. Two Englishmen a generation younger than Cayley, William Hensen and John Stringfellow, after 1842 devised a modern-looking "aerial steam carriage," to be powered by a 25 h.p. steam engine turning two six-bladed propellers. Pictures of it were widely circulated to enthusiastic commentary, and models achieved powered glides from 1845 to1848.

In 1852, two firsts came in Paris: the founding of an aeronautical society (Société Aérostatique et Météorologique de France) and, on September 24 of that year as mentioned in the previous chapter, the first powered airship flight. That was achieved by a 143-foot-long balloon, driven by a three h.p. steam engine which powered a three-bladed, eleven-foot-wide airscrew. Traveling about six mph, it could turn like a ship, and hence inspired the term "dirigible." The designer, engineer, and pilot, Henri Giffard, took off before an enthusiastic crowd at the Hippodrome, and flew about seventeen miles from Paris to Trappes, southwest of Versailles.

Given the importance of the linking of motor power to airframes, 1852 therefore marked the next most important date after the launching of manned balloons in 1783.

The first use of the word "aeroplane" came in 1855, and of "aviation" in 1863, the latter taken from the Latin for "bird" (*avis*) and "action" (*actio*). Gabriel de la Landelle explained in his book, *Aviation ou Navigation Aérienne* (Paris, 1863), "aviation is a word necessary to translate . . . aerial navigation . . . of the ascension and propulsion of a craft [*nef*], traveling in the air." He went on to predict:

> Once practical, aviation will exercise in the world an influence
> one thousand times greater than [previous means of transporta-
> tion]. . . . By aviation, all the isthmuses . . . all the straits will be
> crossed; Suez, Panama, the channel . . . the Bosporus . . . [there]
> will no longer be barriers.

An associate of La Landelle, the colorful photographer, writer, and adventurer Félix Tournachon, known as Nadar, also in late 1863 published the first aviation journal, *L'Aéronaute*, including advertisements for his friend's book. Only about four issues were published, but its sizeable pages revealed a remarkable faith in the future of aviation. A page one quotation from "academician Babinet" stated that "aerial locomotion is today only a question of technology and money."

Nadar himself wrote in the first issue of his "profound faith in the propeller" and "heavier than air machines" rather than balloons for the future of aviation. He nonetheless constructed an enormous "last balloon," the "Géant," to attract crowds to finance his efforts with the *Aérophile* and the Société d'Encouragement pour l'Aviation. He also took the first aerial pictures of Paris, and at one point wrote that "aerial automation, which erases frontiers, suppresses distance, would make wars impossible, and reserve spectacles of other miracles . . ." Another writer in the September 1864 *Aérophile* stated:

> The day will come, and that day has never been so close, where
> the air will be inhabited by men. A day will come where the
> immense space which surrounds us will be occupied by craft of
> such enormous dimensions and extent that our imagination
> today can scarcely conceive of them.

The same year, Victor Hugo proclaimed that flying machines would
make armies "vanish, and with them the whole business of war, exploita-
tion, and subjugation." The next year, George Sand wrote in a preface to
Nadar's *Le Droit au Vol* (The Right to Flight) that now that these "magnificent questions" about flight have been posed, "they cannot remain
long unsolved."

Nadar's preface to the same work taunted his readers: ". . . if you cannot believe, then never fly—and continue to walk—idiot." He then
argued the necessity to move beyond balloons as the future belonged to
bird-like craft that were "heavier than air" machines. He proclaimed:

> If I dream, let me dream . . . of air filled with craft [*nefs*], which
> soar and descend as birds where they wish. . . . The routes of the
> air are charming . . . without the bumps and shakes, or noise,
> fatigue, and dangers of other means of travel . . .

A friend of Nadar's, the far more famous Jules Verne, also in 1863
wrote his first novel concerning flying, *Five Weeks in a Balloon*. In 1872
came *Autour de la Lune* (Around the Moon) and in 1885 *De la Terre a la
Lune* (From the Earth to the Moon), seemingly predicting the 1969
moon flights. In 1886, in *Robur le Conquérant* (Robur the Conqueror),
Verne depicted an electric-powered plane that could control distant enemies, and stated that soon man "will become master of atmospheric space
using heavier than air machines. The future belongs to flying machines
supported by air." In his 1904 sequel, *The Master of the World*, Verne
imagines Robur destroying the American navy before dying in a terrible
storm.

Another popular writer and balloonist, Camille Flammarion, about
the same time imagined a space traveler going half again as fast as light
(300,000 kms per second), and thus looking back on Earth from his

spaceship with a telescope to see the unrolling of previous history. A Russian teacher, Constantin Tsiolkovski, began to write in 1883 of going into space using new types of liquid-fuel rockets, and twenty years later wrote *Exploration of the Universe with Rocket Propelled Vehicles.*

In 1893, came the first publication, *The Advent of the Flying Man,* by the writer who, with Verne, did most to establish visions of flight in modern literature, H.G. Wells. Two years later, he produced *Argonauts of the Air,* then *The Time Machine,* and in 1901 *The First Men in the Moon.* The same year, at the Pan-American Exposition in Buffalo, Frederick Thompson staged a "virtual reality" . . . "aerial ship," to be propelled to the moon by anti-gravity. It inspired President McKinley just days before his assassination, as well as Thomas Edison, who contributed toward Georges Méliès' 16-minute film of 1902, *Le Voyage dans la Lune.*

In 1898, all too presciently, Wells wrote *The War of the Worlds,* and in 1908 *The War in the Air.* It envisaged a light aerial attack on New York City, forcing immediate capitulation by the authorities, while his 1914 book, *A World Set Free,* at least thirty years too soon not only predicted something like the atomic bomb but a world government stopping "global destruction by air." Norman Angell's best-seller on the eve of World War I, *The Great Illusion,* argued further that the increasing interdependence of nations made war altogether senseless. In 1904 and 1907 works, the famous Rudyard Kipling projected control of the globe by the year 2000 by an Aerial Board which would outlaw war and bring air transport to all corners of the world.

With the literary accompaniment came important advances for aviation. The French engineer Etienne Lenoir invented the first proper gas motor in 1860, leading in the next decades to the evolution of the modern engine, compressing and exploding gas in cylinders. As seen, one was fitted to a balloon over Vienna in 1872, and the German Carl Benz equipped "the first practical motor car" with one in 1885. By the next century they were light and powerful enough to enable the momentous take-offs of the Wright brothers and their successors.

In 1864, Count Ferdinand d'Esterno made the first analysis of the difference between soaring and gliding in *Du Vol des Oiseaux* (On the Flight of Birds). Based on that information, later in the decade the Englishman M.P W. Boulton patented a device for ailerons to control turns, while J.W. Butler and E. Edwards proposed delta-wing craft, and Charles de Louvrier and the Russian Nicholas de Telescheff spoke of jet-propelled craft. During these years, at least three French attempted vainly to claim a prize for a five-minute ornithopter flight.

In 1866, Francis Herbert Wenham read a paper to the newly founded Royal Aeronautical Society in London on "aerial locomotion." It advanced the work of Cayley and others to explain how cambered, high-aspect ratio wings produced lift. In 1868 came the first aerial exhibit, at the Crystal Palace in London, where twenty years before Stringfellow had shown his steam-powered model triplane. In 1871 Wenham constructed the first wind tunnel. Others followed, and improved wind tunnels reached the United States by the mid-1890s. In 1881, Louis P. Mouillard, a Frenchman living in North Africa, published L'Empire de l'Air, stressing that man should be able to soar and glide like the birds. Its enthusiasm stimulated many, most significantly the Wright brothers, who, as we shall see, obtained a Smithsonian Institution translation of it at the beginning of their epochal work near the turn of the century.

Two French naval officers actually accomplished brief flights, though without control, as early as 1856. In December of that year, Jean Marie Le Bris briefly sailed his "albatross"-like glider, towed to a claimed height of 100 meters (330 feet) by a horse on a Brittany beach. Several months later, however, he broke his leg on the crash of a second flight from a forty meter cliff. The second, Félix du Temple, aided by his brother Louis, about that time succeeded in flying a model airplane, with forward-swept wings and powered by clockwork springs; but he became far more famous for an 1874 flight at Brest, on the tip of Brittany. There he succeeded in launching history's first manned powered fixed-wing aircraft. It was a bat-like structure which carried a young sailor for a certain distance, possibly using a hot-air motor. But it was launched down an incline and was not followed up.

Nonetheless, that 1874 powered glide pointed to the future, all the more so as that same year the last of the tower jumpers, a Belgian shoemaker named Vincent de Groof, leaped to his death over London while attempting a parachute-rigged ornithopter flight on his "beating wing flyer." Previously, he had glided safely some 450 feet from a balloon on his part-flapper, part-parachute craft, vainly called *espérance*. Also in 1874, an Ohio predecessor of the Wright brothers, W.P. Quimby, proposed ornithopter flight by means of a "species of featherless bird." Slightly later, another American, John Holmes of Kansas, imagined an "improved airship" with some new control features operated by a prone pilot.

Somewhat before these attempts, an English farmer named George Faux had given perhaps the bravest of all the quips about flying by beating the arms and legs, one which De Groof could hardly have appreciated. In September 1862, he jumped from the top of the tallest building in Essex, and despite a furious pumping of his impressively muscular limbs, crashed with various, if not crippling, injuries. Asked why, he replied, "I'm a really good flyer, but I cannot alight very well." Despite his fall, he continued to proclaim his belief that man "will fly like a bird."

In 1871, the first "stable" flight in history, albeit unmanned, had been achieved when another member of a French naval family, Alphonse Pénaud, flew an unmanned "planophore," or sort of helicopter with wings, for over 130 feet in thirteen seconds in the Tuileries Gardens of Paris. The small model was powered by twisted rubber, and its successful flight, together with other Pénaud proposals, as for a "joy stick" and other flight controls, retractable landing gear, dihedral wings, and even jet propulsion, made Pénaud another "father of modern aeronautics." His dihedral wings were an especially important contribution as they helped ensure stability by increasing lift on a wing tipping down, thereby bringing it level again. Pénaud's experiments marked the beginning of powered flight trials. But lacking a proper engine to continue his progress and depressed at continuing mockery of his experiments, in October 1880 he committed suicide. His achievements, however, inspired later aviators, including the Wright brothers.

Another early full-sized "airplane" made several glides at Clamart, near Paris, in 1879, piloted by J.B. Biot. In 1884, the Russian Alexander Mozhaiski claimed to send a pilot, I.N. Golubev, into the air for over sixty feet near St. Petersburg, in a steam-powered monoplane. But like Du Temple's manned glide of 1874, the launch was down a descending slope and could not be sustained or controlled.

The year before, the Frenchmen Alexander Goupil designed a steam-powered "aerial velocoped" with primitive ailerons, which lifted two men, but the flight was controlled by a tether. The Englishman Horatio Phillips demonstrated important proofs of Cayley's writings about lift in 1884, and in the 1890s devised improved types of thick wings to create even greater lift.

Also in 1884, a French officer, Charles Renard, constructed a large dirigible driven by electric motors, and two years later the Austrian David Schwartz devised the first rigid dirigible, driven by a gas motor. Count

Ferdinand von Zeppelin made later models with aluminum frames the most famous flying craft of succeeding years, and they came to bear his name. The first "zeppelin," 420 feet long, flew on July 2, 1900, while the Lebaudy brothers in France also made further improvements for their dirigibles after 1903.

During these years, and into the 1890s and after, numerous would-be pilots experimented with diverse structures and machines: from the Italian Enrico Falamini's proto-helicopter in 1877, to the Australian Lawrence Hargrave's box kites after the late 1880s, to the Scot Percy Pilcher's gliding experiments. The latter sailed up to sixty meters (196.8 feet) on various flights suspended from impressive-looking hang-gliders, but he killed himself on one such attempt in 1899. In 1894, the English-based American inventor of the machine gun that bore his name, Sir Hiram Maxim, with two assistants, succeeded in briefly lifting a giant, four-ton steam-powered test-rig with 100-foot wings, but it crashed and he abandoned further efforts.

In California, L. Gilmore falsely claimed to fly four miles in a powered machine in 1896. In October 1898, Augustus Herring did become airborne briefly in a biplane glider with a compressor motor for fifty and seventy feet over a beach at St. Joseph's, Michigan. But fires, illness, and lack of support delayed his further efforts. A German aviation enthusiast, living in the U.S. under the name Gustave Whitehead (Weisskopf), claimed flights of a half mile, two miles, and even seven and a half miles near Fairfield, Connecticut, before 1904, but so far few have accepted the veracity of his tales. Near Hannover, Germany, the civil servant Karl Jathro flew a kite-like triplane structure equipped with a nine h.p. gas motor 20 yards on August 18, 1903, and three times farther in a biplane configuration two months later, but the take-offs were downhill and lacked control. A so-called Russian "father of aviation," Nicholas Joukovski, about this time constructed a wind tunnel and established an aerodynamic institute which contributed significant work. These efforts caused considerable excitement, but achieved no control or follow-through.

In the 1890s, two bigger names set the stage for the breakthrough of the Wright brothers.

The first, Clément Ader, was born on February 4, 1841, at Murat, south of Toulouse, the future center of French aviation. On October 9, 1890, he actually flew a machine over 150 feet (50 meters), but only inches off level ground; and the flight could not be sustained, over a 200-

meter prepared surface at the Château d'Armainvilliers in Brie, southwest of Paris. The bat-like craft, called *Eole* after the Greek god of the wind, weighed about 330 kilos or 727 pounds, including Ader's 165-pound weight, had wings spanning twelve meters, and was powered by an efficient alcohol-fired, ten to twelve h.p. steam motor, weighing 66 kilos, or about 34 pounds less than the 81.5-kilo, twelve to sixteen h.p. motor of the 1903 Wright *Flyer*. It drove a 2.6-meter propeller. There were witnesses to the "hop," and it was the first steam- powered craft to rise from the ground, but did not achieve control.

Like the Wrights, Ader was early fascinated by bird flight, and engaged in bicycle work as well as work on a new southern French railroad, before beginning to construct gliders after 1872. But until 1887, he devoted most of his time and effort (and profited from) developing the new Bell telephone system for use in Paris. Following the October 1890 trial, and subsequent studies and machines, in 1897 he tried to demonstrate the possibilities of a 400-kilo (258 kilos empty), 16-meter-wide craft before interested military observers at Satory, near Versailles. It was powered by two thirty-h.p. steam engines driving two counter-rotating puller, three-meter-diameter propellers.

On October 14 of that year he succeeded in flying his machine up to three meters high over 200 meters in fifteen to twenty seconds, but then crashed. The effort constituted an "uncontrolled hop," because of the lack of sufficient controls or the skill to deal with wind gusts and crosswinds, which shortly blew him off the track. He had purposely made the runway follow a circle, so that he could keep going until lift off! And in contrast to the Wrights, Ader preferred that there be no wind. The contract had called for the flying of two men for six hours, something not achieved until 1909!

Ader's claim that he was in fact the first to fly, and had flown up to 300 meters (984 feet) in 1897, has received some support in later research. But the fact that observers were unable to see any liftoff, because of the late hour of the twilight flight and dips in the runway, and reported the same, led to decades of disputes. The arguments of his supporters hinge largely on the fact that the wheel tracks of his machines disappeared from their ruts as the craft exceeded about twenty-five kilometers per hour and rose inches or more into the air. Jacques Noetinger, among others, have therefore considered that the 1890 effort marked "the first craft to fly under its own power," and "the first to take off from the ground without wind," carrying a passenger—namely Ader. Other historians finesse the question of whether Ader's efforts constituted the first true flights by alerting that, in any case, his "lifting of a man-carrying machine into the air formed a fundamental stage in the history of aviation."

Ader complained in December 1897 that his "flights" had achieved all that could have been expected of first efforts, and that funding should have continued. Others later speculated that had Ader equipped his craft with a gas combustion engine and had there been a better take-off strip and wind conditions, he might well have gone down as the first to fly. That might also have been the case had he, like the Wrights, developed more pilot skills before his tests. Then he might have been able to recover from the tail wind and sudden gust which apparently caused the October 14, 1897, crash.

As it was, Ader's attempts achieved "jumps" or "hops" and not yet true flight. His fame, however, grew as the French adopted his word, "*avion*," used for models after 1892, instead of "*aéroplane*," a word first used by another Frenchman, Joseph Pline, in 1855 and adopted elsewhere until the shift to "airplane" from 1911 on. In the 1890s, Ader also proposed a remarkably accurate vision of a large aircraft carrier, raising its planes with folded wings to the deck by elevator. Moreover, his prophecy rang all too true, that "who masters the air, will master the world."

As mentioned, the first international aviation organization also had been formed in Paris, in 1852. That was the Société Aérostatique et Météorologique de France, and there followed, in 1863, the Société d'Encouragement pour l'Aviation. In 1866, the English established the British Aeronautical Society, and in 1873 the French upgraded their 1852 organization to the Société Française d' Aviation Aérienne. In 1892, Georges Besançon founded the first professional aviation journal, L'Aérophile, and in 1898 he and other enthusiasts formed the Aéroclub de France. In America the first aeronautical group was founded in 1895, the Boston Aeronautical Society. Then, in October 1905, a more direct ancestor of the twentieth-century aviation organizations was established in Paris: the Fédération Aéronautique Internationale.

If the French took the lead in organizing and preparing for the take-offs to come, the greatest individual steps between Cayley and the Wright brothers were taken by the German Otto Lilienthall. Born in Pomerania in the revolutionary year of 1848, he early became fascinated with the flight of birds, and began the construction of models, again with a brother, Gustave. First attempts at ornithopter flight led him to seek greater knowledge of aerodynamics through a degree in mechanical engineering at Berlin University in 1870. While employed as an engineer, he pioneered the collection of data for wingspan and lift, which, while not always accurate, as the Wrights were to discover, made the greatest advances in the theory of flight so far. His *Der Vogelflug als Grundlage der Fliegekunst* (Bird Flight as the Basis of Aviation) greatly influenced the next generation of enthusiasts.

But it was the more than 2000 glides he made between 1891 and his death on one in 1896 that most advanced and inspired the imminent take-off of aviation. They won him the title of "father of flight testing," and splendid pictures of his flights—made for eighteen variations of his hang gliders—proved to a growing number of people that a man could launch himself into the air and, at least for a while, stay aloft. The photos provided the first substantial linking of the new photography with the acceleration of aviation knowledge and inspired many, most notably the Wright brothers.

Fixing wings up to seven meters wide with tail surfaces for stability to both monoplanes and biplanes (or two-winged structures), Lilienthall proceeded to run down hills to attain the necessary speed to sail into the air. In 1895, near Berlin, he soared some 400 meters. He sought to control the glides by body movement, but without total success as proved by his crash on August 9, 1896, forty miles west of Berlin at Rhinow. He died the next day at a Berlin clinic. He had written, "sacrifices must be made," but "we must fly and fall, fly and fall until we can fly without falling." He elaborated:

> One can get a proper insight into the practice of flying only by actual flying experiments. . . . The manner in which we have to meet the irregularities of the wind, when soaring in the air, can only be learned by being in the air itself. . . . The only way . . . is a systematic and energetic practice in actual flying experiments.

It was, of course, the Wright brothers who used their "systematic and energetic practice in actual flying experiments" to launch the real take-off, to which the key was greater control than had been achieved by their many predecessors.

6

The Triumph of the Wrights

The word "take-off" symbolizes the revolution in patterns of life achieved by the transformation of travel—from passage by foot and boat, to animal, to the machine-powered ships and trains of the industrial revolution, to the extraordinary aircraft of the twentieth century.

Unquestionably the greatest names in the achievement of the "take-off" were the Wright brothers. But like all greatest names in history, they built their achievements on the basis of previous dreams, ideas, experiments, and sacrifices, many of which have been mentioned above.

As a leading historian of aviation, Charles Gibbs Smith explains:

> To bring about this practical flying machine, a number of parallel streams of endeavor and invention had to be born, to develop, and to coalesce, before the Wright brothers could apply their creative faculties to achieve a satisfactory mechanism. These streams were: (1) the science of aerodynamics; (2) the technology of structures and aeroplane configuration; (3) fuel technology; (4) engine technology; (5) airscrew design; and (6) flight control. Thus the age-old dream that human beings would fly through the air by mechanical means was ultimately brought about by citizens of the great nations of the modern world, all working toward a common end, and for the good of humanity . . .

Before exploring the achievements of the Wright brothers, two more names especially need to be stressed.

One is Octave Chanute, another Frenchman, but one who came to the United States at the age of six in 1838. He went on to build a distinguished engineering career in Chicago, and helped the Wrights more than anyone else in the last decade before his death in 1910. The other is Samuel Pierpont Langley, who became the third director of the prestigious Smithsonian Institution in Washington in 1887, and who attempted unsuccessfully to fly a machine just before the Wrights did so.

It was the bilingual Chanute who provided the principal conduit of knowledge of the earlier European advances to the Wrights. This was at first through his 1894 book, *Progress in Flying Machines,* the "first authoritative account of aeroplane history," and then through up to 500 letters exchanged with the brothers. He also helped organize conferences on aerial navigation in Chicago in 1893 and 1902.

Already in 1894, echoing Cayley, Verne, and others cited above, he wrote:

> . . . let us hope that the advent of a successful flying machine, now only dimly foreseen and nevertheless thought to be possible, will bring nothing but good into the world; that it shall abridge distance, make all parts of the globe accessible, bring men into closer relation with each other, advance civilization, and hasten the promised era in which there shall be nothing but peace and good-will among all men.

In 1896, the year of Lilienthall's death, Chanute began his own gliding experiments at the age of sixty-four. He established a camp for gliding on the sand-dune shores of Lake Michigan, and attracted there Augustus Herring and two other American flight enthusiasts who undertook some 1000 glides by 1902. Some of the multi-wing, "katydid"-like craft were considered the most stable and solid flying machines yet built, and achieved flights of several hundred feet. But they lacked the controls devised by the Wright brothers, whom Chanute met in 1900, ten years before his death.

Langley had the theoretical knowledge as one of the nation's leading scientists as well as the wherewithal to have become the first to organize true flight. He naturally received the support of the Smithsonian after becoming its director in 1887, and proceeded to launch a series of experiments flying numerous models. Then, he was able to go on to bigger projects after receiving a $50,000 grant in December 1898 from the War Department in the wake of the victorious war with Spain. But Langley never developed the practical knowledge to master the controls and structures necessary for flight, in part no doubt because he, as Ader before him, never did the necessary experimentation with actual gliding to learn the problems of sailing in the air firsthand, as did Lilienthall, Chanute, and especially the Wright brothers. Rather, he decided to proceed directly from powered models to a full-sized aircraft to be flown by others. An astrophysicist, mathematician, engineer, and architect, born in Massachusetts in 1834, he somehow called his machines "aerodromes," as if he were housing his pilots for extended periods of time.

After building dozens of rubber band-powered models, in 1892 he built the first of his bigger "aerodromes" with tandem fourteen-foot-wide wings, powered by a lightweight steam engine. Tests were unsuccessful until, in 1896, the un-manned *Aerodrome Number Five* was launched by catapult from a houseboat on the Potomac River. It flew a half mile in a minute and a half, and was followed six months later by *Number Six,* which flew 4,300 feet. After delays caused by the Spanish-American War (which, however, encouraged the $50,000 grant from the War Department) he constructed a "*Great Aerodrome.*" It was four times bigger than the previous models, and was designed to carry a pilot. Volunteering to fly the newly completed machine, that weighed only 341.6 pounds (155 kilos), was Charles Manly, the constructor, with Stephen Balzer, of a gas-powered 52.4 hp motor, which drove two pusher propellers. The forty-eight-foot-wide wings were dihedral, or tilted upward, and there were tail surfaces and rudder, but the craft had not incorporated sufficient structural changes to control the great increase in size.

The first flight, on October 7, 1903, did not even become airborne before the craft slid into the water. The next and last Langley-sponsored attempt on December 8, two weeks before the successful efforts of the Wrights, achieved a catapult-assisted launch. But the wings, unable to bear the heavy load, broke and the craft sank. Despite the icy waters of the Potomac, Manly was able to swim to safety, but there were no further attempts, and Langley died broken-hearted in 1906.

Other notable aviation experiments preceding the December 17, 1903 take-off of the Wright brothers included the widely publicized twelve-kilometer (seven-mile) flight of October 19, 1901, from St. Cloud around the Eiffel Tower and back, by a colorful Brazilian living in Paris, Alberto Santos-Dumont. It was in a dirigible, and won its pilot a 100,000-franc prize (about $20,000). In addition, a famous picture from

1901 supposedly demonstrated the flight of a plane with a 3/4 hp motor over Hungary, piloted by Emil Nemethy, but the claims were never otherwise documented or followed up. In California, John Montgomery, a San Diego inventor who had experimented with gliding in the 1890s, made controversial new claims and proposals for launching planes from hot-air balloons. As mentioned, German-born Gustave Whitehead (Weisskopf) claimed to fly his airplane "No. 21" with a two-cylinder steam engine, a half mile over Fairfield, Connecticut, on August 14, 1901, and several times thereafter. Although witnesses have been cited, inconsistencies in the claims have so far left most unconvinced.

In Europe, new interest was generated by glides of army artillery Captain Ferdinand Ferber, who soon opened friendly correspondence with Chanute and then the Wrights. But other French were troubled by reports of the progress of the Wrights. Led by aviation promoter Ernst Archdeacon, a wealthy lawyer and prominent member of the Aéro Club de France, they issued what the *Aérophile* of December, 1903, called "*un cri d'alarme*" at the prospect that the "lead of the Montgolfiers" and other French pioneers might not achieve the first heavier-than-air flight for their country.

Indeed, the first sustained and controlled heavier-than-air flights came in the United States, thanks to the genius of the Wright brothers. Their December 17, 1903 'take-offs made them "the Columbuses of the air."

The brothers were the third and fifth sons of an itinerant preacher of the United Brethren Church, who in 1884 settled in Dayton, Ohio. Wilbur was then seventeen and Orville thirteen. By the mid-1890s, after first jobs helping their father with religious publications and establishing a successful bicycle shop, they turned their attention increasingly to efforts to master the accumulating knowledge of aeronautics. Helped by natural engineering sense and mechanical aptitude, sharpened by family support (their mother had a degree in mathematics) and their work with bicycles, they began systematic researches. The arrival of the first "horseless carriage" automobile in Dayton and news of the death of Lilienthall in 1896 inspired them further. They had first read of the latter's work in the September 1894 issue of *McClure's Magazine*.

In late August 1896, Orville became ill and almost died of typhoid fever, the disease that killed Wilbur in May 1912. However, following Orville's recovery and after local researches and inquiries, on May 30,

1899, Wilbur wrote the Smithsonian Institution for information on the problems of human flight, declaring his belief in its feasibility. The Smithsonian responded promptly, sending its annual reports, including descriptions of the glides of Lilienthall and Chanute, as well as a paper on soaring flight by Edward C. Huffaker, and translated extracts of Mouillard's 1881 *L'Empire de l'Air.* Also included was a list of books, including Langley's 1891 *Experiments in Aerodynamics*, Chanute's *Progress in Flying Machines* of 1894, and James Means's *Aeronautical Annuals* for 1895, 1896, and 1897—all of which they immediately ordered.

Their careful approach to learn all that could be learned of efforts to solve the problems of flight set the stage for the real key to their success— namely, the working out of the problems of control through their own thorough and persistent experiments. Having decided to study all that had been learned by the late 1890s, from 1900 they adopted the commitment to actual flight tests, in complete accord with Lilienthall's statement shortly before his death: "One can get a proper insight into the practice of flying only by actual flying experiments." In a letter to Chanute, Wilbur added: ". . . with the belief that flight is possible . . . what is chiefly needed is skill rather than machinery."

Within a month of receiving the Smithsonian literature on flight, the brothers had constructed a kite-like biplane with five-foot wings, deciding to master the art of flying before finding a motor to power the machine. Fixing cords to the wingtips, which also were linked to the tail surfaces, they already achieved some degree of control. Inspired by earlier studies, and by observations of the wings of pigeons in flight, they used a chance discovery of how a box could be flexed to refine a twisting process, which came to be called "wing warping." A first kite-model flight in August 1899 demonstrated the feasibility of making turns by twisting one wing up and the other down.

Next, with the help of Lilienthall's calculations and an unsatisfactory glide from a small hill in Dayton in 1899, they realized that strong, steady winds of about fifteen miles an hour would be needed to "lift" their glides. They wrote to the weather bureau for information on wind conditions, and in May 1900 queried Chanute for additional information, as "the problem [of flight] is too great for one man alone and unaided to solve . . ."

Announcing plans for a "man-carrying glider with a means of controlling both lateral [roll] and fore and aft [longitudinal] balance," they asked Chanute for advice on sites favoring flights of such craft. Although Chanute recommended California, South Carolina, or Florida, they decided on Kitty Hawk, North Carolina, because *The Monthly Weather Review* informed them that sufficient winds prevailed there and it was closer.

Wilbur set out in September 1900, struggling to find means of transporting the newly constructed glider and a residence for their stay. After an arduous trip of about a week, he found lodging as well as information on how to ship the glider, placed in crates to reassemble on arrival. By early October, 1900 they were ready for the first tests. Already by the 20th, they had achieved over a dozen glides, some of fifteen or twenty seconds and over 300 feet. They lay, belly down, above the lower wing, manipulating cords attached to wingtips for lateral control and the elevator placed in front for longitudinal control.

Returning to Dayton and their bike business in November, Wilbur wrote Chanute a report of their several minutes' worth of glides, and then longer accounts, which were published in July 1901 in the British Aeronautical Society's journal and its German counterpart, *Illustrierte Aeronautische Mitteilungen.* That summer, they undertook the building of a new improved glider, which they showed Chanute when he visited the brothers in Dayton on June 26–27. He lent them a French anenometer to measure wind speeds, and later sent a clinometer to measure angles of elevation and inclination, or angles of attack.

In July 1901, the Wrights again set out for Kitty Hawk, and chose 100-foot-high Kill Devil Hills, four miles away, for their next tests. At Chanute's urging, they were joined by Edward Huffaker, who had worked with Langley, experimented with gliders, and written the pamphlet, "On Soaring Flight." George Spratt, a Pennsylvanian with medical training, also joined them. The four set to work to construct a new glider, the largest yet built, with some 300 square feet of lifting surface, and with the elevator and a rudder for directional control in front. By the end of July, Wilbur made a glide of over 300 feet in nineteen seconds.

With constant adjustments of the curvature of the wing and weight shifts for the center of gravity and pitch control, they made new glides and steady progress. But then came a succession of disconcerting storms, illnesses, and crashes. Indeed, at one point, depressed by the craft seeming to turn in a way opposite to that expected, Wilbur later recalled: "I said to my brother Orville that man would not fly for fifty years."

The brothers and their two assistants broke camp in late August, shortly after a one-week visit by Chanute. Then, in a speech at Chanute's invitation, to the Western Society of Engineers in Chicago on September 18, 1901, in contrast to his expressed doubts in July, Wilbur predicted the success of "soaring flight." He explained how "the machine is permanently sustained in the air by the same means that are employed by soaring birds . . . utilizing the rising current of air blowing up the side of a hill." He was able to offer a photograph partially showing himself prone on the lower wing ten feet or so above Kill Devil Hills, and his remarks were published in the December issue of the Society's journal as "some aeronautical experiments." Widely reprinted, it became, according to aviation historian Fred Howard, "the book of Genesis of the twentieth century bible of aeronautics."

The brothers went on to conduct experiments in a homemade wind tunnel behind their bicycle shop, beginning in November 1901. Creating wind with a fan mounted on a bike wheel that could be tilted at various angles, they made important discoveries of forces of lift and drag, which they called "drift." They discovered inaccuracies in the pressure distribution tables of Lilienthall and became for the first time teachers, rather than pupils, of Chanute.

Returning to Kill Devil Hills in late August 1902, the Wrights built a still bigger hundred-pound glider, thirty-two feet wide, or ten feet wider than the 1901 model. It had a vertical tail, six feet high, which improved stability for turns, and the brothers devised a mechanism for the pilot lying prone to "warp" the wings by moving the hips rather than feet as previously. As in all the early models, the elevator for pitch control was in front of the pilot.

By late October, they had made over 700 glides, including five over 500 feet, and sufficient progress with further adjustments of controls, wings, rudder, and elevator to decide they were ready to attempt powered flight, as urged by Chanute.

Most significantly, they realized—through close observation of turns and the effects of wind gusts, causing stalls, or insufficient lift because of inadequate airflow—the necessity to maintain sufficient air speed, and that another function of the vertical rear rudder was to complement the wing warping for lateral control. They therefore linked the controls for wing warping and rudder and, encouraged by Chanute, in March 1903, decided to file a patent for their work. Earlier, Orville vividly described to his sister, Katherine, the stall* of one of the flights leading to this break-through:

> I was sailing along smoothly without any trouble at all . . . when I noticed one wing was getting a little too high and that the machine was slowly sidling off in the opposite direction. I thought that by moving the end control mechanism an inch or so, I would bring the wing back again to its proper position. I attempted to make the change. The next I knew was that the wing was very high in the air, a great deal higher than before, and I thought I must have worked the twisting apparatus the wrong way. . . . After assuring myself as to what was the proper motion, I threw the wing tips to their greatest angle. By this time I found suddenly that I was making a descent backwards toward the low wing, from a height of 25 or 30 feet, as a result of the machine having turned up at an angle of nearly 45 degrees in front. . . . The result was a heap of flying machine, cloth, and sticks . . . with me in the center without a bruise or scratch.

Meanwhile, Chanute addressed the Aéroclub de France in Paris on April 2, 1903, revealing details of the Wrights' efforts as well as reported-ly exaggerated claims of his own tests and contributions to the Wrights' achievements. The misleading effects of these claims were compounded when the August 1903 issue of *L'Aérophile* published Chanute's descrip-tions and pictures of the gliders, and led to the first disputes between Chanute and the Wrights later in the year, especially over the brothers' denials of inspiration from Ader and Chanute for the working out of their new tail rudders.

In February 1903, the Wrights began construction of what became the famous *Flyer* of the first powered ascents of December. The craft was a 738.34-pound (335-kilo), six-foot-six-inch-wide, 21-foot-long biplane, with a wingspan of 40 feet, four inches, giving a lifting surface of over 500 square feet (48 sq. meters). It had a double front elevator, or "'horizontal rudder," and in the rear a double vertical rudder, linked to the wing-warping controls and maneuvered by the pilot's hips. It was to be

---

*Stalls occur when the speed of the flow of air over curved lifting surfaces on the tops of wings and elsewhere falls to the point where "lift" is insufficient, causing the descent of the aircraft, either flatly, backwards, or in a spin.

launched into the wind from a sixty-foot wooden monorail track and to land on skids.

As the dramatic December flights would show, the craft was eminently airworthy, but the missing link was an effective engine and propellers strong enough to supply the necessary push, yet light enough to be lifted by the onrushing air. With the help of Dayton machinist Charles Taylor, they constructed a motor in the late winter with four cast-iron cylinders, which, placed at the rear of the wings, generated over twelve horsepower at 1090 rpms. It drove two counter-rotating props—necessary to offset the centifugal (torque) forces unleashed by each propellor—some eight feet in diameter which had been shaped according to their wind-tunnel tests for optimum push. Their instruments included a Chanute-supplied new French anemometer to measure wind velocity, a clinometer to measure angles of elevation and inclination, binoculars, camera, stopwatches, tachometers for measuring rpms, and a coil box for starting the motor.

Given the importance of the motors, or engines as they came to be called in English for aviation, a brief digression is necessary about their development. Along with the knowledge of lift, control, and stability, improved knowledge of engine power—the necessary complement for successful powered flight—had also been accelerating. As we have seen above, steam-engine-powered model aircraft had made gliding flights since Henson's and Stringfellow's from 1845 to 1848. In 1860, the Frenchman Etienne Lenoir devised a gas-powered motor, in which gas exploded in cylinders to drive down pistons, enabling lighter, more powerful motors than the necessarily heavy steam engines. Lenoir's countryman, Jean Delouvrier, and the Russian Telechev, even proposed jet engines for aircraft in 1865 and 1867, respectively. In 1876 and 1877, the German engineer N.A. Otto designed an improved four-stroke petrol internal-combustion engine. Then the first practical use of a single-cylinder engine for motorcycles was accomplished in 1885 by Carl Benz, with improvements made the following year by another German, Gottlieb Daimler.

If ground vehicles could be equipped with gas motors, and a gas-driven car appeared in Dayton in 1896, it was only a matter of time to fit them to airplanes, which they would naturally power with more lightness and efficiency than the steam engines such as those used by Ader and other predecessors. On August 28, 1896, in Berlin, a gas motor was used for the first time to power a dirigible, piloted by Wolfert; while in 1901 a 30 hp Daimler was tested on a seaplane in Austria. But it did not power a flight, nor as we have seen, did Langley's last, far more powerful gas motor. So the motor was an essential element, but not sufficient without the necessary expertise and persistence.

Those the Wright brothers had, and their take-off came when they linked their mastery of techniques to achieve control in the air with an efficient gas engine. The latter, again built by their bicycle shop associate, Charles E. Taylor, was "a simplified version of a contemporary automobile motor," though without spark plugs, fuel pump, or carburetor. Batteries supplied the spark for starting, and the engines generated briefly up to sixteen horsepower, which produced, with the props turning at 350 rpms, 132 pounds of thrust, or 40 more that they felt necessary to fly, even if supplying less than the power of Ader's 1897 machine and only one third that of Langley's last machine.

They reached Kill Devil Hills for the fateful tests on September 25, 1903, and the new *Flyer*, named after their bikes (although Cayley had first used the name for a flying machine in 1813), arrived in crates on October 8. Later that month they began gliding tests of the completed machine.

Repeated storms and various mishaps, including cracks in the motor shaft and propellers—for which Orville returned to Dayton for replacements—forced delays, as Wilbur repaired other items. Still, their total costs amounted to only about $1000, in contrast to Langley's costs of over $50,000.

By mid-December they were ready to "go for it." Because of insufficient winds they decided to move their launching rail to the "Big Hill" on a slope of some nine degrees. On the 14th, Wilbur won a coin toss for the first attempt, but over-eager, he raised the front rudder too high, stalling the *Flyer* in about three and a half seconds, 100 feet down the slope, thus necessitating new repairs.

Finally, on December 17, a cold north wind over twenty miles an hour enabled them to move the launching track to level ground. It was Orville's turn, and at 10:35 A.M., he was able to travel 120 feet in twelve seconds against the 27-mph wind, reaching thirty miles per hour airspeed but only about three mph over the ground, given the force of the wind. With a take-off roll of only about 40 feet, the entire flight was far less in length than the Boeing 747's 231 feet, 4 inches. Had it been calm, the flight would have traveled 540 feet! It was immortalized in the picture of John Daniels, one of about a half dozen local witnesses, showing Wilbur just to the right of the machine, then about two feet up: he had been steadying the craft by guiding a wing until lift-off.

Eureka! Man had flown!—and the next flights proved conclusively it was no fluke, all the more so given problems caused by the high wind. Wilbur was next and made some 175 feet, while Orville achieved 200 feet in fifteen seconds on the third flight. At noon came the longest flight of the day, as Wilbur reached a seemingly incredible 852 feet in fifty-nine seconds, against a 24 mph wind. It ended only when Wilbur turned his elevator down too far as a wind gust caused *Flyer* to plow into the sand, smashing the front frame.

Despite the crash at the end, the four flights marked the birth of a new age. Yet the brothers restrained themselves from publicizing the achievement, and headed home for Christmas.

Uncharacteristically, the press generally ignored the great date of the first flights of December 17, 1903. That was due not only to the reticence of the Wrights, but to general deception and derision at the failure of the $50,000 "Langley's folly" two weeks earlier, and to lack of general knowledge of the vital distinction between the new powered airplane and the "air ships," including balloons and dirigibles, such as those then being flown in Europe.

Thus, two hometown newspapers reported only fragmentary accounts, confusing the nature of the flights with those of the dirigibles widely flown in Europe. A local paper even headlined: "DAYTON BOYS EMULATE GREAT SANTOS DUMONT." The brothers denounced the inaccuracies of the *Norfolk Virginian Pilot* story of December 18, which exaggerated from a secondhand account of their telegram home, stating: "Flying machine soars three miles." That story, however, accurately reported that no balloon had been used and that control was achieved. It was picked up by the Associated Press and carried in some five American papers. In Paris, the *Aérophile*, then in its eleventh year, contained on the last page of its December issue a brief paragraph summarizing "foreign" press reports of "success at Kitty Hawk, with an aeroplane using propellers, driven by a tricycle motor, by Wilbur Wright, which traveled five kilometers."

On January 6, the brothers gave a 500-word factual account of the flights to the Associated Press, correcting the reports of distance achieved and other errors. They explained why they were postponing further "trials to a more favorable season," but concluded with the essential point that they were now sure that "the age of the flying machine had come at last." Ten years later, Orville summarized "how we made the first flight":

> . . . faith in our calculations and the design of . . . the machine, based upon our tables of air pressures, secured by months of careful laboratory work, and confidence in our system of control developed by three years of actual experiences in balancing gliders in the air, had convinced us that the machine was capable of lifting and maintaining itself in the air, and that, with a little practice, it could be safely flown.

Indeed, many believe that December 17 was the greatest sign of the beginning of the new century even if three years into it. For 1903 was also the year of Einstein's first professional paper, of the Nobel Prize in physics for the Curies' discovery of radioactivity, of Hollywood's first feature film, *The Great Train Robbery*, as well as the year of the first "tour" of some thirty-four automobiles in the United States, from Pittsburgh to New York City, even as Henry Ford was beginning their mass production in Detroit.

The skepticism continued for some, however. Thus was founded in 1959, the "Man Will Never Fly Memorial Society." Meeting on December 17 each year, the group claimed 5000 members in 1990. It facetiously proclaims that it is "not opposed to flight. Birds do it, bees do it, and even educated fleas do it. But when you stop to think about it, do you actually believe that a machine made of tons of metal will fly?"

Higher, Farther, Faster and Turning

The age of the "flying machine," launched by the Wrights in December 1903, had indeed "taken off," even if it still had a long way to go. It did so with the coming together of the three most essential requirements: the accumulating knowledge of the basics of aerodynamics, especially knowledge of lift, drag, and control forces; the development of efficient, light motors through their application in other fields, especially for the automobile; and the appearance of two brothers who had the necessary mathematical and engineering capacities, and, equally important, the necessary persistence to carry through the years of learning, testing, and refinements necessary to master the control of lift and motion through the air of man and machine.

Then, after their triumph, like many of the geniuses of history, the Wright brothers, thirty-six and thirty-two years old at the time, proceeded both to carry on with their work, but also to obscure it through sometimes over-zealous efforts to protect the patents and profits due their achievement. They also became increasingly frustrated at the lack of support from initially skeptical governments.

In this chapter, accounts of their further exploits will be combined with those of other pioneers on both sides of the Atlantic, who in lesser but important ways also contributed to the development of the art of flying. This art was worked out more-or-less simultaneously by the establishment of ever-increasing records of speed, altitude, distance, and control. The better performances came in military as well as civilian use, and an enthusiastic public played a great role in urging on the pioneers.

In the spring of 1904, the Wright brothers decided to devote themselves full-time to "the flying machine." They would live off of the $4900 surplus so far saved from their profitable bicycle shop, with the well-founded hope of riches to come from sale of their expertise and new

"Flyers."

In January 1904, simultaneous with their first account of the Kitty Hawk flights, they stepped up efforts to secure patents for their discoveries. After their first request was rejected nine months later, they sought the help of a nearby legal specialist, and he wisely advised them to seek a patent for the crucial "three-axis control system" for pitch, yaw, and roll, rather than for the more widely known flying machine itself. Still, then as now, the wheels of the law ground slowly, and approval of the patent did not come until May 1906.

Meanwhile, in the spring of 1904, they were able to secure rent-free use of a half-mile-long, eighty-seven-acre pasture for further flight testing, on condition that they look out for the cattle and horses of the owner, Torrence Hoffman, a Dayton bank president.

The new *Flyer* constructed for these tests was sturdier and eighty pounds heavier than the December 1903 model, with a motor generating sixteen h.p. After various mishaps in May, successful flights of up to 225 feet were achieved in June. But after twenty-four successful flights, an incorrect recovery from a wind gust on August 24 caused an accident which temporarily grounded them.

That, in turn, caused their withdrawal from the proposed big event of 1904, which was to have been an aerial show to highlight the St. Louis World Fair. The famous Alberto Santos-Dumont shipped his seventh dirigible (or "airship," as it was known), in three two-ton crates to St. Louis to compete for the $100,000 grand prize for the completion of a ten-mile (soon reduced to six-mile) circuit. Santos, however, withdrew in anger when never-explained gashes were discovered in the fabric of his airship, considered the most advanced yet. No other contestants had any hope of winning such an ambitious challenge, and the Fair's sponsors reduced the circuit to one mile. The *California Arrow*, a fifty-three-foot airship built by Thomas Baldwin and piloted by Roy Knabenshue, won that reduced race on the last day of October. But, the ill-fated Fair had gone bankrupt and no prize money was available at all.

Meanwhile, the Wrights had constructed a pyramid-like structure, with falling pulley weights to accelerate their craft to offset the lack of wind, which was usually the case on their Ohio pasture. Then in September, they mastered the all-important art of turning the aircraft, decisive proof of their progress with the critical problem of control. After several inadequately controlled half and S turns, on September 20, 1904,

Wilbur flew the first complete circle ever and covered over 4080 feet in one minute, thirty-six seconds. That complete turn* in its way was as important an event as the far more famous "first" flight of the previous December, since to go in a straight line was one thing, but to be able to change direction was equally important. Now the airplane could truly challenge the "dirigible" airship, which turned with rudders or by reducing alternately the power of a motor. Of course the airplane would soon go far beyond the airships in speed and other capabilities.

The September 1905 turns by the Wrights also merited the first news account of a true airplane flight, as against the European accounts of balloons and gliders. That "scoop" was given not by one of the journalists who were increasing their demands for information, but by a beekeeper merchant from nearby Medina, Ohio, Amos T. Root. His story was given in *Gleanings in Bee Culture,* January 1, 1905. It read:

> The machine is held until ready to start by a sort of trap to be sprung when all is ready; then with a tremendous flapping and snapping of the four-cylinder engine, the huge machine springs aloft. When it first turned that circle, and came near the starting point, I was right in front of it; and I said then, and I believe still, it was one of the grandest sights, if not the grandest sight of my life.

---

*Aerial turns are accomplished by the same "lift" that enables the plane's take-off, only it is a pushing to the side by the lower pressures caused by increased airflow across the top of the wing being raised. The Wrights did this by a helical twist of one wing up and the other down, while the aileron, which became the normal device for turning aircraft by World War I, achieves this by setting in motion opposite forces. That is, when the pilot moves his control "stick" in the direction of a turn, it moves a separate surface near the tip of the wing in the direction opposite to the desired turn, forcing the wing up in reaction to the drag induced. Thus, for a left turn, the stick is moved left proportionally to the steepness of the turn desired, which moves the right wing aileron down and the left wing aileron up, thereby causing the wings to move counterclockwise, with leftward lift. To prevent skidding as the plane changes direction, the rudder is also moved, generally in the direction of the turn, but occasionally in the opposite direction to offset gusts of cross wind or sliding. The Englishman M.P.W. Boulton already in 1868 took out a patent for ailerons, but they were not fitted to a glider until 1904 when Robert Esnault-Pelteric tried them near Paris. They were used there on an aircraft in 1906 by Santos-Dumont, and more effectively in 1908 by Henry Farman and Louis Blériot, although they also continued to use wing-warping. Lateral stability had been greatly improved after 1871, when Pénaud had demonstrated that dihedral, or upward angled, wings, would force a falling wing higher because of the faster flow of air over it.

It is nicely ironic that such an eloquent "first" should have come from a man whose living came from the mastery of flying honey-makers. But given the obscurity of that journal and recurring problems which prevented the brothers from demonstrating their progress when Chanute visited in October, the world's press continued to ignore the epochal Wright flights. On November 9, Wilbur circled Huffman Prairie for five minutes at speeds up to thirty-five miles an hour—an achievement that became known as the "victory flight." Then, on December 1, Orville flew his first complete circle.

Yet, incredibly, the U.S. War Department, still sensitive to the fiasco of the Langley Aerodrome, again in January 1905 declined to support the project until the machine "shall have been perfected." The brothers therefore decided to approach European governments to seek financial support. In the years before World War I, they understandably assumed the military would be their best customers even as they expressed hope that the flying machine would end wars, through the terror of aerial guns and bomb drops.

In January 1905, they began correspondence with the British War Office to develop a plane that could carry two persons for fifty miles, but in May, London claimed lack of funds to meet the demand of £500 for each mile covered. Nor at first did contacts with France and Germany produce results.

Meanwhile, they built an improved Flyer with a more powerful eighteen horsepower motor, which became known as the Wright Model A. As in future aircraft, they changed to separate controls for the wing (in 1915, Orville switched to ailerons) and the tail rudder, increasing stability to prevent the side-slipping that had marred earlier flights. They still used hip movements of the prone pilot to pull or loosen cables for wing warping and rudder movement.

After delays caused by their father's church business and a June 1905 accident due to unfamiliarity with the new control system, they made important new advances. These included adjustments to move forward the center of gravity and to inflect the wings to give dihedral or V-shaped angles for greater stability. In September, they solved their last major remaining control problem. This was that extra speed was needed in a steep turn to offset centrifugal forces, discovered when Orville suddenly had to clear a large locust tree in his way on September 28. This also led to the realization that engine torque and the centrifugal force in turns required a rudder opposite to the shift of wing or, later, ailerons. In the same month, Orville was able to fly a figure-eight, or two intertwining circles, which became a standard acrobatic maneuver. Then on October 5, Wilbur flew 24.2 miles in thirty-eight minutes—a record which would stand for several years.

By now it was clear that the twelve-, fifteen- and fifty-nine second flights of December 17, 1903, brief as they were, had indeed signaled the beginning of a new age. The full turns of October 1904, and now a year later, a flight of over half an hour, proved conclusively that the brothers had mastered the basics of flight.

The only witnesses so far, however, had been North Carolina and Ohio residents, and the world remained uncaring or skeptical. In 1905, greatest attention was given to the claims of California inventor John Joseph Montgomery and his pilot Daniel Maloney, an aerial artist and parachutist. Montgomery claimed in March that a glider of the type he had been making since the 1890s had solved the "problem of aerial navigation." The next month the two demonstrated the accomplishment before a hometown crowd at Santa Clara. Maloney cut his glider loose from a hot-air balloon 3000 feet up and sailed, according to varying reports, seven or fifteen minutes to great publicity. There also arose new disputes over stolen ideas and now accusations of sabotage by another California aerial stuntman and airship designer, Thomas Baldwin, who had built the winner of the October 1904 St. Louis World's Fair race. Then on July 18, 1905, at San Jose, Montgomery's glider somehow inverted, went into a dive, and crashed, taking the twenty-six-year-old Maloney to his death.

Wilbur Wright wrote Chanute that he had expected such a disaster, since Montgomery's April 1905 pamphlet "The Aeroplane" misjudged problems of "the distribution of pressures and the travel of the center of pressure with increasing speed . . ." Failures of new Montgomery gliders, and the San Francisco earthquake of 1906 and subsequent depression, ended these California experiments, though some still claim they made important, if unproven, contributions to the "take-off."

To avoid the kind of massive publicity that accompanied and complicated the Montgomery–Maloney efforts, at least prior to procuring patents, the brothers strove to keep the greatest possible secrecy for their work. But when the *Dayton Daily News* and then other papers published accounts of the thirty-eight-minute flight of October 5, 1905, they decided to take the lead in making known their achievements. On October 9, they again wrote the U.S. War Department, and on October 19 to Chanute and the London War Office. Then, on November 17, they sent accounts of their flights to Georges Besançon, the Paris editor of *L'Aérophile;* to Carl Diestbach, New York representative of a German journal; and to Patrick Alexander of the British Royal Aeronautical Society.

The latter read the account at the Society's December 15 meeting in London, and a German translation appeared in the February 1906 issue of Diestbach's journal, *Illustrierte Aeronautische Mitteilungen.* The British War Office, however, had already decided on a new delay, and the Germans became incensed over the previous December publication by *L'Aérophile* of two letters the Wrights had written to French aviation pioneer and artillery captain Ferdinand Ferber. They interpreted Ferber's translations of references to Kaiser Wilhelm as personal insults and proceeded to insult the Wrights. Written in May and October, at the time of the first Moroccan crisis, when Germany challenged French expansion in northwest Africa, the letters referred to the "truculent mood" of the German emperor. The brothers, in turn, were angry at *L'Aérophile* for publishing their private correspondence at all.

Their November 17 account sent to *L'Aérophile* was first published in *L'Auto* of November 30, 1905, stirring considerable controversy over its credibility. The wealthy lawyer patron of French aviation, Ernest Archdeacon, repeated his challenge of the previous March: If the Wrights could fly as well as they claimed, why did they not compete before witnesses for the 50,000-franc prize offered by himself and oil baron Henri Deutsch de la Meurthe, for a closed-circuit one-kilometer flight? Most of the Aéroclub de France shared Archdeacon's skepticism, but Besançon, Ferber, Chanute, and others helped persuade the French government to send a friend of Ferber's, Arnold Fordyce, to Dayton to investigate. He arrived there on December 28, 1905, and promptly signed a contract for a "Flyer" for one million francs on condition it could fly fifty kilometers by the following August. However, the French War Ministry subsequently raised its requirements of speed, altitude, and exclusivity clauses, and the deal fell through, as did a new attempt to sell to the British.

The first confirmed airplane flight in Europe was not achieved until September 12, 1906. It was flown on Denmark's island of Lindholm, by engineer Jacob Ellehammer in a 20hp biplane, but was tethered and went only 42 meters (140 feet). Meanwhile, aviation fever was rampant in France, which in the words of a leading historian of the period, was the "nursery school" of aviation after its birth in the United States.

Several pilots there sought to match the Wrights' achievements that same year. First, a Hungarian, Trajan Vuia, made a short hop of eighty feet in Paris, while the later famous aviator Gabriel Voisin built several unsuccessful craft before an improved third model achieved some success. Alberto Santos-Dumont, already famous for his dirigible tour around the Eiffel Tower five years before, flew a few meters in September and over sixty over the Bois de Boulogne in October. Finally, on November 12, with an improved motor producing fifty hp enabling a ground take-off, he flew his 33-foot-wide box-kite-like craft for 220 meters to win an Aéro Club de France award of 1500 francs for exceeding 100 meters. The *14 Bis* lacked a tail and its wheels collapsed again on landing, but that first sustained flight in Europe forced the Wrights to backtrack from their prediction just before: that besides themselves, "no one will be able to develop a practical flyer within five years." Now Wilbur called Santos-Dumont's flight "the first real indication of progress . . . in France in five years."

Ironically, news of the French flights and of the controversies there over the Wrights' claims stimulated U.S. opinion to look more closely into the beginnings of heavier-than-air aviation. The Aero Club of America was formed in the autumn of 1905, and the following January invited the brothers to join the group, whose other members were mostly millionaires. On April 7, 1906, the prestigious *Scientific American* published a report the Wrights had prepared for the Aero Club, and independently procured confirmation of their claims from eleven of seventeen witnesses queried.

The famous inventor and regent of the Smithsonian Institution, Alexander Graham Bell, was among those becoming fascinated with the new aviation. He gave the most succinctly appropriate answer to the questions about what was so unique about the Wright Flyer: "It flies." But he also believed their aircraft could be improved upon, and at age fifty-eight he began to construct box-kite like structures of tetrahedral cells. One flew briefly in December 1905 with a 165-pound man suspended by a rope, and two years later an elaborate one, fifty-two feet wide and ten feet high with 3,393 cells, reached an altitude of 150 to 200 feet before crashing into the water seven minutes later, dousing the pilot, Lt. Thomas E. Selfridge. That occurred at the test center which Aero Club member Bell had established on his vacation estate near Badeck, Nova Scotia. Along with Selfridge, Bell attracted other leading American aviators, notably Glenn Hammond Curtiss, to his center, and on October 1, 1907, they founded The Aerial Experiment Association.

Like the Wrights, Curtiss also began selling and repairing bicycles. A daredevil who never finished high school, he took up racing, and turning to motorcycles, developed a small motor factory in his hometown of Hammondsport, New York. In 1907, at twenty nine, he set a world speed record of 136 mph on his motorcycle, before injuries and developing interest turned him full-time to aviation. With Thomas Scott Baldwin, who had come to Hammondsport from airship competition with John Montgomery in California, he met the Wrights on September 3, 1907, as they sought to improve their knowledge and give performance flights for the Dayton Fair.

Then Curtiss developed a flying machine, dubbed by Bell, the "June Bug," which won the first *Scientific American* trophy for a straight-line flight of at least one kilometer, at Hammondsport on July 4, 1908. In fact, he flew over a mile, 5360 feet, in one minute, forty seconds, but the Wrights, who had passed that distance in 1905, refused to compete. They were unwilling as yet to change their eighty-foot launching rail and landing skids for wheels as used in Europe and as required for the prize.

That was only one of many "take-offs." In August and September 1907, the Breguet brothers, Louis and Jacques, and Charles Richet, established another first, the lifting of a man by a tethered helicopter, at Douai in the north of France; and on November 13, Paul Cornu achieved the first "free" helicopter flight near Lisieux, in Calvados, Normandy.

On January 13, 1908, a sensation was created by the first officially observed closed circuit or circular flight of one kilometer in one minute, twenty-eight seconds, at the busy airstrip at Issy-les-Moulineaux just outside Paris. The pilot was the son of a wealthy English journalist, who lived most of his life in France, known variously as Henri or Henry Farman. He flew a Voisin biplane with an Antoinette fifty hp motor, to win the Deutsch-Archdeacon Grand Prix d'Aviation, in fact a relatively modest $10,000 (50,000 francs). Farman carried aviation enthusiast Ernest Archdeacon over one kilometer on May 30, 1908, the longest flight yet with a passenger. He had described his first flights the year before as giving ". . . a sort of indescribably joyous feeling that you are independent of the earth."

Another famous French aviator of the time was Léon Delagrange, a Parisian artist and sculptor. He had soloed two days before Farman the previous November, becoming the sixth man on earth to fly a powered aircraft.* In 1908, Delagrange made over forty flights in France and Italy, including one of eighteen minutes, thirty seconds in June, in an improved Voisin aircraft. On July 8, at Milan, Italy, he took aloft the first woman, Thérèse Peltier, another French artist. That flight preceded by several months Wilbur Wright's ascent in France with Mrs. Hart Berg. Then, on October 30, 1908, Henry Farman made the first cross-country flight from Bouy, about 30 kilometers (20 miles) northwest to Rheims (Reims). The next day Louis Blériot completed the first round-trip cross-country flight of about twenty miles, with three stops, from Toury, about fifty miles south-southwest of Paris, south to Arvillers, near Artenay, then back northwest to Santilly, and farther northeast back to Toury.

On February 10, 1908, the U.S. Army Signal Corps finally gave the Wrights a contract, as did the French government in March. In May, Wilbur carried the first passenger, a certain Charles Furnas, ever to go aloft, for 28.6 seconds at Kill Devil Hills. He then departed for triumphant demonstrations of his craft and skills in France, while Orville went to Fort Meyer outside Washington to test another Flyer for the Signal Corps.

Orville began successful flights on September 3 before large crowds, including the twenty-one-year-old son of President Theodore Roosevelt. He set three world records, including the first flight of over an hour—a seventy-minute sojourn on September 11—and the next day one of over nine minutes with a passenger, Major Squier. That followed a previous record of over six minutes with a Lieutenant Lahm. But disaster struck when he agreed to carry aloft on September 17 a third military man, Lt. Thomas Selfridge. On this occasion, Orville's newly installed right pusher propeller cracked, causing vibrations, severing bracing wires, and plunging the craft to a crash 150 feet below. Selfridge, rescued from the fall of Bell's big kite the previous December, suffered a skull fracture that soon killed him, the first victim of a powered airplane flight, although at

*After the Wrights, Santos-Dumont, Gabriel Voisin, and Louis Blériot. In addition to Farman, Voisin's brother Charles, Robert Esnault-Pelterie, the American Glenn Curtiss, and others shortly followed, fourteen having flown by March 1908.

least eight others already had died in balloon accidents. Orville's fifth near-miss with death put him in a hospital for over a month, with scalp wounds, broken ribs, and a fractured left thigh.

Orville's accident followed by a month the first impressive demonstrations of "the Wright stuff" in Europe. To avoid the too-great publicity sure to follow the use of fields such as Issy-les-Moulineaux outside Paris, used by French pilots, he settled on a racetrack 202 kilometers (126 miles) to the southwest, just south of Le Mans. After almost two months spent assembling the Flyer, which had been damaged by over-zealous customs officials, he was ready by August 8, 1908, to begin his demonstrations.

Wilbur electrified the previously skeptical French; enormous crowds gathered at a local race track and, after August 19, at a bigger field east of Le Mans on an artillery range at Camp d'Auvours. The first flights were not longer than those in July of over eight minutes by Blériot and fifteen minutes by Henri Farman, but the facility of his turns, including figure-eights, strikingly demonstrated his control and proved to be the first sustained circular flights in Europe. Then in September, Wilbur steadily increased his performances with flights of over forty-one miles in one hour on the first, thirty-one minutes on the second, and still longer ones on succeeding days. Up to 10,000 spectators gathered, and the soon-to-be-famous Blériot was moved to state that "a new era in mechanical flight has commenced." Wilbur's flights more than offset the news of Orville's accident and of the death of Selden.

Wilbur made over 120 flights that autumn and carried over forty passengers, including such notables as Paul Doumer, an important Governor General of Indochina at the turn of the century; a future prime minister, Paul Painlevé; as well as aviation supporter Henry Deutsch de la Meurthe, and American patrons Mr. and Mrs, Hart Berg. On October 6, he carried another passenger, Ernest Zens, one hour and four minutes, for a new record. Then, following other impressive performances, he climaxed the year on its last day by flying over seventy-six miles (124 kilometers, or 150 counting the turns), at up to a record 375 feet of altitude, in two hours, eighteen minutes to win the Michelin Cup of 20,000 francs.

Blériot and one of Wilbur's most successful students, the balloonist Paul Tissandier, persuaded him to establish a more suitable winter camp six miles out of Pau, just north of the Pyrenees Mountains, and he arrived there on January 14, 1909. Brother Orville and sister Katherine, whom he had met in Paris two days earlier, joined Wilbur on the 16th, ironically surviving a train crash on the way, which killed two people but only delayed the still-recuperating Orville some five hours. By March 23, Wilbur made sixty additional flights including forty with his three leading students, Tissandier, Count Charles de Lambert, and Captain Lucas-Girardvile. "All" Europe, including the kings of Spain and Italy, came to watch.

Next, Wilbur went to Rome, where he trained the first Italian aviator, Lieutenant Calderara, and gave demonstration flights for a $10,000 contract, and a first ride to, among others, the famous poet, patriot, and future World War I pilot, Gabriele d'Annunzio. The visiting J.P. Morgan was one of the spectators, and on April 24, Wilbur took aloft a Universal Newsreel photographer, who filmed the first aerial motion pictures. In addition to sights of Rome, these showed the controls and instruments, including a simple piece of string (later a small horizontal vane) flowing backward to indicate the plane's attitude or pitch. On May 1, the Wrights returned to Le Mans for a farewell banquet. As they were expected in Washington for new demonstrations, they shortly left for England, where they met the Short brothers, Charles Stuart Rolls, and other pioneers. In August and September, Orville returned to Europe for aerial demonstrations in Germany.

The greatest aviation event of 1909, however, was not accomplished by the Wrights, but by the colorful French pioneer, Louis Blériot. On July 25, 1909, he electrified the world with the first successful crossing of the English Channel, some twenty-four miles from southwest of Calais to near Dover in thirty-seven minutes, flying his eleventh machine near the then records of 155 meters (496 feet) for altitude and 76.9 kilometers an hour (48 mph) for speed. Santos-Dumont summarized the excitement, writing to Blériot, "It is a victory for the air over the sea . . . Thanks to you, aviation will cross the Atlantic."

A gregarious, likeable man from Cambrai near the Great War battlefields, Blériot sported a large black mustache, as did Gabriel Voisin. And like the other early greats—the Wrights with their bicycles, Curtiss with his motorcycles, and famous countrymen Voisin and Henri Farman with their new automobiles—he began with work on another aspect of the new transportation: inventing and selling the best car head-lamps yet devised. He spent his considerable earnings from them on a series of mostly unsuccessful airplanes after 1905, nearly killing himself in crashes in 1907 and afterward. Then, with a lucky reward to his wife for saving a wealthy neighbor's child from a fall, he and engineer Raymond Saulnier built a monoplane of the sort pioneered by the French in competition with Wright biplanes. It succeeded in the first Channel crossing, despite the loss of its compass and other problems. This came just a week after engine failure forced down the popular Hubert Latham a third of the way across.

One month later, the mania for new achievements in the air developed still further with the first great aerial fair, held at Rheims in northeastern France. Shows and meetings had been held earlier in the year in London and various French cities, but stimulated by Blériot's Channel crossing and generous donations from the area's champagne producers, the festive Rheims Aviation Week proved aviation's biggest public event so far. Huge crowds, including French President Armand Fallières and English leader David Lloyd-George, arrived, as well as a million spectators. Many new records were broken: for altitude (508.9 feet by Hubert Latham), distance (180 kilometers [112 miles] by Henri Farman), and speed (47.8 mph by Blériot). Where before 1909 only ten men in the world had been aloft for as long as a minute, in that single last week of August 1909 eighty-seven flights went beyond 3 miles, seven over 60 miles, and one went 111.8 miles for the distance record. Some twenty-eight pilots flew in twenty-one French and six Wright aircraft.

But the highlight, coming on the last day, earned the victor the title "Champion Aviator of the World." That was given to the only American at the fair, Glenn Curtiss, who won the featured Gordon Bennett prize of $10,000, put up by the wealthy *New York Herald* publisher of that name. He did it by flying the required 20 kilometers (12.5 miles) in 15 minutes, 50.6 seconds, at the near-record speed of over 46 mph. He now held the distance–airspeed record as he did the land speed record of 136 mph with his 1907 motorcycle victory at Ormond Beach, Florida.

The Wrights, who had just returned to America in May, declined to compete in the Rheims events, although Orville considered doing so between his demonstration flights on a new trip to Germany. Wilbur vetoed the idea and scorned such public displays. Indeed, news of their patent suit against all "copiers" of their machines arrived at the very moment of Curtiss' triumph. Orville flew his longest flight—of one hour, forty-five minutes—on September 18 at Berlin. It failed to break Henri Farman's distance record at Rheims (111.8 miles), but on October 2, before returning to the States, he broke by a good 1000 feet Latham's altitude record of August, reaching an even 1600 feet.

The brothers found competition rapidly increasing in the United States as well. There, a lively aviation magazine, *Fly* (*Flying* after October 1912) had already appeared in November 1908, and claimed 200,000 readers by February 1909. Its covers and numerous illustrations demonstrated the rapidly spreading craze, while noting already in the first issue the inordinate attention given to aviation accidents relative to the far more numerous violent deaths in other types of accidents. Some credit the first aircraft factory in America as being one built in 1908 by Edward Gallaudet, the founder also of a famous school for the deaf in Washington, DC. He had flown airplane models since 1898.

Within two years, there were three "aerial exhibition teams," organized by the Wrights, Glenn Curtiss, and a Texan architect, John Moissant. Another famous Texan, "king of the cowboys" and "Indian fighter" Sam Cody also became a famous pilot, but in England, where he was the first to fly, in 1908. As we shall see in Chapter Nine, these "daring young men in their flying machines" as a phrase of the day put it, were precursors of the famous barnstormers of the 1920s, and were already electrifying growing crowds. One of Curtiss' pilots, Lincoln Beachey, became very famous in 1911, establishing altitude records, "buzzing" grandstands, and even flying under Niagara Falls before an unbelieving crowd of 150,000. Tragically, before one-third that many people, at a San Francisco Exhibition on March 14, 1915, his plane's wings folded as he far exceeded its maximum speed of 103 mph, trying to perform the outside and inside loops describing the figure S. He dove to his death.

Faring far better, as he became hooked on aviation, watching such exhibits after 1909 near his native Enid, Oklahoma, was famous small-plane builder Clyde V. Cessna. He took up flying in 1911 and in 1916 began his airplane factory in Wichita, Kansas. In subsequent years, Lloyd G. Stearman, Walter Beech, and others also established well-known aircraft companies in Wichita. William T. Piper established the third, with Beech and Cessna, of the "big three" of U.S. general aviation: the Piper Aircraft Corporation, in 1937 in Lock Haven, Pennsylvania, and later, Florida.

Following recovery from the September 17, 1908 crash which had

killed Lt. Thomas Selfridge, Orville Wright resumed demonstration tests
for the Army in Washington in late July, 1909. On August 2, he finally
received a contract for the first-ever airplane bought for military service,
the Model A *Miss Columbia*. Then in October of that year, Wilbur made
his first public flights in America. They took place over New York to highlight anniversaries of Robert Fulton's first steamboat ascent of the Hudson
River and of the founding of the city. On the sixth, his ten-mile flight of
twenty and a half minutes over the city won a $15,000 prize and was wit-
nessed by over a million people.

But Glenn Curtiss, too, made celebrated flights for generally lesser
prizes even as the patent wars initiated by the Wrights in mid-August
heated up. The Wrights charged that the increasing use of ailerons
infringed their 1906 patent for wing-warping, and a trial in Buffalo in
December resulted in the judges ruling for the Wrights the following
month. But public opinion became increasingly divided, especially when
the prestigious Smithsonian Institution joined the anti-Wright arguments.

Wilbur, meanwhile, virtually gave up testing his aircraft, leaving that
to Orville, while he increasingly turned his attention to the lawsuits
against Curtiss and others. Before his death, from typhoid, on May 30,
1912, he spent weeks on end in court, and posthumously his testimony
seemed to have won the judgment of the U.S. Circuit Court of Appeals
in January 1914, reinforcing the decision of January 1910. It declared
that Wilbur and Orville, as "pioneers in the practical art of flying heavier-
than-air machines," deserved to have their patents cover ailerons as well
as wing-warping, even though the Englishman Boulton and others had
taken out earlier patents. Curtiss, however, continued to build and test a
craft designed to win the £10,000 prize announced shortly before by the
London Daily Mail publisher for the first aircraft to cross the Atlantic in
less than seventy-two hours without a land stop.

The far greater problem of World War I intervened in August 1914,
and for four years made virtually irrelevant the continuing arguments
between Orville, Curtiss, and others. Indeed, the first previews of war in
the air had already occurred, not only with aerial observations by a pilot
in the Moissant Aerial Circus of Mexican rebels across the Rio Grande
from El Paso in February 1911, but shortly thereafter with the first real
bombardments from the air. By mid-1913, they included relatively large
thirty-pound pipe bombs (many early World War I bombs weighed twen-

ty pounds) dropped by French and American (including a New York Cherokee, John Hester Worden!) mercenary pilots flying for opposing sides deeper in Mexico.

More ominously, in light of European conflicts, Italians used five-pound bombs against Turkish troops in their campaign of autumn 1911 to take over Tripoli (Libya). Early the following year, the French reported "modest successes" with similar small bombs in subduing Moroccan resistance to French control in northwest Africa. The more alarming crises in the Balkans of 1912–1913 also saw the use of bombs and aerial observations by the Turks and others. All that bombing was in clear violation of the 1899 and 1907 Hague Conventions, but unfortunately foretold the future. The Italian Giulio Douhet, made famous by his 1921 book *The Command of the Air*, predicted in 1909 that "the sky is about to become another battlefield," and stated in late 1912 that "a new weapon has come forth, the sky has become a new battlefield."

Before returning to the terrible period of World War I and further acceleration of the take-off of aviation, a review of pre-war records and accomplishments is in order.

On October 18, 1909, the first major city, Paris, was flown over, by the Count de Lambert. The next year, a twenty-five-year-old Romanian, Henri-Marie Coanda, claimed to fly a first jet-powered craft at Paris, but at best it crashed on take-off and many doubt that it ever got that far. Coanda, however, went on to a rich aviation career until his death in 1972, giving his name to some effects of the curvature of airflows. Also in 1910, New York saw the first major hit tune inspired by the new craze, "Come Josephine in My Flying Machine," as well as the first unofficial airmail delivery.

In France, there were even bicycle airplanes, called *aviettes*, with small wings and tail attached. Some achieved short hops, but most "reared up and crashed, or hugged the earth," despite all efforts. On February 18, 1911, a French pilot flew the first official airmail, even if for only six miles, near, of all places, Allahabad, in British India. This was a year after the first radio links were made from an airplane to the ground in the north of France, which in turn came almost a half-century after Thaddeus Lowe had done that from a balloon at Washington, DC.

In May 1911, Jules Védrines won a three-day race from Paris to Madrid, fighting off an attacking eagle over the Pyrenees. The race had been delayed a day, after an accident killed the French Minister of War and injured the Premier when they mistakenly wandered into the path of an onrushing plane. A month later, Curtiss won $10,000 for the longest flight yet in America, 152 miles with two stops, from Albany to New York City; and in June, another Curtiss flyer, Charlie Hamilton, won another $10,000 for a 172-mile round trip from New York to Philadelphia.

The far bigger feat of crossing the entire United States was also accomplished in 1911, although it took about two months. The pilot was thirty-two-year-old Calbraith Perry Rodgers, who had just soloed after only ninety minutes' practice. He took off near New York, September 17, in a frail craft of bamboo, wire, and cloth, and headed west via Chicago and Kansas City, often following railroad tracks and reading the names of towns on towers and hangars. After over seventy stops, untold minor mishaps, including a mid air run-in with an eagle, numerous crash landings, and five major crashes, he reached Pasadena on November 5 and Long Beach on December 10. Despite his heroic effort, he failed to receive the $50,000 prize offered by publisher William Randolph Hearst, as it stipulated a maximum thirty-day flight, which had to be completed by October 10. Four months later, on April 1, 1912, the unfortunate Rodgers crashed to his death after his plane struck a sea gull during an exhibition flown not far from the Long Beach destination of his cross-country trip.

The equally impressive feats of the first crossing of the Alps, and then of the Mediterranean, came a year before and two years after Rodgers' epic flight. On September 23, 1910, Georges Chavez, a Peruvian who was born in and lived most of his life in Paris, succeeded in crossing the Alps over the Simplon Pass to Milan. Two weeks earlier he had established an altitude record of 8487 feet, but now had to pass mountains up to 11,600 feet high, which he did through precipitous gorges, flying much of the way at 6600 feet. Only 10 meters above his landing at Domodossola, his plane broke apart, sending Chavez to the hospital where he died four days later.

In 1908, the altitude record officially was still only 82 feet, although the Wrights had flown much higher. By the end of 1909 the record had gone to 1486 feet and by July 14, 1914, a German biplane piloted by Harry Oelerich soared to 25,755 feet. Fifty thousand feet would be exceeded by 1937 and 100,000 by 1959!

Speed and distance records also fell year by year. Wilbur Wright's stu-

A detail from the sarcophagus of Ramses III, showing the Egyptian goddess Isis. She was the patroness of travelers, and her outstretched wings protected the dead.

A detail of a Tiepolo painting depicting Perseus and Andromeda with the winged horse Pegasus. In the ancient world, Pegasus was a symbol of poetry. (Courtesy of the Frick Collection)

Hypnos (sleep) and Thanatos (death) carry the body of the hero Sarpedon to Zeus. This detail is from a Greek mixing bowl.

The famous Greek statue "Winged Victory" in the Louvre Museum in Paris. Although significantly damaged, the power of this image is undiminished.

A 1638 French print by Marie Briot showing Daedalus and his son Icarus trying to escape from Crete in Greek mythology. Having made wings from feathers and wax, the father succeeds in flying to land, while his son falls to his death because he flew too near the sun.

A fairy rides on the back of a phoenix in this Chinese painting from the Sung Dynasty.

The Marquis de Bacqueville sails into the Seine River, 1742.

An Egyptian engraving showing a Persian "birdman," D'Abdas Ebas Fernas Abou Kassem.

St. Joseph of Copertino levitating before a cross. Many people witnessed his mysterious flights in the 17th century.

Francisco de Goya drew this haunting image of an old witch teaching a novice to fly on a broomstick. The reality of modern flight training has become somewhat less dramatic, with the increasing use of simulators. (Courtesy of Harvard University)

Linda maestra!

J.A.C. Charles and M.-N. Robert are shown departing from the Tuileries in the first hydrogen balloon in 1783, while 200,000 onlookers cheer the ascent. Two hours later, they were thirty miles from Paris.

The balloon "Atlantic" set a distance record of 804 miles from St. Louis in 1859 before crashing in Henderson, New York. John Wise and his crew had hoped to cross the ocean, but perhaps it was better that the journey ended as it did.

In 1783, the Montgolfier brothers launched this huge balloon carrying a sheep, a cock and a duck, all of whom survived.

Madame Blanchard became the first woman to die in an accident involving flight in 1819. She was able to bring her burning balloon down in the Rue de Provence in Paris, but tumbled to her death after she alighted on a roof.

The first aerial photograph taken in America, from a balloon in 1860, shows Boston from 1200 feet.

A poster for a musical of 1898 imagining a future flight over New York.

Thaddeus Lowe about to ascend in a balloon to spy on Confederate forces in Virginia during the American Civil War.

The Wright brothers spent three years at Kitty Hawk learning to glide, as in this 1902 photo.

Octave Chanute designed this glider, and A.M. Herring piloted it on the shores of Lake Michigan in 1896.

German glider pioneer Otto Lilienthal is seen here gliding cver an interested crowd. Before his death in 1896 he was an inspiration to the Wright brothers.

This famous photo shows the moment that the first powered airplane left the ground. Orville Wright is in the machine, and Wilbur Wright is alongside. The first flight lasted 12 seconds and covered 100 feet. (Courtesy of the Smithsonian)

The Old World encounters the New. Wilbur Wright flies over southwest France in February 1909 (before King Alphonso XIII of Spain). The brothers attempted to sell their plane in Europe in order to recoup some of the expenditures incurred during their lonely years of research.

The "Flyer" that Orville Wright brought to Fort Meyer to try to sell to the U.S. Army. The pilot is now seated upright, and the plane is longer and sturdier than earlier models.

The crash that killed a passenger (Lt. Thomas Selfridge), gravely injured Orville, and put a temporary end to Army interest in flight.

Orville and Wilbur Wright, the men who made a reality of the dream of powered flight, in their habitual derbies and suits. Their vision and resourcefulness have been an inspiration to pilots and inventors around the world.

Ruth Law Oliver set a distance record by flying 512 miles from Chicago to New York in 1916.

Harriet Quimby was the first woman to receive a pilot's license in the U.S., as well as the first woman to fly the English Channel.

René Fonck was the top French ace of the Great War with 75 victories, including six in one day on May 9, 1918.

Manfred von Richthofen was the leading ace of WWI with 80 victories. After painting his plane red, followed by fellow pilots, his elite command became known as the "Flying Circus."

The highly-maneuverable Fokker DR-I, the triplane the "Red Baron" was flying when he was shot down in April 1918.

The fast and agile SPAD was a French design that was widely used by
the Allies.

Former race car driver Eddie Rickenbacker was America's leading ace in the Great War
with 26 victories.

The first photograph taken from an airplane in America shows San Diego in 1911 from a Curtiss hydroplane.

The USS *Alabama* is attacked with a phosphorous bomb in a chilling demonstration of air power organized by Billy Mitchell in 1923.

dent, Paul Tissandier, went all of 34.04 mph on May 20, 1909. Two and a half years after Blériot established the new record of 47.85 mph at Rheims on August 28, another French pilot, Jules Védrines, reached over 100 mph on February 22, 1912. Maurice Prévost established the pre-war record of 126,67 mph (203.81 kph), on September 29, 1913.

Distance records went from Henri Farman's officially recorded first kilometer in January 1908, to 233 kilometers (145 miles) by the same pilot on November 4 of the next year. On April 12, 1912, Pierre Prier made the first non-stop flight from London to Paris in four hours, fifty-five minutes, and on September 11 of that year Georges Fourny made the first air trip without stop of over 1010 kilometers (628 miles). The pre-war distance record of 1020 kilometers (634 miles) non-stop was established from Buc, near Paris, in late 1913, by Augustin Seguin, and the first flight to stay aloft for over 24 hours was accomplished near Berlin on July 10–11 by Reinhold Boehm.

After the Rheims Aviation Week of 1909, numerous contests were held. In January 1910, French aviator Louis Paulhan had dazzled southern Californians with a forty-five-mile flight to Santa Anita, after establishing a new altitude record of 4165 feet. On the night of April 27–28 of that year, he narrowly beat the star English flyer, Claude Graham-White, in a hair-raising race to win the £10,000 *Daily Mail* prize for the first flight from London to Manchester. But in October 1910, the latter won the race for speed over 100 kilometers, in sixty-one minutes, 4.74 seconds at Belmont Park, Long Island, outside New York City. On March 8 of that year, the first woman, the Baroness de Laroche, received a license to fly, and on March 28 the first seaplane flight was made near Marseilles by Henri Fabre.

As mentioned in Chapter Four, the first commercial services ever began in Zeppelin dirigibles in 1911, and the first commercial airplane service actually operated in Florida for three months before the war in early 1914. Two Benoist bi-wing seaplanes, carrying one passenger each, made five round trips a day between St. Petersburg and Tampa. Zeppelin's engine-powered dirigibles carried far more passengers in the years before the war. Organized as a commercial service in 1909, by August 1914 they had carried over 10,000 passengers around Germany at speeds of about 40 mph.

French pilot Emil Aubrun made the first night flight on March 10, 1910, in distant Argentina. But a little later compatriots Henri Farman

and Roger Sommer did successive night flights east of Paris, and night flying soon became commonplace, lights and beacons on likely routes being
installed by 1914. That fateful year also saw the first use of flaps, or lowered undersurfaces, to increase lift, although they did not come into widespread use until the 1920s and 1930s. The first retractable landing gear
was experimented with in Germany as early as 1911, but then more practically on a high-wing racing craft in the United States after the war in
1920. Orville Wright made substantial contributions to those developments and American pilots also quickly took the lead in sea flights.

Eugene Ely was the first to take off from a ship. On November 14,
1910, near Hampton Roads, Virginia, he launched from an 83-foot platform on the forward deck of a cruiser, to land two and a half miles away.
On January 18 of the next year, the same pilot took off above San
Francisco Bay to land on a 125-foot platform on another cruiser. Glenn
Curtiss, who employed Ely as an exhibition pilot, shortly demonstrated
the first "practical" seaplane, borrowing features from Fabre's plane of
1910, and by mid-1911 the Wrights also developed their own "float
planes."

Adolphe Pégoud, who would become far more famous for initiating
acrobatic maneuvers, in 1913 also experimented with a hook-and-cable
system for landing a plane on a ship at sea. Then, having observed the
twists and turns of his abandoned plane after a parachute jump, he made
the first inverted flight outside Paris, on September 1. Two days later at
nearby Buc, he executed the first loop, or vertical circle, performed by a
plane, whose speed allowed its completion without stalling at the top,
before beginning an inverted downward descent. He demonstrated his
maneuvers to skeptical fellow pilots throughout Europe in eight major
countries, and within six months some fifty pilots, including, most
famously, Lincoln Beachey in the United States, were looping successfully. The German Max Immelmann, early in the war which would kill him
in 1916, developed the 180-degree climbing turn that bears his name, a
half loop with an inverted half roll at the top.

In 1913 came a series of long distance flights. On June 10, the
French pilot Marcel Brindejonc des Moulinais took off from near Paris,
and with two refueling stops navigated the 845 miles to Warsaw partly at
night. He continued on to St. Petersburg and returned to Paris by early
July, via Stockholm and Copenhagen, with subsequent delays due to bad
weather. In the autumn, Védrines was the first of several French pilots to

make it from Paris to Cairo.

The most famous flight of 1913 was the first crossing of the Mediterranean by the well-known Roland Garros. He did not make it to his destination of Tunis, but arrived at Bizerte after almost nine hours of flight, with ten minutes of fuel, or about one of his 55 gallons remaining! He had left San Raphaël on September 23 and followed the coast of Corsica, where engine vibrations almost forced him down. An hour behind schedule because of head winds and a missing engine part, he kept going and passed his last possible landing spot at Cagliari, driven by a "strange force, stronger than my reason." Garros, Pégoud, Védrines, Moulinais, and countless others did not survive the Great War, but their fame was ensured.

The crucial first parachute jump from a plane was made the next year, on March 1, 1912, by American Army Captain Albert Berry in St. Louis, and by an American woman, Georgia Broadwick, the following year. Pégoud pioneered their use in France. Parachutes obviously contributed greatly to the progress toward safer flight, along with the adoption of seat belts (mandatory in French military aviation by 1913), leather helmets, and other devices.

Also especially important for the later safety of aviation were the first fabrications of gyroscopic stabilizers, and even an automatic pilot, although they were not perfected until the 1930s and after. They came to be named after Lawrence Sperry and his father, Elmer, who had invented the first gyros twenty years before. The Frenchman Raoul Badin had devised in 1911 a lift and-bank indicator, or artificial horizon, which would bear his name, as well as improved anemometers for wind and air speeds, all of which contributed to the Sperry breakthrough. Lawrence Sperry, like so many of the early famous names, died pursuing further knowledge of the great beyond, in a 1923 flying accident. By 1913, he and his father had developed a vertical and horizontal gyro to indicate roll, pitch, and yaw—in effect enabling the first autopilot. It was demonstrated publicly at Bezons, in the Val d'Oise outside Paris, in June 1914.

As will be discussed further, there were also important structural changes giving greater stability and safety, including, as mentioned, the adoption of ailerons for turning, finally by Orville Wright in 1915. By late 1910, the Wrights had changed their skids for the rubber-tired wheels long used in Europe, and by 1911 joined others in abandoning the front elevator in favor of a tail assembly for the only vertical surfaces. The daredevil Lincoln Beachey helped prove the desirability of that when he flew his Curtiss just as well after accidentally tearing off his front boom. More efficient air-cooled rotary engines like the French-built Gnome began replacing previous automobile-type, liquid-cooled engines by 1909.

By 1914 there were over 2000 aviators, not counting over 200 who had died in accidents, including Lt. Selfridge in 1908, four in 1909, twenty-nine in 1910, and sixty-six in 1911.

The early sacrifices made to establish the art of aviation were not made in vain, especially in contrast to the sacrifices of the imminent Great War. On the contrary, they were made while achieving great progress in the post-"take-off" stage of aviation. Flyers had demonstrated possibilities imagined by very few only a decade before, when the Wrights made their first powered flights of December 1903. By the eve of World War I, pilots had exceeded 1000 kilometers (625 miles) in distance, 200 kilometers (124.5 miles) an hour in speed, and 25,000 feet in altitude, for the first time in history truly outflying the birds. The terrible irony was that those achievements were quickly put to use, not for the wonder and ease of travel for which they were proposed, but for the purposes of history's worst war to that time.

8

The Great War and New Records

By 1914, people were flying far, high, and fast enough to persuade contemporaries that aviation was closely bound to man's future. Thereafter, in part accelerated by the wars which followed, increasing numbers of young people took up aviation, and new records of all sorts were established year by year. Many names have already been mentioned, since by their very joining of the small circle of first pilots they deserve reference, but after aviation's initial decade, the wonder of flight can be shown more selectively. From here on, as larger numbers of aviators took to the air—for example the legendary magician Houdini in 1910, who claimed to have made the first flights in Australia, and the great English leader Winston Churchill in 1912—there can be focus on only the very biggest names that make up the next stages of the lore of aviation, and on their stories and contributions to the continuing refinements of the art. There can also be a shift in emphasis to the Americans, who progressively took the lead after the Great War, although aviation remained a very international enterprise.

The year 1914 of course saw the beginnings of history's greatest war up to that time, and aspects of it will be explored even as we try not to lose sight of the aviation wonders which continued along with the unprecedented suffering and carnage. The fears of the military uses of aviation that now gave their first great display were not new. Indeed, almost a half century before the first balloon ascent, the English poet Thomas Gray had seemed to foresee what was to come. In 1737, his poem "Prophecy" stated: "The time will come, when thou shalt lift thine eyes, To watch a long-drawn battle in the skies, . . . England, so long the mistress of the sea, . . . shall bear, And reign the sovereign of the air."

The carnage to come could scarcely have been imagined. In 1917, at the height of World War I, Orville Wright lamented its horrors with the statement: "When my brother and I built and flew the first man-carrying flying machine, we thought that we were introducing into the world an invention which would make further wars practically impossible."

Just before the war's end, he declared, "The aeroplane has made war so terrible that I do not believe any country will again care to start a war," and there were many other such statements.

The first sizeable bombardments struck terror. Whereas the small (five pounds or so) first bombs, dropped by Italy in its 1911 takeover of Libya (Tripoli), caused almost no damage, by the end of World War I, the 500- and 1000-pound bombs were causing considerable losses and more terror. The 300 tons of bombs dropped on England by about a hundred German airship and airplane attacks killed over 1400 people. H. G. Wells, all the more famous for the prescience of his *The War of the Worlds* (1898) and *The War in the Air* (1908), declared in 1917 that "in air raids he was afraid of going to pieces altogether." His friend Arnold Bennett fictionalized in a 1918 novel that "all theories of safety had been smashed to atoms in the explosion . . . the earth swayed up and down. The sound alone of the immeasurable cataclysm annihilated the universe . . ." The most horrific bombing of Paris came in the spring of 1918, with the dropping of an estimated 25,000 kilos (55,000 pounds) on the city, simultaneously with cannon shellings, including a hit which killed close to a hundred Good Friday worshippers at the famous medieval church of St. Gervais.

In all during the Great War, German bombers dropped 27,386 tons of bombs, almost all on the French battlefields, with a few raids on London, Paris, and other cities. The British and French dropped an estimated 16,000 tons on German targets, a tiny fraction of the over two million tons unleashed in World War II, and the still more incredible seven or so million tons of bombs dropped during the American War in Indochina and Vietnam, 1965–1973.

In the long view of history, that terror of aerial bombardment in World War I, and the far worse destruction from the air to come in future wars, marks the most horrific turning point, as we will discuss further in succeeding chapters. Yet World War I, like future wars, also led to great progress in aircraft production and performance, enabled by great infusions of money, energy, and talent. According to varying sources, in August 1914 the French fielded something like 160 airplanes, the Italians 86 (in 1915), the British 63, the Russians 190, and the Germans over

258. Other countries' military aircraft, as Belgium's 16 and America's approximately 8, together with others under repair or in storage, gave a total of about 1000. But by war's end, over 150,000 aircraft, of several hundred types, had been produced by all sides. The French had 3700, the English 2600, and the Germans 2500. Americans were building close to 500 planes a week by November, 1918, but the 1200 or so American airmen at the front were still flying mostly French aircraft.

Thus, the fast expenditure of planes in combat resulted in the development of an aircraft industry of mass production. France produced 67,982 aircraft, England 55,093, Italy 20,000, the U.S. 15,000, and Austria-Hungary and Russia another 5000 or so each. Aviation had encountered the factory assembly-line, just pioneered in the automotive field, although aircraft manufacture quickly became even more complicated. A typical two-seater required up to 50,000 parts and 4000 hours of labor, the early fabric covers often stitched by hand.

Average performances had more or less doubled to near the pre-war records of about 125 mph and 25,000 feet, thanks to more powerful engines and sleeker machines. In 1914, speeds were on the order of 60 to 80 mph in aircraft, which took an hour to climb to 20,000 feet, often powered by 80hp engines, like the Gnome-Rhône rotary. The leading Entente fighter at the end of the war, the Spad XIII, was close to twice the size of earlier models, and weighed 1808 pounds loaded, and was driven by a widely used 220hp Hispano–Suiza engine. By the end of the war, steadily improving fixed-radial engines like the Packard Liberty and the Rolls-Royce Eagle developed up to 400 or more horsepower, and made possible new records in all categories.

On September 18, 1918, a new altitude record of 28,897 feet was established and the distance record went from 634 miles in 1913 to 1936 miles in mid-June, 1919. The pre-war speed record of 126.67 mph went to 171.05 mph on February 7, 1920.

The organization of aviation militarily was also proceeding in leading countries, even as the numbers of airmen were increasing—by ten times in Germany for example. England created the Royal Flying Corps in April 1912, as did France, Germany, and other countries their own flying services soon thereafter. On April 1, 1918, the English, as advised by Generals Jan Smuts and Hugh Trenchard, transformed the Royal Flying Corps into a more independent force, the Royal Air Force (RAF). Russia kept air units under its army and navy until later, as did the United States.

The latter actually established the first military air arm, an aeronautical division under the Army Signal Corps in August 1907. It became an Aero Squadron in March 1913, the U.S. Air Service in World War I, the Army Air Corps in 1926, the U.S. Army Air Forces in World War II, and in 1947 simply the U.S. Air Force.

Proportionately, the United States came farthest, beginning to make up for its lag after the early achievements. At the end of 1913, the Army Signal Corps, which housed the first air units, had fewer than twenty aircraft, and eleven of some forty trained pilots had been killed. Support for American aviation became progressively more efficient, as will be seen, with the establishment of the National Advisory Committee for Aeronautics (NACA) in March 1915. Still, on entering the war on April 6, 1917, the American military had only 55 or so airplanes, and not many more pilots. Some had seen service against Pancho Villa in Mexico during the early spring of 1916. But by November 1918, America had some 767 pilots and 500 observers at the front, and 195,000 personnel in support and other positions in the Air Service. Different sources speak of 35 or 83 or 131 pilots aside from volunteers in Europe, and of 55 or 109 or 250 airplanes available when America entered the war in April 1917.

The U.S. delivered 14,020 airplanes in 1918, and were planning for 40,000 in 1919. In all, some 2500 of 9000–10,000 American pilots received advanced flight instruction, while 23,000 had begun their training. The most famous were some 200 who volunteered to fly for France after August 1914. That French government formed the famous Lafayette Escadrille for about 38 of them, two years before the U.S. entered the war. They adopted two lion cub mascots, "Whiskey" and "Soda," and after beginning combat in the skies over Verdun in May 1915, claimed to shoot down an estimated 199 planes (officially 57), while losing 63, or according to some, 88 pilots. The Lafayette Flying Corps started its engagement with four aircraft, and finished the war with eighteen. Another 172 American volunteers flew in French aviation units. In all, American pilots claimed to down 781 enemy planes and 73 balloons, while losing over 289 of their own aircraft.

At the end of the war, Britain had almost 22,000 airmen, despite the loss of 9378. Some 7755 French pilots were killed, about half in the last year, but the country trained at least 16,000 during the war, and at its end, had 90,000 air service personnel. Italy finished the war with over 5000 pilots, having lost 909 others. Germany began the war with only

500 of them, but finished it with over ten times as many, even though 3128 planes and 5853 airmen were lost. Berlin claimed 7425 "victories," all but 358 on the Western Front.

The most famous pilots, of course, were the "aces," those who had downed five, or later ten or more, enemy craft. First designated by the French press in June 1916 to offset the horrors of the battle of Verdun, they were likened to medieval cavaliers, "the knights of the air." Stories about them made up the second set of "lore" about flying, after that about the very first flights, and before the lore about the long-distance flights of Lindbergh and others. Accounts of World War I aces contributed enormously to later legends even decades later, as for example with the term "top gun," (*oberkanone*) which Germans gave to their pilots with ten or more "kills" or victories.

The German "Red Baron," Manfred von Richthofen, was credited with the most "kills," 80, followed by the Frenchman René Fonck, with 75, the British Edward Mannock with 73, the Canadian William Avery Bishop with 72, and numerous others. Many did not survive. Richthofen's all-red Fokker Dr. 1 triplane was downed by a Canadian pilot on April 21, 1918, shortly after he had completed a book, *The Red Air Fighter*, which sold over a half-million copies. Mannock was killed in July of the same year, but Fonck lived to the age of 59, dying in 1953, and Bishop died in 1956 at the age of 60. About half of all Royal Flying Corps, a third of German, and a quarter of American fatalities occurred during flight training in still-primitive planes. Of fifty-two French military pilots in 1910, three had been killed, three badly hurt, and fourteen requested transfers out of flying even before the start of the war.

In all, some 55,000 airmen—including mechanics, navigators, and gunners—were included in the terrible toll of ten million or so victims of the Great War. Of all French aviators, some 16 percent were killed, with another half put out of commission. The "aces," as of other countries, suffered fatal losses of about a quarter, similar to casualties among the infantry. In some combat zones, pilots survived on average only 17 hours of flight before being shot down. The air services formed about 3 percent of the greatly expanded armed forces at the end of the war, and pilots a small percentage of all air service personnel.

Other famous names who died then or shortly after included the following. Adolphe Pégoud died of wounds still in his cockpit after making it back to friendly territory on August 31, 1915. Famous for his aerobatics before the war, he was the leading ace at the time with six victories, and given a hero's funeral at Belfort. In a telling move, the Germans demonstrated the early chivalry of the war by dropping a message over his burial, "his adversary honors the aviator Pégoud, fallen in combat for his fatherland." Max Immelman was killed on June 18, 1916, apparently when a bullet shot off part of his propeller, which continued to turn, shaking the plane to pieces. Oswald Boelcke, who was the role model for his successor, Richthofen, was the leading German ace, with 40 victories, at the time of his death in a collision, October 28, 1916. The French ace Georges Guynemer (53 victories) went to his death on September 11, 1917. Then the famous Roland Garros, after escaping several years of German imprisonment, was shot down on October 5, 1918, while Jules Védrines and Jean Navarre died in postwar accidents in 1919. The top Italian ace, Francesco Baracca (34 victories) was killed October 28, 1918 while strafing Austrian trenches. The famous poet-patriot, Gabriele d'Annunzio, who would lead the occupation of Fiume in September 1919, leading to the rise of Mussolini, led the dropping of thousands of manifestos on Vienna on August 9, 1918.

Already on August 26, 1914, great publicity was given across Europe to the death of Russian pilot P. N. Nesterov, who had flown the first loop over Kiev almost exactly a year before, after he rammed the plane flown by Austrian Baron Rosenthal. Then, ace A P. de Severski (13 victories) was shot down on his first night bombing flight. The top Soviet ace, with 17 victories, was Capt. Alexandre Kazakov, who joined British forces in the north after the Bolsheviks dropped out of the war. The famous French ace Charles Nungesser, with 45 victories, as we shall see, would later become victim of the fatally unsuccessful effort to be the first to fly non-stop between Paris and New York, May 8–9 1927. French aces were estimated at only 4 percent of combat pilots, but credited with 50 percent of the victories. Only 146 of them survived the war.

The top American ace was Eddie Rickenbacker, who achieved twenty-six victories in French-built Spad fighters, twenty of them in the last two months of the war. The colorful Frank Luke, dubbed a "balloon buster from Arizona," had the most American victories when he was killed in late September 1918 by ground rifle fire. That came after he had downed a confirmed two of a claimed fourteen dirigibles and six German planes. Wounded in the air, he crashed in German territory and was fatally tracked. The third-ranking American ace, Raoul Luftery, posted seven-

teen victories. He had grown up in France and therefore became an interpreter and another hero of the Lafayette squadron, before being killed in
the last year of the war. In all, some 88 Americans became aces, but 237
countrymen were lost in aerial combat and four times as many to illnesses and accidents.

The famous mayor of New York City from 1933 to 1945, Fiorello
LaGuardia, led a bomber group in the Italian theater, while the son of a
Wisconsin senator, William Mitchell, became commander of American
aviators on the St. Mihiel front south of Verdun. He organized the first
bombing blitzes and began his life-long campaign for strategic bombing.
After his demonstration of air power effectiveness by sinking three captured German warships off Norfolk, Virginia, with armor-piercing bombs
of up to 2000 pounds in July 1921, he became a Brigadier General and
Assistant Chief of the Army Air Service. He also sponsored winners of the
1922 Pulitzer and other races, and soon his name became synonymous
with arguments for increasing air power and using it, rather than naval
ships, for the primary defense of America's coasts from enemy attack.
However, understandable naval opposition to such arguments and controversy over his outspoken criticism of superiors for alleged neglect of the
air, led to his court-martial at a famous San Antonio, Texas trial for indis-
cipline in December 1925. "'Billy" Mitchell continued to press his arguments as a civilian, but died prematurely at the age of 57 in 1936.

After the first reconnaissance flights, the famous "dogfights" developed, so-named because of the violent maneuvering for the best position.
That involved various aerobatic moves, attempting to dive out of reach of
opponents' guns and zoom in from under, above, or behind to open fire.
Dozens of tactical maneuvers and conditions or problems affected the
outcome, most importantly the aircraft's performance, weapons, and
ammunition; the skill of the pilots; and the weather. Although the preferred attack force grouped four or six fighters, often there were dozens of
fighters going at each other with wild abandon. A British pilot recalled
scenes over the north of France: "About thirty machines could be all
mixed up together, and viewed from a distance, it seemed as if a swarm of
bees were all circling around a honey pot." They often started off in formation and at different altitudes in order for higher "tiers" to protect
lower ones. On one occasion, over the Ypres battlefield in July 1917,
almost a hundred planes fought at three different levels; seventeen at
17,000 feet, forty at 12,000 feet, and thirty-seven at 8000 feet. On an-

other occasion near the end of the war, another hundred planes "twisted and climbed and plunged like wild things" under a thick cloud ceiling of 3000 feet, trying to avoid each other. Often they came out of the clouds and fog, dodging thick anti-aircraft fire, as they tried to destroy their opponents. German ace Hermann Goering, credited with 22 "kills," described the "dogfights" as being like a "frantic witch's Sabbath in the air." Understandably, there were numerous mid-air collisions, as pilots attempted to close to within 250 meters without being seen, and use about ten seconds to down their target or escape without being hit.

The first great problem to overcome was how to shoot at the enemy without tearing your own plane apart, if there was only one pilot. Two-seaters carried a marksman as well as pilot, and already by the end of 1914 with the deadly machine gun downing planes, beginning with a German Aviatik over Rheims on October 5, some eighty planes had fallen on all fronts. On one occasion in February 1915, the renowned Adolphe Pégoud was able to fly so close to two German planes that his observer was able to kill their pilots with six rifle shots.

The French also developed a system of aerial darts, called *fléchettes*, for dropping razor-sharp missiles about the size of a pencil on ground troops. Then, in April 1915, Roland Garros developed a technique, pro-posed by the Saulnier brothers in 1913, for firing straight ahead through the armor-plated propellers of his Morane monoplane. Given their flight-control problems, this enabled many more French "kills." But soon the precocious Dutch aeronautical designer Anthony Fokker and others bet-ter synchronized the German Maxim gun to fire through the propellers of his steadily improving fighters. That helped give the Germans air supremacy at times in the succeeding months of the "Fokker scourge"— until more aggressive tactics developed by British General Hugh Montague Trenchard and other Allied commanders turned the tide, prior to new reverses in "bloody April," 1917. The development of improved guns, with better sights, firing up to 800 (more normally, 60) rounds a minute, made air battles increasingly murderous. For example, 44 aircraft were downed on the single day of April 4, 1917, in the Battle of Arras, near Douai in the north of France.

In all, over 3,000 German planes were downed on the Western Front, although Allied aces with accumulating exaggerations claimed 11,760 victories. The record downing of six planes in one day by one pilot was achieved in the skies forty kilometers south-southwest of Amiens, near Hétomesnil, well west of his native Lorraigne, by the top French ace Rene Fonck. On May 9, 1918, after downing three Rumpler biplanes by diving under and attacking from below, where their guns' fire was blocked by the lower wing, he then took on five Fokkers and four Pfalzes, under the command of rising German commander Hermann Goering. Flying a Spad XIII with a 220-h.p. engine at altitudes up to 4500 meters (14,400 feet), he picked off three more, one by one, diving through their ranks, with countless twists and turns, almost grazing one victim's wing, and watching the falling leaf configurations of the descending German planes with their distinctive black Maltese crosses on the wings.

Another French aviator achieved a distinction of sorts when he downed a Fokker by deliberately flying into its tail. The propeller chewed it up, and he was able to glide back to safety. Even more astounding was the exploit of Canadian Major William George Barker, who, two weeks before the war's end single-handedly took on some fifty German aircraft, and managed to down four and make it back to friendly territory, though thrice wounded and semi-conscious. Along with such heroics, the main function of the World War I planes nevertheless continued to be aerial reconnaissance to guide artillery fire and track troop movements.

Aces such as those mentioned above, however, best demonstrated the "wonder of flight" in the Great War, as "the winged argonauts of trackless air" proved that the gallantry of previous centuries had not disappeared with the development of machinery spawned by the scientific and industrial revolutions. They therefore became the natural heroes of romantics everywhere. They could be "dashing, devil-may-care types" who were "gentlemen warriors," free to sail above the horrors of trench warfare below, with far less risk of mud or mire, and at least equal chances of survival. They conceived themselves as "artists of the air," and were constantly evoked as "the last warriors endowed with individuality in a war of anonymous millions." They exemplified "the traditionalists' faith in demonstrations of courage and elan" even as they showed "the modernists' emphasis on scientific destruction and the nation in arms."

The aviators also knew of course many of the horrors of the Great War, including the new ones of oxygen deprivation, even greater cold, and of falling to their deaths without parachutes. As American ace Eddie Rickenbacker put it in his 1919 book, *Fighting the Flying Circus*, "Fighting in the air is not sport. It is scientific murder."

As for the Flying Circus itself, this became a legend in its own time, and a model for many future fighter groups in terms of *espirit de corps*. Shortly after the young fighter ace Manfred von Richthofen had taken command of squadron-sized Jagdstaffel 11, "For whatever reasons," he recorded, "one fine day I came upon the idea of having my crate painted glaring red." The pilots under his command, not wishing to see their leader singled out for enemy attention, followed suit and the entire Staffel became crimson, with some smaller parts of the planes painted in a variety of other colors for pilot identification. Richthofen's younger brother, Lothar, commented, "The red colour signified a certain insolence. Everyone knew that. It attracted attention. Consequently, one had to really perform."

Due to increasing Allied numerical superiority, on June 24, 1917, four Jagdstaffeln were combined into Germany's first independent fighter group, Jagdgeschwader (JG) I, under Richthofen's command. This expanded Flying Circus was pitted against the British rather than the French because, as German General von Hoeppner wrote in his memoirs, "Due to his number and his sporting spirit, the Englishman was always our most dangerous enemy." Following the example of Boelcke, Richthofen sought out the best pilots for his command, including such aces as Werner Voss, Ernst Udet and Kurt Wolff, as well as Goering, and "joining the Circus" soon became the ambition of a host of talented flyers. Any pilot who did not at least demonstrate the potential to become an ace was quickly transferred out.

The British, with aces of their own, were unintimidated by the Flying Circus, and, in fact, as designers on both sides desperately sought to invent superior aircraft, individual combats were often decided by which pilot was flying the better plane. The Germans were convinced that the British had designated certain of their squadrons to "get" Richthofen, however this is not borne out by any official records. An account of the Red Baron's last battle, by German Lt. Richard Wenzl, nevertheless contains the part: "Over the lines we attacked seven Sopwith Camels with red noses. The Anti-Richthofen people!"

Richthofen died on April 21, 1918, just short of his 26th birthday, when he apparently became overly fixated on shooting down a Canadian flyer, 2nd Lt. Wilfred R. May, and failed to notice another, Captain A. Roy Brown, coming up behind him. May later said, "Richthofen was firing at me continually, [and] I didn't know what I was doing myself and I do not suppose that Richthofen could figure what I was going to do. . . . I knew I had had it. I looked around again and saw Richthofen do a spin and a half and hit the ground. I looked up and saw one of our machines directly behind."

The"Red Baron," who took a bullet through the heart, had shot down 80 enemy planes, the highest tally of any pilot in the war, and exactly double the score of his mentor, Boelcke. Richthofen's brother Lothar also had 40 victories, but he flew himself out of the war, wounded, after crashing three times, always on the thirteenth day of the month.

In the wake of the horrors and exploits of the war, enthusiasm for aviation produced in succeeding years what many have called "the golden age of flight." Books about the aces became best-sellers, and they and the "lore" they featured influenced many, including great writers such as William Faulkner, Cecil Day Lewis, and Gabriele D'Annunzio. Faulkner learned to fly as a volunteer in the Canadian Royal Air Force near the end of the war, and made it central to some of his writings, such as the 1935 novel, *Pylon*. Lewis' enthusiasm for flying has been cited in Chapter One, while D'Annunzio had already given one of the most eloquent encomiums ever, after his first flight as a passenger way back in 1909:

> Until now I have never really lived! Life on earth is a creeping, crawling business. It is in the air that one feels the glory of being a man and of conquering the elements. There is an exquisite smoothness of motion and the joy of gliding through space. It is wonderful!

More and more enthusiasts took up flying and far more still were caught up in the drama of the story of the post-war rage for new records, aerial shows, and races, which are our next subjects.

The next "aces" to demonstrate the wonders of aviation were those who set speed, altitude, and especially distance records after the war. The pre-war speed record of 126.67 mph (203.81 kph), established on September 29, 1913, by Maurice Prévost, was broken on February 7, 1920 by another French pilot, Sadi Lecointe at 171.05 mph (275.22 kph). The same pilot went to 211.91 mph (341.00 kph) on September 21, 1922, and Italian Major Mario de Bernardi passed all the way to 318.64 mph (512.69 kph) on March 30, 1928. The next big jump came when English Flight Lieutenant G.H. Stainforth reached 407.02 mph (654. 90 kph) on September 29, 1931, while the pre-WW II record of 469.22 mph (754.97 kph) was established by the German Fritz Wendel on April 26, 1939.

Even before the First World War had ended, the 1914 altitude record was raised by over 3000 feet to 28,897 feet by U.S. Army Captain R. W. Schroeder on September 18, 1918. The next year, Frenchman Jean Casale, reached 30,511 feet, and on May 25, 1929, German pilot Willi Neuenhofen added another 10,000-plus to 41,794 feet. Some 51,361 feet was reached by the Italian Mario Pezzi on May 8, 1937, and he established the pre-WW II record of 56,046 feet on October 22, 1938. The next multiple of ten, at 63,668 feet, was not reached until May 4, 1953, by Walter Gibb in a Lockheed Electra, the first American turbo-prop airliner. The decisive one hundred barrier was crossed on December 14, 1959, with 103,389 feet in a F-104C, by American test pilot Joe Jordan, while the Soviet pilot Georgy Mosolov reached 113,890 feet on April 28, 1961, in a MiG-E-66-A. Another Soviet pilot carried that to 123,524 feet in a MiG-E-266-M on August 31, 1977. But meanwhile, the U.S. Air Force's experimental rocket-powered X-15, piloted by Joe Walker, went far above the stratosphere to 354,200 feet on August 22, 1963.

Flight distances went from the pre-war 1020 kilometers (634 miles), flown by Frenchman Augustin Seguin, to the 1936 miles flown the year after its end by British military pilot John Alcock and A.W. Brown in a Vickers Vimy bomber. Moreover, they achieved that over water, on the first non-stop flight across the North Atlantic, taking 16 hours and 27 minutes, June 14–15, 1919, to fly from Newfoundland to Ireland. A month before, U.S. Navy pilots, in one of three 14-ton Curtiss "flying boats," under Lt. Commander Albert C. Read, had gone much farther, from Newfoundland to Lisbon, arriving May 27. But, dealing with numerous problems over eleven days, they had to put down several times at sea and in the Azores before Read's crew reached Lisbon. The other two flying boats did not even reach the Azores. By the end of the year, Australia was crossed by air for the first time.

The first trans-American flight after that of Calbraith Perry Rodgers, in four months in late 1911, was flown by U.S. Army Air Serviceman Lt. William D. Coney from February 21 to 24, 1921, in 21 hours and twenty minutes. The better-known Lt. James Doolittle, to whose exploits we shall return, made one stop between Jacksonville, Florida and San Diego,

California, September 4–5, 1922. Then, the first non-stop cross-country flight from New York to San Diego—2516 miles, although taking six hours longer than Doolittle's flight—was achieved May 2–3 the following year on their third attempt by Lieutenants Oakley Kelly and John Macready. A month later, in June 1923, the first successful refueling in flight, after experiments in 1914, was carried out fifteen times over San Diego for a flight lasting 37 hours and almost 16 minutes.

Already in July 1918, going east and south, English pilots flew from London to Cairo. French pilots made the first crossing of the Sahara in May 1919 and reached Dakar and Timbuktu by March 1920 after a month's flying. Two others made it to Rangoon, Burma in forty seven days after their departure from Paris on October 14, 1919. Even more impressively, English pilots reached Darwin, Australia on December 10 after leaving London on November 12. Another pilot traveled from London all the way to Cape Town, via Cairo, from February 4 to March 20, 1920. Then two Italian pilots made it still farther—from Rome to Tokyo—between February 11 and May 31 that year. Daily passenger service had begun between London and Paris on August 25, 1919, and was established between Amsterdam and London from May 17, 1920.

The first successful commercial air service began in South America also in 1920, when a former German pilot, Dr. Peter Paul von Bauer, commenced 650-mile flights from Bogotá to the Caribbean coast of Colombia. Then, three years after the first crossings of the North Atlantic, the South Atlantic was mastered by Portuguese pilots flying via the Cape Verde Islands off western Africa. They moored their seaplane in the harbor of Rio de Janeiro, June 17, 1922, but took three months to get there, having departed on March 13. In 1924, A Dutch pilot took fifty-four days to make the flight from Amsterdam to distant Java, while French pilots began what soon became a regular run from Paris to Tokyo via Shanghai and other places, between April 25 and June 9, 1924. That same year, between April 4 and September 28, two of the four U.S. Army Air Service Douglas World Cruisers, which set out from Seattle, completed the first tour of the world—even if it took 175 days. Round-trip flights from London to distant Rangoon, Burma, Capetown, South Africa, and Sydney, Australia, began respectively on November 20, 1924, November 16, 1925 and in late spring, 1926.

The far more famous flight of Charles A. Lindbergh (to which we shall return), from New York to Paris, May 20–21, 1927, spanned 3609 miles. American Lieutenants Lester Maitland and Albert Hegenberger made the big flight of some 2439 miles in 25 hours, 50 minutes in the other direction a month later, reaching Oahu, Hawaii from San Francisco, June 28–29, 1927, after several failed attempts since the end of August 1925. (Two weeks later, Ernest L. Smith piloted another plane from there to a crash landing in a tree on the island of Molokai as he ran out of fuel.) The June 28 flight to Hawaii was also notable for the first use of a radio beacon for overseas flight, while Lindbergh's flight had bettered the earlier distance record of the previous October 28–29, by Dieudonné Costes and Georges Ringot, from Paris to Jask in southern Iran, by 250 miles. On October 14, 1927, Costes, who had wanted to try the first Paris–New York flight, instead did the first non-stop crossing of the South Atlantic, from St. Louis, Senegal to Natal, Brazil, with co-pilot Joseph Le Brix. They went on to complete a round-the-world-tour.

Although the claim was disputed later and inconclusively, American Commander Richard Byrd said he reached the North Pole on May 9, 1926 in a Fokker tri-motor, piloted by Floyd Bennett, close to a year after the Norwegian explorer Roald Amundsen came within 158 miles of it. Two days later, on May 11, 1926, Amundsen and the American Lincoln Ellaworth flew over the pole in an airship, and continued on to Alaska. Byrd, his pilot, and two assistants then conquered the South Pole in a Ford tri-motor on November 28–29, 1929, after his 84-member expedition had spent a year of preparations at "Little America," surviving winter cold of –67 Celsius temperatures. The same year, from August 23 to October 31, a Russian plane flew the great circle route over the Arctic from Moscow to Seattle. The year before, in April, 1928, Australian Captain George H. Wilkins had flown over half that distance in the opposite direction, some 2200 miles from Alaska across the Arctic to Spitzbergen and beyond, north of Norway, barely surviving snowstorms and a near-fatal crash.

The important link from England to Australia was flown more quickly than ever before, February 7–22, 1928, by H. J. L. "Bert" Hinkler, and the first east–west crossing of the Atlantic from Dublin to Labrador was achieved that year by a German pilot, Hermann Koehl, April 12–13. Over a month later, Charles Kingsford Smith, as will be discussed further, led a four-man crew to Australia on a famous flight, that began with the fourth successful crossing to Hawaii. Two other English pilots, A.G. Jones-Williams and N.H. Jenkins, made the first non-stop flight from England to India, April 24–26, 1929.

After numerous experiments and crashes of the older dirigible-airships, the Germans developed the huge and famous *Graf Zeppelin,* 774 feet long, which made its first flight on September 18, 1928. It crossed the Atlantic, carrying fifty-five people, in October, via the Azores, and returned non-stop across the North Atlantic with sixty-one passengers. Then, between August 8 and 29, 1929, it made a celebrated round-the-world trip in four stages, with 14 passengers and a crew of 40, starting from Lakehurst, New Jersey.

There, eight years later, on May 6, 1937, a later airship, the *Hindenberg,* caught fire just before landing, killing 35 of its 97 people. It had made its first crossing in 61 hours, 50 minutes, exactly a year earlier, returning in 49 hours, 3 minutes, and other trips after that. But the great consternation over its crash in 1937 led to the grounding for over two decades of the huge, lighter-than-air dirigibles. Seven years before the *Hindenberg* fire, a slightly smaller English airship had crossed the Atlantic in midsummer, 1930, but another crashed in France en route to Egypt and India, with fifty deaths in October that year. There were other such disasters contributing to the ban on such flights after the *Hindenberg* crash.

In 1928, the path to the modern helicopter also made important progress, with the further development of the "autogiro," which had been first flown in 1923 by the Spaniard Juan de la Cierva. It was an "aeroplane with rotating wings," which required only a short take-off run to build up sufficient speed for lift-off. Using flexible hinges for cyclic pitch control to offset varying forces of lift and torque caused by the rotating blades, Cierva was able on September 18, 1928, to fly an improved model 25 miles across the English channel in eighteen minutes at 4000 feet. The next year, other improvements limited the take-off run to 10 to 20 meters, and landings required less than half that. Further progress followed, especially from the work of Louis Breguet in France, of Corrado d'Ascanio in Italy, of Heinrich Focke in Germany, and of Russian émigrés to the U.S. Igor Sikorsky and George de Bothezat. The latter actually saw his X-shaped helicopter, powered by four 6-bladed rotors, make over one hundred ascents at McCook Field in Dayton, Ohio, in 1922–23. Some lifted four people, but no higher than 25 feet or longer than 2 minutes, 45 seconds. In 1936, the twin-rotor Focke-Achgelis FA-61 made the "first practical" helicopter flights, and reached 76 mph. After 1939, as we shall

see, Sikorsky developed a continuing line of increasingly efficient helicopters, as did for fixed-wing craft another countryman, Alexander de
Seversky.

With the world conquered by air to all continents, the next stages of
the "lore" of aviation can be mentioned.

Air mail pilots formed a good part of the next body of that lore. As previously noted, the very first officially noted air mail had been delivered all
of six miles outside of Allahabad, southeast of New Delhi, British India,
on February 18, 1911 by the French pilot, Pequet. It was soon being carried in England and elsewhere in Europe, and after the war accompanied
the development of the new transcontinental flights. In the United States,
regular, if continually interrupted, air-mail deliveries began on May 15,
1918, with a flight from Washington to New York, via Philadelphia. The
following year it struck westward over the "hell stretch" of the Allegheny
Mountains to Cleveland with one stop, and from there to Chicago.

Already, in September 1918, a record crossing—with the wind—of
the 711 miles from Chicago to New York had been established. Two years
later, the service was extended all the way to San Francisco, as four pilots
staged separate flights to reach there from New York, September 8–9,
1920. They stopped after Chicago, in Iowa City, Omaha, Cheyenne, Salt
Lake City, and Reno—flying over 12,000 feet high to cross the Rockies.
Their time beat the then train record between coasts by over a day, despite
numerous delays forced by weather and other problems which extended
the 34 hours, five minutes time in the air to 75 hours, 52 minutes in all.
That made it another historic milestone, far reducing the usual week or
two of most early transcontinental railroad trips. Only five months later,
as seen, another historic relay flight, February 22–23, 1921, narrowed the
lapsed time between San Francisco and New York to 33 hours, 20 minutes, or close to half the record train time of 65 hours. Several years later
that was reduced to about 30 hours eastbound, with the wind, and 34
hours westbound. Night flights soon began, as lights to steer by were
placed on the routes from 3 to 15 or 25 miles apart.

But as one can easily imagine in the days before modern flying
instruments and facilities, these efforts by the U.S. Post Office
Department, which took over from the Army Air Service after the first
flights in August 1918, were extremely dangerous. Indeed, they cost the
lives of thirty-one of the first forty pilots hired! Twenty-six of them died

between October 1919 and July 1921, or over one a month. During one 12-month period of 1920–21, 330 crashes killed 69 and injured 27.

Although safety improved as the sturdy De Havilland 4 biplane became the service workplane, and there were only three accidental deaths in 1924 and one in 1925, Congress decided in February of that year to direct the Post Office to contract out such dangerous work. That was possible by then because of the proven profitability of the air-mail services, which it was reasoned could therefore do without government subsidies. This was a development of great importance for the future of U.S. aviation, for it fostered the search for profits of many aviation entrepreneurs—for example, as will be seen in succeeding chapters, Juan Trippe, the founder of Pan American Airways.

In Europe, the French Compagnie Générale Aéropostale, or simply Aéropostale, as it became known, was organized for mail as the name indicates. It became the most famous of the some hundred air companies that existed by 1927, up from about twenty-seven eight years earlier. In February 1919, it delivered mail (with several crash landings) to Alicante on the southeastern Spanish coast, and two weeks later to Rabat, Morocco. Aéropostale cooperated as well as competed with aviation entrepreneur Pierre Latécoère, who designed his own planes and flying boats and formed a successful company around them. Just after the war, on Christmas Day 1918, he flew in one of his planes from his native Toulouse to Barcelona, and proceeded to develop that and other routes.

Aéropostale, for its part, rapidly developed air-mail routes around Europe and beyond. After the first crossing of the South Atlantic by Portuguese with stops in the spring of 1922, there were widely publicized flights by famous ace René Fonck, and others, in 1924 and succeeding years. Six pilots and two passengers died in crashes on those routes in 1925, three in 1926, and twelve in 1927, the worst year. By September 1926 Latécoère took the lead in developing regular if still dangerous routes from France to South America, via Africa. Then, in April 1927, Aéropostale took over the Latécoere lines.

The famous Jean Mermoz, St. Exupéry, Henri Guillaumet, and others developed the colorful routes to Africa and beyond in the 1920s. On October 10, 1927, Mermoz and fellow pilot Negrin flew non-stop from Toulouse, France, to St. Louis, Senegal. In early 1928, Mermoz and others developed the first links, using fast boats for supplies at sea between flights across the South Atlantic, to distant Argentina some 13,400 km away. Then, on May 11, 1930, Mermoz and two others made the first direct flight from France to Natal, Brazil, via Senegal. They flew non-stop across the South Atlantic, although until the mid-1930s, the transit between Dakar and Natal, continued often to be made by *avisos,* as the boats were called. The first solo crossing of the South Atlantic was made in November 1931, by Australian Bert Hinkler.

Mermoz had crossed the high Andes from Buenos Aires to Santiago in 1928, and went on to numerous dangerous adventures, including being picked up at sea by one of the boats stationed along the route by the French government, 450 miles out of St. Louis, in 1935. The next year, he was not so lucky and went to his death in the crash of his flying boat, a Latécoere Type 300, off nearby Dakar. Six years before that, in June 1930, as dramatized in the 1995 film *Wings of Courage,* Guillaumet had made one of the great survival stories of aviation history, after his Potez 25 was downed in a blizzard in an isolated valley near 20,000-foot peaks in the Andes. Following two days and nights of exposure to minus 20 degrees, he began walking, only to fall 150 feet and suffer frostbite before a lady shepherd took him in and sought rescue.

Aéropostale was taken over by the newly founded Air France in 1933. The latter continued to develop the air mail in combination with passenger services. Air Afrique developed new African routes, while by 1935 Air France was delivering mail and up to sixty passengers to distant Buenos Aires, with two days of flying from Toulouse and other southern French cities. They traveled in mostly Latécoere flying boats, weighing up to thirty-seven or so tons with eleven tons of fuel, and flying stages of 6000 kilometers over open sea and rugged terrain, at altitudes up to 6000 meters over the Andes. The German company Lufthansa also developed air routes to Buenos Aires, linking it with Berlin in early February, 1934. Lufthansa announced its 100th crossing of the South Atlantic on August 25, 1935. Within Europe also, more regular air mail delivery and passenger service developed year by year.

All these achievements were impressive feats, but the most famous long-distance flights were still to come.

9

Barnstormers and Daredevils

If French and European pilots captured most of the "lore" of flying following that of the Wright brothers in the century's first decades, the
next biggest name of all in aviation became that of another American,
Charles Lindbergh. His flight of May 20–21, 1927, from New York to
Paris, created a "frenzy of celebration," first in Paris, then in the U.S. and
around the world.

The French were intimately involved in that flight also. Not only was
Paris the destination, but the prize of $25,000 had been put up seven
years earlier, May 22, 1919, by Raymond Orteig, a French hotel owner
living in New York. Lindbergh narrowly beat out the then far better
known René Fonck, who had crashed on take-off while attempting the
feat eight months earlier, and fellow French aces Charles Nungesser and
François Coli, who disappeared off or over Newfoundland only ten days
before, after almost reaching a safe landing in the New World from Paris
against the wind.

A month earlier, two Americans, Noel Davis and S.H. Wooster, had
been killed in the crash of a plane taking off for Paris from Langley Field,
near Norfolk, and others, including the now-famous American naval officer Richard Byrd, were close to new efforts to capture the Orteig prize.
On June 4, two weeks after Lindbergh's flight, Clarence Chamberlain and
Charles Levine made a flight to near Berlin, 300 miles beyond Paris, and
Byrd and three crew members landed just off the French coast three weeks
after that. But nothing succeeds like success, and after Lindbergh's first
flight completely across the Atlantic, his name became virtually synonymous with aviation in succeeding years. By contrast, the first non-stop
flight between Newfoundland and Ireland almost eight years earlier by
John Alcock and A.W. Brown, on June 14–15, 1919, has been almost
completely forgotten.

A pilot at the age of twenty in 1922, young Lindbergh had already lived a life rich in aviation, surviving four escapes by parachute from doomed aircraft, first as a barnstormer, then in military aviation and flying the mails, mostly from St. Louis to Chicago. He had become known as "daredevil Lindbergh," "lucky Lindy, the lone eagle," and "the flying fool." But he was no fool. Fascinated with aviation since childhood, he acquired substantial mechanical and engineering knowledge, although he was a mediocre and uninterested student in other subjects.

After finishing high school in Little Falls, Minnesota, where he grew up and where his father was a five-time U.S. Congressman, Lindbergh first briefly tried his hand at farming. He resumed his education at the University of Wisconsin, but was dismissed for poor grades in his sophomore year. He then enrolled in a flying school in Lincoln, Nebraska, and there found the first intimations of his true calling. However, he was forced to drop out after only eight hours' flying time, as the troubled school sought money he did not have. He talked several barnstorming pilots into hiring him as a backup performer and assistant. Demonstrating their tricks as far west as Montana, and taking passengers aloft on flights of perhaps ten minutes for a $5 fee, Charles soon became expert, not only at piloting, but at aerobatics, wing walking, and parachuting.

As he had flown only with his mentors, astonishingly he did not solo until April 1923, and that in Americus, Georgia, where he had bought his own $500 Curtiss JN-4 "Jenny." He then decided to enroll in military aviation for more systematic training, and in March 1925 finished top man in his class at Kelly Field, San Antonio. Assigned to a Missouri National Guard unit in St. Louis, he contracted with Robertson Aircraft Corporation to carry air mail, a rapidly developing business. It became profitable enough to offset the great dangers involved, following congressional passage in February of that year of the Kelly Act, which, as seen, established a system for the Post Office to hire pilots to carry their mail. In a year or so, Lindbergh built up over 2000 hours flying time, mostly on five round trips a week between Chicago and St. Louis. He and two other pilots established the best record yet, completing 98 percent of their flights.

On a routine one in late September 1926, he was struck with the idea: Why shouldn't he try for the Orteig prize with a flight to Paris? Using his $2000 in savings and talking his employers and several friends into putting up another $8000 or so, he contracted the Ryan Airlines

Company of San Diego to build a sturdy, single-engine high-winged monoplane, capable of flying 4000 miles with 425 gallons of fuel weighing 2500 of the craft's total weight of 5250 pounds. Christened *The Spirit of St. Louis* and costing $10,580 with its reliable 220hp air-cooled Wright Whirlwind J-5C engine, it met specially ordered requirements for a larger than normal wing span of 46 feet, giving 325 square feet of lifting surface. It was 27 feet, eight inches long, and had one of the five fuel tanks behind the engine, with the cockpit to the rear of that in order to avoid the pilot being crushed between the two as had happened in other crashes. This forced Lindbergh to lean out to the side to see forward, but with the completion of other special features, such as rubber fuel lines to avoid breakages which had plagued less flexible ones, he was ready for the attempt by May 1927. To save weight, he decided to fly dead reckoning without a radio or sextant, and without the parachute which had already saved him four times.

On May 10, he set out from San Diego at 3:55 P.M., soon flying at night in order to practice his dead-reckoning navigation. He almost turned back when the engine missed a few beats climbing to 13,000 feet to cross mountains 12,000 feet high. But he decided to continue, and reached St. Louis the next day. The day after that, he arrived at Curtiss Field, New York. Transferring his plane to the longer runways at Roosevelt Field, near Garden City, Long Island, Lindbergh then had to wait over a week because of unfavorable weather; meanwhile, as the excitement of the press and aviation enthusiasts increased.

Given the atmosphere of observers and the weather, he was unable to sleep more than a few minutes the night before the flight, but receiving a favorable forecast on May 20, he decided to "go for it." The fully loaded airplane took off at 7:54 A.M. (12:54 Paris time). He barely cleared, by twenty feet, telephone lines at the end of the runway as there was a five mph tail wind.

Already without sleep for a day, his greatest problem turned out to be keeping awake, which required a constant shaking of the head and moving about as much as he could in the cramped cockpit. He descended to 200 feet over Newfoundland to be sure of where he was, before setting out to cross the 2000 miles to Ireland. Then he ran into the full panoply of flying problems of those days. Avoiding dangerous cloud turbulence as best he could, he was forced to descend repeatedly from over 10,000 feet to just above the water to escape icing on the wings. He finally spotted the Irish coast, over Valencia and Dingle Bay, amazingly only three miles off his intended crossing, after twenty-eight hours of flight. From there on, fully awakened by his accomplishment, he had smooth going, passing 1000 feet over a small, enthusiastic crowd at Cherbourg, on the coast of Normandy, eight hours later.

At close to 10 P.M. Paris time, he spotted the Eiffel Tower and circled it and the great city. Finally, he had to find the barely lit Le Bourget airfield, the runways of which were not paved for another decade. Knowing it was just northeast of the city, he was guided by the lights of the many cars heading for the triumphant welcome. On landing, he had to avoid a vast crowd of people—estimated at 200,000. He was rescued by the U.S. Ambassador and other officials and guards, soon getting his first proper sleep in sixty-three hours.

He had done it! Although since the first flights with stops, in the spring of 1919, some 92 had crossed the Atlantic by air, the 25-year-old Lindbergh was the first to do so non-stop. Moreover, he broke the previous distance record by over 250 nautical miles, covering over 3400 on a great circle route (about 3610 miles in a straight line), in thirty-three and a half hours, to arrive over two hours ahead of schedule. He could have gone another 700 miles, with over 70 of his 425 gallons of fuel remaining. His airspeeds ranged from about 90 to 100 mph, but his ground speed, with favorable tail winds in the early and late stages of the flight, had been closer to 117 mph.

Immediately, Lindbergh was hailed as the "new Daedalus," receiving the French Medal of Honor and later innumerable other awards, often with overwhelming attention, much of it unwanted. But he continued to make notable flights—to Asia, Russia, South America, and elsewhere. On one, across the U.S. South, a Mississippi black lady put the inimitable question to him: "How much [would it cost] to fly to heaven and leave her there."

In 1932, his first son was kidnapped and killed, to the horror of the entire country. The mother of the baby, and later four other children, was Lindbergh's famous flight colleague and writer, Anne Morrow Lindbergh. Soon, he came into controversial publicity, by expressing admiration for Hitler's Germany and working to keep America out of World War II. But his fame persisted, and post-war work for nature conservation before his death in 1974 largely saved his reputation as the man who "embodied at once the promise of the machine age and virtues of frontier individualism." He also seemed to demonstrate how the love of flying could enable "escape . . . from limitations put upon the free individual," and how America was the best place on earth to accomplish that.

As noted in Chapter Eight, American army aviators Lester Maitland and Albert Hegenberger made the 2400-mile crossing, leaving the other side of the continent, from Oakland to Honolulu, only five weeks after Lindbergh had reached Paris. But the next biggest names in international flights were, first, the Australian Charles Kingsford-Smith, and the Frenchman Dieudonné Costes, and slightly later the Americans Wiley Post and Amelia Earhart.

After three successful crossings in 1927 by Americans from San Francisco to Hawaii, and Bert Hinkler's February 1928 flight from England to his native Australia, Kingsford-Smith, known as "Smithy," organized an ambitious flight all the way from the U.S. West Coast to Australia. During the preparations, as he was already famous as a stunt flyer, he did aerobatics of all sorts for the movies and barnstorming with a flying circus. He chose a three-man crew, with another Australian, Charles Ulm, and two Americans, Harry Lyons and James Warner. They used a Fokker airplane, with three 230hp Wright engines, weighing almost seven tons with a full load of 1304 gallons of fuel.

Christened *The Southern Cross*, after the famous constellation by which they flew on clear nights, they were also equipped with a wireless system giving constant communications with those they could reach. On May 31, 1928, they set out from Oakland across the bay, and in twenty-seven hours, twenty-seven minutes reached Hawaii. Leaving the island of Kauai with its longer runways on June 2, they covered their longest stage of almost 3200 miles in thirty-two hours, flying at 800 feet or less, and avoiding dangerous storms and minor engine problems, to reach Suva, on one of the Fiji islands. They then set off for Brisbane, which they reached in twenty-one hours on June 8, and went on to a rousing welcome the next day in Sydney by 300,000 people, or almost half that city's population. They had gone 7800 miles in three stages, with close to fifty and a half hours of flying.

Three months later, Kingsford-Smith and Ulm made the first round-trip flight from there to New Zealand, arriving back with only three gallons of fuel remaining. On March 30, 1929, those two and two new crew members set out from Australia for London, but crashed. They were rescued on April 5 and continued on to their destination. Then, between June 25 and July 10, they accomplished the flight back to London and new acclaim. A year later, they headed west and reached San Francisco on July 4, 1930, via Newfoundland and New York, completing a round-the-world flight of 33,500 miles after two years and thirty-four days. Kingsford-Smith and others made the flight from Australia to San Francisco two years after that, but in November 1935 his luck ran out. On a flight from Kent, England to Australia, his Lockheed Altair disappeared in a storm over the Bay of Bengal.

Three other "firsts" came in 1929, all in Germany. The first airplane weighing over 50 tons (the Do-X Flying Boat) was also the first to carry over 100 passengers, in fact 169, across Lake Constance. Then the first rocket-propelled plane flew two miles at Frankfurt, a year after a rocket-powered glider flight. The first flight of a liquid-fueled rocket (to which we shall return) was launched on March 16, 1926, by American scientist R.H. Goddard in Worcester, Massachusetts. As seen, the Graf Zeppelin airship made the first round-the-world flight in a dirigible, August 8–29, 1929.

As mentioned also, the French aviator Dieudonné Costes, with co-pilot Joseph Le Brix, made the first non-stop crossing of the South Atlantic on May 11, 1930, as part of a circling of the world—a year after establishing the pre-Lindbergh distance flight with another co-pilot. Then, from September 27, 1929 to November 21, Costes established a new distance record of 7905 kilometers (4941 miles) without stop, as he and Maurice Bellonte completed a well-publicized round trip from Paris to Hanoi and back, via Tsitsihar, northwest of Harbin, northeast China, their first stop after Paris.

More importantly, on September 1–2, 1930, Costes and Bellonte accomplished the first successful crossing—against the wind—from Paris to New York, three years and three months after Nungesser and Coli had disappeared near Newfoundland attempting that just before Lindbergh's triumphant flight. They flew a Breguet single-engine biplane, powered by a 600hp, water cooled, Hispano-Suizza engine, christened *Point d'Interrogation.* The craft, which had flown them to Hanoi the year before, now weighed over 14,000 pounds (6375 kilos), and was 18.3 meters (58.6 feet) wide and 10.7 meters long. Taking off after forty-six seconds of ground roll from Le Bourget at 9:54 Paris time, they varied their altitude between 350 meters (1148 feet) and 2900 meters (9512 feet). Equipped with a radio, they made contact with ocean liners passing below, appropriately including the *America* and the *France*. They passed over Tipperary, Ireland, humming the song they had heard in World War I, "It's a long, long way . . ." Then they flew between Greenland and Labrador and over Cape Breton, Nova Scotia. After thirty-seven and a quarter hours of flight, they reached New York at 7:12 P.M., September 2, with about 100 gallons of fuel remaining.

By 1932, some forty-six flights had crossed the North Atlantic, including many with stops. But 12 of 98 crew members had been lost since 1918, with another 15 rescued after their planes went down at sea. Flights from the United States to distant Buenos Aires were also developed in the late 1920s, and by 1930 the time from there to Miami was reduced to six days.

As noted, there were continuous new time records between cities as speeds increased from 126.67 mph in 1913 to 211.94 in 1922, to 404.02 mph in 1932, to the 469.22 mph of 1939. Perhaps the most publicity was given to "meteor man," Frank Hawks, who established some 200 city-to-city records by 1931, including London to Paris in 59 minutes and Los Angeles to New York in 12 hours and 25 minutes. Already in 1926, Alan Cotham and his mechanic, A.B. Elliott, had made round-trip flights of several months from England to distant South Africa and Australia. In 1929, Frank Hawks became the first to fly solo across the U.S. in both directions. These and other records of course fell year by year with the steady progress of performances. By 1935, records had reached 6587 miles for non-stop flight, 440 mph in speed, and 48,697 feet of altitude.

Challenging the long distance and speed flights for publicity during these years were the Barnstormers, who did everything from wing walking, smoke writing, and trick parachute jumps to climbing or leaping from plane to plane and speeding automobiles and back. Some of the stunts went back to the virtual beginnings of aviation. The first real barnstorming troupe was organized in 1910 in Texas by an architect bitten by the flying bug, John Moisant. After learning to fly at Blériot's school in France, he had already flown a first, somewhat terrified passenger from Paris to Dover and London. He then lured Roland Garros and others to perform with him briefly in Texas and elsewhere, and they stimulated enthusiastic crowds to unleash volleys of gunfire, not always in celebration. Moisant won a 33-mile race across New York City from Belmont

Park in November 1910, but his luck did not hold and he crashed to his death in New Orleans a month later. His pilots continued to fly, however, and performed some of the first military observations and bombings in the Mexican Civil War.

The first American woman to fly, Blanche Stuart Scott, who took off in a Curtiss pusher on Long Island, September 2, 1910, went on to become one of the first stunt fliers in succeeding years. Her stunts included "death dives" from 4000 feet, pulling out 200 feet above the ground, and upside-down flights under New York's East River bridges. As noted earlier, Lincoln Beachey had already achieved great fame for flying stunts in the U.S., stupefying a crowd with his flight under Niagara Falls in December 1911. Earlier he had set an altitude record of 11,600 feet, but in 1913 flew too close to a stand, killing one spectator and injuring three, at Hammondsport, New York. He went on to such feats as landing on the roof of a San Francisco building, and became the undisputed star of pre-war American aviation. But then, he tore off his planes' wings by greatly exceeding its maximum speed of 103 mph, and dove to his death before a horrified crowd of 50,000 at the San Francisco International Exposition, in March 1915.

After the Great War, many of the newly trained aviators decided the closest peace-time equivalent to dogfighting was barnstorming. Joined by new enthusiasts like Lindbergh and, in the U.S., an estimated 500–600 others, they created an enormous new body of the "lore" of aviation. They were able to acquire surplus Jennys, Fokkers, Standards, De Havillands, Sopwith Camels—"the most maneuverable airplane of all time"—and other craft for next to nothing, and stunt-flying groups sprung up everywhere in the nation. However, clearing proper landing and take-off areas, literally "fields" in many places, often required days or weeks of local recruitment of laborers and work before the barnstormers could perform, and still they had to avoid ditches or cope with steep slopes, and constantly repair their planes. Often, they took passengers up for as little as one dollar, or a little gas, using cows as their weather vanes since the bovine creatures stand with their tails to the wind.

Aerial circuses competed for crowds with incredible new stunts. They included standard acrobatic maneuvers, from chandelles to loops to rolls, lazy eights and hammerheads, with many variations at low altitude. There were spins—pulled out of only feet above the ground—jumping from plane to plane or car, and even fake tennis matches with a player on each wing, or headstands, or hanging by toes from trapezes (or twenty-foot-long ropes) suspended from speeding aircraft. There were even planned crashes through the doors of buildings, wrecking the plane even as the pilot walked away unhurt. For "gypsy" stunt pilots, as Martin Caidin recounted in *Barnstorming*, "caution became a dirty word, longevity an object of sneering . . ." Such attitudes were naturally dangerous. By late 1919, eight flyers had been killed attempting various stunts, and, in 1923 alone, 179 accidents cost 85 deaths. Those who survived clearly had to be the best "stick and rudder" pilots with the maximum ability to fly "by the seat of their pants," as the expressions went.

In 1923, nineteen-year-old Benny Howard read a book on how to fly, and quickly set out with an unfortunate passenger in a secondhand Standard he bought at Dallas. He immediately crashed, killing the passenger and putting himself in the hospital. But he belatedly took the lessons he had earlier thought unnecessary, and went on to become a famous barnstormer and racer. He and other survivors went on to glamorous lives, which, along with the high risk were filled with travel, romance, bootleg liquor, and sleeping under aircraft wings in the open air. Some made big money in less commendable ways, with turns smuggling liquor or other goods.

Stories of air shows were innumerable. Slats Rodgers created one at the Wichita Falls, Texas, Air Show of 1923. He did a loop at 1500 feet, dropping a dummy from its top into the crowd below, who quickly called the police. Taken to City Hall, Rodgers and his fellow pilots, known as the "Love Field lunatics" of Dallas, were not arrested, but treated to a celebration of their "fine show." Such performances might earn anywhere from $20 to $2000.

Then there was Smiles O'Timmons, a circus acrobat. One day, he crashed into the side of the blazing water tank he was aiming for, his injuries causing the amputation of one leg and arm and the loss of an eye. His trapeze career over, he decided he could nevertheless still parachute from stunt planes. But on one occasion his artificial leg came off and pierced the roof of the car of a necking couple. In August 1927, over Pennsylvania, his wooden leg got stuck in the wing of a Canuck (the Canadian version of the Jenny), flown by Bob Clohecy. After a half hour of great effort, during which the unbalanced plane almost went into a spin, Smiles was finally able to detach the leg, but in the process lost his pants in the violent slipstream. As Clohecy landed with difficulty, the crowd received a new thrill they had not expected: a semi-nude one-legged man clinging to one wing.

The most famous of all wing walkers, seventeen-year-old Tommy Walker of the Bronx, arrived in Florida in 1932 and learned not only to fly but, with the help of colleagues, to perform astounding stunts once aloft. With two slender wires, which observers on the ground could not see, attached to his belt and the plane, he was able to stick to the wing like a fly, through loops, barrel rolls, and spins. He even played his bugle in the raging air, and at times released his wires to appear to be accidentally falling to sure death, only to open his parachute at the last possible moment. Others flew less ambitious aerobatics without wires, leaning into the wind. Between flights, to earn scarce money in those depression years, Tommy Walker booked prize fights, scoring 26 knockouts in 35 bouts. He also became a famous test pilot of aircraft of the 1930s and 1940s, including the Lockheed P-38. On one occasion he broke his Stimson 35 in half, trying to force it into a spin, narrowly surviving his third emergency bailout.

Another famous barnstormer, Jimmy Collins, became a test pilot, as did many others for the growing airline industry. He described "the exploding crack of those wings tearing off" when he dove a supposedly sound biplane, narrowly surviving as falling debris just missed ripping through his parachute. An unnamed friend fared even worse when his propeller broke apart in a dive, and he broke both legs and an arm smashing into the plane's tail. Yet he used his good arm to pull the rip cord and survived his excruciating descent. Collins was not so lucky on March 2, 1935, when he could not escape his plunging craft, crashing to his death.

The government attempted to tighten controls for licensing, and limited the most dangerous stunts after 1926, but fliers and entrepreneurs refused to give up, though they devised new, more disciplined shows. The Gates Flying Circus, one of dozens formed in the 1920s, for example, organized by Major Ivan Gates of Rockford, Michigan, was able to draw 30,000 spectators to see "the greatest aviators in the world," and sold rides to as many as 100,000 passengers a year by 1927. Gates became known as "the Pope" and "P.T. Barnum of aviation" for his strict but highly publicized promotions, featuring Clyde Edward "Upside Down" Pangborn, an engineer from St. Maries, Idaho, and other colorful daredevils. There were "dives of death," crashes through buildings, fires set in the planes at night, and numberless near-fatal mishaps.

Sensational publicity came frequently, as for the elaborate rescue by three men in two planes of showgirl Rosalie Gordon, after her parachute had become tangled in the wing of Panghorn's plane 2000 feet over Houston. Another famous and tragic incident saw the death of Wesley May when the tree limb he had parachuted onto broke, giving a fatal fall. May had been hired when the parachute of the previous wing walker of the Gates Flying Circus had failed to open—this, after he had sent a telegram to Ivan Gates, which read, WHEN PRESENT WINGWALKER IS KILLED I WANT THE JOB. But the circus organizers of course stressed the safety of their rides, proposing "We will take you high or low, any way you care to go. It's worth a ride to see whether you like it or don't like it . . . The thrill of a lifetime! . . . Fly over your house, see who's visiting your wife . . . Come on up and fly high with the angels." Despite being grounded on several occasions by the new restrictions, in 1928 the Gates Flying Circus flew 273 shows in 75 cities. Then, in 1934, Texaco forced its closing by ceasing to supply free aviation fuel, following a final show with formation loops over Teterboro Field, New Jersey.

Another group, the Thirteen Black Cats of Los Angeles, in the late 1920s flew the following stunts for the right price.

Crash ships (fly into trees, houses, etc.): $1200
Loop with man on each wing standing up: $450
Fight on upper wing, one man knocked off: $225
Blow up plane in mid-air, pilot chutes out: $1500

Later groups, like the Flying Aces of Wichita, Kansas, continued until 1938. The organizer, Jimmie Woods, imposed the discipline necessary to deal with government regulations, such as requiring a minimum of 1500 feet altitude for wing walking, with obligatory parachutes. His wife, Jessie, became famous for sitting on the top wing of Stearmans and Travel Airs, performing loops, barrel rolls, and spins. Finally, new restrictions imposed by the Civil Aeronautics Act of 1938 forced the closing of that last of the flying circuses. The same year, in part because of the earlier loss of his stunt troop, Ivan Gates took his own life, jumping from a New York window.

Then there was flying for the movies, which from early days showed aerial stunts and exploits in multitudinous films. *The Great Air Robbery* of

1919 featured an early "king of stuntmen," Ormer Locklear of Fort Worth, Texas, who developed the jump from the wing of one airplane to another. In the film, among other things, he scrambled up a rope ladder to rescue a drunken pilot, dropped onto a speeding automobile to beat up a crook, and then climbed back into his plane by grabbing the landing gear as it came around again. But the next year, on August 2, 1920, doing a night dive with flares on his wing tips for the film *The Skywayman*, his plane went out of control and he crashed to his death. The film companies nevertheless continued to hire exhibition pilots to feature barnstorming aerobatics or wartime exploits, as in *Ace of Aces* and *The Dawn Patrol*. Seven years later, in 1927, the silent film *Wings*, about two young aviators in World War I, both in love with the same girl, won the first Academy Award for best picture. In 1928, Gary Cooper starred as an English pilot in love with a French farm girl, and in 1929 came *The Woman in the Moon*, directed by Fritz Lang.

The year after that, Howard Hughes began work on *Hell's Angels*, which opened in 1930. It featured Jean Harlow and forty World War I fighters—Fokkers, Sopwiths, and others—flown by some 39 pilots. Hughes, soon to become a famous pilot himself, directed aerobatic dives and passes which ended up taking the lives of three of the film's pilots. The "greatest of all stunt pilots," Frank Clarke, survived the film, but a little later crashed into a tree as he was waving at actress Betty Compson, during filming of *The Woman with Four Faces* at Santa Monica. She and the director rushed over to the wreckage, only to find Clarke calmly smoking a cigarette and asking the astonished two, "Looking for something?" *Flying Down to Rio* in 1933 featured scenes with two starlets doing a veritable aerial ballet. Films of the 1930s, such as *Wings in the Dark, The Bride Came C.O.D., Only Angels Have Wings, Men with Wings, China Clipper*, and *Air Force*, all with famous stars, often featured various Lockheeds or Martins, and others the Stearman biplane. One of the latter, in 1946, contained a scene where the ubiquitous Tommy Walker crashed through a barn at 85 mph only to walk away unhurt despite the plane's wings having been sheared off.

The popular film of that following year, *The Perils of Pauline*, featured aerobatics by pre-war stunt pilot Phoebe Fairgrave Omlie, while the 1965 film *Those Magnificent Men in Their Flying Machines* celebrated the April 1910 prize competition, won by Louis Paulhan, for the first flight between London and Manchester. Many of the planes in these films were supplied and later displayed by A. Paul Mantz and Frank G. Tallman, who formed Tallmantz Aviation Inc. in Santa Ana, California. Another Howard, Hawks, also made many aviation movies. In 1950 came the first more realistic depiction of future spaceflight in George Pal's *Destination Moon*, and in 1957 Howard Hughes' *Jet Pilot* with John Wayne.

Hughes meanwhile had founded his own aircraft company in Los Angeles, as a division of the family Hughes Tool Company in Houston. He piloted one of its first productions, the H-1, to an overland speed record of 352.46 mph on September 13, 1935. He was the first American to set such a record since soon-to-be General William A. Mitchell had accomplished it at 222.98 mph on October 13, 1922. Two years later, Hughes established a record crossing of the United States, in seven and a half hours, averaging 327.5 mph. Then, in July 1938, in a Lockheed 14 Transport with four others, he established a round-the-world record flight of three days, nineteen hours, fourteen minutes, with stops of about eighteen hours. They reached Paris on their first leg in half the time of Lindbergh's flight, and completed the trip with an average speed of 156 mph and a ground speed of 194 mph. After the war, he built the biggest seaplane yet, with a wingspan of 320 feet. Called the *Hercules* and nicknamed the "Spruce Goose," Hughes piloted the 200-ton craft for its only flight of about a mile just above the water off Los Angeles on November 2, 1947. The Soviets flew a still bigger, ten-engine, over 500-ton(!) "surface plane" (*ekranoplan*) a few feet above the water in 1966. It too was soon abandoned, although Russian followers of its designers, Rostislav Alekseev and Robert L. Bartini (an Italian immigrant), continued to work on new huge flying boats.

Howard Hughes went on to increasing fame and eccentricity, dying on a plane carrying him for treatment before reaching Houston, April 5, 1976. Other well-known Hollywood pilots included Merian Cooper, the producer of the famous film *King Kong*, while Mickey Rooney, Shirley Temple, and other stars joined activities, like the "Jimmie Allen Club" for a radio show of that name, celebrating the progress of aviation. Earlier, from 1928 on in America, comic strips like "Buck Rogers," "Smilin' Jack," "Terry and the Pirates" and "Flash Gordon" also reflected and inspired the mania for flying—as from the 1950s on did TV shows like "Captain Video," "Sky King" and "Tom Corbett."

More famous in the 1930s than Hughes were two other Americans, Wiley Post and Amelia Earhart. Post was a native of Texas who became fascinated with flying while growing up in Oklahoma. In 1924, he joined the Texas Topnotch Fliers, but after 99 parachute jumps over the next two years was forced to get more lucrative work in a Texas oil field. On his first day of work there, an accident cost him the loss of one eye, but he went back to flying and became a crack barnstorming pilot. As a friend stated, Post "didn't just fly an airplane; he put it on." Following a stint as a test pilot for the booming Lockheed company, he resumed work as the personal pilot for his friend, wealthy oil man F.C. Hall. The latter bought him a new Lockheed Vega plane with a 500hp Wasp engine, which Post christened the "Winnie Mae" after his wife, Mae Laine, of Sweetwater, Texas.

After winning a 1930 air race from Los Angeles to Chicago, Wiley Post decided literally to take on the world. Others also were planning that feat, and in March 1931, Francis Chichester set off solo from New Zealand, where he had grown up, to become the first to cross to Australia, with several island stops. But setting out for Japan, he crashed on take-off, and gave up the attempt.

Although never successful in two attempts to circle the world, his incredible adventures made James J. Mattern of San Angelo, Texas, almost as famous as Wiley Post in the early 1930s. An airline and stunt pilot, he twice reached Russia, but got no farther in his Lockheed Vega. The first such trip, with Bennie Griffin in July 1932, set speed records for a trans-Atlantic flight and again from England to Berlin, but barely made it into the USSR before a slipped hatch damaged the tail assembly and caused a crash landing, destroying the Vega. Setting off solo June 3, 1933, a month before Post could start his successful effort, "Jimmy" Mattern survived a split wing and stalled engine, which he was able to restart, to set a new solo non-stop distance record of 4100 miles to a Norwegian island. Despite extreme fatigue, a broken gasline, and other mishaps, Mattern reached Khabarovsk, northeast of Manchuria, only to have his oil lines freeze on the way to Nome, Alaska, and endure a new crash. Rescued by Eskimos after two weeks of near-starvation and extreme cold, he made it to a trading post and then Alaska, where he borrowed another Vega and made it to New York on July 30, 1933, 57 days after his departure.

On his first round-the-world trip two years earlier, Post flew with Australian navigator Harold Gatty. They took off from Long Island's Roosevelt Field at five minutes to five in the dawn light of June 22, 1931. After seven hours of flying, they stopped at Harbour Grace,

Newfoundland, to refuel. Crossing the Atlantic to an RAF base near Liverpool, they forgot to check their fuel until after taking off again, which they blamed on fatigue. Once refueled, they set out for Berlin, where they were wined and dined and treated to a good night's sleep. Then they set out for Moscow, which they barely made because of a storm. Not specifying U.S. gallons, they were unable to take off again, as the Imperial gallons used by the Russians overloaded the Vega. After siphoning off the excess fuel, they headed east for Novosibirsk. Next was Irkutsk and then a place called Blagoveshchensk, which they reached following the Trans-Siberian railroad. However, as the airfield there was covered with two inches of water, one of *Winnie Mae's* wheels got stuck in the mud. Horses were able to extract it, and they arrived in Khabarovsk close to five days after their departure, over half-way round the world in about half of their hoped-for time.

From there, after another seventeen hours of flight through heavy clouds and rain, they reached Alaska, landing on a beach near Solomon. After repairing a propeller damaged when they attempted a take-off on soft sand, they were able to find firmer ground and reached Fairbanks. Then they had to climb to 10,000 feet to cross the Rockies and gain Edmonton, where they again found flooded runways. Post landed fast to keep the weight up as long as possible, a basic technique for landing on water. They were able to take off again, after being towed to it, by using the highway out of town. Finally, after a last stop for fuel at Cleveland, on July 1 they reached New York—and a tumultuous reception. They had circled the world in a then-record of eight days, 15 hours, 51 minutes, over a day ahead of schedule. What an adventure, and news of it engrossed the world's press.

The famous stunt flyer Clyde Pangborn, and Hugh Herndon, attempted to best that record, taking off from Roosevelt Field on July 28, 1931. Via Europe, they reached Khabarovsk, only to become stuck in the mud. Continuing without permission to Japan for repairs, they were promptly arrested as spies, a little over a month before that country seized Manchuria (which many consider the true beginning of World War II). But diplomatic intervention secured their release, and October 4–5 they made the first non-stop crossing of the Pacific in close to forty hours. Having jettisoned their landing gear to reduce drag, they crash-landed at Pangborn's hometown of Wenatchee, Washington.

Those years witnessed other notable cross-ocean flights. In July

1931, the appropriately named Alexander Magyar and co-pilot George Endres flew from Detroit, via Newfoundland, to near Budapest to celebrate Hungary's cause. The first New York City to Mexico City flight was completed in June 1930, and another to Panama in November. The first flight from Tokyo to Manila via Okinawa came in November 1935, and from Havana to Seville, Spain, via Venezuela and Trinidad, in January 1936.

Wiley Post did not rest on his laurels. In 1933, he decided to try to repeat or better his round-the-world record, solo! He could envisage this more calmly as the Sperry Gyroscope Company had developed a prototype of the autopilot to keep a plane stable and on course. One was installed on the *Winnie Mae,* and the U.S. Army was happy to place a new radio direction finder for testing. It enabled homing in on target radio stations along the route. Without these instruments, as noted above, Jimmy Mattern, who had hoped to be the first to fly solo around the world, became repeatedly lost and finally crashed in Siberia on June 14, 1933.

A month later, on July 15, Post took off from Floyd Bennett Field in Brooklyn, as it boasted the world's longest concrete runways after its opening in 1931. He made the first non-stop flight to Berlin in 26 hours. After take-off for the east, he discovered he had forgotten crucial maps in Berlin and had to land in East Prussia to replace them. He then needed to return for a suitcase left at that field. Intending to fly straight to Siberia, he had still another unintended stop in Moscow to repair his auto-pilot. Then it was Novosibirsk and Irkutsk with more repairs. Almost running out of fuel, he reached Khabarovsk ten hours ahead of his 1931 flight time with Gatty.

Heading for Alaska Post relied on the auto-pilot to navigate a storm, but then became lost as his radio malfunctioned and he feared running into 20,270-foot Mt. McKinley. Fortunately, through a break in the overcast, he spotted a mining town with a 700-foot landing strip, but ran into a ditch at its end, breaking the right landing gear and propeller. Help arrived from Fairbanks, 300 miles away, and he was able to take off from there, and after weather delays reach Edmonton. Finally he made it all the way to New York non-stop, but only by staying awake in a novel way. Post tied a wrench to his finger and if he fell into a deep sleep, it dropped to awaken him. Fifty thousand people greeted his arrival at 11:50 P.M. on July 22, 1933. He had circled the world alone in seven days, 18 hours and 40 some minutes—almost a day ahead of the 1931 pace—despite the numerous forced stops. Beyond the adventure, *The New York Times* reported its great importance: "With the use of gyrostats and a radio-compass, Post definitely ushers in a new stage of long-distance aviation."

Moreover, the seven days around the world topped previous records by far. These included 1889 and 1913 round-the-world trips by ship, car, and rail, of 72 and 36 days respectively, and air trips in 1924, 1928, and 1929, of 75, 23, and 21 days respectively.

Following new adventures and experiments, including testing the jet stream and work with pressure suits to withstand problems of prolonged flying at altitudes up to 55,000 feet in training for a proposed race to Australia—which Post ended up missing—the Smithsonian bought and displayed the now-renowned *Winnie Mae.* Its owner immediately bought a new plane, an Orion-Explorer, and shortly agreed to pilot popular American humorist Will Rogers, whom he had met after his record 1931 flight, to Alaska in return for an interview on his talk show. Post ordered pontoons to equip the plane for northern lakes, but they were late arriving, and tragically Post allowed over-heavy substitutes to be installed, fearing further delays. They took off from Seattle on August 15, 1935, and came within 20 miles of their destination, Pt. Barrow. But on the next take-off, the engine failed to develop sufficient power to offset the pontoons and the craft stalled at fifty feet, causing a fall to the death of the famous two.

Then there was the immortal "Wrong Way Corrigan." He took off on July 17, 1938, from New York to fly non-stop to California in a Curtiss Robin monoplane. After flying all night, as dawn broke he was shocked to see water below! He soon discovered he had mistakenly flown by the wrong end of his compass needle. But with close to half his fuel gone and without radio or parachute, he decided to continue eastward. After 28 hours, 13 minutes of flight, he landed at Dublin, Ireland. There he greeted an airport officer with a sprightly "Hi! I got turned around in the fog. I guess I flew the wrong way." If so, it was a lucky mistake and Douglas Corrigan became an overnight sensation, greeted triumphantly on his return to New York.

Women and Everyman

Later more famous than Wiley Post, whom she met in 1929, was the most celebrated of all women aviators, and another American, Amelia Earhart. Born in Atchison, Kansas, in 1898, she saw her first airplane at the age of ten at a state fair in Des Moines. Late in World War I, she enrolled as a nurse in Toronto, and then in pre-medical training at Columbia University, New York. But, on a vacation trip to California in 1920, the (later famous) stunt pilot Frank Hawks gave her a ride for $10 at Long Beach, and she was "bitten." Taking lessons, and buying her own plane, she soloed after seven hours in the air in 1922, and the same year set a women's altitude record of 14,000 feet. After the divorce of her parents, she accompanied her mother to Boston and began several years of social and other work.

Unable to stay away from her earlier enthusiasm, however, she resumed her flying in 1927, and accepted the offer to accompany pilot Wilmer Stultz and mechanic Louis Gordon as the first woman pilot to try to cross the Atlantic. They accomplished this on June 17–18, 1928, from Newfoundland to Wales—to the expected acclaim. In 1930, she became the first president of the women's flying group, the Ninety-Nines (after that first 99 of the then 126 licensed lady fliers in the U.S. who founded the organization), and later became aviation editor for *Cosmopolitan* magazine. In 1931, she married the sponsor of her 1928 Atlantic crossing, well-known New York publisher George Putnam.

On May 20–21, 1932, on the fifth anniversary of Lindbergh's flight, she did it solo in the record time of 15 hours and 18 minutes, in a Lockheed Vega, from Harbour Grace, Newfoundland to Londonderry, Ireland. She later recalled that night over the Atlantic seeing:

> the flames lick through [the engine's] exhaust collector ring and wondering, in a detached way, whether one would prefer drown-

ing to incineration. Of the five hours of storm, during black midnight . . . I kept right side up by instruments alone, buffeted about as I never was before. . . . At one point . . . an almost vertical drop of 3000 feet . . . That happened when the plane suddenly "iced up" and went into a spin. . . . I . . . regained flying control as the warmth of the lower altitude melted the ice. As we righted and held level again, through the blackness below I could see the whitecaps too close for comfort.

Not to worry! That is if you were a lady like Amelia Earhart. She promptly flew back to New York against the wind, becoming the first person to ever accomplish such a solo round trip across the North Atlantic. In August 1932, she set a record time of 19 hours, 5 minutes, to cross the U.S., from Los Angeles to Newark, bettering that by two hours the next year. From January 11 to 12, 1935, she made still another first, flying solo from Oakland to Honolulu in 17 hours, 7 minutes. Now known as "Lady Lindy," she returned via Mexico, to another record and a triumphant reception at Newark.

In 1937, she decided to make a final, long-distance flight—around the world! It would be another record, as not around the northern hemisphere, but the 29,000 miles, with zigzags for refueling, required to go around the middle of the earth. She chose a navigator, Fred Noonan, and a new plane, a Lockheed Electra, financed by Purdue University for a "flying laboratory." It had a top speed of 210 mph, a ceiling of 27,000 feet, blind flying instruments, an auto-pilot, radios, and de-icers. She first tested it on July 22, 1936, and then equipped it with extra fuel tanks to enable flying non-stop over 4000 miles.

Announcing her intentions in February 1937, she and her navigator took off from San Francisco on March 17, and established a new record time of just under 16 hours to Honolulu. But the next take-off for Howland Island, midway to Australia, resulted in a crash of the overloaded Electra. Earhart decided to ship the plane back to California for repairs, and then decided to reverse directions and fly eastward.

Reaching Miami, she and Noonan took off on the fifth anniversary of her solo flight to Ireland, and the tenth of the Lindbergh flight to Paris. They headed for Fortaleza, northeast Brazil, via Puerto Rico, Venezuela, and Georgetown, in then British Guiana. Crossing the South Atlantic, they reached Dakar, Senegal, on June 7. They continued eastward to a landing strip cut from the jungle at Lae, New Guinea, proceeding via Fort Lamy (Chad), Khartoum, Aden, Karachi, Allahabad, Calcutta, Rangoon, Bangkok, Singapore, Java, Timor, Port Darwin, and other stops.

They had covered 22,000 miles to reach Lae, the site of what would be a decisive March 1943 battle, and had 7000 to go. Yet the most difficult lay ahead, with 2556 miles of open ocean ahead of them before finding the two-mile-long island of Howland, two-thirds of the way to Hawaii. The take-off at 10 A.M. on July 2, 1937, was dramatic enough, clearing the 3,500 foot strip by only fifty feet. Then, after a last radio message establishing their position at "157 dash 337" or on compass lines 157 southeast by 337 northwest, they disappeared—to the consternation of the world. Intensive searches by U.S. naval vessels and others failed to turn up any good traces, until March 15, 1992, when investigators claimed to find fragments of the plane on another small island 350 miles to the south of Howland Island, halfway to Hawaii.

A last message to Putnam had declared, "I am quite aware of the hazards," but "I want to do it," because "women must try to do things as men have tried." That was "as near a complete reply as I could devise" to the question of "Why?" She also cited "'the aesthetic appeal," as the "lure of flying is the lure of beauty." Those reasons seem far more convincing than other speculations, including a later charge that the flight was also engaged in a spying mission on Japanese bases in the Far Pacific.

Amelia Earhart deserved her fame, but there were many other women pioneers in aviation—beginning with a niece of the first parachutist, André Jacques Garnerin, twenty years after his first jump in 1797. In the 19th century, women were prominent in aerial displays from balloon and parachute. Then, by March 1910, the first woman gained a license to fly, French baroness Raymonde de Laroche. In September and October of that year, as mentioned, Americans Blanche Stuart Scott and Bessica Raiche made solo flights, and the next year their compatriots, Harriet Quimby and Matilde Moisant, the sister of first barnstormer, John, as well as two English ladies, all became licensed. In 1912, Quimby was killed in a crash near Boston, and Matilde Moisant barely survived one in Texas. Blanche Stuart Scott and Bessica Raiche survived numerous such scares, but soon gave up flying. Still, others continued not only to fly, but took up the new stunts, as did Katherine Stinson and Ruth Law Oliver, who were the first women to loop the loop, in 1915. The latter broke the then distance record with a 512 mile flight from Chicago to New York, November 19–20, 1916.

Just after the war, inspired by stories of the aces and a barnstorming show, a 26-year-old black woman, Bessie Coleman, born in Texas and living in Chicago, decided to try her luck. Refused permission to learn in the U.S. because of her race, she saved enough to go to France, where on June 15, 1921, she became the first black woman to earn her wings. Returning to the United States, she gave instruction and acrobatic exhibitions before falling to her death on April 30, 1926, near Orlando, Florida, while preparing for a May Day show. In an accident remarkably similar to that which had killed Harriet Quimby, Coleman was performing a dive from 5000 feet when the plane inverted, throwing her to her death as she had neither fastened her seat belt nor worn a parachute. In those early days, many of the first female pilots, including Scott and Quimby, had faced similar problems getting started, not because of their race but simply because they were not men. For the same reason, Ruth Law Oliver and others were refused permission to perform as military pilots in the Great War.

In the 1920s and 1930s many women, including as noted Mabel Cody, Phoebe Fairgrave Omlie, and Helen Richey, became famous barnstormers and racers. The latter became the first female commercial pilot, flying a Central Airlines Ford tri-motor from Washington to Detroit on New Year's Eve, 1934; United Airlines had hired the first stewardesses in the spring of 1930. Some 34 of 4690 licensed pilots in 1929 were women.

The barnstormers not only performed aerobatics and aerial stunts, but even danced on wings, hung below, or transferred to another plane or to a car. Three English ladies, among others, became famous names in the late 1920s, making highly adventurous flights between South Africa and London, and as far as Japan. In November 1929, Americans Bobbi Trout and Elinor Smith stayed aloft with refueling for 42 hours, but failed by far to break the men's endurance record then of 172 hours, established by Reg Robbins over Fort Worth, with refueling and resupplying. Also in 1929, May 28–29, Lockheed test pilot Herb Fahy set another endurance record without refueling of 36 hours, 56 minutes and 36 seconds over Los Angeles.

Earlier, the then-15-year-old Elinor Smith had won fame flying under New York's East River bridges, and sister New Yorker Laura Ingalls performed an incredible 714 consecutive barrel rolls over St. Louis and

980 loops over Muskogee, Oklahoma a few years later. In 1934, Ingalls became the first to fly solo between some 23 Latin American countries, while in August 1932, Louise Thaden and Frances Marsalis stayed aloft for over eight days with refueling.

Women also became leading aerial racers. In August 1929, Louise Thaden had come in first among 15 women completing the race from Santa Monica, California to Cleveland to inaugurate the National Air Races there. Humorist Will Rogers dubbed it the "Powder Puff Derby," while the press spoke of "petticoat pilots," "ladybirds," and "flying flappers."

Ruth Nichols of New York became briefly more famous than Amelia Earhart, with record cross-country flights in 1930, and an altitude record of 28,743 feet the next year. But she and another Ruth, Elder, failed in attempts to cross the Atlantic, leaving Amelia Earhart, in May 1932, as the first to do so. The numbers of women pilots continued to grow from some 472 in the U.S. by 1932, when there were 17,226 male pilots, to over 3,000 by 1942, reaching an estimated 43,000 of the 655,000 pilots in the country by 1989. Some 500 of the about 50,000 American airline pilots by then were women.

As for why so many women wished to share the wonder of aviation, another barnstormer, Margery Brown, gave the eloquent answer: "Halfway between the earth and sky one seems to be closer to God. There is a peace of mind and heart, a satisfaction that walls cannot give . . ."

The "British answer" to Amelia Earhart was Amy Johnson, five years her junior. Getting her license in July 1929, she set out for Australia on May 5, 1930 in an attempt to beat Bert Hinkler's record of fifteen days. She was ahead by two days on reaching Karachi, but bad weather and forced landings and repairs delayed her arrival in Sydney until May 24, over nineteen days out, and ten days longer than the solo record established the following year. In July 1932, she married the pilot of that exploit, Jim Mollison. He promptly set a record of five days to reach Cape Town, and then established a new record westward crossing of the Atlantic from Ireland. But Amy then bettered by a day his time to Cape Town, November 14–18, 1932.

After numerous other adventursome flights, both solo and together, and equally numerous problems of health and crashes, followed by the Mollisons' divorce, Amy joined the Air Transport Auxiliary (ATA) to help with the war effort. She, Pauline Gower, and over a hundred other women from many Allied countries, as well as England, made important contributions from the Battle of Britain onward, ferrying 120 types of aircraft, including four-engined bombers. Fifteen of the one hundred or so pilots of the ATA gave their lives in the effort. Most famously, in January 1941, three and a half years after Amelia Earhart, Amy Johnson also disappeared in mystery, delivering a twin-engined Oxford trainer from Prestwick, via Blackpool, to Kidlington. She had taken off in marginal weather and probably ran out of fuel trying to find a break in the clouds, in those days before instrument landings. It is known that she was able to parachute out, but she was never found. Again, there was much publicity and speculation about the never-explained accident.

In 1936, two other women pilots became famous, New Zealander Jean Batten and Kenyan Beryl Markham. Taking off from London on October 5, 1936, the 27-year-old Batten covered the 14,000 miles to Australia in under six days, and between October 19 and 24, 1937, returned solo to England, bettering the then record by over 14 hours. She made numerous other notable flights and received numerous awards, becoming known as the "Garbo of Aviation" in tribute to her good looks.

Also beautiful, as indeed were many of the early lady aviators, Beryl Markham turned from assisting her father's training of race horses to flying the mails and passengers in East Africa. In March 1936, she completed her sixth trip from Nairobi to London, and on September 4, 1936, became the first person to fly solo non-stop across the North Atlantic from east to west, all the way from Abingdon, England. However, she was forced to make a crash landing in Nova Scotia, twenty-one hours and twenty-five minutes later. Her book, *West with the Night*, is considered one of the classics of aviation literature. It includes passages such as, on page nine: "I have lifted my plane from the Nairobi airport for perhaps a thousand flights and I have never felt her wheels glide from the earth into the air without knowing the uncertainty and the exhilaration of firstborn adventure. . . . So far as I know I was the only professional woman pilot in Africa at that time."

There were many other heroines of the air publicized in these years. They included French pilot Marie-Louise Bastie, who set an endurance record in 1930, flew to Russia in 1931, and became the first woman to fly from Paris to Tokyo in 1934. The Australian Nancy Bird, known as "Little Bird," became the first barnstormer down under in 1935, and made numerous celebrated medical, educational, and entertainment flights to the distant outback. In 1937, the wife of a French garage mechanic, Andrée Dupeyron, broke the women's record for a distance flight in a straight line, and inspired the movie of that year, *Le Ciel est a Vous* (The Sky Is Yours).

In 1938, Valentina S. Girsodubova, known as "The Soviet Union's Amelia Earhart," and two other women flew almost 4000 miles to the east of Moscow to a crash landing in Siberia and a new record. Following the German invasion of Russia in June 1941, a Soviet woman, Lilya Litvyak, was credited with downing a dozen German planes before being shot down to her death at the age of 21. She was given one of the 32 Hero medals awarded to the several hundred Soviet women military pilots. On the other side, before the war, in 1937, Hanna Reitsch had become a military test pilot for Hermann Goering's Luftwaffe. Famous for gliding records, she helped develop gliders towed by three- or four-engined planes, able to carry up to 200 troops and their weapons. She tested newly developing helicopters, and even an experimental rocket plane—one that reached a speed of 500 mph in seconds and 30,000 feet in a minute and a half. But on her fifth test, in 1943, she could not jettison the undercarriage, and crashed to near-fatal injuries. She resumed her flying only in the last year of the war and, after a year's imprisonment, resumed gliding, establishing a new women's world record the year before her death in 1978.

In America, the most famous pilot after her friend Amelia Earhart was Jacqueline Cochran. Born in North Florida about 1906, she acquired her license in 1932, and became the second woman to win the Bendix Race in 1938. After the U.S. entered the war, she organized several dozen of the most experienced of the then 700 American women pilots for airlifts to England and elsewhere. Prior to her return to the States, another well-known American "ladybird," Nancy Hawkins Love, after two years of efforts, finally secured Army Air Force approval to organize the Women's Auxiliary Ferrying Squadron (WAFS). On November 10, 1942, it ferried its first Piper Cubs from Lock Haven, Pennsylvania to Mitchell Field, Long Island, on October 22, 1942, and in all transferred some 12,650 planes of 77 different types across the country and to England and beyond.

Cochran meanwhile had been asked to form on November 16, 1942, the Women's Flight Training Detachment (WFTD), with an initial class of 28 at Howard Hughes Field, at Houston. Like WAFS, it grew impressively, and on August 5 the two units were joined to form the Women's Air Force Service Command, or WASPS. Prior to its disbandment on December 20, 1944, when sufficient new male trainees had become available, some 1074 American women earned their wings to serve as WASPS, and 38 of them gave their lives for their country. After the war, in 1953, Cochran became the first woman to fly supersonically, and in 1959 set speed records in the Mach 2 F-104. In all, she set an astonishing 69 records, more than anyone else, before her death on August 9, 1980.

Rivaling Jackie Cochran in fame after the war was another Jacqueline, the daughter-in-law of Vincent Auriol, the Socialist President of France from 1947 to 1954. After prominent roles in the Resistance and in the social whirl of the Elysées Palace, an overdose of politics influenced her to take up flying. Receiving her license in March 1948, she went on to aerobatic and other demonstrations and still more publicity. A crash in a prototype amphibian piloted by another laid her up for two years with numerous operations. But then, using her high-placed connections, she became a test pilot at a military center, and in 1951 broke Jackie Cochran's four-year-old speed record by 69 mph at 510 mph, in a British Vampire jet. She became the second woman to break the sound barrier in a Dassault Mystère II, and then Mach 2 in a Mystère III. Between 1951 and 1963, she made five women's speed records, each time bettered by Jackie Cochran. Her June 14, 1963 time of 1266 mph (2038.7 kph) was reached in a Mirage IIIr, while Jackie Cochran topped that at 1310.8 mph (2097.266 kph) on June 1, 1964, in an F-104 G. Jacqueline Auriol continued nonetheless to fly on to other exploits and continuing fame.

After the introduction of food on commercial flights by the early 1920s, the first stewards were introduced, and in 1930 the first stewardesses. On May 15 of that year, a Boeing-United flight from San Francisco to Cheyenne, Wyoming, was served by a trained nurse, Ellen Church, and thereafter the idea of female attendants spread rapidly. Movies on flights were also experimented with as early as 1925, and became routine after TWA first showed *By Love Possessed* on a 1962 flight.

All these services, adventures, records, aerial shows, races, and meetings spawned increasing numbers of "light airplane clubs" and sport fliers. In England after 1925, the De Havilland "Moth," and, in the U.S., planes manufactured by Curtiss, Aeronca, Fairchild, and later Beech, Cessna,

Piper, and other aircraft companies produced increasingly sound and inexpensive planes for the growing number of private aviators. In Germany, Klemm, and in Czechoslovakia, Avia, and others elsewhere developed increasingly attractive light planes. They were used mostly for personal convenience or adventure, but also for odd jobs such as spotting schools of fish and whales.

The airplane seemed on the verge of becoming available to everyone and in the 1930s the idea that anyone might fly seemed increasingly feasible. In the U.S., aeronautical engineer Fred Weick, at NACA's Langley Field near Norfolk, Virginia, after 1931 designed a two-seat, all-metal plane that he argued would not stall or spin, and used simplified controls and the more manageable tricycle ground gear, for "foolproof flight." But it did not "take off," because potential customers soon realized that he had traded off too much maneuverability and power in flight for "easier operation by neophytes." Relatively few "Ercoupes," as they were called, took to the air.

Eugene L. Vidal, the father of the writer Gore, had better luck. He was able to use his influence as director of the Bureau of Air Commerce, from 1933 to 1937, to advance plans for a "poor man's airplane," which would also be a "safety plane," with improvements such as those worked out by Weick, including the spin-proof design and tricycle landing gear, which improved stability on the ground. With assembly-line production, it was supposed to sell for $700, or less than most automobiles, and lead to "an airplane in every garage." Several prototypes were produced, and some even operated as cars on the ground as well as like airplanes in the air—an idea first tried in 1914 with the Curtiss "autoplane." Others imagined wings that could fold up or back to facilitate storage as later on aircraft carriers. But understandably, it was found that the "air cars" were less efficient than cars or planes, especially helicopters, and they failed to go into mass production. Some hope for a workable flying automobile by the next century, however, and the more conventional production of small planes, pushed their number from close to 3000 purchased in the U.S. in 1937, to 33,254 just after the war in 1946.

In France, the Potez, Caudron, and Morane-Saulnier companies were prominent, but it was the *pou de ciel*, or flea of heaven, immortalized by Henri Mignet's best-selling book of 1934, *L'Aviation de l'Amateur, Le Sport de l'Air*, which became the continental rival of the English "Moth" and American Beeches, Cessnas, and Pipers. Known as the "Flying Flea," it was a do-it-yourself craft, designed to be built in about 30 eight-hour days. Weighing only 220 pounds, it cruised at 62 mph, with a top speed of about 80 mph, and landed at only 19 mph. It took off for the first time on September 10, 1933, and went on to great popularity. But accidents of unprepared amateurs proliferated, claiming eleven lives in the year after September 1935, and the government banned its use.

Mignet's words about it, however, entered aviation literature. They included:

To fly! To live as airmen live! Like them to ride the skyways from horizon to horizon, across rivers and forests! To free oneself from the petty disputes of everyday life, to be active, to feel the blood renewed in one's veins—ah! that is life. . . . Life is finer and simpler. My will is freer. I appreciate everything more, sunlight and shade, work, and my friends. The sky is vast. I breathe deep gulps of the fine, clear air of the heights. I feel myself to have achieved a higher state of physical strength and a clearer brain. I am living in the third dimension!

His enthusiasm did much to advance the craze, claiming as events would temporarily prove wrong, "There is definitely less risk than by the road." He also gave sound advice: "What is it in fact, this learning to fly? To be precise, it is 'to learn NOT to fly wrong.' To learn to become a pilot is to learn—not to let oneself fly too slowly. Not to let oneself turn without accelerating. Not to cross the controls. Not to do this, and not to do that. . . . To pilot is a negation." But once aloft, despite problems of cold and the like, "'I no longer want to go down. I never wish to be happier." One day he reported, "At 1,300 feet the foggy look disappears, and I find myself in beautiful clear sky. . . . I make a few turns round the pretty little town, and wave . . . to my friends . . ."

More importantly for our subject, flying was advancing aerodynamically by leaps and bounds, although many of the new discoveries, as of front wing slats to supplement the increased lift given by rear wing flaps, would not come into widespread use until the development of bigger airliners. Those became possible with the improvements in structures, engines, and cockpits of the 1920s and after. Flaps had been tested from 1914 on, with split-wing flaps developed after 1919, and slats for additional airflow by

1921. But their extra requirements of cost, parts, and other complications delayed wide application until the 1930s, despite the great gains in lift enabling slower landing speeds and other advantages.

As seen, wheels replaced skids after 1910, and by the mid-1930s retractable gear were rapidly becoming standard for more advanced aircraft. As early as the 1870s some French had experimented with retractable wheels on models, and in 1920 a Dayton-Wright R.B. racing monoplane first used them. A Verville-Sperry R-3 cantilever, or strutless wing monoplane with retractable gear, won the 1924 Pulitzer race. The tricycle-type wheel arrangement began with the first helicopters, and then with the small planes of Weick and others after 1931, becoming universal after the war. As planes increased in size and speed, systems were developed to use hydraulic pressure to generate the ever-increasing forces necessary to control flaps, other surfaces, the retraction of wheels, and the like.

Other big improvements of these years included the transition from the earlier wire-braced wooden skeletons, covered with fabric, to the further streamlining of fully and rigidly covered fuselages, known as stressed-skin, metal monocoque constructions. From 1912 on, Hugo Junkers and others were increasingly encasing planes in corrugated metal, later smoothed out to reduce drag, with the use of aluminum and alloys such as alclad. By the 1930s, fuselages were made of internally braced stressed-skin, enabling the elimination of external struts. By then also, single-shell monocoque-construction monoplanes were rapidly replacing the previously dominant biplanes. This was spurred by the racing victories of planes such as the Lockheed Vega, designed by Jack Northrop. It was the first monoplane that did not use external struts, and became the first to fly non-stop from Los Angeles to New York, in a record 18 hours, 58 minutes, on August 19–20, 1928. The Vega, and later Lockheed models such as the Sirius, Altair, and Orion, continued into the mid-1930s to be built partially with wood, but increasingly with aluminum and other metals.

The single-wing monoplanes needed stronger materials and, at first, structural supports such as spars and struts. The many wings of the biplanes and triplanes could be rigged to support each other and could lift far bigger payloads relative to their weight. But their greater drag ensured that the higher speed of the monoplanes would make the latter dominant by the 1930s. They progressively adopted the new, lighter and streamlined fuselages and wings, flaps, retractable landing gear, variable-pitch propellers, engine cowling, and other new features.

Improved wind-tunnel research at the National Advisory Committee for Aeronautics (NACA), established at Langley Field near Norfolk, Virginia after March 3, 1915, was especially important for a series of improvements in engines and aeronautical knowledge. By 1928, engineer Fred Weick had developed the "NACA Cowl" to complete the nacelle enclosure of the engine, and thereby greatly reduce drag. He and his team also worked out the aerodynamically correct placement of engines in front of the wings, enabling the development of the new multi-engined airliners and bombers. Similar advances were being developed at institutes in Europe, and at Washington's Aeronautical Research Division and other centers. Engineers of the Army Air Service's Aeronautical Division at Dayton, Ohio, and the Naval Aircraft Factory at Philadelphia were especially important sources for the new knowledge.

Then, after 1925 and 1927, respectively, research by the Daniel Guggenheim School of Aeronautics at New York University and the Fund for the Promotion of Aeronautics under Daniel's son Harry, a former naval pilot, made important new discoveries in the rapidly expanding field. The Fund supported important research at the California Institute of Technology, and was instrumental in hiring famed Hungarian aerodynamicist Theodore von Karman to teach there by the late 1920s. He later went on to important contributions for Jack Northrop's proposed flying wing and numerous other projects. The importance of the correct positioning of the center of gravity was established, and work began on creating "laminar flow control" to further reduce drag.

The designs and technological improvements of European manufacturers like Anthony Fokker, Hugo Junkers, and Pierre Latécoère, and in America of William Boeing, the Lockheed brothers, Glenn Martin, Jack Northrop, and Donald Douglas, as well as of many others, continued to push the new stage of take-off. Drag, for example, was greatly reduced with engines placed in forward wing nacelles and enclosed by cowling. Improved carburetors using turbines to increase airflow were developed by the new Pratt and Whitney Corporation after 1925. Improved ball bearings, cantilevered wings, lighter and stronger, up to 1000 or so hp radial air-cooled engines with sleeker protective cowling, and improved, variable pitch propellers for increased thrust at varying speeds and altitudes, had all come into widespread use by the mid-1930s. On multi-engine aircraft, if one engine failed its propellers could be "feathered" to reduce drag.

As we shall see in greater detail later in the discussion of the commercial revolution in aviation, such steady progress spawned the first truly successful airliners incorporating these improvements. The engineers of the budding Boeing, Douglas, Lockheed, Martin, Northrop, and other companies themselves made new breakthroughs as well as incorporated what they learned elsewhere. In the late 1920s, the Ford Tri-Motor designed by Anthony Fokker, the Northrop Alpha, and the Boeing Monomail especially provided important examples of these improvements. Then the real take-off toward the revolution in passenger air travel came in and after 1933.

The twin-engine Boeing 247 was said to be the "first modern airliner" after its first flight in February of that year. Under the supervision of Boeing's chief engineer, Clairmont L. Egtvedt, who through his development of the B-17 later in the decade also would become known as the "father" of the four-engined aircraft of the future. The 247 used the all-metal monocoque fuselage with cantilever wings pioneered in the U.S. by Jack Northrop, as well as controllable-pitch propellers and retractable wheels. It was the first airliner to use engine cowling, turbo-supercharged engines, and pneumatically operated rubber linings on leading edges for de-icing. The smaller Lockheed Electra after 1933 combined many of these developments, as did the also twin-engined and bigger DC-2s and 3s, which added multi-span wing construction and variable-pitch propellers to attain still greater efficiency. Five years later, the Boeing 307 Stratoliner introduced better means of preventing carburetor icing—another devastating problem for the earlier piston engines in cold weather or at high altitudes. All these aviation breakthroughs were worked out through years of experimentation, mostly with smaller airplanes and increasingly in the United States.

By the late 1930s, refueling with another plane lowering a sort of hose—first experimented with in 1923 and later called a "flying boom,"—was coming into increasing use. Fuels of 100 octane began to be used by 1938 to give engines still greater power, while air brakes were first used on a Martin B-10 bomber in August 1936. The all-important cabin pressurization for higher altitudes was another innovation of the Boeing 307 in 1939, and it was used on all big airliners by 1947. The Stratoliner also had the first flush toilets as well as drinking, dining, and sleeping facilities.

The first modern airliners had arrived. The Douglas DC-3, which first flew in 1935, carried 21 passengers at 190 mph, and came to dominate the U.S. market, supplying over three-quarters of the airline fleet by 1940. It was widely copied or modified around the world, and had carried 600,000 people by 1960 to become one of aviation's classic planes. Including its military model, the C-47, over 12,000 were built and some were still flying a half-century later.

Racing contests sponsored many of these improvements, especially in the heady days between the wars. Speeds, as mentioned, had gone from the 126.67 mph of 1913, to 171.05 mph in 1920, to 211.91 mph in 1922, and to 318.64 mph in 1928. Most astonishingly, the last was achieved in a seaplane (a Macchi M-52 bis), as had the previous record, and as speed records would be down to 1939. A principal reason seaplanes like the 1934 record-setting (440.69 mph, 709.07 kph) Macchi MC-72 could exceed the speeds of land craft for over a decade was the fact that they had unlimited take-off and landing areas. That enabled them to reduce drag with shorter wings and use ever more powerful engines, like the 2800hp Fiat with two counter-rotating propellers of the Macchi MC-72. Also, close to the water, there was said to be even less air resistance than with the close-to-the-ground "effect." Pilots naturally sought to profit from such "air cushions."

By the mid-1920s, Americans, British, and French had further streamlined fuselages, equipping them with pontoons, while Mussolini subsidized Italian aviation to best all competitors, especially for the famed Schneider Cup. Jacques Schneider, the son of a French arms manufacturer, had earned a pilot's license in 1911, and also set a balloon altitude record that year. Two years later, he used some of his father's money to sponsor races of the "hydro-aeroplanes" he had become fascinated with. The first was held at Monaco in June 1913, and was won by Maurice Prévost, the only pilot to finish the 174-mile course. He averaged 61 mph in a Deperdussin monoplane, which had one of the first monocoque fuselages, and was equipped with twin floats.

After the war, the Schneider Cup became the most sought-after in aviation and led to intense competitions between American Curtiss seaplanes, Italian Macchis, British Supermarines, and others. The winning country hosted the next meet, and sites alternated between the Continent and England and the United States. Interest was enormous, and some

200,000 gathered to watch an Italian victory along the Lido at Venice in 1927, and still more the race of 1928, also won in record time by Major Mario de Benardi. Then Henry Royce, the outstanding English designer of engines with Charles Rolls, developed superchargers to greatly increase engine power, and won the race of 1929. Close to a million jammed the coast around Portsmouth to watch a Supermarine win a third consecutive race in 1931 at 407.02 mph. That ended the Schneider Cup, when the trophy was given to England for its three victories in a row. Ironically, a new Macchi-Castoldi 72, flown by Francesco Agello, established the all-time seaplane record of 440.69 mph, in Italy on October 23, 1934.

Although seaplanes were fastest in the decade after 1928, land racers naturally drew still more fans to ever more events. The first to use retractable take-off and landing gear, designed by Alfred Verville, won numerous races after 1920, and inspired the gear's increasing use. The most famous races after the Schneider Cup were sponsored by New York publisher James Gordon Bennett from 1909 to 1920, and in the early 1920s by the widow of the early French aviation enthusiast Henri Deutsch de la Meurthe, and the St. Louis publishing family, the Pulitzers. From 1928, 1930, and 1931, respectively, the most celebrated became the National Air Races, begun in 1924. The Thompson Races, sponsored by a Cleveland automotive manufacturer, and organized by Cliff Henderson in 1930, as well as the Bendix Cross Country Races, sponsored the following year by New York aviation industrialist Vincent Bendix, also drew famous contestants and large crowds of spectators. The times of the Thompson Races went from 201.96 mph to 283.41 mph in 1938, and of the Bendix, between Los Angeles and New York, from eighteen hours, twenty-one minutes in 1931, as flown by Jimmy Doolittle, to Howard Hughes' seven hours and a half in 1936.

The longest race ever, for $60,000 put up by Australian MacPherson Robertson, was won by a De Haviland Comet in 1934, narrowly edging out the new Douglas DC-2. Only nine of twenty planes completed the 11,323 miles across twenty-one countries, between Mildenhall, England and Melbourne, and the winning time of not quite seventy-one hours drastically cut the previous times. Also most impressive during these years were the mass trans-oceanic and continental flights organized by Mussolini's Air Minister, Italo Balbo. They included a flight of ten Savoia seaplanes from Italy, via West Africa, to Natal, Brazil, in January 1931, and of twenty-four from Orbetello, via Iceland, to a world's fair in

Chicago, July 1–15, 1933.

The most publicized of the race organizers in the U.S., Cliff Henderson, actually began his flying as a general's chauffeur in France in World War I, and organized a barnstorming group of stunt pilots known as the Black Falcons on his return to Santa Monica, California. He mixed other stunts with racing, and helped organize a National Air Race at Los Angeles in 1929, over a fifty-mile closed circuit. In 1929, he was asked to stage the next National Air Races at Cleveland. "Gladiatorial in concept," Henderson began them with a "racehorse" start, in front of a grandstand holding 80,000 people. With planes taking off fifty feet apart, ex-barnstormer Doug Davis won the feature race in a Beech Travel Air Model R. The races were interspersed with daredevil stunts that one spectator likened to "an elephant skipping rope." In 1930, Henderson repeated the show at Chicago, with Charlie Thompson providing the backing in return for the speed race bearing his name. Charles Holman won it in a Laird biplane at 201.91 mph.

Another Laird biplane won the first Bendix Cross-Country the next year, but was the last biplane to win a famous race. Most subsequent Thompson Races were held in his hometown of Cleveland. The later speed prizes required flights around closed circuits marked by pylons and simulated speed and maneuverability, while the distance races stressed the monoplane's endurance and reliability, as well as speed.

Most significant of the racers by the 1930s were Americans Jimmy Wedell, Benny Howard, Frank Hawks, Roscoe Turner, and especially Jimmy Doolittle. Wedell, of Louisiana, won the Thompson Trophy in 1933 at 237.95 mph, and was considered a genius at making his own racing craft out of his head. He took to signing letters, "Speedily yours," before being killed in 1934 when a student caused the stall of his Gypsy Moth. United Airlines Captain Benny Howard also raced, but was banned from it by a new company policy, only to become famous for constructing the only airplane—which he called *Mister Mulligan*—ever to win both the Thompson and Bendix prizes the same year, 1934.

Lockheed Vegas, Altairs, and Orions won most of the races in these years, and their streamlined features influenced the development of other planes and airliners. But the most infamous racing craft was undoubtedly the Bee-Gee, designed by the Granville brothers of New Hampshire and Springfield, Massachusetts. With a high stall speed and a tendency to spin, it has been considered, by Martin Caidin among others, "among the most dangerous airplanes ever flown." But it was fast! A model flown by Lowell Bayles did the ten-mile laps of the 1931 Thompson Trophy with a winning speed of 236.23 mph, and the next year Jimmy Doolittle's new model, with a 535 h.p. Pratt & Whitney Wasp engine, averaged 252.68 mph. Bayles was killed shortly in the crash of a Bee Gee, as were other top pilots. Then, in 1938, Frank Hawks, who, as mentioned, had set 200 city-to-city records, was killed in another show-stopper, the "aircar," built in part from an Oldsmobile by Joe Gwinn, who was his passenger. It plunged uncontrollably into power lines while trying to land in upstate New York for a sales pitch of the supposed land-air vehicle. Jimmy Doolittle fortunately survived such experiments, for, famous as he already was, he would go on to great new landmarks in aviation history.

Roscoe Turner, of Corinth, Mississippi, was not only a big man, over six feet tall and weighing 225 pounds, but a master showman. He created his own flying circus, and became known as the "best dressed" aviator, sporting a needle-pointed waxed mustache and specially designed blue tunics and riding breeches to impress his audiences. Decking out his 18-passenger Sikorsky transport as a flying "cigar store," after 1925 he took society ladies up for tea and other stunts. In 1928 he headed for Hollywood and, after flying for the film *Hell's Angels*, established a Los Angeles-to-Reno air service, with one of its Lockheed Vegas styled "The Alimony Special." He gave rides to famous movie stars such as Carole Lombard and Loretta Young, and in 1930 strapped a lion into his co-pilot seat, equipped with its own parachute. He won the National Air Race that year and compiled 30,000 miles in the air with his famous pet, before the lion's growing size forced its retirement. He won the 1934 and the last two Thompson races in 1938 and 1939. Along with Jimmy Doolittle, Turner was the only pilot to ever win both the Thompson and Bendix Trophies. He won the former three times, as he did the Henderson Trophy for speed. He also won the Harmon Trophy as "America's premier aviator" in 1932 and 1938.

As noted, few of these remarkable flights could have been achieved without the structural and technical improvements and other advances in the knowledge of aerodynamics. Perhaps the aviator who demonstrated the validity of the improvements more than any other was James H. Doolittle.

Born on December 14, 1896, at Alameda, California, he spent his childhood in Nome, Alaska, where his father had gone to try his fortune in the gold rush. His mother took him back to Los Angeles in 1908 for further schooling. Encouraged to put his extra energies into boxing, young Doolittle won the amateur bantamweight championship of the Pacific Coast at fifteen. He then dropped out of the University of California to enter the Army Air Corps, earning his wings in March, 1918. Thereafter, he was never long on the ground, and performed many bold, if not reckless, experiments, adventures, and crashes. He participated in Billy Mitchell's bombings of captured German ships off Norfolk in July 1921 and, as mentioned, on September 4, 1922, became famous with his record crossing of the country from Pablo Beach, Florida, to San Diego, with one refueling stop at Kelly Field, San Antonio, in 21 hours, 20 minutes. In 1925, he earned one of the first doctorates given in aeronautical engineering, at prestigious M.I.T.

Then, between his record speed flights for, respectively, the Schneider, Bendix, and Thompson trophies of 1925, 1931, and 1932, Doolittle demonstrated on September 24, 1929, one of aviation's most important firsts. Sponsored by the Guggenheim Fund for the Promotion of Aeronautics, he flew a two-seat Consolidated NY-2 on a blind rectangular course entirely on instruments, in and around Mitchell Field, Long Island. Flying with a light-proof hood that prevented outside vision, his fifteen-minute trip at up to 1000 feet in the specially equipped plane made the front page of *The New York Times*, which declared it the "greatest single step forward in safety" so far for aviation. Bad weather flying thereafter became increasingly commonplace.

Named director of the Guggenheim-financed Full Flight Laboratory in 1928, Doolittle had spent the year before mastering the best instruments of the day—there were then eleven in use, most importantly the Sperry artificial horizon and directional gyro, improved altimeters, airspeed devices, and a radio device to establish position relative to transmitting antennae. Another pilot accompanied him on the September 24 instrument flight in case of need, but Doolittle alone flew, guided by his illuminated instruments. On January 14, 1935, he set a new record of 11 hours, 59 minutes, for a transcontinental flight from Burbank, California, to Floyd Bennett Field, New York. As we shall see, his greatest fame came in World War II, when he led the April 18, 1942, carrier-launched B-25 raid on Tokyo.

Another convincing demonstration of the great progress in aviation was the beginning of passenger service all the way across the Pacific, even before that was accomplished across the Atlantic! Following Kingsford Smith's 1928 flight from San Francisco to Australia and the early 1930s flights to Japan and beyond by Pangborn, Post, Hughes and others, still other aviation entrepreneurs naturally began to imagine the aerial linking of the Americas with the earth's most populous continent, Asia.

Pan American Airways, the first effective big airline to make regular long-distance flights, took the lead. It began in the early 1930s to organize trans-Pacific flights to complement its burgeoning service to Latin America. In 1931 it established a flying school in Miami, specializing in cross-ocean flights. The next year it ordered its first four-engined flying boats, three Sikorsky S-42s and three 48-passenger Martin M-130s, and then in 1936 twelve of Boeing's B-314 flying boats, called "Pullmans of the Sky." The latter weighed 50,000 pounds empty and were capable of carrying seventy passengers with sleeping berths and dining areas. The planes were known variously as "California," "Honolulu," "Pacific," or, most popularly, "China Clippers," capable of flying non-stop from California to the islands of Hawaii, Midway, Wake, Guam, and beyond. Staging posts and runways were prepared on the latter islands from 1935 on.

The first Clipper reached Hawaii in 17 hours, 46 minutes, April 16–17, 1935, and returned to San Francisco five days later in 20 hours, 22 minutes. In the summer, clippers reached Midway, Wake, and Guam on successive flights, and between November 22 and 27, a Martin China Clipper with a crew of six went all the way to Manila with two tons of mail, in 63 hours, 24 minutes on a flight of over 8201 miles. It returned to San Francisco, October 2 to 6, with a cruising speed of 130 mph. A year later, the first seven passengers were taken to Hawaii on October 21, 1936. Six months after that, on April 28, 1937, a Sikorsky S-42 extended the service to Hong Kong. By October 1, 1937, 2000 passengers and two million letters had been lifted, mostly to Hawaii, but many all the way to the gates of China, some 8700 miles west of California. The film *China Clipper,* starring Humphrey Bogart as the pilot, further popularized and romanticized the achievement. In December 1937 a second route was inaugurated to New Zealand via Samoa, but a month later chief pilot Edwin Musick and his crew tragically disappeared when the plane exploded in mid-air north of Pago Pago. A second Pan Am crew disappeared between Guam and the Philippines on July 29, 1938.

The first "regular" Pan Am flight with passengers from New York to Southampton, England, via Bermuda, in a Boeing 314 "Yankee Clipper" flying boat did not come until June 28, 1939. Later bi-weekly flights cruising over 180 mph reached there via Newfoundland and Foynes, Ireland, while other Pan Am flights reached Lisbon and Marseilles via the Azores. By 1945, when Pan Am ceased to use amphibious airliners, it had flown some 15,000 crossings of the Atlantic, while TWA had flown another 10,000. As seen, by the mid-1930s, German Dornier and French Latécoère seaplanes were pioneering routes to South America, as were "Short Flying Boats" to the far reaches of the British Empire. Graf Zeppelins increased passenger services to the Americas in 1935 and 1936, but suspended them after the tragic explosion of the 804-foot-long *Hindenburg* on May 6, 1937.

The far greater tragedy of history's worst war began a little over two months later in China, and two years after that in Europe. Before returning to the triumph of passenger travel after 1945, the next two chapters will explore aspects of the terrible uses of military aviation in that and other wars.

The Fear of Flying and of Bombardment

Before considering new aspects of the wonder of aviation amid the aerial holocausts of the Second World War and other wars, it may be noted again that fear of flying has always been present. Indeed, it contributed to the enormous forward strides of aviation in the continuing quest for greater safety. Many fear flying, instinctively wondering if they will fall from the sky, thinking that what goes up must come down, and possibly not as intended. Acrophobia, or the fear of heights, makes some people fear *any* climb, but for most, that affects going up a ladder or looking out from the roof of a tall building, or the like, far more than sitting in the snug comfort of a modern airplane. Some people, however, are terrified at any sense of not being on familiar ground, and many feel forced to take special courses to overcome the fear of flying. This is most noteworthy when well-known stage or screen stars, or business executives, are forced to fly—to their regret—to meet the frequent engagements required by their professions. In the air, they grab whatever seems most secure, and hang on for dear life, with white knuckles and faces, heavy breathing, and sometimes worse symptoms.

As mentioned, the very first U.S. aviation journal, *Fly*, noted in its premier issue of November 1908 the disproportionate attention given to flying accidents, even if far fewer died in them than in other disasters. But it has always been so, especially if the crash involved the deaths of citizens of the country whose press reported the accident. Such publicity has accentuated natural fears and all too frequently obscured the progress of aviation safety.

By the late twentieth century, if an American was to travel 100 million miles, or the equivalent of 4000 times around the equator, the chances of dying in an air crash would have been on the order of one tenth (depending on the year) that of going such a distance by car, and close to a quarter the risk of going the same distance by train. It was not always so, and air-mail pilots in 1920, for instance, died at the rate of 7.62 per million miles flown. Two years later that figure fell to 0.57, which would have been 5.7 for 100 million miles, but that was still nineteen times as dangerous as scheduled air flights a half century later. The distress call "Mayday" from the French, *m'aidez* (help me), must have been heard all too often in those years, especially after its adoption by the International Radio and Telegraph Convention of 1927.

By 1985, however, major airlines in the U.S. registered only 0.3 deaths over the previous six years for passengers going 100 million miles, and commuter lines 1.27. Automobile accidents by contrast inflicted 2.8 deaths per 100 million driver miles in 1982, declining to 1.8 ten years later and 1.7 in 1993. Other measurements included 0.8 deaths in jets and 0.9 in propeller-driven planes for every one billion passenger kilometers.

Certainly, considering the time of travel, the safety differences between traveling by airplane or on the ground are far less in the air, given the far greater speeds. In 1990, for example, in the United States there were only seven accidents, not all of them fatal, for every 100,000 hours of flying time. Even pilots in advanced military fighters enjoy surprising safety. The supersonic F-5 and its two-seat trainer version, the T-38, for instance, had only 2.1 deaths per 100,000 hours of flight in the 1980s, and the F-14, 5.93 deaths per 100,000 hours in the 1990s.

Before 1983, the world's regular airlines suffered about twenty fatal accidents annually, with a record of forty-two in 1972, killing 1210 people, while twenty-nine in 1974 killed 1299. In 1988 1182 people died in about two dozen air crashes world-wide, as had 1083 in 1987. In the U.S. the 68 commercial air crashes of the decade 1965–75, declined to 32 from 1976 through 1987. There were 231 deaths caused by air accidents in 1987, and 278 in 1989, but then only 39 in 1990. By contrast, tens of thousands have died every year in car accidents, although highway deaths also have been declining, from the U.S. record of 56,300 in 1972, to about 40,000 a year in the 1990s. Late in the century, over 80 percent of Americans still travel between cities by car, as against over 10 percent by air. But the discrepancy between news about major air crashes involving perhaps hundreds, and the far more numerous deaths incrementally, caused by autos and other disasters, is still striking.

In large part, of course, that is because of the drama of the airplane crashes: as when a B-25 slammed into the Empire State Building, killing 14 in New York on July 28, 1945; or when a record 582 died in a runway collision of two 747s on the Canary Islands on March 27, 1977; or when 520 died in the crash of an overloaded 747 into a mountain in Japan on August 12, 1985. Many other airplane accidents killed hundreds, including the U.S. record of 275 deaths in a DC-10 take-off at Chicago on May 25, 1979. Of course, another reason for the publicity given air crashes is the relative frequency of big-name victims, since famous people travel so often by air. In the 1930s, these included entertainers Will Rogers and Carole Lombard, as well as Notre Dame football coach Knute Rockne. Recently, this was true for the great publicity given for the crash of an Air Force version of the 737 attempting to land at Dubrovnik, Croatia on April 3, 1996, that killed U.S. Commerce Secretary Ronald H. Brown.

The hijackings of airliners to places like Cuba or Arab countries also struck terror. They reached a peak of 33 successful ones out of 40 attempts in 1969. Then the installation of metal detectors and X-ray scanners to prevent the bringing of weapons onto planes largely solved the problem in subsequent years. The successful Israeli rescue of an Air France jetliner en route from Tel Aviv, which had been kidnapped to Entebbe, Uganda, in June 1976—led by Jonathan Netanyahu, a brother of the Israeli leader elected in May 1996—signaled the near end of hijacking.

The latest hazard in the air, as on the ground, has become political terrorists with their planting of bombs. On December 21, 1988, a hard-to-detect plastic explosive blew apart an America-bound Pan Am 747 over Lockerbie, Scotland, killing 270. The incredibly painstaking work of investigators, who collected wreckage from over 850 square miles of countryside, indicated Libyans were responsible for that. Another explosion, on July 17, 1996, blew apart a TWA 747-100 off Long Island, killing 230 people on their way to Paris, and investigators were forced to collect clues from the sea. Little evidence remained after the June 23, 1985 explosion of an Air India Jumbo-Jet off Ireland, with 329 killed, although this was considered to be the work of Sikh separatists.

Yet in the year of Lockerbie, 1988, a mathematical study concluded that the chances of Americans dying of terrorism if they had flown abroad was one in 1.6 million, as against one in 168,100 of dying in other air crashes, and one in 5,300 of dying on the highway.

The record of improving safety for aircraft, in motion at airports or in the air, is due to the work of many factors and people. They include not only the pilots and technicians, but ground maintenance personnel and air controllers, and of course, ever better equipment. Airline pilots have mandatory medical checkups every six months and must retire at age 65, while commercial aircraft are inspected on average once every 39 flights.

In June 1995, there were 48,000 employees of the Federal Aviation Administration, including 2600 inspectors and 17,415 air traffic controllers in the U.S., 12,000 of them at "full-performance level," capable of any relevant assignment. This was 1000 fewer than a decade earlier, when there was 28 percent less traffic, and came about because of the dismissal of 11,400 air controllers in the United States in 1981 after disputes over illegal strikes. Still, the 473 million Americans who traveled by air in 1992, of the 1.166 billion worldwide, continued to enjoy unprecedented safety, down to 0.0006 deaths per million miles flown. Over 1.5 million people a day took commercial flights in the U.S. in 1994, but only 237 suffered air crash fatalities that year, and only 1 in 1993.

Air Traffic Control (ATC) normally maintains, under both Visual Flight Rules (VFR) and Instrument Flight Rules (IFR), about five or up to fifteen miles horizontal and 1000 feet vertical separation between big planes at cruise and three to five miles and 1000 feet vertically in approach and take-off patterns within about 20 miles of airfields. Without the problems of wake turbulence and higher speeds, the minimum separation for smaller aircraft can be as low as 1.5 miles. At times separation also is done by time, planes taking off often three or five or ten minutes apart; and since the 1940s modern planes have been equipped with Automatic Direction Finding (ADF), Inertial Navigation Systems (INS), Distance Measuring Equipment (DME), VHF Omni Range (VOR), Instrument Landing Systems (ILS), and other devices for radio and radar fixes of ground position and direction. Weather radar systems and storm scopes to detect turbulence and wind shear have been continuously improved, as have navigation and control systems. By late in the century, the latter included, among others, INS (Inertial Navigation System), Loran (Long Range Navigation System), a space-based information network for Global Positioning System (GPS), and the Traffic Alert and Collision Avoidance System (TCAS).

When there are accidents, the 30-pound "black box" flight recorders (which in fact are bright orange, with reflective yellow stripes!), giving details of up to 100 kinds of data, as well as of all cockpit conversations, are analyzed for all possible lessons to be learned, assuming they can be found. By the 1990s there were well over 100,000 flights a day by all types of aircraft in the U.S., up to 4200 of them in the air at one time. In 1994, they carried over 481 million passengers within the country, And American aircraft carried another 47 million overseas, many on the 100,000 trans-Atlantic crossings a year. Therefore the relative safety of contemporary flying in busy thoroughfares is no small feat. For example, from New York, there are over 3000 arrivals and departures a day, frequently with 300 aircraft approaching or circling at any one time for the three big local airports. At John F. Kennedy International Airport, more than at most, planes also had to contend with a huge bird population. From 1979 to 1994, some 2800 planes in or out of approach there struck over 3500 birds, mostly gulls. They caused no fatal accidents, but damaged engines and leading surfaces as to a lesser extent do bugs of all sorts.

Flying is said to be twice as dangerous in Europe as in the U.S., three times as great in Latin America, four times as great in Africa, and who knows what in Russia since the breakup of the Soviet Union. Military and general aviation, including small private planes and commuter services, is also considerably more dangerous than flying the scheduled airlines, which maintain the highest standards of training and equipment. Bad weather, including icing on wings and tail, turbulence with wind shear, micro-bursts, vortices, and severe storms, causes about 2 percent of air crashes, but human error a full two-thirds of those accidents, with mechanical and engine failures, including flame-outs, the rest. Over 73 percent of U.S. jet airliner accidents from 1959 to 1994 were said to have been caused by flight crews. In Europe these problems were still complicated as late as 1993 by 22 different systems of control, operated from 42 centers, as against the single system used by 20 centers in the U.S. By then, French controllers were handling up to 5000 flights a day. The safety levels of flying are all the more impressive when one considers that the Boeing 747 has some 4.5 million moveable parts with 135 miles of electrical wiring. An average of about ten hours of normal ground maintenance is required for every hour of an airliner's flight, and there are regular partial and complete overhauls.

In any case, whatever the toll of one or all air crashes, it pales beside that for the hundreds of thousands of deaths inflicted by aerial bombs, bullets, and missiles. Exact figures are not possible, but certainly the estimates of air deaths suffered in travel are dwarfed beside the tens of millions killed in the horrific wars of the 20th century. As mentioned already in Chapter Eight, the menace of hurt or death from the air understandably struck terror in all battles of the air age. By the 1930s, the fears encompassed the imagined total destruction of the major cities. A 1934 English publication stated: ". . . mankind is Frankenstein, and Science, especially the science of aviation, is his monster." Even Orson Welles' infamous broadcast of Halloween Day, 1938—borrowing H. G. Wells' title of forty years before, *The War of the Worlds*, to imagine a Martian invasion of New Jersey— seemed all too believable. Such fears were not without reason, as estimates of air deaths include the following: 2,081 English killed by German bombs in World War I; and in World War II, some 60,000 English, 330,000 Japanese, and 593,000 Germans killed. The Japanese nickname for American B-29 bombers came to be "birds of hell."

There are no reliable estimates for victims of air strikes in the post-1945 wars in Korea, Indochina, Algeria, Afghanistan, Iran, Iraq, Lebanon, Bosnia, Chechnya, and elsewhere. But some exist for particular offensives. Some 52,000 Vietnamese were said to have been killed by Operation Rolling Thunder, 1965–68, but those raids were responsible for only about two-thirds of the one million tons of bombs dropped on North Vietnam, which were a fraction of the four million tons dropped on the South, one and a half million tons on Laos, and a half million on Cambodia in the American war in Indochina, 1964–73. That was the greatest bombing in history, while the 88,500 tons dropped on Iraq, January 17 to February 28, 1991, was the most concentrated. Estimates of Iraqi victims in the Gulf War ranged from a few thousand to 150,000. Still, although there can be no adequate apologies for those victims other than to say "War is war," and "All is fair in war," there were also innumerable new stories of the "wonder of it all" in the terrible wars of the 20th century.

Even before the greatest of all wars, from 1937 to 1945, there were many adventures in combat in diverse places. Any flight is an adventure of sorts, and in earlier days, with the greater problems of malfunction and accidents, this was all the more true. But, obviously the greatest dangers came when to normal possibilities of falling out of the sky were added the risk of exploding flak or bullets whizzing by. In the earlier guerrilla wars in Mexico and elsewhere, mercenary pilots did not face formidable antiaircraft weapons. Nor did Japanese pilots attacking Manchuria in 1931, and China six years later, nor Italians in subduing Ethiopian resistance in 1935–1936.

But that changed in the Spanish Civil War, from July 1936 to June 1939. There, General Francisco Franco won against the popular front and loyalists, with the help of ground and air forces sent by Mussolini and Hitler. However, the combination of that fascist support with the hero-ism of the defenders made the war a cause célèbre for most of the world's peoples. Especially praised were the heroics of various groups of volun-teers who fought against Franco. They included such famous names as writers André Malraux, Antoine de Saint-Exupéry, Arthur Koestler, George Orwell, John Dos Passos, and Ernest Hemingway. Pilots Bert Acosta, Whitey Dahl, Albert Baumler, and Frank Tinker were among the 3100 Americans making up the famous "Abraham Lincoln Brigade," which fought with over 30,000 other volunteers from some 50 countries. The authors all wrote best-selling works about their experiences, includ-ing Malraux's 65 missions as a bombardier-gunner and Saint-Exupéry's new flight adventures, which conclude his famous aviation memoirs, *Wind, Sand, and Stars*. Hemingway's fascination with Spanish culture, and Koestler's and Orwell's political preoccupations, informed some of their most famous works.

Tinker, who used the name Francisco Gómez Trejo, downed eight enemy planes to become the top American "ace" of the International Brigade, or Escuadrilla España as the foreign fliers were designated. Ironically, the first confirmed kill by an American was achieved by a Communist newsman, Ben Leider, and that without firing a shot as the German plane he was chasing crashed into the ground trying to escape. He also became the first American to die in the war, when his plane was shot down by German He-51 biplanes a few days later. Dahl achieved fame when his showgirl wife, Edith, with an impassioned letter to Franco, saved him from a firing squad after his capture. Albert Baumler made five kills after he had been dismissed by the Army Air Corps for "failure to show proper flying proficiency." He was soon severely wounded, while after his return home, Frank Tinker shot himself to death in a nearby Little Rock hotel room not long after hearing of the surrender of Republican forces to Franco on June 13, 1939.

Bert Acosta, already famous as a test and racing pilot, thereafter be-came the most famous American survivor of the battles against the German Condor Legion and its Ju-87 Stuka dive-bombers and Dornier

17 bombers. The latter were made infamous by Picasso's picture of the April 26, 1937 bombing of the Basque town of Guernica, killing a fourth, or 1654, of its inhabitants. Other intensive bombings hit Barcelona and Madrid, while in the fighter war German Me-109s arrived to replace the outclassed He-51. Eventually the 700 Italian and a similar number of German planes proved decisive against the more numerous 1947 loyalist aircraft, 1407 of which were supplied by the Soviets.

Still closer to the most horrific battles in history, which began in China after July 1937, was the famous group of American fliers who became known as the "Flying Tigers." Their commander was Claire Chennault. Born in Texas in 1890, he served in the Army Air Corps in World War I, but was delayed in learning to fly until the great flu epidemic of 1919 created the opening he sought. He went on to become a well-known advocate of aggressive combat tactics as well as a skilled aerobatic pilot. He was appointed head of the Air Corps' own team, known as the "Flying Trapeze" after the popular song of the early 20th century. They were the "daring young men" who swung through the air "with the greatest of ease." But stubbornly independent and high-spirited, like Billy Mitchell before him, Chennault was involved increasingly in disputes with superiors, which, together with medical problems and transfers of other participants grounded the group in 1936.

The timing, however, gave Chennault the chance for his greatest fame. One of his last aerobatic flights had impressed a visiting Chinese general, who recommended him to Soong Mei ling, the Wellesley-educated wife of China's leader, Chiang Kai-shek. She was just then overseeing the Nationalists' attempt to build up their air arm in the face of Japan's aggressions, and asked Roy Holbook, one of the twenty American flight instructors already there, to invite Chennault to help. He arrived in June 1937, and quickly gained the confidence of the Nationalist leaders. He also quickly became aware of the severity of China's needs, with only about 100 combat-ready aircraft. They faced not only far superior Japanese forces, but the enormous problems of their own history, including crushing defeats in Imperialist wars and subsequent warlordism throughout the previous decades, as well as the great difficulties in trying to modernize their vast and backward country.

An earlier episode illustrates just how bad the problems of China were, as does another example, albeit a negative one, of a "wonder" of aviation history.

A self-proclaimed hero of World War I's Lafayette Escadrille, Bert Hall, dropped out of sight until he co-authored the best-selling 1929 book, *One Man's War*. He then proceeded to China to various adventures and great publicity, with *The New York Times* on April 27, 1930, proclaiming him "the most outstanding aviator soldier of fortune . . ." In fact, he was something of a pirate, and as adviser to a General Chang Hui-chang, he swindled some $100,000 from the general to buy nonexistent Douglas bombers. Promptly jailed on his arrival in California in August 1931, he was released when the Chinese dropped the charges out of fear of losing too much face with further revelations about how an American was able to pull off an old Chinese trick, commonly practiced by the war-lords themselves and their henchmen. But Hall tried again with another Chinese general in 1933, only to be arrested on his way home in Japan. He was returned to Shanghai for trial and was deported to two and a half years imprisonment in Washington State. A more respectable American, colorful Julius Barr, served as Generalissimo Chiang Kai-shek's personal pilot in the early 1930s before becoming a test pilot for the Boeing Corporation.

Also tasting foreign adventure was America's most famous pre-war black aviator, Hubert Fauntleroy Julian, known as the "black eagle." He became a stunt flier and parachutist in various barnstorming groups and was invited to Ethiopia to perform for Haile Selassie's 1930 coronation. The latter appointed him commander of his fledgling air force, but then deported him for violating orders regarding the use of the Emperor's plane, a De Havilland Gypsy Moth. Returning to the States and great publicity, Julian blamed envious subordinates for his misfortunes in Ethiopia, charging them with trying to poison him, and other acts of sabotage. Mussolini's invasion of Ethiopia five years later was another step to the outbreak of war the next year in Spain, and after 1939 throughout Europe.

The first really heavy fighting of World War II came to China with the Japanese invasion after July 1937. Before that, Chiang Kai-shek's Nationalists had finally begun to reduce the chaos of many years of war-lordism and to make some progress toward modernization. But Japan's conquest of the coastal areas gravely weakened them, and together with continuing Nationalist mistakes and Communist gains, finally resulted in the country's submission to Mao Zedong's forces in 1949.

In the more than four years before Pearl Harbor, following the Japanese attack in the autumn of 1937, the only foreign help received by the Chinese Nationalists—about $250 million worth—came from Russia, which also sensed a threat from the Japanese and still remembered its losses to Japan in the 1904 war. Moscow also sent about 500 "advisers," including its own version of a Flying Tiger group. In those first war years, another dozen or so pilots from other countries came to fight in China, and some new planes were procured. But they were far from adequate, and the situation became increasingly desperate, even before Hitler's invasion of Russia in June 1941 forced an end to that country's aid.

In October 1940, Chiang Kai-shek decided to send Chennault to Washington to seek more aid against the vastly disrupting Japanese bombings of the wartime capital of Chungking and other Chinese targets. The Lend Lease Act of March 1941 began much greater U.S. aid to China, and President Roosevelt's Executive Order of the next month accelerated Chennault's recruitment of over 300 American volunteers, including about 100 pilots, 200 maintenance personnel, and 2 nurses. The International Air Squadron was renamed the American Volunteer Group, or AVG. A small number of volunteers set sail in June 1941, some 150 in July and others in September. But continuing Japanese advances and bombings by late 1941 forced many of them initially to stay in their first war-front destination of Burma.

An American businessman, William Pawley, who three years earlier had supplied two dozen Vultee V-11 bombers to Chennault, again took the lead to deliver more than 90 Curtiss P-40 "Tomahawk" fighters to the American Volunteer Group in China. They were procured from planes designated for England, their mission being described as including defense of British Singapore. The fighters soon began to adopt the distinctively gaping tiger shark's maw, painted just behind and below the propellers of their planes. A 25-year-old volunteer, Eric Shilling, ironically inspired by a picture of Luftwaffe Messerschmitts, similarly decorated for the Germans' Mediterranean war theater, convinced Chennault to so decorate his planes. Henceforth they were universally known by the more decorous name of "flying tigers." They spoke of themselves, however, as "sharks," fighting the Japanese "bandits."

The successful, if belated, American effort to defeat Japan produced some of the great examples of the "wonder" of aviation, not least the exploits of the Flying Tigers. Two of Chennault's pilots, David Lee "Tex" Hill and James H. Howard, were sons of missionaries to China, and they needed all the prayers they could get. Only one Flying Tiger, Albert J. Baumler, had had combat experience, with five "kills" in the Spanish Civil War, and he only arrived months later. But the group, including famously in addition to the above three Charles Bond, Gregory Boyington, Robert Hedman, Bob Neale, Robert Lee Scott, and others, soon more than proved themselves.

At the beginning, they also had more than a few troubles. Establishing themselves first at a base 100 miles north of Rangoon (Yangon), they lost three pilots to accidents before Pearl Harbor Day. Another proclaimed himself a "Japanese ace," as he cracked up five American aircraft in training missions. Although for over a year there were never more than forty-nine planes available for combat and seventy pilots fit to fly them, they were divided into three pursuit squadrons, dubbed "Adams and Eves," "Panda Bears," and "Hell's Angels." The first two soon transferred to Kunming, southwest China, while the last remained as long as possible north of Rangoon and saw most of the early action. In their first tangle with the Japanese on December 20, 1941, the Flying Tigers proved their stuff, downing nine of ten opposing Mitsubishis, which they surprised several hundred miles south of the Japanese target of Kunming, China

The first American victim in the air, Henry Gilbert, came three days later in the developing battle for Rangoon. Two days after that, Robert "Duke" Hedman became the first American "China ace," downing five enemy planes out of the nine fighters and fourteen bombers shot down that special Christmas Day. However, the Japanese ground forces continued to advance and took Rangoon two months later, forcing the Tigers to move to northern Burma and then into China.

The P-40s, with their superior armament and guns and great speed, approaching 500 mph in a dive, enabled successes at first of twenty or more Japanese planes downed for every one of their own lost. The Americans' aggressive flair greatly contributed to these early victories, but then the Japanese developed similar maneuvers, splitting their formations and executing tight half-loops, split S-dives, and the like to attack the American planes, reducing the overall American kill ratio to under ten to one.

Their new tactics became even more effective with the arrival of more maneuverable Mitsubishi type 96 and Nakajima type 97 fighters, and then the redoubtable Mitsubishi "Zero." Some Flying Tigers expressed a preference to go against the Zeros rather than the 96s and 97s, but the Zero became by far the most infamous of the Japanese planes. Armed with two 7.7-mm machine guns or two 20-mm canon, the Zeros were highly maneuverable, and could climb quickly to 34,000 feet and cruise at 330 mph. The P-40, with heavier armament of four .30 caliber and two .50-caliber machine guns and armor plating, could not match the Zero's climb rate, maneuverability, or top speed, but it could dive faster and out-shoot them. The Tigers therefore never tried to dogfight the Zeros, but rather to gain altitude advantage and dive on them—"hit and run"—often from their maximum height of 21,000 feet.

Antics of the high-spirited Americans sometimes caused new prob-lems. The propeller of one pilot's plane chewed up Chennault's car in a taxiing accident. Then a more damaging incident occurred when Gregory Boyington, an ex-Marine pilot and one of the most colorful of the Flying Tigers, disrupted a reception at the group's Kunming headquarters for Generalissimo Chiang Kai-shek and his wife in early 1942. He and six others made an upside-down fly-by that passed so low that the honored guests felt forced to dive to the ground, with embarrassing loss of face. Then, escorting the VIPs back to the wartime capital of Chungking, the Americans ran out of fuel and crash-landed on a graveyard, the only avail-able clearing, but the most sacred of Chinese sites.

More serious, of course, were the problems caused by Japanese advances, and the resulting exacerbation of the common morale problems of young military men serving in distant places, frequently facing odds of five or ten or more, against the 700-odd Japanese planes in the Burma theater. As Rangoon fell by March 6, 1942 and the Burma Road supply route to the Nationalists was closed shortly after that, General Joseph W. Stillwell, the American commander in China and Chief of Staff of Chiang Kai-shek's Allied staff, demanded that Chennault use his men as ground support for the retreating Chinese troops, and the effort to re-open the Burma Road. The Flying Tigers and their chief argued that that would be a misuse of their mission. After all, prior to the fall of Rangoon, in thir-ty-one encounters over their first six weeks, the Tigers had destroyed 217 planes, and possibly 43 more, while losing only four of their pilots and sixteen P-40s in air-to-air combat. Why should they waste their time bombing and strafing?

Those new demands contributed to their declining morale, which compounded other problems, including extensive maintenance for the P-40s. The climax of morale problems came with an April 18, 1942 refusal of 28 of 34 pilots to conduct a strafing mission over Chiang Mai, Burma. That in turn led Stillwell and higher authorities to step up their demand for the integration of the Tigers into the U.S. Army Air Corps, as a way to enforce greater discipline.

Still, Flying Tiger exploits continued, as with the downing of twenty-two enemy aircraft without a single loss ten days later, as the Japanese tried to destroy them on the airfield near Lashio, the southern terminus of the Burma Road and the northern terminus of the railroad from Rangoon. They had attacked dummy airplanes rigged up on the ground by the Chinese, and were then surprised by the P-40s attacking from above.

But the Japanese ground troops continued to advance, taking Lashio by April 21 and crossing into southern China on May 1. This forced the Flying Tigers to operations out of Loiwing, about a hundred miles north of Lashio, where the second and third squadrons were assigned. Next, they moved farther northwest into China to Pao Shan, Yunnanyi, and Kunming, where headquarters was maintained. The latter was 165 miles east of Yunnanyi, and 1000 feet lower in altitude at 6000 feet. Later operations also took off from bases over 300 miles farther east and north, at Kweilin, Hengyang, Chungking, and some other bases in southwest China. The squadrons were rotated periodically, with the first assigned to Kweilin and the second to Chungking in June.

On July 4, the Flying Tigers were enrolled into the Tenth Air Force of the Army Air Corps as the twenty-third fighter group, or simply the China Air Task Force (CATF). They inherited fifty-four P-40s and three P-43s, but only twenty-nine were "operational." Only thirty- four ground personnel and five pilots stayed on in China with Chennault. But they and new recruits continued the free-wheeling guerrilla style of aerial fighting the Flying Tigers had made famous. Understandably, they continued to be known by their popular nickname, and in March 1943 they regained much of their independence when the unit was placed under the Fourteenth Air Force, and once again under the command of General Chennault.

Already by July 1942, the Flying Tigers had been credited with the certain downing of 299 Japanese planes, destroying another 200 on the ground, and possibly another 153. Their own losses were only a dozen planes in the air and sixty-one on the ground. They claimed to have killed 1500 Japanese with the loss of only ten of their own in air combat, the same number in accidents, and three to bombs. Twenty-nine Flying Tigers became "aces," with five or more "kills," topped by Robert Neale with fourteen and Tex Hill with twelve.

Many of those who had departed in the late spring of 1942 out of fatigue and frustration at the increasing difficulties and restrictions went on to exploits elsewhere. One, Dick Rossi, set the record of over 750 flights over the "Hump," while Pappy Boyington and Jim Howard downed, respectively, twenty-eight and thirty enemy planes over the Southwest Pacific and Germany, scores close to those of the leading aces in their respective theaters. Charles Bond served as personal pilot to wartime Ambassador Averell Harriman in Moscow, and he and many others continued important jobs in military and commercial aviation following the war.

The primary mission of the China Air Task Force after July 4, 1942, became the protection of American and Chinese bases for the mounting American war effort. In October, they had to operate with fewer than fifty P-40s and a dozen B-25s, but Chennault convinced a Washington conference a little later to move to a tripling of the fighters, including P-38s and P-51s, and still bigger increases of bombers, including B-24s. Receiving over half of the increasing Hump tonnage, they notably increased their bombing of Japanese targets. In the first year of its existence, the Fourteenth Air Force dropped almost 2000 tons of bombs on enemy targets, as against the total of 299 tons dropped before by the China Air Task Force.

There were incredible new adventure stories of the aviators in China, as well as of their continuing hardships, suffering, and death. The missionary John M. Birch, whose name was taken by the notorious anti-Communist group after his murder by Chinese Communist guerrillas in August 1945, offered his services and joined the CATF in July 1942. The group profited from his skills as interpreter and chaplain. Pilot John Petach, who volunteered to stay on for two more weeks, in part because he had just married one of the U.S. nurses, was killed in the explosion of his plane on July 10 of that year.

Colonel Robert Lee Scott fared far better. After being transferred from his preferred smaller aircraft to flying transports over the Hump because his thirty-four years exceeded the twenty-eight-year limit established for fighter pilots, he was able to overcome that objection and joined the Flying Tigers in the spring of 1942. He even became its operational commander as General Chennault moved up, Scott taking command of the Fourteenth Air Force nine months later.

On Scott's first command flight, July 3, he and his twenty-eight men downed thirty-four of ninety-six Japanese planes which again had been fooled into attacking Chinese-made dummy P-40s on the ground at their Kweilin base. The next day they lost two of their own, but downed another twenty-eight enemy planes attacking Yunnanyi. Scott became a double ace by September, and claimed 100 kills after a year heading the China Air Task Force. After reassignment to the States, he returned for new exploits in China during the last months of the war. Another incredible story came on December 12, 1943, when Lt. Donald S. Lopez downed a Nakajima "Oscar" fighter by ramming it, but was able to make it back to a base near Hengyang, despite having lost three feet of a wing.

After the spring 1942 closing of the Burma Road and its Chinese extension, the Ledo Road, supplies for the Chinese had to be transported 500 or more miles over what was called the "Hump," across the world's highest mountains, the Himalayas. They flew from Chabna Airfield near Dinjan and Sadiya on the Brahmaputra River in Assam, extreme northeastern India, to Kunming. Later, some took off from Moran to the south and in the last months of the war, some B-29s made deliveries all the way from Calcutta. On the most-flown route, it was about another 1100 miles from New Delhi to Sadiya, and 400 miles from Kunming to the Nationalist wartime capital of Chungking.

At first, two-engine C-47 "Gooney Birds," the military equivalent of the DC-3, were the workhorses of this airlift under the China–Burma–India Command, called the Assam–Burma–China Ferry Command or Task Force Aquilla. They carried some 6000 pounds of cargo and battled fierce winds and storms over 16,000-foot passes to reach airfields, often built by hand by thousands of Chinese. The 6000-foot, hundred-foot-wide strip at Kunming, for example, was built with several layers of stone and earth placed on top of rice fields. At times, due to monsoon storms and other problems, the planes could make only several round trips, delivering less than a 100 tons a month. By November 1943, however, deliveries over the Hump reached 13,000 tons, despite the loss of

375 pilots on the dangerous route that year. The number of planes increased to about 100, as the U.S. Army Air Corps Tenth Air Force operated over seventy-five, and the China National Aviation Corporation, half-owned by Pan American Airways, another twenty-five. The cargo planes came to include the Curtiss C-46 with its four-ton payload, a quarter again as large as the C-47s, then the four-engined Douglas C-54, and the Consolidated C-87s which could carry up to five tons of cargo or passengers. The military version of the C-87, the B-24, was also used at times for military protection against attacking Zeros.

It took eighteen tons of supplies for Chennault's planes to drop one ton of bombs, and six planes crossing the Hump laden with drums of fuel just to supply enough fuel for one B-29 to bomb Japan, which they did on twenty occasions after June 1944. Astonishingly, U.S. forces in China, which totaled 60,369 people by August 1945, required as much as 53 percent of new money printed by the Chinese government to cover its costs during the war's last eighteen months.

Tonnages delivered across the Hump climbed to 39,000 tons a month by November 1944, and some 650,000 tons were delivered that way by the end of the war. The record of 71,042 tons was delivered in July 1945, and the best day's load was 5327 tons carried by 1118 flights on August 1, two weeks before Japan's surrender. But it took another forty to seventy days, for example, for Chinese coolies to transport from Kunming to Kweilin, the approximately 400 pound, 55-gallon drums of aviation fuel. Each P-40 used 200 gallons, or 1340 pounds for every two and one half hours aloft. The Hump and other trickles could only supply about 6 percent of the country's pre-war imports.

The Hump remained extremely dangerous. It was said that "for every 3000 tons flown into China, three Americans gave their lives." Yet, interservice and governmental rivalries and red tape led to other problems as well. In the spring of 1942, the Hump pilots, led by Colonel Scott, had to stage a rebellion to deliver the vitally needed fuel and munitions rather than the less essential items designated by theater commander General Joseph Stillwell, which ranged from mops to Chinese paper money—printed in Brooklyn! Scott had been able to turn that to his advantage to win Chennault's gratitude and the coveted admission to the Flying Tigers, flying P-40s instead of C-47 Gooney Birds.

Near the end of the war, following Stillwell's recall from China the previous October and continuing disputes, Chennault himself was transferred back to Washington. But by the end of the war a month later, his Fourteenth Air Force had climbed to 20,000 men with a thousand planes. They claimed to have destroyed 2600 enemy planes and 75,000 troops as well as extensive transportation and other Japanese complexes in China, while losing fewer than 500 of their own men.

If the Mitsubishi Zero gave the Flying Tigers new problems after the first battles, it also tested the mettle of the Navy's Grumman F-4F Wildcat, the standard American carrier-launched fighter until 1943. In America's first year of the war, the Wildcats shot down 40 Zeros to a loss of 41 of their own. Then, with the capture of distant Pacific islands, the land-based Lockheed P-38 "Lightning," first used extensively in the autumn of 1942, soon established air supremacy in the Pacific campaigns. The first dozen delivered to the China Air Task Force, however, were all shot down by more agile Zero pilots, who took advantage of the early inexperience of the Americans, led by football hero Tom Harmon. He was rescued by Chinese guerrillas.

Later, the P-38's superior speed, maneuverability, climbing and diving capacities, and 20-mm cannon and four .50-caliber machine guns, rapidly achieved control of the Pacific skies. Its two Allison 1425hp liquid-cooled engines gave it a top speed of 414 mph, and made it the first airplane to approach the speed of sound in a dive. Over 10,000 were produced for all theaters, making its image of two parallel fuselages joined by wings, cockpit, and tail one of the most distinctive of the war.

One of the most dramatic exploits of the P-38 was the fatal downing of Japan's top admiral, Tsoroku Yamamoto, the planner of the Pearl Harbor attack. That came in the midst of the famous battle of Guadalcanal on April 18, 1943. Four days earlier, code-breakers had learned of the Admiral's planned inspection tour, from Rabaul to Kahili on Bougainville, in the lower Solomon Islands. Flying 435 miles from their base on Henderson field on the American-controlled part of Guadalcanal, sixteen Lightnings under the command of Major John Mitchell spotted their targets near the destination. Captain Thomas G. Lanphier "put a long, sturdy burst into the right engine" of Yamamoto's Mitsubishi bomber, and "saw it break into flames. Just as I came into range of its tail canon, the wing tore off, and the plane plunged into the jungle and exploded."

By 1944, carrier-based Grumman Hellcats and Chance Vought Corsairs, with speeds of 380 mph and 417 mph respectively, together with the land-based P-38s and P-47s, had complete control of the Pacific skies. The Republic P-47 "Thunderbolts," advanced models of which, with a 2500hp Pratt and Whitney engine, could reach over 400 mph, also were heavily armed with eight .5-inch machine guns.

Even by the time of the April 1943 U.S. revenge against Admiral Yamamoto, the war had turned around in Asia, as in Europe after the Russian victory at Stalingrad two months before that. Nowhere did the Allied victories come easily, but without the airplane they might not have come at all.

12

Aviation and the Victory Over the Axis

Demonstrations of the immense destructive force available through air power came one after the other in those terrible years. Although the Japanese invasion of China had already been in progress since 1937, the unleashing of full-scale war in Europe came on September 1, 1939, when Hitler's Germany invaded Poland. Thus, scarcely two decades after the last of millions of bodies from the Great War had been laid to rest, the continent of Europe was once again aflame.

From the beginning it was clear that the new war would not repeat the stationary mass bloodletting of Flanders and Verdun, but would instead involve more mobile bloodletting, much farther dispersed. The Germans had devised an offensive technique called "blitzkrieg," which, rather than compelling men to run toward a machine gun, or sit beneath artillery fire, employed aircraft and tanks to surpass and surround an enemy's front. While some planes would still be devoted to their traditional role of trying to destroy the opposing air force, others were used as flying artillery to burst key points in the enemy line with sudden, pinpoint attacks. Still others hit population centers and refugee columns in order to sow chaos behind the front.

The attack on Poland began with some 300 Stuka Ju-87s, dropping 500kg (1102 lb.) bombs to devastate the defenses on the frontier. Two weeks later the Russians, according to a secret agreement between Hitler and Stalin, moved in from the east, thus once more erasing the brave Polish nation from the political map of Europe. Russia then spent the following winter in bitter fighting against Finland, which finally submitted, after inflicting about a million casualties on the ineptly led Soviet attackers.

The "phony war" in the West ended after April 9, 1940, with German attacks first against Denmark and Norway, and a month later against, successively, the Netherlands, Belgium, and France. All but the last had fallen by May 20, and Britain was forced to pull some 338,000 of its and Allied troops from the continent by June 4.

The German response to the British evacuation at Dunkirk has been considered curious, since by ordering his panzers to halt short of the beaches, Hitler missed his best—and only—chance to knock Britain out of the war. (Such a large number of POWs at that stage, in unscrupulous hands, would by themselves have been a bargaining chip to force political concessions.) In those days, before the growth of the Waffen SS provided Hitler his own military arm, the traditional German Army was his only viable competition for power, and further was an institution that couldn't be dealt with by employing the Nazis' usual gangster methods. With its remarkable triumph over the Allies in France, the prestige of the Army had reached new heights and in the dictator's mind no doubt threatened to become too powerful for him to control. The Luftwaffe, on the other hand, was headed by a Nazi, ex-WWI fighter pilot Hermann Goering, and as a much younger service was more infused with Hitler's own ideology. In 1940 it was clear that the speed, armament and airframe strength of the planes were immeasurably greater than those of the previous world war, but it was not yet known how profound a strategic effect aircraft could have on operations.

After issuing his "panzer halt" order, Hitler bestowed the "honor" of wiping out the British Expeditionary Force (BEF) at Dunkirk to the Luftwaffe, which then proved inadequate to the task. Controversially, the British had held back some of their fighter squadrons when the battle for France began to slide, and these were now available to help save the BEF. Although the British troops lined up on the beaches took terrible punishment from bombing and strafing German planes—the common refrain being "Where the hell's the RAF?"—Fighter Command was in fact waging a fierce battle out of eyesight of the troops to hold many of the Germans off. Further, with the tremendous strength of the Royal Navy mobilized and innumerable private craft from the English coast employed, the BEF was brought back largely intact, although without its heavy equipment. On the 10th of June, Mussolini attacked France from the southeast, and Paris fell to Hitler's troops on June 14. The country surrendered a week later.

With the bulk of continental Europe under Nazi control, or allied with them, Britain was now the only nation that remained defiant of

Germany, and in July 1940 the two nations began a face-to-face battle that was unique in the history of great power conflict, because it was fought in the air.

Although previous antagonists of Britain had been foiled by that thin slice of water called the English Channel that had traditionally protected Britain from foreign aggressors, the 2670 planes in the western air fleets of the Luftwaffe could zip across the water and arrive over English soil in minutes. RAF Fighter Command, numbering some 600 Hurricanes and Spitfires, which could be vectored using data from a coastal radar net, was the first line of defense and simply needed to survive the onslaught, because without total air superiority an actual German invasion across the Channel could not be attempted.

It's ironic that Germany would be the first nation to attempt a strategic decision with air power, since the Luftwaffe had been specifically designed as a tactical force, intended to coordinate its operations with the Army. While the British were busy developing heavy Lancaster, Stirlings and Halifax bombers (the Americans had had the B-17 since 1935 and would soon have the B-24), the Germans abandoned production of their only four-engine bomber, the He-177, before the war. (The Fw-200 "Condor," that later menaced Allied shipping, was a converted airliner.)

In the Battle of Britain the Stuka dive bombers, which had proven so successful in abetting land operations (and would continue to provide good service against Russian tanks) became lumbering prey for the nimble British fighters and soon had to be withdrawn. Likewise, the twin-engined Me-110 Destroyer, meant to be a devastating fighter, soon came to need its own fighter escort in daylight operations. Heinkel 111 and Dornier 17 two-engined bombers were effective when able to sneak past the RAF defense net, but quickly became victims when caught by a fighter. When British pilots penetrated the bomber streams, wholesale devastation would ensue as the medium-weight German bombers lacked adequate defenses.

Messerschmitt Bf 109s flew high overhead of the formations, looking to bounce British pilots before they could reach the bombers. The British were under strict orders to avoid the German fighters, but the young men of the RAF did not always heed the rule. When Me-109s came tearing through their formations, many pilots mixed it up with them. The superior maneuverability and 365 mph speed of the Spitfire was able to offset the faster climbing and diving of the 354 mph Me-109;

however, in terms of pilot skill, as in the Great War, the British and Germans seemed evenly matched.

In the beginning, the Germans targeted the British ports and coastal areas, softening these up for an invasion of the island. They then switched to hitting the RAF airfields and on August 15, the busiest day of the battle, launched 1786 sorties—a victory was in sight.

On August 24, however, one He-111 became disoriented and dropped its bombs on London. The new Prime Minister, Winston Churchill—no amateur at the psychology of warfare, and seeing his fighters being gradually worn down through casualties and strain—promptly ordered RAF's Bomber Command to launch a retaliatory raid, of 81 bombers, against Berlin. This was a crucial turning point in the battle, because on September 7, by way of revenge, the Germans commenced the "blitz" on London and other English population centers, inflicting heavy casualties on civilians, but saving Fighter Command from further direct attacks. In a stratagem, the Germans assembled some 250 fighters in a way that would resemble a bomber formation on British radar screens, hoping that a large number of RAF fighters could be lured into combat. The British weren't fooled.

After particularly heavy losses of aircraft on September 15, Hitler postponed and later canceled his planned invasion of Britain. It was then that Churchill made his famous accolade of the British pilots: "Never in the field of human conduct was so much owed by so many to so few. All hearts go out to the fighter pilots, whose brilliant actions we see with our own eyes day after day . . ." By the time this major phase of the battle petered out, November 3, though continuing in one form or another through the rest of the war, the Germans had lost 1/33 planes (the British 915), and the Luftwaffe had been gravely weakened.

By following an aggressive strategy in the early years of the war, Germany was able to record another "first" the following May, when it conquered the island of Crete with an airborne invasion. After the evacuation of Greece, some 40,000 British Empire troops—primarily Australians and New Zealanders—had occupied Crete, including the two airfields on the island. On May 20, 1941, German paratroopers came floating and gliding in, dropped or towed by three-engine Ju-52 transports. At first it was an unmitigated slaughter. The Germans were mown down as they landed and the survivors had scarcely enough time to organize themselves into units. They seized the airfields, but as Junkers attempted to land with reinforcements and supplies they were shot up by Allied troops holding the surrounding hills. Eventually, however, Germans in small groups managed to clear the hills around the airfields and the reinforcement stream commenced. Seven thousand Germans flew in on the first day, 22,000 by the end of the week, and the Allies then surrendered. Offshore, meanwhile, the Luftwaffe had attempted to hold off the Royal Navy, sinking three cruisers and six destroyers. The final toll for the Germans was 5600 dead paratroopers (as well as over 5000 more reinforcements sunk at sea). Hitler was appalled at the losses, and although German paratroopers continued to be identified as such, throughout the remainder of the war they would primarily be used as ordinary infantry.

As England held on, Hitler committed his most fatal blunder with the invasion of Russia, June 22, 1941. As unprepared as Russia had been in the wake of Stalin's purges and the general disbelief that the latter's fellow megalomaniac could repeat Napoleon's fatal error, Moscow had made a saving move two months earlier. That was to sign a Neutrality Treaty with Japan in April. If Japan had attacked from the east simultaneously with Hitler from the west, even Russian courage and "General Winter" might not have staved off an Axis victory. Nevertheless the offensive was rewarded with unprecedented success in its early stages.

After the first day, the Luftwaffe had basically destroyed the entire Soviet air force in the west (mostly on the ground) in a performance unmatched until Israel's surprise attack on Arab airfields in June 1967. Soon, however, the strength of Soviet reserves and the power of the Russian weather brought things to a halt. Moscow was bombed throughout the fall of 1941, rather in a feeble attempt to repeat the psychological effect of the bombing of Warsaw two years previously, but the German armies had run out of strength. In December 1941, they lay frozen and exhausted outside the city limits of the capital; further, on the seventh of that month a huge event was taking place on the other side of the world. By the time the smoke had cleared, the United States was in the war.

For Americans, the Japanese attack on Pearl Harbor on December 7, 1941, struck home the first overwhelming revelation of the destructive force of air power. There, of course, it was the Japanese planes that made history. The planner of the sensational attack was Admiral Isoroku Yamamoto. He had fought the Russians in 1905, subsequently learned to fly, and had gone on to study at Harvard and serve two tours in

Washington as Naval Attaché. In 1939, he became overall commander of the Japanese Navy, and soon began to plan for the strike he felt could cripple the America he thought he understood.

With the impasse in negotiations between Tokyo and Washington in the autumn of 1941, Yamamoto assigned Admiral Chuichi Nagumo to prepare to lead a fleet of six carriers northeastward. They set out November 26, and were given the final go-ahead on arriving 200 miles north of Hawaii. The U.S. had "penetrated" but not yet cracked the code ordering the strike, and Washington's latest order to "'be on alert" was blocked by atmospheric static. This was compounded by the failure of responsible officers in Washington to recognize the importance of their information. A recent study concludes that "the American failure to prepare . . . was the result of errors, jealousies, and catastrophic mistakes in judgment."

Thus, U.S. forces were tragically surprised when some 353 planes under Commander Mitsuo Fuchida struck just before 8 A.M. on that fateful "day of infamy." Strafing by Mitsubishi Zeros and hits by 550 lb. bombs dropped by Aichi and Nakajima bombers killed 2403 Americans, destroyed 247 planes, and sank three battleships, including the *Arizona*, damaging four others. They wounded another 1178 personnel and sank or damaged an additional eighteen ships. But they failed to destroy submarine, fuel, and repair complexes, and the U.S. carriers *Lexington* and *Enterprise* were away delivering planes to distant Midway and Wake islands. The U.S. recovery and mobilization of production and recruitment was rapid, and in less than four years would prove decisive for the defeat of Japan as they were for that of Germany and Italy.

That was not evident for several months, however, as 3000 naval planes with 3500 pilots accompanied Japanese forces to launch their own "second blitzkrieg," after the one four years earlier in China. The very next day, December 8, 1941, the Japanese staged "little Pearl Harbor," destroying another 100 planes at Clark Air Force Base in the Philippines. Two days later, Japanese aircraft based near Saigon found the British battleship *Prince of Wales* and the battle cruiser *Repulse* in the South China Sea off Malaya, and sent them to the bottom with a loss of only four planes. Imperial forces went on to the destruction of much of the Allied Pacific fleet and the rapid conquests of Hong Kong, Malaya, Singapore, Burma, and all of the Philippines by April 1942. But on the 18th of that month, American pilots were able to strike Japan for the first time.

This was the famous "thirty seconds over Tokyo" raid of eighty air-men led by Jimmy Doolittle. The big problem in those early days of American involvement was that Japan controlled all possible land bases big enough for long-range bombers to do the job. With special training, nevertheless, it was found that medium, North American B-25 bombers, powered by two 1700hp Wright engines, even if loaded with five-man crews, extra gas tanks, and four 500-pound bombs, could take off from an aircraft carrier. Each take-off with full power and flaps had to be timed to take advantage not only of the wind but of the rise and fall of the ship. Once off, they could not land on the 467 feet of available deck, however, and with the installation of extra gas tanks would have to make it to two primitive landing strips in Nationalist-controlled parts of China, several hundred miles southwest of Shanghai.

The USS *Hornet,* making twenty knots into a thirty-knot wind, launched the sixteen planes one after the other, starting with Doolittle's at 8:20 A.M., April 18, 1942, some 824 miles east of Tokyo. Proceeding just above the waves to avoid detection, the 25,000-pound craft then climbed to 1200 feet or so and dived on their targets at Tokyo and four other cities. Their bombs did little damage, but the psychological effects were great. Continuing on to the southwest, seven of the eighty airmen were lost, four in crash landings off the China coast and three who were exe-cuted by the Japanese after parachuting into enemy territory in China. Because it was sighted by Japanese ships, the *Hornet* had been unable to reach the planned 450 miles from Japan, and the greater distance forced eleven of the crews, including Doolittle's, to bail out before intended, as fuel supplies were exhausted. Another four B-25s crash-landed in or near Nationalist-controlled China, and the sixteenth made it to Vladivostok just northeast of Korea, where the crew was interned by the Soviets.

The effort and the incredible sufferings of the survivors were immor-talized by Captain Ted Lawson in his 1943 book and the movie which fol-lowed, *Thirty Seconds Over Tokyo.* It recounted the training, the raid, the crash of his plane off the Chinese coast south of Shanghai, and the sur-vivors' miraculous escapes. Badly hurt in the crash, his leg became infect-ed and had to be amputated near Japanese lines without anesthetics in conditions difficult to imagine. Still, he and most of the others were able to make it out, on Chinese-carried stretchers and trucks, to Hengyang, and then by plane to Kweilin and Kunming, then to India and beyond. Another 13 of Doolittle's 80 raiders, in addition to the initial seven fatalities, died in other actions during the war.

By early May 1942, the U.S. won its first victory against Japan in the war's greatest naval battle to that time, in the Coral Sea to the northeast of Australia. It was also the first to be decided by air power alone as the opposing fleets were never in direct contact. The American flattops were the *Yorktown* and *Lexington*, each carrying about twenty Grumman F-4F Wildcat fighters, and another fifty or so dive and torpedo bombers, such as the Douglas Dauntless and Devastators, and reconnaisance planes. (Other carrier-based planes, such as the Hellcat, "the most successful carrier-based fighter in history," and Corsair, which arrived a little later, could fold their wings to increase storage space.)

On May 7 the U.S. fleet was in position to block a Japanese invasion force headed for Port Moresby, New Guinea, from which it would be within striking distance of Australia. American planes found the light carrier *Shoho* and sent it to the bottom. The Japanese likewise sank the U.S. oiler *Neosho*, having mistaken it for a carrier, as well as its accompanying destroyer. On May 8 the battle came down to *Lexington* and *Yorktown* against the heavy Japanese carriers *Shokaku* and *Zuikaku*. The Japanese torpedoed the *Lexington*, dooming over half of the sixty-nine U.S. aircraft lost that day, and lightly damaged *Yorktown*; however they lost some eighty-six planes and *Shokaku* was severely damaged. Although the battle itself might have seemed close to a draw, after months of inexorable Japanese success the Americans had finally stopped their southward advance. The invasion of Port Moresby was abandoned.

The Japanese then sought in early June to destroy the U.S. fleet and bases far to the northeast, in the Aleutians, and at Midway Island, northwest of Hawaii. Although the Japanese took and held Attu and Kiska in the Aleutians in attacks from June 3 to 7, the graceful Consolidated Catalina flying boats, Lockheed P-38 Lightnings, Martin B-26 Marauders, and other U.S. planes limited the Japanese gains. More important, based on increasingly accurate intelligence and code-breaking, the U.S. learned of the progress of a huge Japanese fleet toward Midway, and dispatched its surviving three carriers to intercept it. The Japanese combined fleet was the largest yet deployed anywhere, and the cream of its naval air force aboard four carriers was by now battle-hardened and accustomed to victory. It seemed that for the Americans aboard the *Enterprise*, *Yorktown* and *Hornet*, the battle would be, at best, a near thing.

The Japanese opened the battle by attacking Midway Island, while B-

17 Flying Fortresses based there sallied out against their fleet—without success. The American carriers remained undetected and so launched wave after wave of planes against the Imperial Fleet, only to have most of them splashed by ships' fire and the Japanese fighter screen. The protective Zeros had just come down to the deck to disperse a torpedo plane attack when a flight of Dauntless dive bombers arrived above. On board the carriers the Japanese were feverishly attempting to switch the armaments on their planes for an attack on the American fleet when the dive bombers came screaming down. One, then another, then another Japanese carrier was hit, all in a space of five minutes, and each suffered fires and explosions that raged out of control. The remaining Japanese carrier, the *Hiryu*, launched her planes in two waves and they succeeded in sinking *Yorktown* (finished off by a submarine the next day), but then *Hiryu* herself was chased down and sunk.

Although at Midway the Americans lost 147 of 233 aircraft, as well as 307 airmen, just six months into the war the Japanese naval air force had been gutted. Aside from the four carriers, they had lost 411 planes and most of their aircrew who, along with an estimated 4800 sailors, went down with their ships.

In July 1942 came the first of many island landings by U.S. Marines: on Guadalcanal in the eastern Solomon Islands northeast of Australia. During one stage of this epic, multi-faceted campaign, the Japanese carriers *Shokaku* and *Zuikaku*, repaired since the Coral Sea, once more took on two of their American counterparts, this time the only two remaining U.S. fleet carriers in the Pacific, the *Enterprise* and *Hornet*. In the swirling Battle of the Santa Cruz Islands, both Imperial flattops were damaged, however *Hornet* was lost and the *Enterprise* had to leave the battle area for repairs. Marine pilots were meanwhile flying Wildcats out of an airfield cut in the jungle of Guadalcanal, Henderson Field, which became the centerpiece of the land effort. Bitter fighting and intensive air strikes went on until Japanese abandonment of the island the following February.

As the American buildup accelerated and materiel arrived in the Far Pacific, a half dozen operational air forces under the overall command of General Douglas MacArthur and Air Corps General George Kenney proceeded methodically toward Japan. The Fifth, Seventh, Thirteenth, and, from mid-1944, the Twentieth Air Forces directed bombing campaigns and support operations against eleven island groups. The downing of Admiral Yamamoto on the first anniversary of Doolittle's Tokyo raid,

April 18, 1943, assumed symbolic significance, while the taking of Tarawa in November 1943, and of Kwajalein in February 1944 established control of the vast stretches of ocean between Australia, Midway, and Hawaii. By then the U.S. Navy was operating 12 aircraft carriers in the Pacific war.

By the middle of 1944, the U.S. was able to establish the first air bases within striking distance of Japan itself, with the conquests of Guam, Tinian, and Saipan, a thousand miles to the east in the southern Marianas. All these campaigns were accompanied by intense fighting with Japanese who fought to the last man, and by bombing-strafing runs. Samuel Hynes, with over 100 bombing missions in the spring of 1945, flying single-engine Douglas Dauntless dive bombers, gave one of the best accounts of a pilot's view of the carnage below caused by these missions: ". . . In an air war you are not very conscious of your enemies as human beings. We attacked targets—a gun emplacement, a supply dump, a radar station— not men. . . . I never saw a single Japanese soldier on the ground."

There were also innumerable dogfights over the island battles as opposing aircraft tried to establish air supremacy. The U.S. developed new tactics for this, notably the "Thach weave," devised by Lt. Commander J.S. Thach in 1942 to offset the greater maneuverability of the Zeros. It involved coordinated banks inward and crossovers by pairs of Grumman Wildcats and Hellcats, Chance-Vought Corsairs, and other fighters. These maneuvers threw off Japanese targeting and enabled the Americans to come in behind the enemy aircraft. Using such tactics in 146 missions in P-38s between September 1942 and December 1944, Richard Ira Bong became America's top ace with forty kills, followed by Thomas McGuire with thirty-eight. Numerous compatriots scored dozens of victories, but the Japanese Shoichi Sougita and Saburo Sakai said they downed even more, claiming 120 and 64 victories, respectively, against American planes.

The last gasp of the Japanese naval air force came in the Battle of the Philippine Sea, more commonly referred to on the American side as "The Marianas Turkey Shoot." Vice-Admiral Jisaburo Ozawa sortied on June 19, 1944 with Japan's nine remaining carriers, and the assistance of about 100 other planes on Guam, his intention to destroy the American Pacific Fleet and its own now-fifteen carriers. After a gigantic, day-long air battle, 346 Imperial planes were shot down, as compared to only 30 U.S.

Navy fighters. Eighty more American planes ditched in the sea after running out of fuel on their way back to the carriers, although this was exactly the kind of loss the United States was uniquely positioned to afford. Adding insult to injury, the next day U.S. submarines destroyed two more Japanese carriers, including the redoubtable *Shokaku,* and Ozawa finally returned to base with only 30 planes remaining from his original 450.

One of Japan's problems was that its system for pilot training—the most rigorous in the world prior to the war—did not serve the Japanese well once their first elite cadre had been killed in battle and they suddenly needed thousands of quick replacements. By 1944, not only were American aircraft superior in performance, but the new U.S. pilots were better flyers than their opponents. After the "Turkey Shoot," the Japanese decided that instead of expecting their men to fly with the Americans, they would simply request new pilots to crash their planes onto enemy ships, a skill considered well within their capabilities.

In Europe, meanwhile, Nazi Germany's hopes for victory depended on being able to subdue the Soviet Union before the rapidly growing strength of the Anglo-American coalition caught them in a vise. From 1941 until mid-1943, the only major land fighting in the west took place in North Africa, where the Germans had placed a good general, Rommel, with several panzer divisions, who managed to keep the Allies busy for almost two years. Basic to the Axis strategy was the continual supression by the Luftwaffe of the British air and naval base at Malta, which sat astride their supply route from Italy.

The air war in Africa, fought mostly by fighters, was lively but had little strategic influence until after the decisive defeat of Rommel at El Alamein, when growing numbers of Allied aircraft became a scourge for Axis columns, which, in the desert, had nowhere to hide. During the last stages of the Axis defense, when their ships no longer had hopes of making it across the Mediterranean, the Germans attempted to resupply their forces with Ju-52s and motorized MC323 Gigant gliders, skimming low across the waves; but scores of these were lost to Allied fighters screening the coastline.

In July 1943 the Allies took another step by combining all their air, sea and land forces for the invasion of the island of Sicily. Having been victimized by German glider and paratroop assault in Norway, Holland and Crete, the Allies now employed their own airborne forces, although not without some initial difficulty. The British 1st Airborne Division, swooping down in Waco and Hortha gliders, became widely dispersed, and of 147 gliders only 12 hit their drop zones, a full 69 aircraft crashing into the sea. The American 82nd Airborne was next, and fared somewhat better, also missing their targets but at least coming down on land instead of water. Since airborne troops are invariably elite soldiers, such a wide dispersal of men might even have worked to the Allies' advantage by way of spreading alarm in the enemy rear areas, although this was not to the advantage of the paratroopers themselves.

The real tragedy occurred on the night of June 11, when an American gunner in a fleet that had fought off repeated Luftwaffe attacks all afternoon spotted a bomber-like plane coming toward his ship and opened fire. Other AA gunners started firing in the dark, and soon the entire fleet plus machine guns on shore were filling the night sky with bullets against a large stream of aircraft. This was unfortunately the second wave of the 82nd Airborne, and 23 paratrooper-laden C-47s were lost, another 37 damaged in the gigantic storm of "friendly" fire. Following this incident, the Allies, like the Germans after Crete, wondered whether airborne attacks were practical.

In Russia, the war was being fought on a mammoth scale, the Germans and Soviets locked in a death grip on a thousand-mile front. The German offensive in summer 1942, this time toward the south, found easier going than the prior year's attack. Hitler became convinced that the Soviets had been irretrievably weakened, and German armies extended themselves hundreds of miles, to the Volga and into the mountains of the Caucasus. When winter came, however, the Soviets once again struck back with unexpected strength and the German Sixth Army, numbering at least 250,000 men, became surrounded in the city of Stalingrad.

At this point in the war the Germans were already experienced with encirclement battles and Hitler asked the chief of the Luftwaffe, Goering, if the troops could be kept supplied by air, as 100,000 of them had been at Demyansk the year before, until which time other Axis forces could break through the ring. Goering assured his Führer that the Luftwaffe transport force could do the job.

In any case, Stalingrad became one of the most pitiful sieges since medieval times—a desperate, starving army deteriorating in stages. On only one day during the siege did the Germans manage to get in the minimum supply requirement. The road to the airfield was lined with wounded, limping or crawling to reach an aircraft in the hope of evacuation. The Ju-52s that managed to run the gauntlet of Soviet fighters and AA fire to land on the debris-covered runways unloaded their supplies and then took on as many wounded as they could carry. Once the battle had been decided, the Germans ordered the evacuation of valuable specialist personnel, and airfield security escorted these through the injured and dying so that they could get out to fight on other fronts.

Throughout the war, German Me-109s and, later, 412 mph Focke-Wulf 190s, had the advantage of the Soviet Ratas, Yaks and MiGs in air-to-air combat, and some pilots in the east ran up huge victory totals, led by Erich Hartmann's claimed 352. (All his victims were Soviet except for seven, American Mustangs, who by 1945 were ranging over Romania.) Russia's top ace, I. Kozhedub, was credited with 62 victories, followed by Alexander Pokrychkine with 59. Although the German fighter pilots who spent most of the war in Russia ended up with by far the highest numbers of kills (nine finishing with over 200), the "top gun" of the Luftwaffe was probably Hans Joachim Marseilles, who, stationed in North Africa, totaled 158 victories, nearly all of them British. Marseilles died at age 23 when his cockpit began filling with smoke as he returned from an otherwise uneventful sweep over Cairo. His fellow pilots urged him to hang on until they got back over German lines, which he did, but after finally turning his Me-109 over to bail out, his body fell lifeless to the ground. He had either lost consciousness at the moment of bail-out or perhaps had been slammed into the tail section of his plane.

The climax of the war in Russia came in July 1943 with the German offensive at Kursk. Thanks to excellent intelligence, provided by the "Lucy" spy network in Berlin, the Soviets had advance warning of the enemy plans and the battle began with a preemptive strike by Soviet planes against German airfields. A newly installed radar system alerted the Germans in time, however, and enough fighters were able to scramble into the air to beat back the threat. The launch of German bombers, for what then amounted to a second strike, marked the movement of the "irresistible force" against the "immoveable object." For nine days, the German and Russian armies slaughtered one another on either side of Kursk, while aircraft swept in against tanks, infantry and artillery. German Stukas had been re-armed with anti-tank cannon; Russian Sturmoviks, nearly impervious to machine-gun fire, raced in against German armor.

By the eighth day, in the center of the southern front, three Waffen SS Divisions had clawed their way through successive Soviet defense lines, only to be met by the Russians' major reserve, the Fifth Guards Tank Army. After the ensuing largest armored battle in history—some 800 Soviet tanks against 450 German—both sides had lost about half their strength, but for the first time in the face of a good weather offensive the Russians hadn't broken. The arithmetic of an attrition battle arguing against further attacks, the Germans called off the offensive, girding themselves instead for the gigantic counterattacks that were sure to come.

In the Pacific, by late 1943, medium B-25 and B-26 bombers, P-38 and P-47 fighters, as well as heavy bombers—first the Consolidated B-24 Liberators and Boeing B-17 Flying Fortresses—were able to use Guadalcanal and other new bases for their missions. Then, from the Marianas by the autumn of 1944, under the new Twentieth Air Force, the new 65-ton Boeing B-29 Superfortresses, the biggest and most advanced heavy bombers yet, readied to begin their devastating raids against Japanese targets.

Twice as big and with twice the range of the predecessor B-17s, the Superforts' 4200-mile range allowed for increasingly deadly raids on the Japanese islands 1500 miles to the north of Guam, Saipan, and Tinian. The first raid was launched by fourteen B-29s on October 28 against a Japanese base in the Truk islands to the southeast of Guam, and on November 24 they hit Tokyo. After the reconquest of the Philippines in early 1945, and of Iwo Jima and Okinawa in the most bitter battles of the Pacific from March to June 1945, some 334, then over 700 B-29s began the heaviest bombing yet seen in Asia. The huge bombers took off mostly from Saipan, and after April, from Okinawa. By the late spring of 1945, almost 6000 sorties a day were being flown.

Attempting to allay their increasingly desperate situation, in late October 1944, in the battle for the Philippines, the Japanese began their quixotic Kamikaze missions. These were named after the "divine winds" that destroyed invading Mongol fleets in 1274 and 1281. Over 1100 of some 1321 Kamikaze attacks came in the biggest single battle of the American war in the Pacific, that of Okinawa. In it, some 12,000 U.S. planes supported over 500,000 American troops on about 1000 ships to take that sizeable island 450 miles south of Japan. The Kamikaze pilots struck 322 U.S. ships in all, sinking 34 of them. Other sources speak of 1465 such attacks, mostly by Zeros diving at close to 600 mph onto their targets, sinking 26 ships. Another 936 returned without finding targets. But the fanatical heroism of many Japanese could not offset the awesome American firepower. And by March, Washington decided to use incendiary bombs, partially justifying this by the fact that the Japanese had already been doing so against Chinese cities for six years.

On the night of March 9–10, 1945, under the command of Twentieth Air Force chief General Curtis LeMay, 130 Superforts, each carrying six tons of incendiary bombs, set fire to sixteen square miles of Tokyo. The destruction was immense, burning one-quarter of the city's very flammable bamboo and wooden buildings and killing over 100,000 citizens. In April and May, another eleven square miles of Tokyo were razed, with the city's population more than cut in half from its pre-war five million. Some 90 other cities were also ravaged, 20 of them over half destroyed. In all, about 668,000 Japanese civilians were killed and 2.3 million homes were gutted in those raids.

While Allied offensives in the Mediterranean Theater proceeded apace, and the Germans struggled to postpone their Götterdämmerung in Russia, the British and Americans were meanwhile creating a strategic air capability that would greatly weaken the German war machine. The first heavy British raids had begun the last night of May 1942, when 1046 twin-engined Wellingtons and other bombers struck Cologne. At a time when German armies had not yet been defeated, the fact that Britain was hitting back against the enemy with "Thousand Bomber Raids" had an uplifting effect on British morale.

English raids became more damaging with the acquisition of more advanced Lancaster and four-engined Halifax bombers, carrying up to four tons of bombs each. The most devastating bombing yet began with the arrival of four-engined U.S. B-17s and B-24s after July. The first strike by U.S. aircraft against Germany actually was launched from a Khartoum base, established in East Africa for the supply route to China. This was June 12, when thirteen B-24s struck the Ploesti oil fields in Romania. Eight of the planes returned, one crashed, and four were diverted to Turkey, but Ploesti would see far more American bombers in the coming years.

On July 4, 1942, using a dozen twin-engine Douglas Havocs of the RAF, U.S. pilots struck German targets for the first time from England. Three were shot down, and another, piloted by Captain Charles C.

Kegelman, made a miraculous escape. His right engine on fire from a direct hit, the plane's right wingtip struck the ground, but bounced back into the air and the plane struggled back to the base in the east of England. The first raid by U.S. planes based in Britain came on August 17, when a dozen Flying Fortresses struck the Rouen railyards in Occupied France. Other raids in succeeding weeks struck nearby targets there and in the Netherlands. The first flown by over 100 heavy bombers— some 108 B-17s and B-24s, escorted by 156 Spitfires and P-38s—hit Lille on October 9.

But then attention was diverted to supporting the American invasion of North Africa, which came on November 8. Bombardments of Axis targets to the north soon began from African and later Italian bases under the Ninth and Twelfth Air Forces. On April 4, 1943, B-24s struck Naples with one raid made famous by its only loss, of the *Lady Be Good.* By May, sorties increased to 2000 a day with the conquest of Tunisia, and B-17s blasted Palermo as the invasion of Sicily in July neared. On July 19, 1943, some 500 U.S. aircraft attacked targets in Rome, carefully chosen to avoid its many artistic treasures. The shock of that raid and allied advances in Sicily led to the resignation of Mussolini on the 25th, but glider-borne German stormtroopers kidnapped him off a mountaintop and set him up again two months later.

A new massive raid had again been launched against the Ploesti oil fields, from Benghazi, in Libya, on August 1, 1943. Fifty-three of 177 B-24s were shot down, with the loss of 446 airmen, and only thirty-three of those planes returned fit to fly again.

But it was from England, turned into a "vast, stationary aircraft carrier," that the most devastating use of air power yet proceeded. This was orchestrated by the addition to British Bomber Command of the U.S. Eighth Air Force, established there after February 1942, first under the command of General Carl A."Tooey" Spaatz, then after his assumption later in the year of command of the Twelfth Air Force in North Africa, under General Ira Eaker. Together with the Ninth Air Force, which arrived in England to give tactical support after the expulsion of Axis troops from Africa, the strategic Eighth Air Force came to include over 400,000 men and 11,500 aircraft on over 100 bases. Close to another 1700 aircraft in Italy under the new Fifteenth Air Force and other units worked in close support.

Some 50,000 or more of those American airmen lost their lives, as against over 30,000 in Asia. British Bomber Command lost over 55,000, not to mention the many thousands more forced to spend part of the war in POW camps. On many dangerous missions one quarter of the planes failed to return, and on at least one occasion 12 of 13 were lost. In any case crews faced, as the Eighth's final commander, Jimmy Doolittle, would later put it, innumerable acute high-altitude problems with an average of "six hours on oxygen, intense cold [including frequent frost bite], deafening noise, constant vibration, and a one-in-three chance of completing their tour."

By 1943, the Allied bombing attacks, under the overall command of General Henry Harley "Hap" Arnold in Washington and Sir Arthur "Bomber" Harris in London, were taking a heavy toll. The British usually flew at night at lower altitudes to avoid flak, but the Americans flew by day, with precision bombing from altitudes high enough to avoid the heaviest enemy fire. In March, the Eighth Air Force's then 125 big bombers in England made their first successful raids into Germany against railroad yards and submarine building complexes in the Ruhr valley. By the end of May, U.S. heavy bombers increased to over 300 despite the loss by then of 188 B-17s and B-24s. They fell to heavy flak and to aggressive new tactics by German fighters, including straight-in, "line abreast" firing runs with closing speeds over 600 mph by Me-109s and FW-190s. Some 279 U.S. bombers struck German targets on May 29, and more heavy raids came in June. Still heavier raids were carried out in "Blitz Week," the last week of July. On July 24, some 309 Flying fortresses struck targets in Norway and on three other occasions that week over 300 hit German targets. On the night of July 24–25, some 791 RAF bombers fire-bombed Hamburg, killing over 70,000.

On the first anniversary of the U.S. strike against Rouen, on August 17, 1943, a huge armada of 376 B-17s struck ball-bearing and Messerschmitt factories at Schweinfurt and Regensburg, losing respectively 36 and 24 of their number. Those attacking the latter target in southwest Germany flew on to bases in North Africa on the first "shuttle" mission of the war. On that and the next six days, some 148 bombers were lost and by mid-October 1943 U.S. heavy bomber losses stood at 723.

But U.S. production, which went from manufacturing 6000 military aircraft in 1940 to 19,000 in 1941, to 47,836 military aircraft in 1942, to 85,898 in 1943 and 96,318 by 1944, rapidly replaced them. Throughout the war America produced an incredible 300,000 or more military airplanes, including 18,188 B-24s and almost 13,000 B-17s. Some 4750 of the latter were downed, but they and other Flying Fortresses, flying up to 36,000 feet at up to 318 mph, unloaded 640,036 of the 1,556,088 tons of bombs dropped on German targets—a third again as much as the B-24s. Of those bombs, the Eighth Air Force dropped 701,300 tons, but lost 43,742 crewmen and 4456 bombers as they did so.

Another famous phrase of the war, "on a wing and a prayer," was coined about the story of another B-17 which struggled back to England on one engine, October 8, 1943. German flak had knocked off half its tail and tore gaping holes in its wing and fuselage. Heavy losses then and on other days, however, made that period become known as "Black Week." Fourteen B-24s were lost, for example, on October 1 raids against factories in Augsburg, Germany and in Austria. But the aviators knew what they were in for, that "some . . . will inevitably be killed." One B-17 pilot later stated a thought shared by many: "The razor's edge of difference between what they called life and death was what gave combat its incredible beauty." Two Eighth Air Force officers, Captain Bierne Lay and Major Sy Bartlett, wrote the popular novel *Twelve O'Clock High,* about some of those experiences.

A second raid was launched against Schweinfurt in west central Germany on October 14 by 383 bombers, 92 of which were forced to turn back and another 60 of which were shot down. At some points along the flight path there were so many parachutes in the air that civilians on the ground thought it was an airborne invasion. In mid-December, some 637 bombers escorted by 500 fighters made a three-pronged attack against Bremen, Hamburg, and Kiel.

On January 11, 1944, just after Jimmy Doolittle assumed command of the Eighth Air Force and Tooey Spaatz of all U.S. Air Forces in Europe, some 800 U.S. bombers and fighters roared against German targets, with a loss of 60. Another huge raid struck January 24, and in "Big Week," a month later, thousands of Allied planes, now including some from new bases in Italy, blasted German targets. On February 20, over 1000 U.S. heavies and 900 fighters hit aircraft factories, two as far away as Posen, Poland, while 600 RAF bombers struck Stuttgart that night. The U.S. lost 41 bombers and 11 fighters that day, and another 64 on February 25, when 400 bombers of the Fifteenth Air Force from Italy joined the Eighth in attacking targets in southern Germany. In all that week, the U.S. lost 226 bombers and 28 fighters on some 3800 sorties. Still, the bomber loss rate was 3.5 percent as against 9.2 percent the previous October. Moreover, it was estimated that the Germans critically lost 434 pilots that week, and perhaps 1000, or close to a third of their total strength between January and April, 1944.

On March 6, over 1000 tons of bombs were dropped on Berlin. That set off one of the epic air battles of the war, as some 400 Luftwaffe fighters tangled with 800 Allied fighters and 660 bombers, of which the Germans downed 11 and 69, respectively. But on the entire Western front, Germany lost 800 fighters during the heavy bombing strikes of February and March.

Then came the massive bombardments accompanying the D-Day invasion of June 6 and after. The Allies used some 12,837 aircraft, while Germany had only some 319 on that front. Up to 2500 bombers struck German targets around St. Lô several times later in the month, and subsequently continued to pursue retreating Nazi troops and targets. There were some deaths from "friendly fire" as Allied fighters flew ground support missions for the fast-moving tank columns of General George Patton and other forces. Bombs also fell in the wrong places and on one occasion killed a U.S. Army General, Lesley McNair. On another occasion a B-17, whose crew had been killed by heavy flak, crashed into a British ammunition dump, setting off a huge explosion.

Especially crippling for Germany was the near total disruption of its oil supplies. From April through August 1944, B-24s struck the principal source at Ploesti, Romania, nineteen times, and huge raids were launched against refineries in Germany. On May 12 and 28, 1944, respectively, the Eighth Air Force sent 935 and 1282 heavy bombers against plants near Leipzig. By the end of the war over 90 percent of Germany's energy sources, as well as most of its steel production, had been destroyed. Yet, hurt as Germany was, it still produced an estimated record 25,000 fighters in 1944, and by then was in better shape with fighters than with pilots. Like the Japanese, the Germans suffered from a rapid deterioration in the quality of their new pilots as the war went on, in their case because there simply wasn't enough fuel to give the new recruits flying hours.

As their cities and industry were becoming methodically destroyed, the Germans came up with a new invention, and after June 11 and September 1944, respectively, they sent thousands of the terrifying V-1 and V-2 rocket bombs against England. The supersonic V-2 was especially devastating. In all, including aircraft, which by the later stages were primarily the fast Ju-88, the Germans dropped 71,000 metric tons of bombs on Britain, killing some 60,000. Without the protection of radar, English losses would have been far greater. Although patented by a German as early as 1904, radar was not made workable until 1936, first in Britain. Within four years the English established some forty-six radar stations which could detect planes fifty miles off. They also installed devices on some planes, beginning with their Blenheim night fighters.

The final defeat of Hitler's forces came after the Normandy invasion, which was the largest in history. Over 3000 of the 5000 U.S. combat planes in England, which included over 2000 heavy bombers, flew an incredible 8700 sorties that day, and the RAF another 5700. (On hearing of the assault, two Me-109s managed to strafe the beaches.) Some 176,000 men in 5000 ships the first day and one million within a month, under the overall command of U.S. General Dwight Eisenhower, successfully crossed the English Channel to land in Normandy. The invasion was preceded by a huge airborne assault behind the beaches—its strategic value laying largely in the belief that whatever confusion took place in the drop zones would probably be doubled among the enemy trying to figure out what was going on.

The last of the great airborne assaults took place on September 17, 1944, after the surviving Germans had fled Normandy. This time, three divisions of airborne troops were integral to the operation because they would drop behind the enemy lines in Holland to hold bridges for Allied armor that would simultaneously break through the frontier.

While considering the plan, a British officer wondered whether they might be going "a bridge too far," thus inspiring the title of Cornelius Ryan's famous work. The American 82nd and 101st Airborne managed to seize their bridges, as did the British 1st Airborne, landing near the farthest bridge, in Arnhem, however the "Red Devils" then became surrounded by two SS Panzer divisions that Allied intelligence had failed to detect. Despite the assistance of the 1st Polish Airborne Brigade, which flew in as reinforcement, the British were nearly annihilated and the promised armor never reached them. Although the record of massive airborne operations in World War II is one of mixed success, the exploits and demonstrations of bravery by the paratroopers are impressive.

Enormous new bombings accompanied the last great battle in the West, as the Nazi counterattack in the "Bulge," near World War I battlefields, was repulsed. Like the German Army, the Luftwaffe saved its last major effort for this offensive, and was able to launch 700 planes in a pre-emptive strike on Allied airfields just prior to the assault. The Germans were further assisted by overcast weather during the entire first week of their surprise attack, which began on December 16. On December 24, however, the skies cleared and over 2000 heavy bombers and almost 1000 Allied fighters struck 11 airfields, 14 communications centers, and count-less traffic-jammed roads with some 5000 tons of bombs. More heavy raids followed, and by January 12, 1945, 16,312 sorties dropped about 40,000 tons of bombs on 19 airfields, 64 railway yards, and 54 other complexes, and destroyed 468 German planes.

The most controversial Allied bombing of the European war came in February, with the devastation of Dresden. On the night of February 13–14, two waves of 772 and 550 British Lancasters used saturation fire-bombing to destroy that refugee-swollen city. This could not have been totally unexpected, since the British had long before determined that cities were the only targets large enough for their bombers to hit—given their dedication to bombing at night—and "Bomber" Harris had openly advocated the necessity of destroying the enemy civilians' "housing." The next day, however, as the civilians were attempting to dig themselves out, 1350 U.S. heavies, previously devoted to precision daylight bombing of industrial targets, escorted by 900 fighters, repeated the British attack, together totaling close to 3000 tons, to level 85 percent of the city.

The damage was enormous, as immortalized in Kurt Vonnegut's 1969 novel, *Slaughterhouse Five*. Deaths were estimated at anywhere from 40,000 to 175,000, since no one knows how many refugees were crowd-ing the city after fleeing the Russian front. Since Dresden was not an industrial center, and the effort to destroy it so immense, one explanation for the attack is that the Allied intention was to create a "signpost" for the rapidly advancing Red Army, in the event Stalin, flush with his recent suc-cess, had any doubts about the effectiveness of Allied air power.

Darmstadt and other cities were also fire-bombed, and a strike against Berlin on February 3 was said to have killed some 25,000. Huge new raids followed, with a record 30,358 sorties in March, dropping a record 67,365 tons of bombs the last week of that month. March also saw the dropping by RAF planes of a few of the biggest-ever bombs of 22,000 lbs., dubbed "earthquakes," to down previously impregnable bridges. The Germans in their final desperation developed their version of Kamikaze attacks, their leading fighters, the constantly upgraded Me-109s and FW

190s, ramming the planes they could not shoot down. An estimated eight U.S. heavy bombers were lost to such attacks.

By then, RAF Spitfires and Typhoons, and American P-38s, P-47s, and P-51s, had established basic control of the Western skies. It was the last, dubbed the Mustang, that became, with the slightly slower but highly maneuverable British Spitfire, the most effective Allied fighter of the war (although America's top ace in Europe, Francis "Gabby" Gabreski, flew P-47s). Designed by North American Aviation and first flown in 1940, the P-51 was steadily improved, 1943 models reaching 440 mph at 30,000 feet, powered by Allison, later Rolls-Royce, liquid-cooled 1200 and 1695 hp engines. Capable of long range, up to 1700 miles with extra gas tanks, it was so agile that one pilot recalled: "flying it was a sensual pleasure." They and P-38s began to arrive in Europe in November 1943, and over 15,000 P-51s were built.

One of the most famous groups of P-51s was flown by black aviators in the segregated U.S. Army Air Corps under the Fifteenth Air Force. It was established with the advance into Italy, and the group became known as the "Red Tail Angels" after they painted the tails of their Mustangs vermillion. They downed or damaged some 400 enemy aircraft, while never losing an escorted bomber. Especially famous were their commander, Lt. Colonel Benjamin O. Davis, the first black to win military pilot's wings, and Captain Armour G. McDaniels, who fell to jet-powered Messerschmitt 262s in a raid on Berlin, March 24, 1945. After the war, survivors popularized as their name "The Tuskegee Airmen," after their place of training in Alabama. A 1995 movie of that name dramatized their 95 Distinguished Flying Crosses and the fame of members, including a future mayor of Detroit, a borough president of Manhattan, and other well-known African-American leaders.

The jet will be the main subject of a later chapter, but here its origins and relation to World War II can be mentioned. Astonishingly, as with many of the world's great inventions, the first jet-powered aircraft were achieved almost simultaneously, but obviously independently, in Britain and Germany. The Englishman Frank Whittle actually patented the idea in 1930 but could get no substantial support until the war. The German, Dr. Hans-Joachim von Ohain, took out his patent in 1934 and was aided by work on the all-important engines by Junkers and BMW. A Heinkel 178 with a centrifugal-type engine became the first aircraft to fly on jet power, if only for 50 seconds, above Rostock, August 27, 1939—just four days before the invasion of Poland. Whittle was able to ground-test an engine the same year, and two years later both countries put jets to more extensive tests.

A Heinkel 280 was fitted with an ejector seat, the first ever, and made an initial flight April 2, 1941. On the 18th, the pilot Fritz Schafer broke the April 26, 1939 speed record by almost 20 mph at 485 mph. On May 15, 1941, Whittle's Gloster Meteor jet flew smoothly for 17 minutes at the RAF's Cranwell field. High-speed demonstrations followed, but there were delays, in part caused by industrial competition at making the necessary engine improvements. Finally, by July 1944, the RAF received the first two Meteors, and they and new arrivals saw some limited action. After the war, on November 7, 1945, a Gloster Meteor F4 set a new speed record of 606.38 mph. The U.S. made rapid progress after its first jet flight by a Bell XP-59A Airacomet in October 1942. The breakthrough Lockheed P-80 Shooting Star flew first in January 1944, and over 100 were produced by the end of the war, with another 400 in 1946.

The German jet fighters, delayed fatally by one of Hitler's major blunders, as he demanded that the new jets be equipped for bombing rather than air combat missions, finally were equipped with superior axial flow engines. They powered the twin-engined Messerschmitt Me-262 fighter bomber, which first flew on October 3, 1944. The Heinkel He-162 jet fighter reached a new record speed of 520 mph in early 1945, and the four-engine Junkers 287, with forward swept wings and rocket as-sisted take-off, could fly over 500 mph and became the world's first heavy jet bomber. But by then it was too late, although the superior firepower and speed of the German jets caused some late alarm in Allied commands, as did the V-1 and V-2 rockets sent against Britain after mid-1944. Once the Me-262 had been approved for fighter purposes, German General of Fighters Adolf Galland organized a squadron of aces to fly the jets against Allied bomber streams. In March 1945, Me-262s downed 24 B-17s, and by the end of the war 52 big bombers and 10 fighters.

Along with the heroic morale of all the Allied forces, the productive capacity of the United States was clearly decisive for the imminent victory in Europe, with the surrender of Germany on May 8, 1945. This was true not only for the machines of war but for personnel. Where there were only about 8000 American military pilots in 1941—a figure not much higher than that of 1926—by the end of 1944 there were almost

300,000. That was close to the 304,139 military aircraft produced by U.S. industry from 1939 to 1945. And it was the use of some 75,000 of those planes, available late in the war in all theaters for bombing and strafing, that was both the most punishing to the enemy and the most unique, as no previous war had been decided that way. As Jimmy Doolittle stated about the final defeat of Japan, three months after that of Germany, "Our brave infantry had the men and the guts and the leadership to have invaded Japan; our Navy had the ships to storm the beaches; our Air Force made it all unnecessary." And as a recent major study of American air power stated, "Only a full appreciation of . . . the massive [bombing] campaigns of World War II . . . can establish how the problem of air war became acute long before the nuclear age."

Following the Allied victory in Europe in early May 1945, the U.S. decided to finish off Japan's resistance with its newly invented atomic bombs. They fell on Hiroshima, August 6, and on Nagasaki, August 9, the day after Russia's invasion of Manchuria. Japan surrendered on August 15, but debate understandably has continued about the dropping of the bombs, the most terrible single destruction ever to fall from the air. After the successful test of a twenty-kiloton plutonium bomb in New Mexico, on July 16, Washington decided it must use the fearsome new weapon to avoid having to invade Japan and even more deaths.

Taking off from Tinian Island in the Marianas, Col. Paul W. Tibbetts commanded the Superfortress *Enola Gay*, named after his mother, to release at 8:15 local time the first approximately 9,000-pound uranium-235 bomb, "Little Boy" (10.5 feet or 3 meters long, 29 inches or 0.7 meters in diameter). Falling from 31,600 feet at 328 mph, 43 seconds later it detonated 1900 feet up with a force equivalent to 12,500 tons of TNT. This almost totally destroyed over five square miles of Hiroshima, killing over 100,000 persons at once and another 50,000 in its aftermath. Three days later, the 10,000-pound "Fat Man," almost 12 feet long and 5 feet in diameter, exploded 1650 feet above Nagasaki with the still bigger force of 22,500 pounds of TNT, killing about 75,000, with another 25,000 dying later of radiation effects.

The use of air power, as we have seen, finally ended the greatest war in history with the surrender of Japan, August 15, 1945. Pictures of the mushroom clouds showing the brilliant fireballs, some 8000 feet across and rising to over 50,000 feet, electrified the world.

A new era had begun!

13

The Commercial Revolution

Another wonder is that mankind has survived at all, given not only the
horrors of World War II, but the threat of nuclear annihilation in the
four decades of the Cold War. Fortunately, the engineers and scientists
who gave us the new tools of destruction have been able since 1945, with
the help of their fellow citizens and leaders, to avoid the use of new
weapons against civilian populations to anything like the extent of World
War II, as well as to prevent the sort of nuclear accident that might well
have undone all the precautions of the politicians and statesmen.

Undoubtedly the further development of aviation and the launching
of spaceflight, with the enormous commitments of energy, money, and
scientific knowledge involved for the cutting edges of economies and
technologies, have been critical factors in preventing a new and final holo-
caust. The sharpening of skills and widening of human knowledge
required by the now vast aviation and space world has clearly played a
great role in producing the pool of experts with the logic, methodology,
and precision to avoid that ultimate catastrophe. Of course, as mentioned
above, small countries such as Afghanistan, Iraq, Korea, and Vietnam suffered enormously from devastation by air power in more recent decades.
Indeed, the over seven million tons of aerial bombs dropped mostly on
rural Indochina before 1973 will surely remain the record for aerial bombardments, being over three times all the explosives dropped from the air
in World War II. However, terrible as that and other post-1945 wars and
problems have been, they could not compare in effects with those of the
Second World War, which killed over fifty million people.

More recently, most of the world's people have come to see aviation,
not as the instrument of war it has been for too much of this century, but
as something altogether different: the best means to enjoy new horizons
of speed, travel, and adventure, and the only means for rapid transporta-

tion to distant places.

As mentioned in Chapter Seven, over 10,000 paying passengers flew around Germany in Zeppelin airships from March 1911 to the outbreak of World War I, while in Florida, several hundred flew between St. Petersburg and Tampa on Benoist seaplanes over the first three months of 1914. Following new beginnings of commercial aviation after the Great War and modest development in the 1920s and 1930s—100,000 Germans having flown by 1928—the real take-off of mass travel by air came in the late 1940s with the first piston-powered engines strong enough to transport bigger numbers of passengers at what were previously record speeds, and then at several times those speeds once jet engines and structures were mastered in the 1950s (the subject of our next chapter).

Where in 1926 only 6000 Americans traveled by air, millions began to do so in the 1930s. By 1930, the third amendment to the Kelly Air Mail Act of 1925, changing pay scales from poundage to miles flown, had encouraged airlines to carry more passengers with their mail. Some 522,000 people were flying in the U.S. by 1931, and by 1941 their number reached three million, then twice that in 1945, and 12.5 million in 1946. This was only the beginning, and by 1961 the number was 58 million and close to ten times that a generation later.

By the mid-1950s, Americans traveled more and more by air. This was in large part due to the reduced costs of air travel. Whereas in 1929, the cost per passenger mile was still 12 cents, it fell to 5.1 cents a decade later—still three times the cost of bus travel, and twice that of travel by rail. In 1940, 456 million Americans traveled by train, a number exceeded for travel by air by the 1990s, with over 528 million (including over 47 million abroad) airline passengers in 1994. Over 80 percent of Americans still travel by car, going an estimated 1.5 trillion miles a year, and in the mid-1990s, 352 million traveled by train. The percentage traveling between cities by air has risen from 2 percent in 1950 to over 10 percent, and one third of American adults were flying at least once a year by the 1990s.

Worldwide, the statistics for increases in air travel are equally dramatic. The number of people traveling by air soared from 2.5 million in 1937 to 45 million in 1952, 90 million in 1957, 325 million in 1971, 750 million in 1980, and 1.1 billion by 1990. By late in the century, there were over a million passengers flying on about 20,000 flights every day in the United States. Yet, where Americans made up over 50 percent of international air travelers before 1946, that percentage declined with the development of other economies and aviation industries. In 1992, the 473 million Americans taking to the air made up about 40 percent of the 1166 million airline passengers that year, as against 31 percent who were Europeans. About half of them were flying on business trips, and about half for pleasure. In international travel, America's decline was much steeper, from a near monopoly in 1945 to under 18 percent in 1980. It will decline further as growth in air travelers to and from and in Asia, for example, is projected to pass 300 million a year by the new century.

The striking increases in air travel dictated new organizations and techniques to handle its many complexities. Air Traffic Control (ATC) came into use first at Newark Airport outside New York in 1935, where there was already a take-off or landing every ten minutes. Other airports soon followed, trained personnel staggering the flights in accordance with the rules of national aviation authorities as best they could, given the then-still-primitive equipment.

To coordinate such rules and air traffic around the world, after World War II the International Civil Aviation Organization (ICAO, OACI in French) was formed through the work of a series of conferences in Chicago, Havana, and Bermuda from 1944 to 1946. It established its headquarters in Montreal, with the primary function of coordinating international air routes, working in conjunction with the already existing International Air Transport Association (IATA to all). The latter had been founded in Holland in 1919, then was based in Paris. It, too, was reorganized in 1945, with offices in Montreal and Geneva, to facilitate other aspects of cooperation between the burgeoning international airlines, which numbered over 100 flying over 13,000 aircraft by late in the century.

The international organizations naturally had to work closely with national aviation organizations such as the various air transport associations and air traffic control centers (ATCC), controlling and maintaining the separation between flights within the respective countries. There were also groups such as the Fédération de l'Aviation Internationale (FAI) and the International Airline Passenger Association, which had some 110,000 members by 1994. By then, close to 500,000 people were working in the American aviation industry. These included over 53,000 pilots, 87,000 flight attendants, 59,000 mechanics, 17,415 air controllers, 48,000 employees of the FAA, and over 240,000 in various service jobs. In 1990, they were controlling or flying over 7000 commercial airplanes, including 4149 turbojets, 1595 turboprops, and 1419 commuter aircraft, as well as up to 200,000 private planes, including 7397 rotor craft, when they entered controlled airspace.

In the United States, on August 23, 1958, the Federal Aviation Act had taken effect, creating the Agency of the same name, the FAA, to supersede the functions for the control of aviation that had been organized by the Commerce Department with the Air Commerce Act of 1926, the Civil Air Regulations of 1937, and the Civil Aeronautics Authority (CAA) after 1938. The latter became the Civil Aeronautics Board (CAB) in 1940 and the Airways Modernization Board in 1957. Until 1984, the CAB continued to be responsible for economic regulation and the investigation of accidents, but after 1958 the FAA assumed primary responsibility for most aviation operations, while the National Transportation Safety Board took over responsibility for accident investigations after 1984. The FAA, for example, established 40-mile-wide (later reduced to 10nm) transcontinental and other airways under 20 or more Air Route Traffic Control Centers (ARTCCs), for the some 2000 commercial airliners flying in the U.S. at the time of its formation, as well as rules and prohibited zones for military aviation and testing. Other countries established similar agencies and controls, coordinated internationally by the ICAO and IATA.

The system still used for landing in bad weather under Instrument Flight Rules (IFR)—the Instrument Landing System, or ILS—first came into use in England in 1944. It projects radio beams, known as localizers (LOC), to guide planes in the air in accordance with Air Traffic Control (ATC), for take-off, cruise, and on approach, the latter normally on a Glide Slope (GS), captured by the second ILS antenna, of 3 degrees toward the airport in question. By and after the war, ILS and Non-Directional Beacons (NDBs) or AM radio facilities tuned in by aircraft Automatic Direction Finders (ADFs) were becoming widely installed at leading centers.

Aircraft and airports were progressively equipped with new avionics, including, most importantly, the Altitude Director Indicator (ADI) and the Inertial Navigation System (INS). They also included Distance Measuring Equipment (DME), Doppler radio and radar systems, Long Range Navigation (Loran-C), Omega-Very Low Frequency (VLF), Very

High Frequency Omni Range (VOR), Tactical Air Navigation (TACAN), and other new navigational systems. Still newer, often computer-based systems, digital avionics, with simplified cockpits housing Flight Management Systems (FMS), a new precision Distance Measuring Equipment (DME-P), Omega (navigation system), laser gyroscopes, Microwave Landing Systems (MLS), Electronic Flight Instrument Systems (EFIS), the Engine Indicating and Crew Alerting System (EICAS), Full-Authority Digital Engine Control (FADEC), Stormscopes, and Traffic Collision and Avoidance Systems (TCAS) were linked to airport Standard Automatic Terminal Information Systems (ATIS), Precision Approach Radar (PAR, formerly Ground Control Approach or GCA), Cathode Ray (CRT-TV screens), Direct Access Radar Control (DARC) and, in the U.S., some 250 Terminal Radar Approach Control (TRACON) sites, establishing ever better management of general aviation and "flow control" for the higher-speed jets. Many airports in turn also came on-line with the Internet, called Aeronautical Telecommunications Network.

By the late 1980s, the most accurate system (to within 21 feet or 7 meters) of all these "computer controlled integrated avionics," the satellite-based Global Positioning System (GPS; in Russian, Glonass), supplemented by the Wide Area Augmentation System (WAAS), began to become available. It enabled landings in actual zero visibility as against the virtual ability to do that given by the ILS and earlier systems, and even "free flight," with less dependence on ground controls and more in-flight autonomy for pilots, as in the days before radio and electronic ground controls. Still, in bad weather, although the jetliners came to be held at departure for "flow control," to minimize fuel consumption and other problems before landing at their destination, at times it still remains necessary to "stack" airplanes at 1000-foot intervals to accommodate excessive numbers of aircraft at peak periods, since the ILS often handles about 15 or 20 or so planes an hour as against up to perhaps 75 in clear weather. The improved equipment and coordination of Air Traffic Control, however, has steadily and greatly reduced waiting times at busy airports. The record of an airliner stacked 5 hours over Washington, DC in the spring of 1946 will surely not be exceeded.

The Cold War in its way provided a sort of transition between the horrors of World War II and the more peaceful future. It also linked the advances in military aviation with civilian uses. Douglas Aircraft, the leader in pre-war commercial aviation, for example, supplied most of the planes used in that incredible airlift that saved the 2.5 million people of Berlin from complete Soviet takeover, with the cut-off of all land access to the West from June 24, 1948 to May 12, 1949. The airlift continued to the end of September and, in all, Douglas C-47s (DC-3s) and C-54s (DC-4s), as well as some Boeing C-97s ("Stratocruisers"), and various RAF and other planes, carried a total of 2,343,000 tons of supplies into the city on 277,264 flights. The biggest workhorse of the airlift, as of the earlier Hump flights, was the four-engined C-54, the military version of the DC-4, which was precisely the first hugely successful big commercial airliner.

With basic improvements in the prototype which had first flown in June 1938, the DC-4 "Skymaster" (C-54) took off in February 1942, and rapidly established a predominance reminiscent of its predecessor, the DC-3, to be discussed below. By 1945, some 1100 had been produced and its four 1350hp Pratt and Whitney radial engines carried a crew of six, and over 40 passengers, at up to 250 mph (400 kph). The overseas division of American Airlines began flights in it between New York and London in 1945, while in the U.S. airline companies stressed the amenities of the DC-4, with its first tricycle gear for such a big plane, and passenger comforts including soundproofing, upholstered seating, steam heat, air conditioning, comfortable toilets, and electrical outlets for personal appliances.

Then, by 1947, the further great improvement of cabin pressurization, pioneered by the Boeing "Stratoliner" after 1939 and the Lockheed "Constellation" after 1944, was added for the new version, the DC-6. It could carry over 50 passengers at over 312 mph (500 kph) as far as 3750 miles with its four powerful, 2400hp Pratt and Whitney engines. By 1953, the further-improved Douglas DC-7 could carry up to 95 people at 362.5 mph (580 kph) for 5000 miles. That cut the pre-war transcontinental flights of over 16 hours by the DC-3 to about 8 hours, but it still took up to 15 hours, even with favorable winds, to cross the Atlantic from New York to London or elsewhere. The DC-7 made the first commercial transport flights against the wind without stop from the East to the West Coast. Such performances, as well as those of rivals like the Lockheed Constellation to be discussed below, represented the apogee of pre-jet aviation performance. As before the war, Douglas continued to far outsell its rivals. Almost 600 of the DC-4s, 6s, and 7s were sold, as against some 200

Constellations and 55 Boeing 377 Stratocruisers.

The man responsible for the Douglas airliners was Donald W. Douglas. Born in Brooklyn on April 6, 1892, he became hooked on aviation watching the flights of Orville Wright in 1908, and later of Glenn Curtiss and others. He enrolled in the Naval Academy, but then decided to transfer to M.I.T., where he earned a degree in mechanical engineering in 1914. The next year he moved to Los Angeles to become the chief engineer with Glenn Martin's new aviation company. After the United States entered World War I, he briefly headed the Aviation Section of the Signal Corps. Frustrated with bureaucratic problems, Douglas returned to work with Glenn Martin, but now in Cleveland, where Martin had established his operations for a few years.

In 1920, Douglas decided to return to California and set up his own company—initially in the back of a barber shop! With the development of an effective biplane, the "Cloudster," which was the first aircraft ever to lift more than its own empty weight, of a torpedo plane for the Navy, and in 1924, the world cruiser DWC, which, as we have noted made the first round-the-world flight, he was well on his way. Douglas also wrote articles in prestigious journals like *Scientific American*, discussing the advantages of airplanes for travel and the carrying of cargo. But his real take-off came with the development of the first DC (Douglas Commercial) airliners after 1933.

The instigator of that take-off, as would be the case for some of the first big jet transports two decades later, was an airline executive, himself an experienced pilot, Jack Frye. A founder of Standard Airlines in California in 1926, he became vice-president of Trans World Airlines (then Transcontinental and Western Airlines, which became TWA) and convinced fellow directors of the need for a bigger, longer-range plane than yet existed. In August 1933, Frye wrote the leading manufacturers requesting a plane that could carry 12 people for 1000 miles at 150 mph. The next year, February 18, 1934, to protest the temporary order for the U.S. Army to carry air mail, Frye and the even more famous new vice-president of Eastern Transport, World War I ace Eddie Rickenbacker, teamed up to fly a TWA DC-2 from Los Angeles to Newark, with the last cargo of civilian-carried air mail in the near record time of 13 hours, four minutes.

Douglas, meanwhile, set to work and won the order for the first Douglas Commercial airliners. Only one DC-1 was produced in 1933 with changes leading to the DC 2 the next year and the DC-3 in 1935 and 1936. Douglas and his engineers, including Ed Heinemann and Arthur Raymond, incorporated the new information in aerodynamics for the DC-2. They used the example of the "first modern airliner," the Boeing 247, which had begun flying in February 1933, and they also used a stressed skin, metal monocoque fuselage, and variable-pitch propellers for greater efficiency at different speeds and altitudes. Cowling around the engine reduced drag, and wing flaps enabled a slow landing speed of 58 mph. The first flight of the DC-2 was May 11, 1934, and its two Curtiss Wright engines enabled the 24,000-pound plane to transport up to 14 passengers at 178 mph.

From 1936 on, the DC-3s with two 900 to 1200hp Cyclone twin wasp radial engines carried up to 21 passengers at 195 mph. As mentioned, they achieved almost complete domination of commercial aviation before the war, making up 260 of the 322 in the fleet of U.S. airliners in 1942. They also made up all 74 of the fleet of American Airlines, which had been instrumental in getting the development of the DC 3. Far more flew as the military C-47, and over 12,000 were built and continued to fly in many countries for many decades. Boeing, which became the number-one plane maker of the jet age, almost achieved that much earlier. But loyalty to United Airlines, which began to fly its Boeing 247 on March 30, 1933, dictated the refusal to sell its eight-passenger 247 when Frye requested 20 of them for TWA a little later. That led to the order in August 1933 for the Douglas DC-2 and the subsequent dominance of the DC-3.

Thus, not only was aviation a very international enterprise, but clearly there was also much beneficial interaction as well as competition between the airlines. As Donald Douglas confessed, "It was the challenge of the 247 that put us into the transport business." While there were over two dozen airline companies in the U.S. in 1934, most passengers were already carried by those that remained the biggest carriers for decades afterwards, namely American Airlines, Eastern Airlines, Pan American Airways, and United Airlines. All were in existence by 1930, and played huge roles in aviation developments thereafter—although not all survived the turbulent competition of the late century.

Before further discussion of them and some others, a review of the later developments of Donald Douglas and his company is in order.

Despite fierce competition from other manufacturers, Douglas achieved record profits with its DC-6s and 7s, until Boeing captured the bulk of the jet airliner market after 1958. The year before that, at age 65, the senior Douglas turned over his corporate positions to his eldest son, Donald Jr. The company soon was forced to seek new financing for the enormous costs of developing new models, as its DC-8s and 9s failed to match the sales of Boeing's 707s and 727s. This led to its 1967 merger with the McDonald Company of St. Louis, founded before the war by James Smith McDonald, like the senior Douglas a former engineer with Glenn Martin. McDonald was famous for its F-4 Phantom jet fighter developed by the early 1960s, and the new McDonald-Douglas company became an even more formidable organization, with its F-15 and F-18 fighters, the latter produced in partnership with the Northrop Corporation. The senior Douglas ran into his hardest times after 1967. A famous yachtsman and distinguished gentleman, he suffered increasing health and family problems and died of cancer in 1981.

As mentioned, both Donald Douglas in the teens, and James McDonald in the twenties, had served as engineers with Glenn Martin before starting their own companies. And, indeed, Glenn Martin was with the other Glenn, Curtiss, one of the biggest names in aviation history after the Wrights. Born in Macksburg, Iowa, January 17, 1886, Martin accompanied his parents to Santa Ana, California in 1905. Two years after that, inspired by Octave Chanute glider designs, news of the Wright brothers, and glider demonstrations by greater Los Angeles neighbor John Montgomery, he began his own experiments as he earned a living in automobile service and sales.

In 1909, Martin made a short hop in a biplane glider to which he attached a Ford car motor. Then, after the January, 1910, nearby air show, he began his own flying exhibitions even as he continued designing work and money-raising efforts. By August 1912, he got enough financing to incorporate the Glenn L. Martin Company. After 1915, with the help of Donald Douglas among others, he was able to sell a trainer to the U.S. Army and to Holland, and become the third airplane manufacturer after the companies of Orville Wright and Glenn Curtiss. Following a brief merger with the Wright Company of Dayton, Ohio, Martin got backing from wealthy Cleveland industrialists and incorporated in that city, in September 1917. In 1929, he moved his operations to near Baltimore, where he died in December 1955, two years after his mother, who had given him lifelong support—as well as controversy over her domination of her famous son.

The Martin company's greatest profits, like those of its competitors, came during World War II, when it sold 8983 planes to the Army and Navy. As in World War I, that was again third, now, to the sales of military aircraft by Douglas of 30,980 and by Lockheed of 19,077. But Martin planes included such famous models as the MB-2 bombers, which General Billy Mitchell used to sink the German battleships in July 1921, the B-10 bomber of the later twenties, the M-130 "China Clipper," the B-26 Marauder, and the B-57, a version of the English Canberra twin jet bomber. But Martin's post-war effort to compete for sales of big airliners failed, as the M-202 sold only 20, mostly to Northwest Airlines, and its last plane, a Navy anti-submarine patrol plane, was produced in 1960. The next year, it merged with the American Marietta Company, and the Martin Marietta company manufactured mostly missiles and diverse other products, including some space hardware.

Bigger for those manufacturers and near top place for the manufacture of advanced aircraft since the early days, is the Lockheed Corporation. It has grown out of the company founded by another pair of brothers, Malcolm and Allan Loughead. Born near San Francisco in 1887 and 1889, respectively, by the early 1930s they changed the spelling of their name to its phonetic equivalent, the more familiar Lockheed. Red-haired Allan was plagued by bad health as a child, and never even finished grammar school. But he received substantial tutoring from his talented mother. Simultaneously, older half brother Victor, a disciple of John Montgomery and author of some widely read publications on airplanes, introduced his younger brothers to the possibilities of aviation. Victor worked as an engineer in Chicago, and found work there for Allan, who in 1912 managed to coax a Curtiss 35hp pusher plane off a snow-covered field on his first try. He went on to become a flying instructor and exhibition pilot until a near-fatal accident induced him to shift his enthusiasm to the making of airplanes. Returning to work with cars in San Francisco, he built his first plane there the following year. It was a tractor-type amphibious biplane. He went on with Malcolm to found the Loughead Aircraft Manufacturing Company in Santa Barbara in 1916.

Although three years later Malcolm moved and went into the business of manufacturing the automobile brake he had invented, Allan and engineer Jack Northrop (about whom more shortly) helped to develop a first "Flying Boat," a small sport plane in 1919, and in 1927 the famous Lockheed "Vega." After various Depression-induced financial problems and deals, and the 1928 reestablishment of the company in Burbank, California, Allan followed Malcolm's earlier example in the 1930s to move progressively to other pursuits. But the Lockheed Corporation under the leadership of brothers Robert and Courtland Gross, and brilliant chief engineers, notably after Jack Northrop, Gerard Vultee, Richard A. Von Hake, Hall Hibbard, and Clarence L. "Kelly" Johnson, continued to develop outstanding aircraft. These included the airliner "Electra" in 1934, a military version of it, the "Hudson," which was sold to the RAF in World War II, and the famous U.S. military fighter the P-38. The four-engined, three-tailed C-97 became the equally famous Constellation which, after the war, achieved temporary dominance in big airliner sales because its 300-mph speed was some 50 mph higher than that of the rival DC-4. Then, in 1955, the "Super Constellation Starliner" competed successfully for awhile with the still faster DC-6s and 7s.

The company's chief designer after the war, Clarence Johnson, with the help of outstanding test pilots like Tony LeVier, developed the first successful U.S. jet fighter, the F-80 "Shooting Star," the record-setting F-104 "Starfighter," and after 1955 and 1964, respectively, the incredible very-high-altitude (over 80,000 feet) spy planes, the U-2 and SR-71. All these were produced at the famous Advanced Development Products Division, or "skunk works," in Burbank. It took its nickname from the imaginary still for producing moonshine in Al Capp's famous comic strip "L'il Abner."

The SR-71 holds the all-time speed record for a ground-launched plane, of 2193.17 mph, flown July 28, 1976. Among other record flights, it reached Washington, DC from Los Angeles in an astonishing 64 minutes, two seconds, at 2144 mph. Only the B-52-dropped X-15 has gone higher, into the fringes of space at 354,200 feet in August 1963, and faster, some 4534 mph, on October 3, 1967. Lockheed also manufactured the Air Force's leading transports, the C-130 "Hercules," the C-141 "Starlifter," and the then world's largest transport, the C-5 "Galaxy." The latter first flew in June 1968, a year before Allan Lockheed died. He was succeeded by another dynamic leader, Daniel Haughton, who secured the take-off on November 16, 1970, of the Lockheed 1011, a three-engined airliner carrying up to 400 passengers.

Probably the most famous early aeronautical engineer of all was John

K. "Jack" Northrop. Born in Newark, New Jersey on November 10, 1895, his family moved to Nebraska and then to Santa Barbara, California before he was ten. Seeing his first flight at age 16, he began his life-long commitment to building airplanes. After high school, he served briefly in the Army Signal Corps, with the chance to study the planes they were responsible for, and then, like so many of the pioneers, he took work in a hometown automobile garage. When the Lockheeds moved their operations to Santa Barbara in 1916, he was able to devote all his time to his first love. As mentioned, his talent contributed greatly to the first successful Lockheed planes, and he became famous after bringing out the Vega with Allan Lockheed in 1927. It carried a pilot and six passengers for over 500 miles at 135 mph.

Northrop also was a prime developer of the new monocoque fuse-lages and, working with the Douglas Company from 1923 to 1926, he developed the multi-cellular wing and later, with Edward Heinemann and others, dive flaps and other improvements that enabled the DC airliners and other aircraft to fly so well. In the late 1920s he again became Lockheed's chief engineer and then after 1929 with diverse partners, including Kenneth Jay and Lloyd Stearman, he formed what would become a decade later the Northrop Corporation. In the early 1930s, he produced the all-metal, stressed-skin construction "Alpha" and other sophisticated aircraft.

Along with "his many design breakthroughs that helped make possible" modern aviation, Northrop also became obsessed with the development of a flying wing. He made models for it from the late 1920s, and in the late 1940s, one, the XB-35, and its jet model, the YB-49, came close to adoption. The ultimate in air drag efficiency, with neither fuselage nor tail, the flying wing had other problems, however, including range and adaption to jet engines. A fatal crash at Muroc, California on June 5, 1948, temporarily ended flying-wing experiments. One of the victims of that crash was USAF Captain Glenn Edwards, for whom the famous Edwards Air Force Base was named. Three decades later, as the Air Force was moving to a similar idea for the Northrop Corporation's "Stealth Bomber" to avoid enemy radar, Jack Northrop died on February 18, 1981, able to believe that his vision for the flying wing had been vindicated. Famous Northrop jets included the F-89 "Scorpion," which first linked autopilot and fire-control radar, the F-5 "Freedom Fighter" and its supersonic trainer version, the T-38, as well as the F-20 "Tigershark."

The other most famous pioneer designer and builder of aircraft, William Boeing, also began his work very early, after about 1910; but since that work would lead his company's name to become synonymous with big jet airliners, the Boeing company will be described later in the transition to discussion of the jet age.

But there were numerous other names who also made their contributions to the principal subject of this chapter, the commercial revolution in aviation.

A mushrooming of new aviation companies took place during and after the late 1920s, and some of them remained big names in both military and civilian aviation. A World War I naval aviator and post-war test pilot with an engineering degree, Leroy Randle Grumman founded the company of his name in 1929 and from 1932 on was producing the fighters that became synonymous with naval aviation. They included the World War II attack bombers, "Avenger" and "Intruder," as well as the F4F "Wildcat" and F6F "Hellcat" fighters, and later the twin-jet F 14 "Tomcat." The company's commitment to aviation and quality was well shown in its inscription for its 1943 calendar:

> The pilot never rides alone. With him . . . go the mind and heart and energy of all those who had wrought the miracle of the mechanism which gives him mastery over gravity and space. . . . The plane he flies is not merely a thing of organic and inorganic material . . . the plane is a creature of man's genius, endowed with motion. Each fitting, part, and rivet; every fairing, calculated stress, and computed force is integrated into a machine that comes to life . . .

Back in the 1920s, another famous manufacturer of military airplanes was launched when New York financier Clement Keys began National Air Transport, which grew into North American Aviation. In the 1930s, under the leadership of James Howard Kindelberger and Lee Atwood, it began development of the famous World War II planes the P-51 and B-25. After the war, it produced the most celebrated early jet fighter, the F-86, and the record-setting X-15. Before World War II, of course, as preparations for war proceeded, many other aviation companies in the belligerent countries were manufacturing the fighters and bombers used all too much, as discussed above, before the Allied victories of 1945. Another California firm specializing in military aircraft was Consolidated Vultee, popularly known as Convair. Overseas, Vickers Ltd. began operations way back in 1911, and produced planes, culminating with the Wellington bomber and Spitfire fighter in World War II. De Havilland and Handley Page were other famous early British aviation companies. In France, the Morane-Saulnier company, also founded in 1911, produced famous military planes thereafter, as did the Junkers, Heinkel, and Messerschmitt companies in Germany, and others elsewhere.

In civil aviation before and after the Great War, what became the national airlines of many nations, especially in Europe, were instrumental in beginning the commercial revolution in aviation. People were flying between leading cities less than a year after the Armistice. The Farman brothers made the first passenger flight from Paris to London on February 8, 1919, and began sustained service between Paris and Brussels on March 22—activities taken as the beginnings of what became the national airline, Air France, in 1933. The Belgian airline, Sabena, also had its beginnings in 1919, while a predecessor of what became the German airline Lufthansa began domestic service within Germany as early as February of that year. A predecessor of British Air began service from London to Paris on August 25, 1919, and, after the founding of the Dutch airline, KLM, on October 7, 1919, the British cooperated to establish regular service between London and Amsterdam. A Franco-Romanian air service began service between Paris, Prague, and Warsaw in 1920, and shortly to Berlin, and then all the way to Bucharest and Constantinople.

In the Soviet Union, Andrei N. Tupelov (1888–1972), called the "father of Soviet aviation," produced his first plane, an AN 2, in 1923. The Russian immigrant to the U.S., Alexander de Seversky (1894–1974), also became well known. A former naval pilot, he founded an American aviation company in 1931 that produced the prototype of the famous World War II fighter, the P-47 Thunderbolt. In England, the Supermarine Aviation Works Ltd., founded in 1912 and bought by Vickers Aviation Ltd. in 1928, under their outstanding engineer-designer, R.J. Mitchell, produced a series of superior aircraft culminating in the equally famous Spitfire.

By the mid- and late 1920s, most European cities were linked by air and, as we have seen, adventurous aviators extended flights to the far corners of the world. Passengers soon followed those pioneer pilots, and by the 1930s there were passenger flights between the leading European cities and distant cities in Asia, Africa, and the Americas. New airlines started up around the world—in China, Japan, Argentina, Brazil, Colombia, Italy, Sweden, Switzerland, and elsewhere.

But it was in the United States that the commercial revolution in the air went furthest, given the vast distances of the country and the relative wealth of its citizens. By 1931, as noted, planes were already transporting some 522,000 people by air as well as 4400 tons of mail. Before discussing the biggest American enterprises fostering the commercial revolution in aviation, let us begin with mentions of some of the lesser-known.

In 1928, the brothers Paul and Thomas Braniff founded in Tulsa, Oklahoma, an air passenger service to Wichita and Kansas City that would become Braniff International Airways. By the time of longtime chairman Thomas Braniff's death in 1954, it was flying to several continents. But with higher fuel costs and increased competition from rivals abroad and in the U.S., especially after the deregulation act of 1978, Braniff was forced into bankruptcy in 1982 and ceased operations in 1989. The demise came despite moves such as hiring famed artist Alexander Calder to design colorfully and imaginatively painted fuselages.

Other successful American airlines whose origins go back to the 1920s include Delta and Northwest. A veteran pilot of World War I "Jennys," Collet Everman Woolman founded a crop-dusting service in 1924, and in 1929 began passenger service between Dallas and Jackson, Mississippi. He expanded to cover routes to Atlanta and Charleston, and incorporated Atlanta-based Delta Airlines in 1934. Postwar mergers and expansion brought Delta to third place, behind American and United, in passenger miles by 1989. In fourth place that year was Northwest Orient Airlines, which also took off first with air mail contracts for the vast territory from the Dakotas to Seattle. It offered support services to the North Pacific in World War II, and continued expansion after the war. The fifth-place airline in 1989 was Continental, which started slightly later. It was incorporated in 1934, at first under the name of its founder, Walter Varney, who began services between Denver and El Paso. The airline shortly flew to Wichita and Tulsa, and after the war to both coasts and abroad. U.S. Air, which temporarily ranked third following its linking with British Air in 1992, was incorporated in Delaware in 1937 by

Richard C. du Pont of the famous family of that name. Previously, U.S. Air had absorbed Allegheny Air in 1979 and Piedmont and Empire Air in 1986, the same year Northwest absorbed Republic and other airlines. In the 1990s, there were other linkups of international airlines, including American Airlines with British Air in June 1996, following the latter's with U.S. Air, United with Lufthansa, Northwest with KLM, and others.

There were numerous other small beginnings and some 44 airlines about 1930. Some merged to form new ones but most disappeared with no traces beyond the memories of their crews and passengers. Still, they, too, made big contributions to the spreading of the "air-mindedness" of the "winged gospel" that was increasingly dominating the U.S. and other countries.

The number-one U.S. airline in later decades grew out of no fewer than 84 companies of the late 1920s, taking the name American Airways Company in 1930. In 1934 it was incorporated as American Airlines, under the AMR Corporation, later based in Dallas, as was the Braniff International Company. Shortly after that its new leader, Cyrus Rowlett "C.R." Smith, encouraged Donald Douglas to create the DC-3. By late 1936, American was flying up to 14 passengers in sleeping berths installed in the DC-3 across the country in 16 hours eastbound and 18 hours westbound. By 1942, American used only that plane for its fleet of 74, which topped United's second-place total in the United States of 62 airliners, including 49 DC-3s. American held its own into the jet age, where we shall return to it, as to United Airlines and other aviation companies.

United, which at times topped American for the most passenger miles flown, also grew out of various mergers of the late 1920s and early 1930s. Most famously, its partners included Varney Air Lines and the Boeing Company, with the latter introducing air-to-ground radio and in 1930, as noted, stewardesses. In December 1934, eight months after American, they and several other companies incorporated United Air Lines under the direction of William "Pat" Patterson, with its headquarters in Chicago.

The company prospered with its use of the "first modern airliner," the Boeing 247, in 1933 and then the DC airliners, as well as from its close ties with Pratt and Whitney for advanced engines. As early as April 1940, it was the first airliner to introduce cheaper coach service, and after the war it was a principal supporter of the four-engine DC-4s, 6s and 7s. In 1954, it was the first airline to employ flight simulators for pilot training, and in 1961 it absorbed Capital Airlines. In 1967, it was the first airline company to clear $1 billion in annual revenues, and after 1993 United pioneered wider ownership with its staff as a way to overcome financial and efficiency problems. It also started West Coast shuttle flights between San Diego and Seattle, as did various airlines between European cities.

In 1971, United's 25,512,953 passengers topped American's 19,244,730, and all but one or two of the world's then over 106 airlines. Until the breakup of the Soviet Union, with its state monopolies, Aeroflot, with over 3000 planes and 600,000 employees, was the largest of all. Founded in 1923, by 1991 it was flying some 138 million passengers, and still over 60 million on some 45,318 flights in 1992. But by 1994 it had broken up into hundreds of separate air carriers. In the remaining big Communist country, however, CAAC (Civil Aviation Administration of China) continued to expand its flights, on some 350 airliners by 1995, for the vast Chinese population as well as for foreign flights.

Slightly older than still-prospering American and United , which continue to alternate leadership in passenger miles, and more famous than them into the jet age, are other famous corporate names, at least two of which, Pan American and Eastern, were forced into bankruptcy in the 1980s. Established, as was Pan Am, to profit from the delivery of air mail after the U.S. Congress sanctioned private entrepreneurship for this in 1925 was the company that became Eastern Airlines. In that year, Harold Pitcairn flew his own "mailwing," and in 1928 won profitable monopolies of the New York to Atlanta and Miami routes. In 1929, North American Aviation bought the company and changed its name to Eastern Air Transport.

In 1934, after the temporary shifting of air mail back to military deliveries exacerbated other financial problems and takeovers by General Motors, the company was reorganized as Eastern Airlines under World War I ace Eddie Rickenbacker. A racing car driver before the war, he had founded Florida Airways before taking work with General Motors. Now he equipped the Eastern subsidiary with DC-2s and 3s, got the financing to purchase the company from GM, and took it to third place behind American and United by 1942. Dominating service in the southeast of the U.S., the company organized World War II troop transport to Brazil and beyond. After the war it continued its growth, and in 1961 organized the first shuttle service between Boston, New York, and Washington, DC. New services to the Caribbean, and the succession as president of astronaut Frank Borman in 1975, at first brought success. But the Airline Deregulation Act of 1978 brought problems for Eastern, as for other U.S. airlines. Acquired by Texas Air Corporation in 1986, as four years earlier Continental Airlines had been, Eastern staggered from crisis to crisis. Despite moves such as giving 25 percent of its stock to employees, it became bankrupt in 1989, and ceased operations in January 1991.

Still-surviving TWA was incorporated in 1928 as Transcontinental Air Transport (TAT) after the merger of several companies. In August 1930 another merger, this time with Western Air Lines, created the first TWA: Transcontinental and Western Air Lines. The company used Charles and Anne Lindbergh to reconnoiter routes, as did Pan American, and in 1933, as mentioned above, its vice-president, Jack Frye, was instrumental in getting Donald Douglas to launch the DC airliners. By 1942, TWA was in fourth place among American domestic airlines, after American, United, and Eastern, and it stayed close to that position, though with difficulty, later in the century. In May 1950, it changed its name to Trans World Airlines, and is still universally known as TWA.

The greatest name of all twentieth century airlines, Pan American World Airways, did not survive. It too grew out of a series of earlier attempts and mergers in the 1920s. Its creator, Juan Terry Trippe, was one of the principal organizers of the commercial revolution in aviation. Learning to fly in a World War I version of the reserve officer programs for college students, he returned to Yale for a 1920 degree. But after two years in a New York bank, Trippe decided to commit his life to expanding the use of aviation. Of an old American family and named for an aunt Juanita, he used his father's inheritance to start, in 1923, Long Island Airways, with nine surplus Navy "Jennys." This beginning failed to generate sufficient business, while the next venture, Colonial Air Transport, won the New York to Boston air mail contract, but then became one of the companies which merged to form American Airlines.

In 1928, after new mergers, a new company won the profitable Key West to Havana air mail route, soon expanded to some Caribbean islands, and took the name of Pan American Airways. A new merger in 1930 with the New York, Rio de Janeiro, and Buenos Aires Air Line, led to the doubling of its fleet of three-engine Fokkers, Sikorsky S-38 "flying boats," and other aircraft, and the landing of an even more profitable South American air mail contract. Until the mid 1930s, over three quarters of the company's revenues came from delivering air mail, but Pan Am soon became the world's largest passenger airline as well. As discussed in Chapter Ten, Trippe organized Pan Am's expansion to the Pacific, with air mail and passenger flights to Hawaii and Manila in 1935 and to Hong Kong by April 1937. By June 1939, Pan Am flights were reaching London, via Newfoundland, and a little later Lisbon and Marseilles, via the Azores. In World War II, Pan Am was the biggest civilian troop carrier and devoted up to three-quarters of its resources to the war effort. Pan Am was close to being America's national airline, and Trippe enjoyed very close ties with the country's most powerful citizens.

After the war, Trippe invested heavily in new planes to increase overseas flights to all continents, in competition especially with TWA. Then, he was more responsible than any other corporate figure for the successful launching of the jet age.

On October 13, 1955, when other airline executives were still skeptical of using big jets, following the crash in early 1954 of two of the first to fly, BOAC "Comets," he ordered 20 of the recently tested Boeing 707s, and encouraged Donald Douglas to enter the competition with an order the same day for 25 DC-8s, still in the planning stage. As he put it, "We ordered the big jets as quickly as we could; then asked our engineers and economists to prove that we had made the right decision." He also made possible the fulfillment of the development of the Boeing 747, which first flew in February 1969, with his order of 25 for $525 million on April 13, 1966. Pan Am later ordered another 21 of that fabulous "wide-body" four-engine jet airliner.

Trippe's retirement in 1968, however, shortly coincided with the first crises of the huge airline. Increased competition, the soaring of fuel prices after 1973, and other problems, including those of the 1963 landmark Pan Am Building in Manhattan, led to escalating financial crises. Pan Am's final death blows followed its 1980 acquisition of National Airlines, whose domestic routes did not coordinate with the 81,430 miles of international routes flown by the larger company. The 1985 sale of Asian routes to United Airlines, and the 1986 beginning of a rival to Eastern's shuttle flights on the East Coast of America, sold to Delta Airlines in 1991, could not prevent the declaring of bankruptcy that same year. To the dismay of its many fans, Pan American Airways ceased all operations in January 1992.

Pan Am's demise was the biggest shock attributed at least in part to the Essential Air Services Program, as the Deregulation Act of 1978 was called. That act expanded greatly, but turbulently, aviation competition in the United States. If airlines were to survive, all thereafter depended on their lowering the cost of air travel per passenger mile. That cost had gone from about five cents a mile with many services in 1970 to over 11 cents a mile with fewer services by 1988.

In addition to the higher fuel and other costs, there were also the costs of the constant expansions thought to be necessary to keep up. Employees of the major airline companies went from 330,495 people in 1982 to 540,412 ten years later. As aircraft sales declined prior to a reversal of that with replacement orders near the turn of the century, on the other hand, jobs in aviation manufacturing temporarily declined, from 1.3 million in 1990 to under one million in 1993. Airline employees included, in 1992, 84,071 flight attendants and 50,852 pilots. The latter had numbered 28,144 ten years before and now relied on some 58,670 mechanics, or about 15,000 more than in 1982. By the 1990s, the 3300 or so planes flew from 425 or more of the some 14,000 airfields in the country. Chicago's O'Hare, handling 66,435,252 passengers on 882,112 flights in 1994, remained the busiest on earth, while Memphis, Tennessee came in second, mostly for 1,653,289 metric tons of freight and the express mail system centered there after 1973 by Federal Express.

Trans-ocean services also illustrated new cost-cutting efforts. The colorful English World War II veteran pilot, Freddie Laker, worked his way to the chairmanship of British United Airways in the 1960s, and in the early 1970s set up his own company to fly "skytrains" between London and New York. But the bigger lines competed with their new APEX fares, offering cheaper service if purchased in advance, and still cheaper travel if the passenger took a chance on "stand-by fares." After considerable success in the late 1970s, Laker Airways ran into increasing headwinds and had to cease flights in February 1982. British Caledonian's extensive air tours also were unable to survive, although disciples of Laker, Tower Air and Virgin Atlantic Airways, held out longer. The oldest of the trans-Atlantic "bargains," on Iceland Air, was still going strong at the end of the century. Icelandic, as it was then called, began cheap flights between America and Europe in 1955. By the 1990s, Virgin Atlantic Airways was a leading low-cost carrier to and from its base in London.

Airlines in the U.S. in the 1980s, like People's Express, cut services even more drastically and reduced their costs to about seven cents a mile, but still did not survive. Some 161 companies went out of business after the deregulation of 1978, while 39 began to fly after 1989. These included: Air South, Carnival Air Lines, Kiwi International Airlines, Mesa Air, Midway Airlines, Nations Air, Tower Air, Valuejet Air Lines, Vanguard Air Lines, Western Pacific Air Lines, and especially Southwest Air Lines. Their average cost per mile continued to climb, but in mid-1996 a revived Pan Am claimed to have cut costs further still.

In the effort to lure more passengers to fill empty seats, various promotions increased the number of passengers but, in the process, American airlines' discount fares went from 36.9 percent of all flights in 1977 to 91.3 percent in 1987, and by 1993 free trips given for "frequent flier miles" made up 7 percent of air traffic in the nation, further cutting into airline profits. In the last quarter-century, U.S. airlines also began to reorganize their routes around "hub" cities as well as to organize flight and passenger planning with ever more powerful computer-based data systems. Both gave greater efficiency for the periodic checkups, substitutions, and scheduling problems arising from the enormous complexity of airline operations. Delta Airlines pioneered the "hub and spoke" system, organizing flights out of its Atlanta base and, by the 1990s, American Airlines' principal hub, the Dallas–Fort Worth airport, for example, was employing 35,000 workers to service 2100 flights a day. Many companies also found it cheaper to lease than to buy airplanes, and by the mid-1990s, close to a third of America's commercial fleet was rented from the International Lease Finance Corporation in California, the Irish GPA Group P.L.C., and some 130 other companies, including competing airlines.

The American airline manufacturer which succeeded best of all, producing up to 60 percent and more of the fabulous new jet airliners, was the Boeing Company of Seattle. The company's origins go back to the early part of the century, when William E. Boeing became hooked on flying after seeing the 1910 Los Angeles Air Show. He proceeded to enroll in Glenn Martin's flying school and took a $10,000 Martin seaplane to his home near Seattle in 1915.

Boeing had been born in Detroit in 1881 of a prosperous timber merchant, and after several years of additional schooling in Switzerland

and in engineering at Yale, made his way to the West Coast the very year of the first Wright brother flights in 1903. In Seattle, he established a lumber and furniture business as well as other enterprises that helped him through the inevitable hard times, such as those following World War I. Then, with a naval officer friend, Conrad Westervelt, he proceeded to build two twin-float B&W seaplanes, which they felt would be superior to others of the day. In May 1916, Boeing flew the first and proceeded to incorporate the Pacific Aero Products Company in July. Westervelt was soon transferred out of Seattle, but William Boeing had found his calling and soon showed his genius.

The time of course was just before America's entrance into World War I, and an improved model C tandem-seat twin-float seaplane was adopted in 1917 by the Navy, with the purchase of over fifty for its expanded training programs. New models designed with the help of brilliant engineers, including Clairmont L. Egtvedt, Philip G. Johnson, and Mike Pavone, were sold to the Army and the firm's name was changed to Boeing Airplane (the second word dropped in May 1961) Company.

After the war, Boeing began cooperation with a former Army flight instructor, Edward Hubbard, who flew the first international air mail in 1919 from Seattle to Vancouver. Boeing made new military sales of bombers and fighters, and by the time of Hubbard's premature death in 1928, the company was in the big leagues, having launched its successful air mail and commercial models, the 40, 80, 204, and Monomail. They flew more and more passengers, some 12 on the Model 80, as well as the profitable Chicago–San Francisco air mail route, and developed other impressive civil and military aircraft. Its subsidiary, the Boeing Air Transport Company, carried about 30 percent of America's mail and passengers by 1930.

Although William Boeing decided to retire in 1934, his dedication to the best research and experimentation and organizational skills ensured the company's success. As he had put it five years before:

> I've tried to make the men around me feel as I do, that we are embarked as pioneers upon a new science and industry in which our problems are so new and unusual that it behooves no one to dismiss any novel idea with the statement that it "can't be done." Our job is to keep everlastingly at research and experiment, to adapt our laboratories to production as soon as practicable, to

let no new improvement in flying and flying equipment pass
us by.

Before his retirement, he had organized close cooperation with the
Pratt and Whitney Engine Company, the Hamilton Propeller Company,
the Stearman Aircraft Company, and other aviation specialists, ensuring
top-of-the-line performance. With his immediate successor, Clairmont
Egtvedt, and Chief Engineer Charles Montheith, he developed, by
February 1932, "the first modern airliner," the 247, with its streamlined
metal fuselage, retractable landing gear, two reduced-drag Hornet engines, and variable-pitch propellers. It was one of the first airplanes to
undergo "static," or deliberate stress, testing, and was adopted by the predecessor of United Airlines.

Boeing had helped form that airline with Edward Hubbard among
others, just before the latter's death in December 1928. Hubbard had also
been instrumental in many other early breakthroughs of the company,
while Boeing's acquisition of the National Air Transport Company, and
other deals, enabled the incorporation of United Airlines in December
1934. Just before that, however, 53-year-old William Boeing resigned all
his aviation posts to protest the June 1934 ruling of Congress that airline
manufacturing and the then 44 existing passenger services had to be kept
separate. That coming on top of the February 1934 presidential transfer
of air mail delivery to U.S. Army aviation—though suspended March 10
after the death of 12 unprepared military pilots—induced Boeing to
avoid any such further political frustrations and quit while he was ahead.

Although, as seen, Douglas with its DC airliners achieved dominance
in commercial aviation into the 1950s, Boeing's 247, 307 Stratoliner, and
314 China Clipper in the mid- and late 1930s, and then the B-17s and
B-29s engineered by Egtvedt as the "father" of the four-engine bombers
of the Second World War, ensured the company's continuing prosperity.
Its engineers had been reduced from 90 to 70 and workers from 1700 to
700 in 1934, but these soon began to increase again. The leadership of
Egtvedt's successor Philip Johnson, as Boeing chairman (prior to his death
in September 1944) furthered still more the company's reputation, as did
outstanding new engineers like Ed Wells, Wellwood Beall, John Steiner,
and George Schairer, and test pilots like Edmund Allen. By 1945,
Boeing's workers had reached 35,000 prior to being reduced to 6000 with
the ending of orders for Flying and Super Fortresses. But, even before its

further take-off in the jet age after the late 1940s, the Boeing 377 Stratocruiser, despite engine and propeller problems, made substantial gains and points; for example, with the popularity of its bar with spiral staircase, in competition with the Douglas DC-4s, 6s, and 7s, and Lockheed Constellations. The company's chief lawyer, William M. Allen, became Boeing president in 1945, and oversaw the continued climb out until his retirement in 1969. We shall return to more about Boeing and other leading aviation companies in the next chapter on the jet age.

Growth in general aviation, or private and commuter flights, accompanied the explosion of flying in commercial aviation. Following a temporary decline in the late 1940s, with the dissipation of the dream of "an airplane in every garage," expansion soon resumed. By 1989, in the United States for example, there were well over a half million licensed private pilots. Of the total of close to 700,000 pilots, there were about 58,000 airline pilots and another 50,000 or so in the armed services, while of the 43,000 female pilots, some 500 were airline pilots and another 625 served in the military. In 1994, an active 283,700 private pilots were flying about 200,000 aircraft, most of them still built by Beech (acquired by Raytheon in 1980), Cessna, Piper, and also Mooney, Pitts, Socata (formerly Aerospatiale General Aviation), Diamond and others. The all-time best-sellers, with over 36,000 produced, were the Cessna 172 Skyhawk and the Piper Cherokee 140. Commuter and executive services, flying Lear jets and other aircraft, also expanded greatly, although the actual production of new small planes declined temporarily, or even ceased for a while, due to legal and other problems. In additon, thousands of modern adventurers witnessed some basic aerodynamics by sailing their gliders, hang gliders, parachutes, paratrekkers, and by sky diving. Many more millions sailed their Frisbees, boomerangs, and rings through the air. Modern versions of Frisbees with up-to-date materials and airfoils began to be marketed after 1957, before long with record throws of over 600 feet.

In addition to the pleasures and convenience of their own aerial ventures, pilots were especially inspired by new record-setting flights, such as Max Conrad's 1961 circling of the world at record speeds above 120 mph in a Piper "Aztec," although taking longer than Wiley Post's somewhat shorter flight of seven days, 18 hours, and forty some minutes in 1933. In 1978, Robert S, Mucklestone established a new round-the-world record of seven days, 13 hours and 13 minutes, from Seattle to Seattle, in a Cessna 210. In mid-June 1993, three French pilots lowered that to three and a third days (80 hours) in a TBM-700 business plane filled with extra fuel and powered by a single Pratt and Whitney 700hp engine.

Taking longer, but making a far more triumphant flight, was the December 14 to 23, 1986, tour of the world in just over nine days without stop by Richard Rutan and Jeanna Yeager in a remarkable 2680-pound craft carrying some 7000 pounds of fuel. It was the first-ever circumnavigation of the world without air-to-air refueling—although understandably taking a bit longer than a flight of three B-52s which on January 18, 1957, with four aerial refuelings, circled the world in 45 hours and 19 minutes. An Air France Concorde bettered that against the wind from Lisbon in 32 hours, 49 minutes, with six stops, October 12–13, 1992, and with the wind to the east from New York in 31 hours, 27.8 minutes, August 15–16, 1995. A Lear Jet completed a tour of the world from Denver to Denver in 49 hours, 21 minutes in February, 1996.

Rutan and Yeager, veterans of supersonic F-100 and helicopter flight, respectively, landed at Edwards Air Force Base on December 23, 1986, after nine grueling days, three minutes and 44 seconds, with a scant 18.3 gallons of fuel remaining. Richard's brother, Burt, already a famous designer with his own factory at Mojave, California, and a stable of imaginative airplanes with wings in front (canards), hinged and tilt wings, and other aeronautical experiments, had proposed the flight as early as 1981. He went on to lead the creation of the largest composite construction civilian airplane yet built, appropriately titled "The Voyager." It was an incredible, catamaran-like twin wing and tail construction, with two streamlined fuel shells sandwiching the central fuselage, which housed the pilots and two engines. One was a pusher in the rear, producing 117 h.p., while the puller propeller in the front delivered 130hp, both delivering great fuel economy. A shorter front wing and 111-foot main wing achieved an astonishing lift-drag ratio of 132 to 1, as against the average of about 20 to 1. Its Hexcel honeycomb construction with new extremely strong and light composite materials such as graphite, and glass and carbon fibers, had been pioneered in the late 1970s.

Other manufacturers sought to perfect "laminar flow" wings and flexible or asymmetrical wingtips to further reduce drag, while airframes built with such techniques by Paul MacCready and others had no motors at all, but were to be driven by solar power, or by human energy. On June 12, 1979, Bryan Allen pedaled one the 22.5 miles from Folkestone,

England, to Cap Gris-Nez, France, in 2 hours and 49 minutes, to equally great astonishment.

Along with these demonstrations of individual heroics, as repeatedly noted above, the veteran surviving airlines of course continued to fly more and more passengers, up to 1.166 billion of them in 1992, and more each year after that. By far the majority of those traveled in the jet airliners. The beautiful and incredibly efficient big jets culminated the revolution in commercial aviation and, with the military jets, are our next subject.

14

The Jet Age

The third greatest miracle of man's taking to the air, after those of the first men in balloons in 1783 and of the Wright brothers in their fixed-wing plane in 1903, is undoubtedly supplied by the jet engine. As children we have all marveled at our rubber balloons sailing across the room when released without tying the nozzle. But how could air pushed out of an engine develop the force to lift hundreds of tons high into the air at such great speeds? As discussed in Chapter One, that is achieved if the engines can provide thrust equal to at least a quarter of the plane's weight, generating the speed necessary for a sufficient rush of air to create the lift for take-off. Propellers do that by using, among other forces, the same pressure differential that generates the lift of the wings and other surfaces. But the low pressure in front of the turning blades in horizontal flight produces forward, not vertical, pressures. In both cases this results from the reactions to the falling pressure given by the faster passage of air across the front and upper surfaces than across the rear and lower surfaces.

The jet engine eliminates the drag and torque of the propellers and produces far stronger forces of propulsion, which are measured in pounds of thrust rather than the horsepower of prop engines. Thrust varies greatly with speed and altitude, and at sea level, moving only one mph, one horsepower is equal to about 375 pounds of thrust. But at 375 mph, the two become about equal and 5000 pounds (2265 kg) of thrust equals 5000hp. Near the speed of sound at 750 mph (1210 kph), 5000 pounds of thrust equals 10,000hp. Conversely, thrust decreases as planes climb, to about half at 25,000 feet, but that is related to and offset by decreasing air pressure and drag. For speeds above about 350 mph, the turbofan becomes markedly superior to propeller engines; above 640 mph, the turbojet is increasingly superior; and above about Mach 3, no compressors are needed at all, given the rush of incoming air. Such engines for ultra-high-speed flight are called ramjets. As will be discussed below, turbine engines using compressed air to drive propellers, or turbo-props, have been widely used also, especially for lower-speed aircraft.

Whereas the huge post-war bomber, the B-36, of the Consolidated Vultee Aircraft Corporation, known as Convair, which first flew in August 1946, had the strongest prop engines yet, six 3800hp Wasp Major engines (the Boeing C-97 "Stratofreighter" and B-50 bomber, successor to the B-29, used four 3500hp Wasp engines, and the DC-7 and Super Constellations, four 3400hp Wright Turbo-Compound engines), the Boeing 747's four Pratt and Whitney JT-9 or General Electric CF-6 engines produce close to 60,000 pounds of thrust each at take-off. The two Airbus 330 Rolls Royce RB-211 engines are rated at 70,000 pounds of thrust, while the two GE-90 or Pratt and Whitney PW 4084 engines for the Boeing 777 have been tested at up to 105,400 pounds of thrust each, although more normally they are rated from 76,400 to 77,200 pounds or so. Indeed, the belief of great engineers—earlier in the century, Sanford Moss of General Electric, and later for the jets, Clarence "Kelly" Johnson of Lockheed, Perry Pratt of Pratt and Whitney, and Ed Wells of Boeing—that ideally airplanes should be built around a good engine or engines, rather than vice versa, seems indisputable. Not surprisingly, with the advance of engine technology, this increasingly became the case for successful planes. As one saying has it, "If the engine is strong enough, it can fly a bathtub."

The jet engine produces its enormous power by harnessing the precision technology and advanced materials of the post-industrial revolution to the Newtonian principle "to every action there is a reaction." The action is produced by the gas-powered turbines that compress and heat the enormous amounts of entering air, which are then expelled by combustion at still higher heat and speed through the engine's tail pipe or nozzle, which is reduced in size to further increase expulsion speeds. That enormous thrust backward thereby drives the airplane forward with increasing speed and efficiency. With fewer working parts, the jet engine also is far more reliable. Where pre-jet age piston engines had a failure about every 4000 hours of flight on average, the jets fail far less often. Advanced turbofan engines have brought the failure rate in cruise to under one every 200,000 hours.

Engine compressors, at first mostly of the centrifugal and later increasingly of the axial type, turning at very high speeds—for example, up to 13,450 rpms in the F-15's Pratt and Whitney 100 engine and even higher in other engines—have achieved pressures as high as 28 times that of the entering air. The air is then compressed still further, up to 1000 pounds or so per square inch, by fuel-fired combustion at temperatures over 1000 Celsius. The compressors operate on the same principle as the piston-engine superchargers developed by the 1920s for more efficient operation at higher altitudes, but in the jet engine the air is not only compressed within the engine but also expelled backward at hundreds of feet per second. As leading authorities put it in John Taylor's *The Lore of Flight*:

> . . . air is drawn in at the intake in a steady stream, is compressed by a compressor, fed to a combustion chamber and heated by burning fuel, and then passes as white-hot gas through a turbine which drives the compressor. The gas may then simply be expelled through a nozzle to provide thrust, or additional turbine stages may be added to extract shaft power to turn a propeller [in turbo-prop aircraft] or other device . . . [such as afterburners to fully burn all of the air for additional thrust but at the cost of much higher fuel consumption].

The fuels used, which also have been continuously improved, are various blends of kerosene with petrol. Most commonly in the early decades of jet flight, they were called Avtur (aviation turbine fuel), JP-1, or Avtag (aviation turbine gasoline), and later JP-4 or 5. Then JP-7 was developed to withstand the very high temperatures of ultra-high-speed flight. The early jet engines consumed fuel almost two-thirds again as fast as the prop engines they replaced. But the efficiency of these engines by the late 20th century enabled the generation of up to eight or more pounds of thrust for every pound of engine weight. The air expelled backward converts its heat and pressure into kinetic energy driving the plane forward with increasing efficiency until it reaches the designed cruising speed. Jets are most efficient in cold, dense air, thrust declining as altitudes or temperatures rise.

The F-16's Pratt and Whitney 200 turbofan, for example, weighs over 3000 of the plane's 14,567-pound empty or 37,500-pound fully loaded weight, but produces close to 25,000 pounds of thrust with afterburner, enabling near-vertical climb or driving the plane to its maximum speed of 1350 mph (Mach 2.050). At a cruising speed of near .9 Mach, the engine produces 15,000 pounds of thrust. In 1903, by contrast, the Wright brothers needed about 13 pounds of engine weight for every horsepower they produced, a ratio that has been improved to better than one hp per pound in advanced piston and turbo-prop engines, but to nowhere near the ratios achieved in the jet engines. The average car motor produces about a half pound of horsepower for every pound, whereas Rockwell International's fuel pump motor for the Space Shuttle turns out 100hp per pound of weight.

Problems such as flameout, or the cessation of combustion for the jet engine, have been mostly solved, and the latter's efficiency has also increased many times. One of the first successful jet engines produced, the Bristol Olympus of 1950 weighed 3520 pounds and produced 9140 pounds of thrust. By contrast, the Boeing 747's four engines each weigh about 9000 pounds and produce up to 60,000 pounds of thrust. The climb rates of military jets well illustrate that increasing efficiency. Where the F-86 of the early 1950s could climb at a 45 degree angle and the F-4 of the 1960s at a 70 degree angle, the F-15s and 16s by the 1970s could go virtually straight up for a certain time. In early 1975, the two Pratt and Whitney 100 engines of 23,930 pounds each of thrust rocketed an F-15 to 65,616 feet (20,000 meters) in 2 minutes, 2.94 seconds.

Much of the increased efficiency for high-speed subsonic flight came with the development of the turbo-superchargers in the 1930s, and by 1958 of the turbofan or fanjet, pioneered by Adrian Lombard of Rolls-Royce. In such engines, larger compressor blades bypass additional air around the engine core, simultaneously increasing thrust and reducing noise and fuel consumption. The most powerful engines are turbofans with high bypass ratios leading to maximum thrust. Pure jets such as the Rolls-Royce/SNECMA (Société Nationale d'Etude et Construction de Moteurs d'Aviation) "Olympus" are used for supersonic craft like the Concorde and, as mentioned, ramjets for still higher speeds above Mach 3 or so. The turbine blades have had to be constructed with new alloys to withstand temperatures up to 1180 Celsius or more and stresses up to 35,000 pounds per square inch as the blades rotate at speeds up to 100,000 rpm!

The expertise and care going into these advanced machines can be illustrated by the fact that 500,000 hours of testing was done for the General Electric CF-6 turbofan. Another example can be imagined from the July 1995 test to see if a Boeing 777 CE-90 engine could cope with the ingestion of an eight-pound Canada goose being fired into it at full throttle!

As noted in Chapter Seven, a Romanian aviator claimed to have made a "hop" by jet at Paris in 1910, and in the mid-1920s two English engineers proposed the use of gas-powered turbine power to drive propellers which led to the turbo-props of the 1950s. Two decades before that, the first functioning jet engines were being developed in England and Germany, as mentioned in Chapter Twelve. The German Heinkel 178, using the 1934 patent of Hans-Joachim von Ohain, made the first true jet flight of almost a minute above Rostock, on the Baltic, on August 27, 1939, four days before the German invasion of Poland. Improved Heinkel jets, including the two-engine He-280, took to the air in April 1941, immediately breaking existing speed records and seeing some limited military action before the end of the war. A Heinkel 162 set a new speed record of 520 mph in early 1945, and the twin jet Messerschmidt 262 soon carried that to 540 mph.

The Englishman RAF pilot Frank Whittle had been the first to patent a feasible jet engine back in 1930, but had to wait until 1937 to ground-test his machine. On May 15, 1941, his Gloster Meteor jet took to the air above the RAF's Cranwell Field, and by September attained 370 mph with 850 pounds of thrust. After more engine improvements, Meteors saw action in the last year of the war, and a little later a Gloster Meteor F-4 set a new speed record of 606.38 mph on November 7, 1945.

Whittle shared his knowledge with the U.S., shipping a turbojet across the Atlantic. General Electric developed an improved version and the Bell Aircraft Corporation of Buffalo, New York, used it to fly the XP-59A "Airacomet" in October 1942. Lockheed's breakthrough P-80 "Shooting Star" first flew on January 8, 1944, and its model R raised the Meteor's speed record to 623.74 mph on June 19, 1947. It saw military action in the Korean war after June 1950, followed by the Republic F-84 "Thunderstreak" and the North American F-86 "Sabre," which became famous especially for their duels with the first effective Soviet jet fighter, the MiG-15. All these planes advanced aerodynamic knowledge of the rapidly increasing high-speed flight.

By then, experimental planes had mastered the problem of exceeding the sound barrier. That problem had seemed insurmountable, and in the popular imagination almost defeated the promise of jet flight. It had already troubled high-speed dives of the Hawker Typhoon and Tempest, the P-38, 40, 47, 51, and other World War II aircraft. The problem was first noticed in 1938 and widely so by 1941, as buffeting occurred when the air accelerated over wing surfaces to transsonic speeds as diving planes exceeded 450 or so mph. Some had broken up in flight, and just after the war the problem became public knowledge after it appeared to kill Geoffrey de Havilland, son of the aviation pioneer and founder of the English aviation manufacturer of the same name. Taking off from Hatfield on September 27, 1946, in a DH-108 experimental jet named the *Swallow*, with swept wing and tail based on German research, the plane disintegrated half an hour later. Apparently, as he approached Mach 0.875, 7,500 feet up, "violent longitudinal pitching oscillations" created G loads that broke up the plane. A popular 1952 British film, *The Sound Barrier* (*Breaking the Sound Barrier* in its U.S. release), dramatized that and other test flights even as it falsified the solution, which had nothing to do with reversing the controls as in the film.

The problem arose from the fact that as a plane approaches the speed of sound of 761.20 mph at sea level—about 650 mph above 35,000 feet, and over the wings and other surfaces above about 450 mph—the air compresses into a shock wave, or a wall of air unable to adjust to the onrushing plane. At transsonic speeds above about Mach .7 or 532.84 mph near sea level, where airflow is a mixture of subsonic and supersonic, drag and control forces increase drastically and the plane becomes unstable in the turbulent air, which pitches the nose up or down and violently shakes the wing and tail. Once the shock waves pass, giving the sonic boom, with the acceleration of the plane past the speed of sound, the airflow again becomes stable and flight smooth.

New aeronautical understandings and developments greatly improved the ability to master the transition to supersonic flight. Structural adjustments made supersonic flight progressively problem-free and efficient. They included dive flaps installed by 1944 on P-38s and other hot fighters, swept wings already used by German jet fighters such as the Me-262, higher tail and other vertical surfaces, including "ventral" fins under the tail and "dorsal" top fins, and vertical fins under the wings. By the late 1950s, "coke-bottle"-shaped fuselages to reduce drag further smoothed the transition to supersonic speeds and beyond.

The breakthrough came with the development of three Bell X-1 research aircraft after 1945. As its four-chamber, 6000-pound-thrust rocket could sustain only 2.5 minutes of flight, it was to be dropped from a B-29. The plane, with small, strong wings some 3.5 inches thick at right angles to the bullet-shaped fuselage, was first tested in October 1946, over fabled Edwards Air Force Base Flight Test Center in the Mojave Desert 150 miles northeast of Los Angeles. It used its own long runways as well as nearby dry lake beds like Muroc or Rogers. On December 9, it made its first powered flight after being dropped from 27,000 feet, and subsequently a series of tests attained ever greater speeds. On October 14, 1947, then Captain Charles "Chuck" Yeager reached Mach 1.06 (700 mph) at 43,000 feet. He had been released at 20,000 feet and climbed while accelerating through increasing buffeting until nearing the sound barrier and smooth flight.

Although the achievement was kept secret until June 1948, the 27-year-old Yeager rapidly became known as the hottest of the hot pilots, the one with the most "right stuff," in Tom Wolfe's memorable phrase. A World War II ace with over 13 kills, he had trained as a test pilot at Wright Field, Dayton, before making the epochal flight. He was already well known in aviation circles for his wartime dogfighting and post-war test-flying skills, and his West Virginia drawl came to be increasingly imitated by pilots. He was lucky enough to have survived until then, having been wounded and shot down on March 5, 1944; but he had been able to parachute into Occupied France and make a harrowing escape to Spain.

Now in 1947, he enjoyed another stroke of fortune and overcame a nearly prohibitive accident. Arriving at the test center at Muroc, he replaced Bell test pilot Chalmers "Slick" Goodlin, who had performed the early tests, when the army balked at Bell's demands for the civilian's exorbitant "hazard pay." Then Yeager almost goofed it the night before, when he and his wife, "Glamorous Glynnis," after whom he named the X-1 and other planes, decided on a midnight horseback ride outside the Pancho Bar, fabled for its post-flight parties. Galloping back, he failed to see that the yard gate had been closed and as the horse hit it, he pitched over, breaking two ribs. Yet, he was able to find a sympathetic doctor to bind him and an ingenious idea to use part of a broomstick to avoid the pain which would be caused by the necessary stretching of his arm to close the door through which he climbed from the B-52 into the X-1 as it rose above 7000 feet.

Such stories of course illustrate the truism that the greats make their own luck, and Yeager needed to demonstrate that almost immediately with his second try to break the barrier. Again released from a B-29 at 20,000 feet, this time he discovered he had no electrical power and hence could neither ignite his rockets nor communicate his problem. Using an emergency valve by hand to release the 5000 pounds of volatile fuel which would have collapsed his landing gear and exploded, he nonetheless managed to land safely, after a screaming dive with neither power, assisted controls, nor the ability to make known his plight.

Yeager went on to break the sound barrier over a dozen times, reaching Mach 1.45 on March 26, 1948, before the Air Force made the flights public in June. An improved version of the DH-108 that had killed Geoffrey de Havilland two years earlier passed the sound barrier in England on September 9, 1948, but in a dive. Speeds continued to increase, and in mid-December 1953, Yeager piloted a new improved X-la to Mach 2.4 (1612 mph) at 74,200 feet, bettering the record Mach 2 just set by another famous test pilot, Scott Crossfield, in a Douglas Skyrocket.

The year 1953 also saw the first level supersonic flight by a ground-launched airplane, the North American F-100 Super Sabre. On August 20 it streaked to a new world speed record for a ground-launched plane of 822 mph (1323 kph) above Edwards Air Force Base, California. New "Century Series" supersonic fighters from the mid-1950s progressively went faster and more smoothly, with "coke-bottle" fuselages and other aerodynamic advances. The Convair delta wing F-102 and 106, the Republic F-105 Thunderbird or "Thud," and the Lockheed F-104 Starfighter were especially exciting aircraft.

As we shall see with the transition to the space age, Crossfield was one of the principal testers for the X-15 and SR-71, planes that were transitional between the traditional planes and space ships. Crossfield, Joe Walker, Bob White, Joe Engle, Iven Kincheloe, and others were, with Chuck Yeager, standouts among the some 540 test pilots—from whom were also chosen the astronauts in the late 1950s, the subject of our succeeding chapters.

Flying much "lower and slower" but making their own contributions to the new knowledge of flight were the turbo-props and helicopters.

Given the almost two-thirds-higher fuel consumption and longer runways required by the jets, the turbo-props seemed an attractive alternative in the early 1950s. They used gas turbine engines to turn propellers, a gear box linking the two, and used less fuel and created less noise than the early jets. They were especially efficient at what seemed in the early 1950s the ideal speed of perhaps 300 to 450 mph. The Rolls-Royce Dart, used in a British Lancaster bomber in 1947, became the first practical turbo-prop, producing initially 990hp and eventually 2,000. It was used the following year on the first successful turbo-prop airliner, the four-engined Vickers Viscount, which entered widespread service by 1953, using Darts by then improved to 1480hp. A Bristol Britannia carrying up to 139 people entered service in 1957, soon making the first turbine-powered flight across the North Atlantic.

The similarly sized Vickers Vanguard, with four Rolls-Royce Tyne engines, first flew in 1959, as did the same year the most successful American turbo-prop airliner, the Lockheed Electra (not to be confused with the 1934 two-engined Lockheed craft of the same name). It was powered with four Allison turbo-props, and Lockheed used an improved version of that engine to power the still widely used military transport, the C-130 Hercules. Like the Soviet Union's Antonov 12 and later models, it could carry a 44,000-pound payload, or some 92 troops. After its first flight with Aeroflot in 1961, the Tupelov TU-114, with four double-bladed engines, became the largest turbo-prop airliner in service, matched later by a similar Tupelov "Bear," for military use. Later U.S. transports included the high-bypass turbofan jet-powered Boeing C-135, Lockheed's C-5A and C-141, and by 1994 the McDonnell Douglas C-17.

In the West, the French-Italian Avions Transport Regional (ATRs), British Aerospace (Jetstreams), Canadair Avroliners and Challengers, Embraer Brasilias, Fokker, Saab, Grumman, Beech, Cessna, Fairchild, Piper, Astra, and others all introduced smaller pressurized turbo-props—as well as "junior jets"—in and after the 1960s to dominate many of the commuter airlines. So did Lear, Lockheed, Falcon, Gulfstream, Bombardier, Starcraft, Visionaire, and others for corporate jets. William Lear, who died in 1978, designed the first successful auto-pilots in the late 1940s, and went on to pioneer the development of smaller jets. The company founded in 1919 by aviation pioneer Anthony Fokker, who had died in December 1939, also was especially important for the expansion of passenger services. Its 44-passenger F-27 "Friendship," after 1956 was one of the most fuel-efficient turbo-props, as were its F-28 and F-100 jet transports. Despite recent financial problems, the Fokker company continues to pioneer new techniques for the use of composite materials of glass and carbon fibers, new structures, and still more fuel-efficient "propfan" engines.

Boeing and McDonnell Douglas also gave much attention to the new propfans, in part to argue that their new planes would achieve up to 40 percent more fuel efficiency than Airbus and other rival airliners. By 1994, U.S. airlines, especially for flights of under 500 miles on over 375 routes, were going back to the use of prop-jet or propfan aircraft carrying 65 or so passengers. One such, a French-Italian ATR-72, crashed south of Chicago on October 31, 1994, killing all 68 aboard. By the mid-1990s, such planes were carrying over 50 million passengers in America, or some 10 percent of domestic traffic, at costs less than a third those of the small est jet airliners. By the new century, propfans, with counter-rotating propellers fixed behind jet engines, are expected to become increasingly prominent.

The pure jet engine, however, was and is the wave of the future in aviation. That is the case even for helicopters, the most widely seen of all aircraft, given their uses in the cities of the world. From the 1950s on, engineers also began to apply turbine-engine technology for greatly improved helicopter engines to drive their rotors, which were increasingly made from high-strength composites of fiberglass, carbon fibers, and graphite, sealed with epoxy or phenol-formaldehyde resin. Those developments came mostly after the death in 1972 of the person who did most to develop the modern helicopter, Kiev born Igor Sikorsky.

Sikorsky envisaged such machines even before he became famous in 1913 for the first four-engine craft, a biplane that carried eight passengers aloft in Russia on a record flight of 1 hour and 54 minutes. But his greatest fame came with his development in Stratford, Connecticut, after December 10, 1940, of the VS-300 prototype of the modern helicopter. Its single rotor whirling above the cabin to provide the necessary lift, with a small tail rotor tilted to counteract torque and provide directional control, became the standard model of future helicopters. His Sikorsky S-55, which first flew in November 1949, even flew in stages across the Atlantic from July 13 to 31, 1952. On the last day of May and the first of June 1967, a Sikorsky HH-3C managed a trip to England non-stop, with refueling. A Bell Model 206L staged a round-the-world trip from September

1 to 30, 1982, and another accomplished that solo the following year.

Helicopters, however, have been far more widely used for short flights in and around the growing cities of the world, especially to and from airports and for emergency services. A Bell Model 47 began the first commercial passenger trips by helicopter after March 8, 1946, and they became ubiquitous thereafter. In addition to their short flights to airports and elsewhere, they became essential for emergency work by medical, fire, and police services.

They also saw great service in post-1945 military conflicts. In the Korean War, the Sikorsky S-56 and other helicopters were unarmed, but transported enormous amounts of supplies and wounded soldiers. They first used suppressive fire in the French-Algerian conflict, and far more so in the second Vietnam War. There the Bell AH-1 Huey-Cobra was especially destructive, with up to 2000 a day flying and their 16 barrels able to fire an incredible 6000 rounds a minute. Only refitted DC-3s, the AC-47, sardonically called "Puff the Magic Dragon," and the four-engine Lockheed turbo-prop, the AC-130 Hercules, could throw more firepower at the ground.

Boeing CH-47 Chinooks were used mainly to transport up to 44 combat troops each, and the Sikorsky HH-53 "jolly green giant" for the rescue of downed servicemen. The Soviets built equivalent gunships and used them in Afghanistan, such as the Mikhail Mil MI-26 Halo attack helicopter, which began flights in 1985. It was then the largest operational helicopter, but its 105-foot main rotor spanned less than half that of the earlier Russian twin-rotor Mil MI-12. By the 1990s, there were even bigger military helicopters, such as the 16-ton American Sikorsky CH-53 Super Stallion, capable of carrying 43 soldiers at speeds above 200 mph. It participated in the dramatic rescue of U.S. Air Force Captain Scott O'Grady six days after his F-16 had been shot down over Bosnia on June 2, 1995.

Another Slavic name, Frank Piasecki, son of a Polish tailor who emigrated to the U.S., founded in 1943 a company in Philadelphia which competed with Sikorsky and Bell for the booming market in helicopters. It became the Vertol Aircraft Corporation and was bought by the Boeing Company in 1960. The venerable Bell Aircraft Company became another major producer of the vertical take-off craft, as did McDonnell Douglas. From the 1970s on, turbine-propelled tilt rotors advanced speeds for helicopters like the Sikorsky S-61 and S-92 to up to 300 knots or more, and led to the twin tilt-rotor V-22 Osprey, developed after the late 1980s by Boeing and Bell-Textron. (Textron, a parachute maker in World War II, acquired Bell in 1961 and Cessna and General Dynamics in 1992.) The Osprey, along with the British Harrier vertical take-off jet fighter (about which more shortly), seemed to pioneer the advance toward the ultimate idea of high-speed planes needing no runways.

In the 1950s, as military uses and developments of engine performance progressively proved the superiority of jets for high-speed longer-distance flights, their use in commercial aviation was only a matter of time. As had been the case after the Wright brothers, Europeans took the lead at first, but then were far surpassed by Americans. The first jetliner was Britain's De Havilland Comet. On July 27, 1949, less than three years after the death probing the sound barrier of son Geoffrey de Havilland, the first model took to the air. The following year it impressed, among others, Boeing chairman William Allen at the Farnborough Air Show. It made the first-ever scheduled service by jet on May 2, 1952, with a 6724 mile flight from London to Johannesburg. Its four Ghost turbojets, each producing 4450 pounds of thrust, subsequently carried up to 36 passengers at 490 mph on flights to India, Singapore, and Tokyo.

But then disaster struck, with at least three disintegrations in mid-air. On the first anniversary of the first flight, one broke up in a storm near Calcutta, and on the clear day of January 10, 1954, another exploded even as the pilot was announcing his climb through 26,000 feet over the sea near the isle of Elba, Italy. They were grounded definitively after a third Comet exploded nearby between Naples and Sicily on April 8. Then, a rigorous process of detective work, with the subjection of the plane underwater in a huge tank to the equivalent of almost 10,000 hours of pressurization and depressurization similar to those in flight, caused the thin metal skin to split, proving that metal fatigue was the cause of the explosive decompressions.

De Havilland sought to master solutions for this problem with a fourth model of the Comet, as did new models of Soviet airliners, such as the Tupelov 104, which for a time after it began service with Aeroflot in September 1956 was the only jetliner in service. But it was the Boeing and other American companies which first achieved definitive breakthroughs to prevent explosive decompression caused by metal fatigue, thereby ensuring ever safer jet flight. Using knowledge developed from the pioneering Strategic Air Force bomber, the B-47, which flew initially in December 1947, and from the twice-as-big 480,000-pound maximum-weight B-52, which first flew on April 15, 1951, Boeing used four-times-thicker metal skins braced with titanium at regular intervals as "stoppers" to prevent any tearing apart of its planes. The square windows of the first Comets were replaced by more aerodynamically sound round ones, and other structural and training improvements followed.

Douglas and other manufacturers followed suit, while engine makers General Electric, Rolls-Royce, SNECMA, and Pratt and Whitney pioneered the development of ever-better jet engines. The latter's first commercial jet engine of January 1950 and subsequent models were especially important for opening the way to the miracle of the jet age in commercial aviation. Founded in 1925, Pratt and Whitney four years later associated with the United Aircraft and Transpotation Company, and later in the century became a division of United Technologies.

Before returning to commercial aviation, new aspects of the breakthroughs in military aviation need consideration. After the development of the first jet engines, the sweeping back of the wings offered the most critical improvement in performance. At higher speeds this design change greatly reduced drag, especially for the large wings required for heavy loads, while such top-speed, smaller craft as the F-104, and the experimental X-1 and X-15, had short straight, or slightly swept, wings. The Germans pioneered wing shapes after their first jet flight in August 1939, even producing a forward-swept wing as on the 1944 Ju-287 jet bomber. The Me-262 wing had an 18.5-degree angle, while the Gloster Meteor and De Havilland Comet also had slightly swept wings.

NACA at Langley Field, Virginia, had begun such studies also, and just after the war experts like Boeing's George Schairer initiated further wind-tunnel research into wing shapes. He recommended an angle of 35 degrees as against the maximum of 29 degrees considered best by the Germans (based on the pioneering work of Ludwig Prandtl at the University of Göttingen on the effects of "boundary layer" drag of wings). The idea was carried out for the construction in Seattle of the first Strategic Air Command (SAC) jet bomber, the B-47 Stratojet, which had been designed first for straight wings. Another pioneering innovation, engineered by Boeing designer George Martin and brilliantly demonstrated by the B-47, was the suspension of its six General Electric J-35, then J-47, engines in pods under the wings. They were the first American axial-flow turbojets, and four were hung in two inboard nacelles, the other two farther out. The plane reduced the transcontinental speed in 1949 to a mere 3 hours and 46 minutes. Later big jets, like the Boeing 747, commonly used a 37-degree angle of wing sweep.

On the 44th anniversary of the Wright brothers' triumph, December 17, 1947, jet-assisted take-off (JATO) was used for the first flight of the B-47, to boost by 18,000 pounds its six engines' 24,000 (later 30,000) pounds of thrust. Drag chutes were deployed after touchdown, because of the high landing speed at close to 140 knots by the 200,000-pound bomber, and approach chutes were also tested, but not used until the B-52. The early commercial airline jets then developed "clamshell" shutters, also known as "deflector doors" or "buckets," to divert the outrushing air forward, thereby slowing landing speed. Although at first without much efficiency, they became the standard means of slowing the landing of big jet airliners, and later, engine thrust reversal has improved to up to 80 percent that of the engines' forward thrust.

A more serious problem than its high landing speed for the B-47 as the first big swept-wing aircraft was its stability at higher speeds in flight. Above about 470 mph, the upward lift pressure raised the wings sufficiently to offset the use of the ailerons, creating a reversal-of-controls situation. At still higher speeds nearing the speed of sound, shock waves disrupted airflows and the nose tended to pitch up, possibly inducing a spin with abrupt nose downturns. Near Mach .84, often following corrections to the nose-up indication, there could occur an opposite "tuck under" phenomenon in which the plane began to dive. With the help of information from NACA, which had been long studying these problems, Boeing and other engineers were able to install wing tabs, called vortex generators, and new Mach or pitch-trim compensators that automatically triggered as the plane entered critical numbers above .75 of the speed of sound, establishing control over most of these effects.

The equally serious problem of "Dutch roll," or yawing, usually caused by over-controlling at lower speeds or by turbulence-induced sideslipping, was solved by new training methods and by the installation of yaw dampers on the jets' rudders. Later planes like the 707 used boosters for more rudder power and taller tails to prevent the problem. The name "Dutch roll" apparently derived from an ice-skating maneuver in Holland. Improved types of speed breaks or "spoilers" on the tops of wings were also developed for the new high-speed aircraft, and later, tailerons or tail surfaces which folded outward. By the 1990s, new airliners were equipped with rising wingtips, or "winglets," to add lift and reduce vortices and drag.

Boeing produced some 1400 B-47s, and on Air Force orders, the designs and lessons incorporated into them were shared with rivals Lockheed and Douglas, which manufactured another 700. Therefore, the B-47 became the forerunner of commercial jet airliners to come, while its bigger successor, the B-52 Stratofort, made known still more lessons of high-speed swept-wing flight for even bigger planes.

More than twice as big as the B-47, with a gross take-off weight of 480,000 pounds, the B-52's eight Pratt and Whitney J-57 fanjet engines were improved to 17,000 pounds of thrust each and drove the giant machine to 50,000 feet at 600 mph. The Air Force insisted on changing the B-47's tandem seating for pilot and co-pilot to the more convention-al side-by-side arrangement. Then the giant plane refined aerial refueling methods, as demonstrated by the 24,325-mile trip, in January 1957, around the world in 45 hours, 19 minutes by three Stratoforts using four refuelings by C-97 tankers.

Boeing produced some 744 of the giant bombers in eight different models, culminating in the B-52H. The awesome strength of the enor-mous airplane was demonstrated by a maneuver developed to escape any possible release of a nuclear weapon at low altitude, namely a Cuban Eight half-loop followed by a half roll to change direction a full 180 degrees in the minimum time. The first B-52 flight was on April 15, 1951, and some were still flying 40 years later in the Persian Gulf War. The release of their 30-ton bomb loads on some 126,615 sorties made up about a third of the weight of bombs dropped on Indochina from 1965 to 1973.

Boeing's success with the B-47 and B-52 after 1947 and 1951, respectively, put it into the best position to seize dominance of the soon-to-boom commercial jet airliner market. From its inception, transferring the superior performance of its military bombers to the civilian field was the vision of its leaders. As noted above, after founder William Boeing's retirement in mid-1934, leadership passed to fellow engineers Clairmont Egtvedt and Philip Johnson before the succession of lawyer William M. Allen for the launching of the jet age. On Johnson's death in 1944, Allen became President the next year, Egtvedt remaining chairman until retir-ing in 1966, three years before Allen did.

Following their impressive performance with the B-47 and observing early successes of the De Havilland Comet, on April 22, 1952, the Boeing directors decided to "go for it." They authorized the beginning of work on a jetliner that, powered by four increasingly powerful Pratt and Whitney turbojets, could carry almost three times the Comet's original 36 passengers. That was ten days before the latter plane's first flight, but two years before its grounding due to the fatal "metal fatigue" disasters. The 1954 Comet crashes naturally unnerved Boeing, as well as Douglas, which had begun studying the possibilities of jet airliners. But their engineers, now helped by those of De Havilland and elsewhere, were already solving the problems of the "explosive decompression" due to "metal fatigue" which doomed the Comet, and they were ever more confident that big jets represented the future of commercial aviation. Lockheed and Convair would soon follow.

The problem of convincing the big airlines to buy the new planes, after the crash of the Comets, however, remained enormous, complicated by new problems of noise control and the need for up to two-mile-long runways. For a time after the grounding of the Comet in April 1954, the 50-passenger Tupolev 104 was the only jetliner in service. It first flew on June 17, 1955, and the Soviet Union's Aeroflot began seven-hour, one-stop flights with it from Moscow to Omsk and Irkutsk on September 15, 1956. But the breakthrough of the Boeing 707 was not far off. And if the decision to go ahead with the work for it in April 1952 was the biggest gamble in Boeing's history, the October 13, 1955, decision of Pan Am's Juan Trippe to buy 20 of the B-707s, as well as to order 25 of the still-to-be-tested Douglas DC-8s, was the biggest gamble in any airline company's history, given the enormous financing required for a then seemingly risky product.

Boeing won its bet with Trippe to produce the airliner ahead of schedule, and Pan Am soon ordered another 25. In 1956, Boeing's civil airline orders topped those of Douglas for the first time. Then, on October 26, 1958, three weeks after a BOAC Comet 9 made the first trans-Atlantic crossing in a smaller jet, it inaugurated the jet age of the future with a flight from New York to Paris on a Boeing 707-121. The first commercial jet flight in the U.S. came six weeks later, on December 10, 1958, from New York to Miami. By mid-1964, Pan Am was flying 214 jet flights a week across the Atlantic, as well as others to all corners of the world. In August 1969, chief competitor TWA sent a 707 around the world in 60 hours, including stops. But the share of profitable trans-

Atlantic flights of Pan Am and TWA steadily dropped—from 80 percent in 1947 to 32 percent by 1962 and less thereafter. Pan Am also helped launch the Boeing 747 with 25 orders on April 13, 1966.

As discussed in the previous chapter, that prestigious airline folded in 1992 and competitor TWA barely survived. By 1982, Japan Air Lines surpassed Pan Am for international travel, with British Airways, Lufthansa, and Air France leading Pan Am and Japan Airlines by 1990. American, Delta, Northwest, and United Airlines also greatly extended their overseas routes, and American and United carried the most passengers of all, considering domestic as well as international flights. They were followed in order by British Airways (absorbing U.S. Air in 1992), Northwest (linked with KLM), Delta (linked with Virgin Atlantic), and Air France. By 1991, Japan Airlines was in seventh position, with TWA eighth and Lufthansa ninth.

The 1990s then saw a series of mergers to cope with the enormous competition and with the decline of defense orders after the end of the Cold War. The biggest such merger occurred with the Northrop Corporation's acquisition of the Grumman Corporation in March 1994, followed six months later by Lockheed's merger with Martin Marietta not long after their separate acquisitions of parts of General Dynamics and General Electric Aerospace. The new Lockheed-Martin Corporation superseded McDonnell Douglas as America's largest defense contractor and became second to Boeing in overall aviation manufactures. Also in 1994, the German consortium Deutsche Aerospace acquired the venerable Fokker Royal Netherlands Aircraft Factories, and there was continuous talk of other mergers both of manufacturers and airlines, including by November 1995 that of America's two largest aviation companies, Boeing and McDonnell Douglas. The next year, the two biggest engine companies, General Electric, in partnership with SNECMA of France, and the Pratt and Whitney division of United Technologies, began cooperation to construct a more powerful engine of 72,000 to 84,000 pounds' thrust for a new model of the Boeing 747.

The miracle of the incredible take-off of commercial jet aviation after 1958 was almost aborted when a Pan Am 707-120 narrowly escaped crashing into the North Atlantic in December 1958, only two months after the beginning of service. Flying from Paris to New York at 35,000 feet, it suddenly went into a spin. Apparently the Mach trim device failed to function, or had not been set properly, and the plane "tucked under" as it neared the speed of sound. Making matters still worse was the fact that the commander, Captain Waldo Lynch, was chatting with happy passengers in the rear at the time, bragging about the wonders of the new airplane. Crawling back to the cockpit, he and co-pilot Sam Peters, with great difficulty, were able to level the wings of the plunging plane and stop its dive, but not before it had reached 6000 feet. One can imagine the panic on board. The plane reached Mach .95 and sustained G forces beyond the design limit of 3.75, creating among other effects a bend in the wings and two black eyes for the pilot. The tail stabilizers, wing panels, and ailerons were damaged. Yet the plane was able to make it to Gander, Newfoundland, and then back to Seattle for repairs. The near-tragedy in fact proved the astonishing solidity of the plane and may have salvaged the jet age itself.

Similar stories kept occurring, if with declining frequency, as transsonic and other new flight problems became better understood. But the computers used increasingly in the jet age from the late 1950s on sometimes caused other problems. One of the most dramatic came on February 19, 1985, when a China Airlines 747 flying from Taipei to Los Angeles plunged 32,000 feet below its cruise altitude of 41,000 feet.

The nightmare began after the plane's right wing began to dip as it flew through turbulence nearing the California coast, and moved sharply down when the computer tried to compensate for the quitting of a right engine after the auto-throttle varied the output of the four engines to cope with the turbulence. It is thought that had the pilots, who had been flying for ten hours already, fully disconnected the auto-pilot and taken full manual control in time, they might have prevented the escalating series of events. As it was, the auto-pilot over-compensated for first the turbulence, then the engine failure, and forced the plane into an "aileron roll." Its other engines quit and it spun upside down for some two minutes before the pilots, who had finally assumed manual control, were able to recover and restart the engines, 9000 feet above the Pacific. What an approach for the landing at San Francisco! All passengers and crew were safe, but badly shaken, as one can easily imagine. Naturally there followed improvements in both the computer-based auto systems and the pilot training necessary to cope with such emergencies.

Something one could try to avoid but not prepare for struck a British Airways 747 flying over Indonesia about the same time. Ash from a recent volcanic explosion caused all four engines to flameout and they could be restarted only at 12,000 feet after descent from over three times that high. Another British Airways flight had an equally narrow and bizarre escape on June 10, 1990. The pilot, 41-year-old Timothy Lancaster, was sucked out into the slipstream of his De Havilland Bac 111 Trident en route from Birmingham to Malaga, Spain, when his cockpit window burst at 23,000 feet. The co-pilot and other crew members were able to grab the legs of the captain, whose clothes were immediately stripped off by the wind, and hold on until an emergency landing in the south of England!

There have been innumerable other stories of narrow escapes— whether missed approaches and go-arounds, fallen engines or exploded doors, clear air, jet wash, and storm turbulence or wind-shear buffeting and countless other aviation adventures, not to speak of the inevitable crashes. But surely no story can top that of the Aloha Airlines Boeing 737 which lost one-third of the roof of its fuselage and still landed safely on April 29, 1988. With the sudden decompression at 24,000 feet, one flight attendant was sucked out of the gaping hole, and two-thirds of the 89 passengers were injured, but the safe landing fifteen minutes later of that flight by pilot Robert Schornstheimer on the beautiful island of Maui midway from Hilo to Honolulu was another miracle of flight. Pictures that flashed around the world showed what looked like half a plane blown away. The remnants holding everyone except the unfortunate attendant had been able to survive only because the rest of the 20-year-old fuselage held together. That had not been the case of a Far Eastern Air Transport which blew completely apart in 1981, killing all 110 aboard. Both episodes were apparently due to the same metal fatigue that had doomed the Comet a quarter-century before. Today, better knowledge and exper- tise together with new inspections, maintenance, and refinishings are able to prevent more such incidents almost entirely, and, as we have seen, fly- ing is the safest of all means of transportation, given the distance traveled.

By the late 20th century, the European commercial aviation companies achieved near-equal prominence with the American giants, which is pre- dicted for Japanese and other Asian enterprises in the future. As there have been frequent references to such non-American contributions to the history of aviation, it remains to supply additional information on Airbus Industrie, the consortium of France (37.9 percent ownership by Aéro- spatiale), Germany (37.9 percent ownership by Deutsche Aerospace), and

England (20 percent ownership by British Aerospace), with a Spanish company holding the remaining 4.2 percent. By the 1980s it was producing Boeing's biggest competition for jet airliners. Formed in December 1970, the group also had participation from other European countries and their aviation companies, such as Germany's Daimler-Benz Aerospace (DASA), Holland's Fokker, Italy's Alenia, and Spain's CASA.

As seen, British Aerospace had already been responsible for half the achievement, with Aérospatiale, of the Mach 2 Concorde. That astonishing plane, almost a decade in the making, flew first on March 2, 1969, and entered service on January 21, 1976, with simultaneous departures from Paris and London, for Rio de Janeiro and Bahrain respectively. Miraculous aspects of its flight have been discussed in Chapter One, while here we may note the delay of the United States and Russia to develop supersonic commercial aviation. The Soviets actually were the first to fly a supersonic airliner, the slightly larger TU-144, on December 31, 1968. But they soon grounded it due to vibration, fuel, and other problems—climaxed by the crash of a demonstration model at the Paris Air Show of 1973, it is thought because of pilot error. In the U.S., despite extensive research and design by Boeing, Douglas, Lockheed, and the government, begun as in England and France in the mid-1950s, no supersonic airliner has ever flown in the 20th century. Massive publicity about possible pollution, noise, sonic booms and other problems prevented even the testing of a prototype, as Boeing had planned for 1976.

With their flagship Concorde, France also was the biggest builder of the Airbus series in its factories at Toulouse. Airbus Industrie did most of the designs, cockpits, and avionics there, and assembled parts flown in from its European partners on specially designed transports known as "Super Guppies." For example, fuselages and tails were usually constructed in Germany and wings in England.

Airbus Industrie was able to build on France's extensive contributions to the early history of flight, and the genius of later aviation designers like Marcel-Ferdinand Bloch. After World War II, he founded Avions Marcel Dassault, taking the *nom de résistance* of his brother, Dassault (literally, "on the attack"). In 1967, he bought the firm founded by pre-war pioneer Louis Breguet, the name becoming Avions Marcel Dassault-Breguet Aviation. It proceeded to develop successful military fighters, beginning with the Ouragan (Hurricane) in 1951, the Mystère in 1954, the delta-wing Mirage series from 1955 on, and in the 1980s, in cooperation with the British, the Jaguar and Rafale European fighters.

Dassault, Breguet, and others already in 1951 proposed the medium-sized jet airliner that became the Caravelle. Produced by Sud Aviation, it became the world's first jetliner with engines in the rear: initially two Rolls-Royce "Avons," each with 10,500 pounds of thrust. Flying first on May 27, 1955, the Caravelle entered service four years later and sold widely, some 278 models, through the 1960s. That was also the case with the De Havilland-designed, Hawker Siddeley-built, three-engine Boeing 727 look-alike, the Bac 111 Trident.

The first Airbus, the twin-engine, 42-ton A-300, made its maiden flight on October 28, 1972, and entered service with Air France on May 24, two years later. Its successors, the A-310, A-320 (and bigger version, the 321), and A-330 were all powered by two under-wing Rolls-Royce, German MTU, or General Electric engines, linked with France's SNEC-MA engines of increasing power. By 1995, GE/SNECMA was planning new CFMXX engines of 43,000 pounds thrust to power the first four-engine Airbus, the A-340.

Its maiden flight came in October 1991, and it entered service two years later. The A-310 was the smallest of the series, the A-320 having pioneered the first "fly-by-wire" system of Commandes Electriques, eliminating or reducing in size traditional controls, like mini-control sticks installed on either side as in advanced fighters, in favor of computer switches, thereby enabling the reduction of crews to a pilot and co-pilot. Already great fuel efficiency was improved by the automatic transfer of it to maintain center of gravity, as against doing that by changing trim, which increased drag.

The best-selling model, the A-320, had close to 900 orders by 1990, and the new, smaller A-319 sold well later in the decade. Airbus sales had climbed to nearly 30 percent of the world market by then, while Boeing's share had dropped from a peak of over 70 percent to under 60. In 1994, Airbus won 110 orders for airliners as against 111 for Boeing. Nearing the new century, McDonnell Douglas had declined from its previous dominance to selling close to 10 percent of commercial airliners, with all other aircraft manufacturers the remaining fraction. Of course, there have been significant annual changes in such figures, as well as over longer periods of time, as is now projected for the fastest-growing markets, in Asia.

With the rise of Airbus Industrie, U.S. companies like Boeing, supported by the government, charged that excessive subsidies of over $25 billion from the three big countries were violating international free-trade accords. The Europeans countercharged that the military and space contracts for the U.S. firms amounted to up to 72 percent of American aerospace costs, and more than offset any such government help for Airbus Industrie, which was largely ended anyway when the industry became profitable. Agreements in the 1990s supposedly reduced subsidies worldwide for developing new aircraft to about a third and to only 5 percent after sales began. New disputes over landing rights and other matters inevitably soon arose, however, given the complexities and vagaries of the business, and such disputes prevented the inclusion of air travel in the 1994 GATT accords for world trade.

The real competition, of course, was over the superiority of the various planes for the roles for which they were designed. There, American firms, especially the Boeing Corporation, maintained an overwhelming, if declining, advantage. After the decisive breakthrough of the Boeing 707, which sold close to 1000 models, came other remarkable Boeing planes. The all-time best-seller was the two-engine Boeing 737, which made up close to a quarter of the U.S. commercial air fleet in the early 1990s. The first flight of a 99-passenger 737-100 model, soon followed by the 200, had come on April 9, 1967, after two years of development. By late in the century, close to 3000 Boeing 737s had been sold, most of them after the 1984 introduction of the 140-passenger model 300s, followed by the 400, 500, 700, and 800 models. The equally remarkable three engine Boeing 727 was four years older than the 737, flying first in February 1963. Carrying at first 189 passengers, it became the second best-seller of all time, some 1831 by the end of its production in 1984. The incredible, 300-, then 400-ton Boeing 747, already discussed in Chapters One and Thirteen, entered service in January 1970, and by 1993 Boeing had delivered close to 1200 of them to the world's airlines, almost half the advanced model 400.

The first flight of a Boeing 747 had been scheduled for December 17, 1968, to mark the 65th anniversary of the epochal flight of the 605-pound *Flyer* of the Wright brothers, but problems forced a delay of the first test flight to February 9, 1969. These included: construction of the world's largest enclosed space to house construction of the giant plane, across some 40 acres at Everett, north of Seattle; four new hydraulic systems for each 747, to operate the enormous control surfaces; and above all, new low-weight, high-bypass ratio (up to 8 to 1) engines, with water injection and afterburner, to generate up to 59,000 pounds of thrust at take-off. General Electric had pioneered such engines for the Lockheed C-5A cargo plane, lifting 769,000 pounds off the earth in June 1968. As noted in Chapter One, the improved CF-6, and the Pratt and Whitney JT 9, are most commonly used for the 747, although at first consideration was also given to the superb Rolls-Royce RB-211, which powered the Lockheed 1011.

The first commercial flight of the huge plane came on January 21, 1970, when 324 passengers were carried from New York to London. Thereafter, the 747 was improved year by year. For example, the instrumentation on its flight panel was reduced by the mid-1990s from 971 to 365 lights, gauges, and switches.

After the enormous successes of the early Boeing jetliners, in direct response to the growing competition from Airbus Industrie as well as new McDonnell Douglas and Lockheed planes, Boeing delivered two new twin-engine, fuel-efficient, "fly by wire" aircraft, the Boeing 757 and 767. Designed to carry from 150 to 230 or more passengers and thereby fill the niche between smaller planes and the huge 747, they went into service after 1982, and by 1994 had sold more than 400 each, as had rival DC-10s and MD-80s.

With the new, and slightly bigger, three-engine McDonnell Douglas MD-11 and four-engine Airbus 340 entering service in the early 1990s, Boeing decided it had to develop an airplane to meet their competition for the next size passenger group. The Boeing 777 flew first on June 12, 1994 and entered service June 7 the following year with a United Airlines flight from London to Washington, pioneering a whole new set of breakthroughs. Its two Pratt and Whitney 4084 engines, generating over 70,000 pounds of thrust, enable the transportation of from 292 to 550 passengers, depending on the model, some of them ten feet longer than the 747.

Boeing used the input of leading clients like United to ensure still greater wide-body comfort. Most astonishingly, the 777 was the first-ever plane to be designed entirely by computer. The company pioneered "Design-Build Teams" (DBTs), running "Computer-Aided Three Dimensional Interactive Applications" (CATIA) at over 2000 work stations, which handled some 3500 billion bits of knowledge. All workers had access to that staggering amount of information for one "blueprint," which thereby succeeded in eliminating many previously demanding steps of trial and error. The Boeing 777 achieved the lowest cost per passenger mile yet, with the latest in design, aerodynamic airfoils, composite materials, and "fly by wire" efficiency with a crew of only two.

The technological excellence of the Boeing 777 largely offset its delay in responding to the launching of the Airbus 340 and MD-11. By 1995, it was getting 70 percent of the market share for planes of its class. Delays had been still more the case with the decade-long lag between the 757 and 767 and their competition for the 250- to 350-seat market, opened in the early 1970s by the Douglas DC-10 and Lockheed 1011, both of them with three engines in the rear. The Lockheed 1011 Tristar first flew in November 1970, but had early problems with its Rolls-Royce engines and failed to sell more than about 250 before the plane was discontinued in 1981.

The DC-10, however, sold some 446 models after its first flight on August 29, 1970. Despite the involvement of a DC-10 in the worst aviation disaster in U.S. history, when an engine failure on take-off from Chicago's O'Hare Airport caused a crash killing all 275 on board, improved versions of the DC-10 were still widely used in the 1990s. But Boeing remained clearly far ahead in the competition for commercial airliners in the jet age. While in its early years after 1958, the DC-8 sold 556 versions, the Boeing 707 sold 999. Then, Douglas delivered some 900-odd each of its two-engine DC-9, and the later version, MD-80, as against Boeing's delivery of 1831 models of the 727 and some 3000 of the best-selling 737. Although the 737 suffered highly publicized crashes, one killing 132 people near Pittsburgh on September 8, 1994, its safety record remained better than normal, with only one fatal crash per million take-offs.

In January 1993, Boeing reached an agreement with Airbus Industrie to cooperate for the building of a four-engine super-jumbo airliner capable of carrying 530, 600, or even 850 passengers with full-length double decks. Before long, however, predictable financing problems and some skepticism developed over costs and plans for it, as well as for a planned second-generation supersonic airliner. In July, Boeing announced plans for a stretched 747 to carry 500 or 550 passengers in place of the super-jumbo, even as plans proceeded for a supersonic "High Speed Civil Transport," perhaps to be built by a consortium of eight big aviation firms, Boeing, Aérospatiale, Alenia (Italy), British Aerospace, Daimler-Benz

Aerospace Corporation (Deutshe Aerospace or DASA), McDonnell Douglas, Tupolev, and a Japanese company. In the summer of 1996, Boeing purchased Rockwell, thus acquiring that company's tradition of innovation and expertise in not only weapons systems but aerospace.

Later developments on the fates of various planes and manufacturers obviously are not yet known, but by the late 20th century, it has become very clear that mass travel at jet-age speeds is one of the greatest miracles of human history.

Vertical and Military Flight

Although the rather emphatic ending of the Second World War has discouraged great powers, much less superpowers, from direct conflict with each other since, military aviation in recent decades has nevertheless continued to progress, and reveals numerous links between traditional aviation and the space age, as well as many more "miracles" of flight at sub- and supersonic speeds. One such link of course was the simple vertical ascents of the helicopters and all the more so of the new Vertical Take-Off and Landing (VTOL) craft. While space ships went into hundreds-of-miles-high orbits, the VTOLs went to tens of thousands of feet as against helicopters' normal hundreds or several thousand feet. The biggest breakthrough came with the development of tilt-jet aircraft like the British Aerospace Harrier and the tilt-rotor Bell-Boeing V-22 Osprey.

By the 1950s some 30 different schemes for vertical or very short take-off and landings (V/STOL) aircraft were actually flying in the U.S., England, France, and Russia, over 20 of them successfully. They included some 15 different approaches, ranging from tailsitters (at first called "flying bedsteads") to vectored thrust. The crucial problems were to have sufficient thrust forced downward to drive the craft upward and then to make the transition to level, high-speed flight. For the lift-off, thrust had to exceed the weight of the ship, but in cruise could be reduced to a fifth or tenth of that weight.

In August 1954, an Allison propeller engine-powered tailsitter, the Convair XFY-1 Pogo, was able to ascend vertically outside San Francisco, and in November to make the first true VTOL flight with transition to horizontal flight, followed by a vertical descent. A Ryan jet-powered tailsitter had risen in November 1951 and, after four years of work, an improved version made the first jet-powered VTOL flight on December 10, 1955. The McDonnell compound Autogyro XV-1 started hover tests in 1954 and achieved transition to horizontal flight on April 29, 1955, with 200 mph speeds the following year. Due to the progress of helicopters flying over 200 mph (a Lockheed XH-51a compound helicopter flew 302.6 mph in 1965), the program was abandoned in 1957, but provided valuable knowledge for the tilt-rotor programs. Various forms of flying engines (coleopters, or platforms), looking like amusement-park rides, were also developed, but the biggest breakthroughs came with the ability to vector the jet or tilt the propellers.

After various experimentation in the early 1950s, a Bell helicopter, the XV-3, made full transitions from vertical to horizontal flight by the end of 1955, and achieved 350 knots with further improvements by the 1960s. In the 1970s the larger model XV-IS climbed to 25,000 feet. Other companies, including the venerable Curtiss Wright Company, made important contributions, but the ultimate in tilt-rotor aircraft, the V-22 Osprey, began as the X-22A, and developed further out of the collaboration in the 1980s between Bell Helicopter Textron and the Boeing Company. The tilt mechanism to turn the huge propellers, driven by two Allison turbine engines, from vertical to horizontal, enabled it to lift off like a helicopter and then fly like a plane. Its first lift-off came in March 1989, and the transition from helicopter to airplane flight in September of that year. With a length of 57 feet, it uses two 38-foot-diameter rotors attached to swiveling engine pods on the tips of its wings to lift its 40,000-pound gross weight. The Allison turboshaft engines produce 6000hp each and will be strengthened to 10,000hp, enabling it to cruise at 275 knots up to 30,000 feet, with a top speed of nearly 350 mph, and to increase the gross weight to 59,000 pounds if using a short take-off roll of 500 feet. This enables the carrying of more than 24 troops or 15,000 pounds of cargo.

The British Aerospace Hawker Harrier jet also takes off vertically or with a short roll, but can go supersonic as well. It, too, developed from the mid-1950s on, with key advances made after the early 1960s by the Hawker Siddeley "'Kestrels." The new designation "Harrier" hovered first in August 1966, and was flying by late the next year. It entered Royal Air Force service in early 1969 and demonstrated its incredible performance on May 8, 1969, with a flight from central London to mid-Manhattan, New York. Using vertical take-off and landing, with refueling in flight, it arrived in 5 hours, 57 minutes, and returned—with the wind—26 minutes faster. The Concorde makes that crossing in about 3 hours, but then passengers must get to and from the airports.

The French-built VTOL Dassault "Balzac" and Mirage IIIV (vertical) also made important advances. One of the latter used eight Rolls-Royce lift engines and a SNECMA turbofan, capable of 20,000 pounds of thrust with afterburner, to reach an astonishing Mach 2.04 on September 12, 1966. Subsequent crashes and financial constraints, however, hampered further development. The Soviets developed their V/STOL planes, most famously the Yakovlev 38 Forger, using two liftjets and a horizontal propulsion engine, and there were also German VTOL jets.

All these solved the critical problems of developing sufficient thrust both to lift and drive forward the aircraft at great speeds. But the British Hawker Siddeley firm's mastering of the ability to "vector" its increasingly powerful, from 8000 to 21,500 pounds thrust, Pegasus engines, proved a better solution to the problems of going from vertical to rapid horizontal flight than the use of separate lift and propulsion jets. The culmination came the Hawker (taken over by British Aerospace in the mid 1970s) developed "Harrier." By attaching four nozzles to the engine, controlled by a single lever near the throttle, the plane is able to go from vertical take-off to speeds of up to Mach 1.3 and beyond. Two nozzles on each side project either downward or backward, according to the desired motion. They are placed under the front and back of each wing where they join the fuselage. In the mid-1970s, in cooperation with McDonnell Douglas, a more powerful Harrier II, its Pegasus engine generating up to 34,000 pounds thrust, was developed. Designated the AV-8A and 8B, it became a principal weapon of the U.S. Marines, and the Royal Air Force used it for 2376 missions in the war between Great Britain and Argentina over the Falkland Islands in the spring of 1982. Bill Gunston, in a recent book on the jet, spoke of the Harrier as having pioneered "vectored thrust as the way that future land and sea fixed-wing airpower will surely go."

The greatest use of such aircraft, of course, came for places without airstrips or for use off aircraft carriers. Even the normal launches and landings on carriers require maximum reflexes. The "Sea Harrier" could rise vertically, but other planes had to be catapulted. Advanced Navy and Marine corps jets, up to some 70 or more of them, would be fixed one by one to a hook behind the steam-powered catapults, to hold them in place as the engines were put on maximum power with afterburner. The powerful catapults then hurl planes weighing 38,000 pounds or more, like the

Grumman F-14 "Tomcat" and McDonnell-Douglas/Northrop F-18 "Hornet," to over 150 mph in about 250 feet, less than two seconds later. That is near the take-off speed of about 140 knots (161 mph) of both planes, and with the forward speed of the ship into the wind, enables maximum climb to the desired altitude.

Anyone who has ever landed in a jet aircraft on a runway must marvel at the ability of naval pilots to bring their planes down on ships at sea. To land such high-speed planes on the incredibly small surface available—at most 1000 feet on a top-of-the-line carrier—the key is for the plane to catch the "trap" of the four restraining wires accurately enough for the still-speeding plane to stop within the 750 or so feet of length of an average modern carrier. Beginning their approach about three miles out, the landing jet streaks by the carrier 800 feet up at over 300 knots, and breaks sharply left with the wing pointed straight down at the water, the pilot pulling up to 6 or so Gs depending on the plane's velocity. Slowing in a descending turn around the ship, as guided by the Landing Signal Officer (LSO), the pilot then must touch down at about 130 knots (149.5 mph) exactly in place to "trap" the arresting wires that will stop the hurtling jet. They will be missed if the incoming plane is even a foot or so too high, and the jet will be forced to go around. The LSOs grade each "trap," from the best, an underlined "OK" or 5, to "unsafe" or 0. Yet such landings can come only 37 seconds apart, as the hustling crews follow their clockwork precision handling of the carrier's planes.

There could be even less time for an incoming plane if a problem occurred at the wrong moment. Thus, the first woman F-14 pilot, Kara Hultgreen, had only 12 seconds from first perception of a compressor stall in the left engine of her F-14 approaching the carrier *Abraham Lincoln*, off San Diego on October 25, 1994. This caused her death as the plane yawed left and was waved off out of control, without the time for her safe ejection, although the rear-seat RIO (Radar Intercept Officer) was able to get out safely.

Night landings on carriers are almost always terrifying, although from the 1950s on the pilots and LSOs had the assistance of optical glide slopes, light beams, mirrors, manually operated visual landing aid systems (MOVLAS), and automatic carrier landing systems (ACLS), replacing the earlier, luminous amber "meatballs." The LSOs also continued to use hand signals, brilliant orange or other color suits, and luminescent flags to guide the finding of a moving, perhaps two-football-field-sized landing strip. There was always the question of a high-speed landing on a tiny, often rocking surface. As navy pilot, then astronaut Alan Shepherd, put it, "At night, in rain, and fog and nasty winds, it is like being thrown into a rolling cement mixer . . . coming home in a 'controlled crash.' "

Such rectangular landing patterns, with a high-speed passover of the runway, breaking left two more times onto the downwind and base legs, and then again onto the final approach, are also used by land-based military jets. But given the narrowness of the margin of error for landing on surfaces as small as those of even the biggest carriers, such flying undoubtedly comes closest of all "normal" aviation to the requirements of advanced aerobatic maneuvers. For the F-14, like the F-18 with two seats, engines, and tails, but entering service several years earlier in 1974, there is the additional complexity of sweeping the wings back for greater speeds and then forward again for the approach and landing. In the same way as the earlier Vought F-8 Crusader and the USAF's bigger twin-engine, two-seat, but single-tail General Dynamics F-111, which began flying a decade earlier, the wings are swept back for take-off only about 16 percent, then to about 26 percent for the climb at 350 knots, and to the optimum 35 percent for Mach .74 cruise. For maximum speeds up to Mach 2.2 or 2.3, the sweep is extended to its maximum of 72 percent.

This use of aerodynamic flexibility gives maximum maneuverability for such over Mach 2 aircraft, but also adds steps for already busy pilots, monitoring up to 300 control switches with all possible precision. The B-1 bomber, as well as the English Tornado, Soviet MiG-23, Su-24, Tu-26, and other new planes also use "variable geometry" with different sweeps to the wings. The new ultra-high-performance jets, with their great speeds giving G forces up to seven or so times normal gravity, also add a "biological barrier" to the pilot's tolerance of outside forces, which has superseded the old "structural" and "mechanical barriers" of earlier aviation.

The most famous aerobatic displays in the United States and other advanced countries are also performed by Navy and Air Force pilots, all trained in acrobatics, especially for new versions of fighter combat. The elite pilots of the Navy's Blue Angels, flying F-18s by the 1980s, and the Air Force Thunderbirds, by then flying F-16s, give spectacular demonstrations of precision aerobatics with planes only three feet apart. Most commonly they group in four-plane Diamond or six-plane Delta formations, for Cuban 8s, chandelles, Immelmanns, loops, rolls, split S's, and other group maneuvers. Even normal solo aerobatics, such as Milton

Thompson described with an F-104 doing a loop starting at Mach 2 at 35,000 feet and climbing vertically to top out at 60,000 feet, raise quite a few hackles. But the most hair-raising are the high-speed crossovers by two or more jets, where precision timing and placement are necessary to avoid obviously fatal collisions.

Perhaps the most spectacular crash associated with such modern versions of the old barnstorming displays and dogfights came in early September 1988. On that occasion, the solo Messerschmitt-Bolkow-Blohm MB-339A jet of the ten-plane Italian "Frecce [arrows] Tricolori" team passed too low and a fraction of a second too soon, slamming into a crossing colleague, the number two of the left group of the formation, which caromed into a third plane, also traveling at about 350 mph, some 200 feet over the USAF's Ramstein base about 70 miles southwest of Frankfurt, Germany. The Italians had been flying the maneuver since 1955, before up to some 18 million people a year, but it was the worst air show accident ever, killing not only the three pilots but over 47 spectators when one of the jets cartwheeled into the middle of the concession stands. Another 350 or so were injured. The spectacular demonstration featured two groups of four and five planes passing each other from opposite directions, trailing smoke of the Italian national colors of red, white, and green. The tenth jet had intended to cross through the others to form the "heart" that would have climaxed the maneuver.

Even without the risks of such aerobatic formation flying, pilots on high-performance missions face high risks. Career Navy pilots, for example, earlier faced up to a 23 percent chance of auguring in, although, as in commercial and general private aviation, the military accident rates also have been declining.

For the military jets, the biggest safety device of all came with the development of the ejection seat, which enabled the use of parachutes at speeds so high that pilots could not climb out on their own. The Germans pioneered this and over 60 of their early jet pilots made such emergency ejections in World War II, using seats powered upward by compressed gas. Small rockets to power the ejections, controlled by a handle in the cockpit, proved more effective, however, and were shortly developed by the victorious allies, England, France, and the U.S. Early testing of the devices, with many variants, had to overcome numerous problems. Thus, America's top Pacific Theater ace, Richard Bong, was unable to eject from the P-80 he was testing in California on the very day of the first atomic bomb drop, August 6, 1945. An ejection seat was first successfully tested by pilot Bernard Lynch, flying his Gloster Meteor jet at 320 miles per hour over Chalgrove, England, in July 1946.

By a decade later, most problems with the ejection seats had been solved. Still, if the ejection was at too high a speed, the airflow would knock the ejectee unconscious. Later aircraft, starting with the F-111, could also be rigged so that the explosive charge would eject the entire cockpit "capsule" into the air, enabling it to slow down enough for a safe parachute descent. Another most important jet-age safety feature came with the development of pressure suits to protect pilots from the excessive G forces of maneuvers at high speeds; these forces could drain enough blood from the brain to cause unconsciousness.

There have also been many advances in "avionics," with the application of the enormous advances in electronics for aviation. New "laser radar" made possible an unprecedented ability to see incredible details up to two miles away, whether for terrain clearance with zero visibility, for avoiding other planes, or for target sighting.

Invaluable for training pilots to avoid danger, as well as for saving money and time, has been the development of simulators, especially ground-based representations of the flight deck and instrument panels at various stages of flight. Beginning with the simple representations of cockpit and instruments with rotations to imitate flight in the Link Trainer, first used by Binghamton, New York inventor Edwin A. Link in 1929, simulators in the computer and electronic ages have come close to producing the "virtual reality" of flight without leaving the ground. Using six or more axes for movements and realistic visual displays, they can produce all possibilities of flight, without the cost and dangers of the real thing. They are also used in flight to imitate what projected new aircraft will encounter, and on the ground have expanded in size to resemble something like planetariums with their projections of scenes.

Such bigger, fully developed simulators can show approaches and landings, fighter combat, and any imagined emergency. The ability to train for all such possibilities in the air, without leaving the ground, or with smaller simulators in planes, has become an increasing part of aviation, although some still insist, with some logic, that there is no substitute for the real thing. But they come close! As Bryce S. Walker describes in his recent book, *Fighting Jets*, about the use of simulators to train for the F-18:

. . . Though the pilot is stationary [on the ground], he has the illusion that he is flying. To complete the illusion, as he manipulates the controls to bank, the computer tilts the [image of] the horizon. And when the pilot closes in on his target, the image automatically enlarges and the pressure on his G suit increases, just as it would if he were actually accelerating.

Aerial refueling became another essential component of flying, especially for military jets on long missions. The workhorses for this in the late 20th century were the Boeing RC-97, after 1956 the KC-135 Stratotanker, a cousin of the 707, and by the 1980s a version of the DC-10. The latter feeds from its up to 31,200 gallons through a 50-foot or so hose or "boom," after the drogue nozzle has been fitted with a "probe" to the fuel tank of the plane waiting below.

Work toward the next generation of ultra-high-speed and altitude aircraft has paralleled the march into space and therefore provides the transition to our next chapter, on the space age. All airplanes have undergone modifications to improve their flight, but with the quantum jumps in technology by late in the century, these have enabled airplanes to become quasi-"space vehicles." By the late 1980s, the advanced countries had launched projects for hypersonic passenger planes, imagining speeds up to Mach 25 (16,500 mph), not far below the 17,500 mph required to go into orbit, and at altitudes over 100,000 feet. Such "Trans Atmospheric Vehicles" (TAV), like the American X-30, or "National Aerospace Plane," will obviously go far beyond the British and French Concorde. The "Orient Express," for example, is expected to link the U.S. and Japan in two hours. So will the new smaller military aircraft, designated the "Advanced Tactical Fighter" (ATF), or in another version, the "Fighter Support Experimental" (FSX) plane, go far beyond the late 20th-century fighters. They will use new fuels—where possible, the most efficient, super-cooled (to –423 Fahrenheit) liquid hydrogen—as well as the "vectoring" of thrust for supersonic ramjets, called "scramjets," to enable much greater flexibility, maneuverability, and the slowing of speeds for landing.

The X series in the U.S., of which there have been over 30 since the Bell X-1 broke the sound barrier on October 14, 1947, have pioneered these breakthroughs. Experimentation for relatively slower flight has test-

Omar Locklear, famed daredevil, strikes a pose atop a DeHavilland Jenny. He fell to his death while stunting in a movie in 1920.

Four aviation pioneers met by chance at the Lockheed factory in 1935. They are, from left: Amelia Earhart, Wiley Post, Roscoe Turner and Laura Ingalls. (Photo by Albert L. Bresnik, courtesy of Madonna M. Turner)

The dapper racing pilot Roscoe Turner, standing next to his Wedell-Williams, in which he won the 1932 Thompson trophy.

Charles and Anne Lindbergh speaking with the press before a flight. Note their heavy insulated suits to cope with the frigid temperatures of open cockpits. (Courtesy of the Smithsonian)

These lighter-than-air dirigibles were used by the U.S. Navy in the 1920s and '30s, before a series of crashes soured the government on the notion. In the 1980s the idea was revived to track smugglers. (Courtesy of the Smithsonian)

Jimmy Doolittle stands next to his crashed plane during one of his cross-country flights. "Any landing you can walk away from . . ." (Courtesy of the Smithsonian)

Three Curtiss B-2 Condors above Yosemite National Park in California during the 1920s. El Capitan is on the right.

Corporal Garland Cain reaches for his ripcord as he falls from the wing of a plane in this early demonstration of parachuting.

A "China Clipper" passes over early construction on the Golden Gate Bridge on its first flight across the Pacific in 1935. (Courtesy of the Smithsonian)

CHINA CLIPPER OVER SOUTH TOWER OF GOLDEN GATE BRIDGE FIRST WESTBOUND FLIGHT NOVEMBER 22, 1935

NC-14716 WRECKED IN WEST INDIES - 1945

The world's first jet plane, the Heinkel 178, flew just prior to WWII, on August 27, 1939. German jet fighter squadrons were formed too late, however, to change the outcome of the conflict. (Courtesy of the Smithsonian)

A Curtiss P-40, of the type made famous by the American "Flying Tigers" who fought in China.(Courtesy of the Smithsonian)

A captured I-16 Rata of the USSR reposes on an airfield next to its superior adversary, a German Me-109, somewhere on the Eastern Front.

A B-25 takes off from the *Hornet* for the famed "30 Seconds Over Tokyo" raid, led by Jimmy Doolittle. The short deck made for a white-knuckle launch, but the raid was a stunning boost for American morale. (Courtesy of the Smithsonian)

Hawker Hurricanes seek out the enemy during the Battle of Britain. Though less glamorized than its cousin, the Spitfire, RAF pilots termed the Hurricane a "wizard kite."

Ju-52 transports skim across the Mediterranean to deliver the world's first fully airborne invasion. Though Crete eventually fell, the initial carnage on the drop zones dissuaded the Germans from further such attempts.

Although they succeeded in devastating German cities and industry, some 80,000 Allied airmen were lost during the WWII bomber war. Here a B-17 "Flying Fortress" attempts to shake off a pursuing Messerschmitt.

A B-24 breaks up over Germany while its mate looks on helplessly. Laden with bombs and gasoline, flak could turn these bombers into incendiary wrecks.

A split second until impact as a Japanese Kamikaze closes on an American ship. As their situation became increasingly desperate, the Japanese sent their young pilots on one-way suicide missions in which they caused extensive damage, but were unable to turn the tide in the Pacific War.

Allied bomber crews breathed a little easier when the high-performance, long-range P-51 Mustang arrived to provide escort against German fighters. The Rolls-Royce-powered Mustang is still active in pylon racing.

The Boeing B-29 "Super Fortress," a 60-ton long-range bomber, delivered devastating attacks against the Japanese homeland.

A B-29, the *Enola Gay*, dropped the atomic bomb that destroyed Hiroshima. As the apex of the philosophy of "total war" from the air, this, along with another bomb dropped on Nagasaki a week later, ended WWII.

The devastation caused by an atomic blast. Only concrete structures have survived. This horrifying vision was to haunt the world throughout the following decades.

A Piper J-3 Cub, one of the most successful small plane designs of all time. (Courtesy of the Smithsonian)

A captured German rocket being tested by the United States in 1950. Tests like these helped pave the way to the moon.

The Bell X-1 in which Chuck Yeager broke the sound barrier. He called it *Glamorous Glennis*, after his wife. (Courtesy of the Smithsonian)

The North American X-15 being dropped from a B-52. The main engine of the X-15 has just ignited. (Courtesy of the Smithsonian)

The SR-71 Blackbird, one of the best spy planes ever built and the holder of many speed records. (Courtesy of the Smithsonian)

The F-16 by General Dynamics is a modern fighter that is "fly-by-wire," meaning a computer must help the pilot.

Neil Armstrong became the first man to stand on the
moon, in 1969. (Courtesy of NASA)

A space shuttle lifting off toward the next frontier of
flight. (Courtesy of NASA)

A Boeing 777 takes off. This latest airliner is replete with a host of electronic aids, the latest in lightweight materials, and every advantage known to science; it still, however, needs a human in the cockpit to arrive safely. (Courtesy of Boeing)

ed everything back to the Wright brothers. From 1984 on, the Grumman X-29 began to test forward-swept super-thin, graphite-epoxy wings and canards at speeds up to Mach 1.6. There have even been experiments to seemingly rewrite the rules of aerodynamics, for example with the post-1990 X-31's use of vectoring jet propulsion to fly high-speed sharp turns and "post-stall" maneuvers. Others, as those done by the Freewing Aircraft Corporation, founded in 1987, envisage the use of hinged, "floating," or "oscillating" wings with variable angles of attack to avoid stalls and other flight problems, while new micro-electromechanical (MEM) systems are being installed to further reduce drag and turbulence.

The new generation of fighters, such as the Mach 2.2 Lockheed (with Boeing and General Dynamics) F-22 and the Advanced Research Projects Agency X-32 in the U.S., the Russian I-42, the Japanese-U.S. FSX, and New European Fighter Aircraft (NEFA) like the EF-2000, incorporate all these breakthroughs, especially for avionics, maneuverability, and the evasion of enemy radar to go far beyond the previous generation of near-Mach 2 aircraft, the F-15s, F-16s, F-18s, and their European equivalents, the Jaguars, Tornados, Gripens, Viggens, MiGs, Sukhois, Mirages, and Rafales. Even fighters like the F-16, over 3400 of which had been produced by 1995, demonstrated many superlatives. But the advances keep coming, and they will go into the new U.S. "Joint Strike Fighter" for the 21st century.

Highly Maneuverable Aircraft Technology (HIMAT), with thrust vectoring for almost right-angle turns, for example, was advanced by the X-31 and Remotely Piloted Research Vehicles (RPRV) from the late 1980s on, while the capacity to evade radar was pioneered in the 1980s by the "stealth" technology of the Lockheed F-117 fighter and the four-engined North American Rockwell B-1 and Northrop B-2 bombers. The first and last of these in ways went back to Jack Northrop's conception of the "flying wing." But they were also able to use the new composite materials and still closer blending of engines and wings into the aircraft structure to render the planes virtually invisible to radar. By late in the century, the X-32 had demonstrated vertical landings after high-speed flight, and there were plans for a new X-34 shuttle to be launched by the reusable X-33 rocket. Before the B-1 and 2, work toward Advanced Technology Bombers (ATB) like the B-70 and the hypersonic Dyna-soar had already advanced such futuristic knowledge. But most important of all for the breakthroughs in ultra-fast and high-altitude aviation were the flights of the SR-71 "Blackbird" and the X-15.

Developed for Lockheed by Kelly Johnson and Ben Rich at the legendary "skunk works" in Burbank, California, the prototype A-12 first flew on April 26, 1962, and the SR-71 in late December 1964. The intermediate model YF-12A set a new speed record of 2070.1 mph (3331.51 kph) in May 1965, and then the SR-71 established the all-time confirmed speed record for a ground take-off plane of 2193.17 mph (3529.56 kph) on July 28, 1976. On September 1, 1974, it also set a trans-Atlantic crossing record of 1 hour, 54 minutes, at an average speed of 1806.963 mph (2908.026 kph), as well as new cross-country records at over Mach 3. The incredible SR-71 was used mainly for high-altitude reconnaissance at 80,000 feet and up to 100,000 feet, cruising at over 2000 mph (3220 kph) causing temperatures up to 300 degrees Celsius (572 Farenheit). Such altitudes and speeds enabled avoiding a new incident such as occurred when the Soviets shot down a predecessor Lockheed spy plane, the U-2, flying about 60,000 feet above Sverdlovsk on May 1, 1960.

The 102-foot-long, needle-nosed, twin-tailed, all-titanium Blackbird, with rear delta wings spanning 55 feet 7 inches, weighed 60,000 pounds empty and 120,000 at full weight. Two 32,500-pound thrust Pratt and Whitney J-58 turbo ramjet engines powered it to take off at near 230 knots. After up to 2500 miles without refueling at Mach 3, it landed at about 155 knots using a 40-foot-diameter brake chute to stop. Despite its extraordinary successes, including photography of unprecedented accuracy and detail, with the ending of the Cold War and financial constraints, the 15 or so Blackbirds remaining of the 50 (32 of which were SR-71s) that had been built, were for the most part grounded after March 6, 1990. The Lockheed TR-1 successor to the U-2, with a much more modest speed of 580 mph, continued to fly high-altitude reconnaissance missions.

Different but equally impressive leaps to the fringes of space by manned airplanes, even if rocket powered, began after 1958, three years before the first Soviet and American astronauts, with the flights of the North American X-15. Although dropped from a B-52 flying in the stratosphere, the X-15's incredible records, capped by NASA pilot Joe Walker reaching an altitude of 354,200 feet on August, 22, 1963, and the Air Force's William "Pete" Knight achieving a speed of Mach 6.72 (4534 mph, 7297 kph) on October 3, 1967, will stand for a very long time, if not forever, for non-space vehicles. For ground-based planes, the comparable records are, as mentioned, for speed, the SR-71's 2070.1 mph (3331.51 kph), and for altitude, some 123,492 feet (37,650 meters), established by Soviet pilot Alexandre Fedotov in a MiG E-266M on August 31, 1977.

Such performance required much time and many resources. Already in 1951, the designer of the X-1, Robert J. Woods, proposed to NACA a plane that could fly above Mach 5. With designs worked out under John Becker at NACA's Langley, Virginia headquarters until the mid-1950s, and then by North American Aviation after September 1955, the X-15 took shape with a sleek "black-bullet" needle-nose fuselage, having a small 22-foot span, rear wings, and a square-looking ventral cruciform tail. Where the SR-71 had two tails, one above each engine, the X-15 had one above and slightly below the rear of its 50-foot-long fuselage. It used inconel-x chrome-nickel skin that could withstand temperatures up to 1200 degrees Fahrenheit, and rear skids with a nose wheel for landing.

From the Edwards Air Force Base Flight Test Center, the X-15 made its first unpowered free fall flight from a B-52, at 38,000 feet, in June 1958, and a first powered fight from one flying Mach 0.82 at 45,000 feet on September 17, 1959. Both caused problems that North American's chief test pilot, A. Scott Crossfield, overcame with his legendary skills. Already famous as the first person to reach Mach 2, on November 20, 1953, at 62,000 feet in a B-52-launched, all-rocket Douglas D-558 2, he was then hired by North American to supervise the testing of the X-15. On the first flight, he found the craft very unstable as it began to porpoise in great arcs. Crossfield was able to land it with the perfect timing necessary to catch the upturn simultaneously with his touchdown, on one of the Mojave Desert's dry lake beds, and modifications in the coordination between the control and hydraulic systems fixed that problem. Then on the first powered flight 14 months later, using the X-1's XLR-11 engine, a fuel pump malfunction and explosion caused violent buffeting and another emergency landing which, this time, broke the craft in two. Crossfield somehow emerged unscathed.

Further modifications and the fitting of a more powerful Thiokol XLR-99 rocket engine burning 1000 gallons of liquid oxygen and 1,400 gallons of anhydrous ammonia to produce 57,000 pounds of thrust, by November 1960 made possible successive speed and altitude records. By late 1961, the X-15 was reaching Mach 6 and 200,000 feet of altitude, and it then went on to the all-time records mentioned above: an altitude of 354,200 feet in August 1963 and a speed of 4534 mph on October 3, 1967. The latter, the equivalent of about 6700 feet per second, or twice the speed of a rifle bullet, topped the previous record of the Air Force's prime pilot for the X-15, Bob White, who five years earlier had first gone over Mach 6 at 4093 mph, or some 6600 feet per second! The X-15 could climb at 4000 feet per second at its peak!

It also did the most extraordinary testing yet, from ejection seats workable at ultra-high speeds to different control sticks for different aspects of flight, executed on a "high range," extending 485 miles from the huge Edwards complex, 13 miles long by 4 wide, all the way into Utah. New pilots arrived and received initial training on rocket-boosted versions of the two-seat Lockheed F-104 Starfighter which, prior to the X-15, was the sleekest plane yet, with a similar 50-foot length and thin 7-foot wings toward the rear. It could do Mach 2.2 in level flight, and not only served as chase plane to monitor X-15 flights, but as a pilot training simulator; for example, for 200-knot landings. The X-15 flights normally lasted only about ten minutes.

Such flights of course were not without their dangers. In the 1950s, experimental planes had already claimed the lives of two of the most famous American test pilots. Iven Kincheloe, who had made the first flight beyond 100,000 feet in altitude, to 126,200 feet, in an X-2 on September 7, 1956, was killed shortly afterward, when the engine of an F-104 he was testing at Edwards Air Force Base quit at the most danger-ous time—just after take-off—preventing his use of its downward ejec-tion seat, which understandably was later changed to a safer system. His successor as chief test pilot for the X-2, Milburn Apt, died after bailing out when his plane went out of control just after setting the first speed record over Mach 3: Mach 3.2 (2094 mph) at 65,500 feet on September 27, 1956.

After the first crash landings of the X-15 came one in November 1962 that seriously injured pilot Jack McKay. Then, the record speed of 4534 mph on October 3, 1967, raised temperatures so far above accept-able limits—to some 3,000 degrees Fahrenheit—that it burned holes in and charred the surface of the X-15. On that occasion, record-breaking pilot Pete Knight was able to land safely, but a month later an ultra-high-altitude flight ended fatally. On November 15, 1967, Air Force pilot Mike Adams reached 266,000 feet, but the plane went out of control, descended through 230,000 feet, and entered a Mach 5 spin! There was a partial recovery 100,000 feet below that, but then the control system failed and pitching oscillations broke up the plane at 62,000 feet.

Such sacrifices were not in vain, and as leading aviation historian Richard P. Hallion put it, "without question, the X-15 constituted the most successful research airplane of all time," contributing over two dozen "major advances in aerospace technology." But those contributions having been made, and with the space programs over five years old, it was decided to end the X-15 series. The last and 199th flight of the series was made by the 81st flight of the first X-15, on October 24, 1968. It was no accident that the first man to step on the surface of the moon on July 20, 1969, Neil Armstrong, was one of the dozen X-15 pilots.

16

Into Outer Space

The last great miracle of aviation is, without question, the sending of humans into "space."*

That came after a first complete orbit of the earth by a Russian, Yuri Gagarin, on April 12, 1961, followed almost immediately by the suborbital flight of American Alan Shepard. Gagarin circled the earth from 112.4 to 203 miles up, in an elliptical orbit, for 1 hour and 48 minutes, narrowly avoiding spinning out of control just before a successful landing over 500 miles east of Moscow to the south of Kazan. Shepard's 15-minute flight on May 5 went 297 miles across the Atlantic from Cape Canaveral, Florida, with an apogee of 116.5 miles. Both flights came less than four years after the Soviet Union had launched on October 4, 1957, the first object to circle the earth every 90 minutes in an elliptical orbit up to 569 miles high. It was an aluminum sphere, weighing 83.6 kilograms (184 pounds) and called Sputnik ("satellite"). A new word, "sputnik," entered the world's vocabulary, and the words "cosmonaut" and "astronaut"—to designate space travelers—soon followed. They derived from the mythological Argonauts, who sailed the ship *Argo* to seek the flying ram's golden fleece. (Already, in 1880, a European science fiction work spoke of "astronauts," or star sailors.)

The space age had begun and, powered by the Cold War competition between the United States and Russia, developed with extraordinary rapidity. It reached an initial climax not even 12 years later when two Americans were able to land on the moon on July 20, 1969. Another ten

---

*"Space" is defined as "above the atmosphere." According to the Fédération Aéronautique Internationale (FAI), that is above 100,000 meters (328,000 feet, or about 63 miles). The United States Air Force awarded astronaut wings to the X-15 pilots who flew above 50 miles (264,000 feet), while astronauts speak variously of space as above 60 or 80 miles.

Americans accomplished that millennial dream, while the Russians established endurance records in space. Two Soviet cosmonauts first exceeded a full year there before returning to earth on December 21, 1988, 366 days after their ascent. Already, with the launching of re-usable space shuttles by the U.S. after 1981, the way seemed literally open to the planets, if not the stars, although that would have to await the establishment of an extremely costly space station, to be supplied by the shuttles.

As we have seen, the dream of going to the moon goes way back to ancient times, but the possibility had to await the new knowledge of the sky and the development of engines powerful enough to accomplish such a feat. Those engines were new types of rockets, which produced far more reactive thrust by using the action of burning liquid oxygen, hydrogen, and other new fuels such as nitrogen tetroxide and monomethyl hydrazine. For over a 1000 years, earlier rockets had been powered by "black powder," formed of a mixture of charcoal, saltpeter, and sulphur. The 20th century rockets increased their thrust to the 7.5 million pounds (equivalent to over 160,000 million horsepower!) that the Saturn V rocket threw out to propel the up to 6,407,000 pounds of lift-off weight— over 90 percent of which was fuel—needed to carry the American astronauts the 238,000 or so miles to the earth's only satellite! With an elliptical course, the moon's orbit around the earth varies from 253,000 miles at apogee to 221,000 miles at perigee.

The early dreams of going into space became more realistic with the pioneering studies of the use of liquid-fuel rockets for imagined space travel by the Russian school teacher Konstantin Tsiolkovsky. He published a book on the subject in the phenomenal year of 1903, and continued work on it until his death at 78, in 1935. Hermann Oberth, a Transylvanian who was born near the border of Romania and Hungary but spent most of his long life (1894–1989) in Germany, followed up these ideas and in 1923 published the influential book, *Die Rakete zu den Plantenraumen* ("The Rocket into Interplanetary Space"). But the first successful launching of a liquid-fuel rocket, to an altitude of 41 feet, 184 feet away, at 60 mph, was accomplished by the American father of the new rocketry, physicist Robert Goddard, from a field near Auburn, Massachusetts, on March 16, 1926. He received some small initial funding from the Smithsonian Institution, but then public skepticism and limitations imposed by local safety officials induced him to move to New Mexico.

There, near Roswell, between 1930 and his death at 62 in 1945, he and assistants worked out many new firsts for rocket flight and achieved ascensions to 9000 feet. A spaceflight center at Greenbelt, Maryland, near Washington, DC, would later be named for him, as followers realized his saying, "The dream of yesterday is the hope of today and the reality of tomorrow."

But the biggest steps in pre-war rocket development came in Germany following the work of Hermann Oberth and others. By 1937, the brilliant 25-year-old engineer Wernher von Braun was appointed director of the secret military center at Peenemunde, north of Berlin on the Baltic coast. There, he proceeded to develop the team which constructed the fearsome V-2 rockets, over 3000 of which fell on England and Allied targets during the last year of the war. They killed over 5000 people, but their use coming only after September 1944 could not prevent the defeat of Germany seven months later. They were the first true space rockets, proving definitively the possibility of efficient aerial operation in the vacuum of space. Standing some 46 feet tall and weighing 27,000 pounds, they used 25.4 tons of thrust to arc to about 60 miles up before descending with one ton of explosives on their targets. U.S. forces were able to remove some 300 box loads of V-2 parts before the arrival of Russian troops, and Von Braun and most of his associates elected to continue their work in America. Others chose to go to Russia, and the Soviets were able to acquire most of the Peenemunde documents relevant for rocket development, so that the space programs of both superpowers had a substantial input of German rocket expertise.

If until 1945, rocketry, even more than other aspects of aviation, developed to meet the military demands of World War II, the next stages similarly accelerated due to the demands of the Cold War. Missile and space programs developed rapidly in both the U.S.S.R. and the U.S. In America, centers were established first at White Sands, New Mexico and Huntsville, Alabama, and then by the late 1950s at Cape Canaveral, Florida, and at Houston, Texas. In the then-Soviet Union, testing and launches began near Volgograd (Rapustin Yar) and then at Baikonur (Tyuratum), about 300 miles north-northeast of the Aral Sea in Kazakhstan, and later also at Plesetsk, south of Archangelsk. The first priority in both the United States and the Soviet Union was for the development of missiles carrying the new and ever more fearsome atomic weapons. When the Soviets tested an Intercontinenal Ballistic Missile

(ICBM) in August 1957, it was evident that space ships were not far behind, and Sputnik I used a similar rocket for its spectacular launching in October 1957. An improved SS-6 ICBM, producing 900,000 pounds of thrust, sent Gagarin into orbit in 1961.

The Soviet program was conducted in strictest secrecy, but their "chief designer," as he was called, was identified on his death in January 1966 as Sergei Korolev. Already on November 27, 1953, a member of the Soviet Academy of Sciences, A.N. Nesmenyanov, announced the "real possibility" of launching an "artificial earth satellite"; using their big military rockets, they proceeded to do so less than four years later. The U.S. had announced the study of that possibility even earlier, in December 1948, but then made the wrong choice in the late 1950s of working with smaller rockets like the Vanguard and Viking to try to orbit satellites such as the Discoverers, Explorers, Pioneers, and others, rather than more powerful military rockets like the Redstone, Agena, and Atlas to launch heavier loads. The Soviets increased their launching power for space missions to over a million pounds of thrust by the early 1960s.

Prior to the American triumph of landing men on the moon from 1969 on, the Soviets achieved almost continuous space firsts. In early November 1957, a month after the orbiting of Sputnik I, they launched the much heavier, 1120-pound Sputnik II with a dog, Laika, on board. Laika died from lack of oxygen two days later. But then, less than four months after Gagarin's single first orbit of the earth in April 1961, his backup pilot, Gherman Titov, looped the earth 17 times in 25 hours. Vostoks 3 and 4 followed America's entry into manned spaceflight by several months, and on August 11 and 12, 1962, flew within three miles of each other.

Following the Cuban Missile Crisis of October, and the Cold War's closest brush with armageddon, the Soviets pulled off a new and double space spectacular, June 14–16, 1963, when Vostok 6 claimed a first rendezvous in space with Vostok 5, and moreover was commanded by the first woman in space, Valentina Tereshkova. Vostok 5's pilot, Valeri Bykovsky, carried on to complete 81 orbits and almost five days in space, while a year later Tereshkova married the cosmonaut of Vostok 3, Andrian Nikolaev. Americans, however, doubted that the Vostoks had achieved enough control or proximity to prove a true first rendezvous.

Given the tensions of the Cold War, the U.S. reacted with disbelieving shock to the Soviet successes beginning with Sputnik I. Congress greatly expanded funding and on July 29, 1958, President Eisenhower authorized the centralization of the venerable NACA and other aviation agencies in the armed services and government under the National Aeronautics and Space Administration, or NASA. By 1962, its headquarters and Space Task Group were established in Houston, while work continued at other centers, notably at NACA's old site of Langley, Virginia, the Goddard Space Center in Maryland, and the Jet Propulsion Laboratory in Pasadena, as well as at the leading aviation companies on Long Island, in St. Louis and on the West Coast, and—for the needed rockets—at Huntsville, Alabama. The Soviets also centralized their space efforts with the 1960 creation of the Strategic Rocket Force (later the Russian Space Agency) on the same level as the armed services, just after establishing a central cosmonaut center at Star City (Zvezdny Gorodak), 30 miles northeast of Moscow, and a control center between the two at Kaliningrad.

Following the embarrasing failure in December 1957 of a Vanguard rocket to develop enough thrust for a successful firing, on January 31, 1958, the U.S. used a new Juno 1 rocket to launch into orbit from Cape Canaveral its first satellite some four months after Sputnik. Weighing only 3.25 pounds, Explorer 1 was promptly dubbed by Russia's leader, Nikita Khrushchev, "America's grapefruit satellite." But it made an important scientific discovery, of the Van Allen radiation belts, or concentrations of radiation particles trapped by the earth's magnetic field.

New satellite launchings followed, and with the appointment in March 1960 of Wernher von Braun as director of the Marshall Space Flight Center at Huntsville, there was rapid progress in the development of more powerful rockets. These were, in succession, the Redstone, Jupiter, and Atlas, then the Titan 2 for the two-man Geminis, and finally Saturns for the three-man Apollos. As in any testing, new problems also arose. On July 29, 1960, came a spectacular explosion of a rocket launch at Cape Canaveral, and in December a highly publicized, so-called "popped cork" fiasco. This occurred when a congressional delegation observed the computer-ordered shutdown of the firing of a Redstone rocket, which then settled back on its pad with a final popping into the air of a part of its nose tip, like some absurd firecracker.

The new NASA space team, under the leadership of Robert Gilruth, James Edward Webb, Chris Kraft, Max Faget, and others, however, was well on the way to the launching of the first American manned space program, dubbed "Mercury." The first passenger, to the chagrin of many, was in fact a chimpanzee, Ham, who flew to his recovery near Bermuda at the end of January 1961. New problems occurred with tests of the Redstone rocket and Mercury capsule, but then came the successful and almost identical sub-orbital flights of Alan Shepard on May 5 and of Gus Grissom on July 21, 1961.

The first orbital flight by an American, future Senator John H. Glenn, on February 20, 1962, foreshadowed the coming of the great American space triumphs. His Mercury 6 space capsule weighed 4265 pounds and completed three orbits in 4 hours, 55 minutes. Following delays from the scheduled launch on December 20, and repeated waits for better weather, the lift-off by a 95-foot-high Atlas 6 rocket, powered by kerosene and oxygen, came at 9:47 A.M. After three orbits, finding the automatic control system inoperative, Glenn was able to manually fire the retrorocket and descend safely, to land 166 miles east of Grand Turk Island in the Bahamas. Among other fascinating reports from his ascent into the heavens, Glenn reported, as would others after him, seeing "fireflies" or "flicker flashers," described as "a big mass of very small particles that are brilliantly lit up like . . . little stars . . . they swirl around the capsule . . ." It turned out they were ice crystals formed by moisture emerging from the capsule.

Glenn's highly publicized success—the New York ticker-tape parade witnessed by millions was considered the most elaborate since that for Lindbergh 35 years before—and the installation of hand controls after Shepard's first trip into space partially overcame both the astronauts' frustrations at being only "a man in a can" like the first monkeys, as well as the feeling that "backward" Russia had upstaged the U.S.

Three more Mercury flights followed, with M. Scott Carpenter's repeat of Glenn's three orbits on May 24, 1962, and then Walter M. Schirra's six orbits on October 3. Deke Slayton had been scheduled as the third American to go into space, but was grounded because of a heart murmur and put in charge of flight crew assignments. The last Mercury flight revealed still greater advances by American space technology, as well as the increasing feasibility of President Kennedy's May 25, 1961, proposal to land a man on the moon before the decade was out. On May 15–16, 1963, Gordon Cooper completed 22 orbits and landed Mercury 9 in the Western Pacific only 4.5 miles from the recovery ship.

But Russia continued to register space firsts. On October 12, 1964, the new Voskhod ("sunrise") series completed 16 orbits with three men on board, including the first two mission specialists, engineer Konstantin Feoktistov, and medical doctor Boris Yegorov. They reported valuable new information and demonstrated a new ion-propulsion device for altitude control. Then, on March 18, 1965, Voskhod 2 dramatically enabled the first human being, Alexei Leonev, to step outside a spaceship through an airlock, some 120 (its apogee was 307) miles up. He remained outside just over ten minutes on a 16-foot (5-meter) tether, and such exhilarating, weightless free-floating in space, with cavorts and somersaults as well as observations and experiments, came to be called "extra-vehicular activity," or EVA. Leonev and Commander Pavel Belyayev almost achieved another less glorious first when their automatic guidance system failed and a first Soviet manually controlled re-entry landed in the Ural Mountain forests near Perm. They had to spend the night in the capsule to escape attacks by wolves before rescue the following day!

The two Voskhods were the heaviest spacecraft yet, 11,525 and 11,730 pounds respectively, as against the some 10,430 or so pounds of the Vostok series. Also, they were able to land with their craft retrofiring above the earth, whereas the earlier Vostok cosmonauts as well as some later ones descended by parachute. They were also the first space trips in which the cosmonauts had the confidence to wear lightweight clothing in lieu of bulky space suits.

The ten flights of U.S. Gemini spaceships, from March 23, 1965, to November 11, 1966, flown mostly by the second group of nine new astronauts, revealed America's steady progress toward landing men on the moon. Using the same conical shape as the Mercury capsules, but bigger (18 feet, 5 inches long and 10 feet in diameter) and with 50 percent more room for the astronauts, they weighed from 7000 to 8509 pounds. The McDonnell Aircraft Company, under the guidance of engineer John Yardley, was the prime contractor as it had been for the Mercury series, and as North American Aviation would be for the Apollos. The ever-improving Atlas, Titan, and finally Saturn rockets powered these space ships into orbits ranging from 100 to 219 miles up. The astronauts rode in the re-entry module of titanium and beryllium, and controlled 16 liquid-propellant rockets for maneuvering and control during re-entry. After the four solid-fuel retrorockets fired with 2500 pounds of thrust, the craft began its descent with parachutes slowing it in the final minutes before splashdown.

After unmanned tests on April 8, 1964, and January 19, 1965, the series began with the launch of Gemini 3 on March 23, 1965, by a Titan 2 rocket producing 430,000 pounds of thrust. This was over 70,000 pounds more than was produced by the Atlas rockets that launched the Mercury series. Rising from Cape Canaveral, renamed the Kennedy Space Center after the assassination of the President on November 22, 1963, astronauts Gus Grissom and John Young completed three revolutions from 100 to 140 miles up. A little over two months later, Ed White performed the first American space walk on the four-day mission of Gemini 4, launched on June 3, 1965, under the command of Jim McDivitt. White was able to use a hand-held gas reaction device to maneuver without a tether for 21 minutes in space during one of the 62 orbits completed. He strapped an 8-pound emergency oxygen pack around an improved 16-pound space suit. The latter's up to 21, as against the normal 4, layers for insulation were critical, to say the least, inasmuch as temperatures in space varied from as much as 250 degrees Fahrenheit at noontime to minus 250 at midnight, and changes of pressure could cause severe bends and a literal bubbling of the blood!

Other critical maneuvers were perfected on the longer flights which followed, including more EVAs, practicing rendezvous, docking, and maneuverability in space. First, Gemini 5 established a new duration record of 120 orbits, August 21–28, and Gemini 7 went all the way to 206 orbits from December 4 to 18, 1965. Gemini 6 actually followed number 7 by eleven days, but then achieved another important first: a rendezvous within one foot of Gemini 7 on December 15. Gemini 6 completed 15 orbits before splashdown in the Atlantic, while Gemini 7 went on to a record 206 orbits until December 18, completing over 20 experiments. By then, Americans had accumulated 1353 hours in space as against the Russians' 507.

There followed on March 16, 1966, the first docking in space when Gemini 8 linked up with an Agena target vehicle in a 185-mile-high orbit. That came 6 hours and 34 minutes after launch as astronauts Neil Armstrong and David Scott achieved a "hard dock," the Gemini 8's cone fixed inside the Agena's docking collar. After a half-hour of steady flight, however, the two craft began to tumble end over end—with over a turn a second! Disconnecting from the Agena, which they thought had caused the problem, the men were alarmed to find the spinning even worse, plus the new danger of a collision with the Agena. Unable to turn off the 16 maneuvering thrusters, Armstrong was forced to use the re-entry rockets on the Gemini's nose to stabilize after a half-hour of efforts. Later, it was found that the problem had been caused by continuous firing of the number 8 yaw thruster; but by now having used fuel reserved for the rest of the mission, at 10 hours, 4 minutes they retro-fired over Central Africa and parachuted into the Pacific 30 minutes later. After three hours at sea, the two were picked up by a destroyer, which then took 18 hours to reach Okinawa, 450 miles to the west.

It was the closest yet to a space catastrophe! Given the recovery from the emergency tumbling and the successful descent without the usual tracking stations and their precise reports, astronauts Alan Shepard and Deke Slayton would later state: "That was a fantastic recovery by a human being under such circumstances and really proved why we have test pilots in those ships . . ."

Then, from June 3 to 6, 1966, Gemini 9, under the command of Navy pilot Tom Stafford, demonstrated new rendezvous techniques to within three feet of the target, enabled a record 2-hour, 9-minute space walk by Eugene Cernan, and landed only two miles from the Gemini's target in the Atlantic. Its 45 circular orbits at 185 miles were called "the most significant" up to that time, although the failure of a computer and the straining of life support systems caused new scares. Using a 125-foot tether for his over-two-hour EVA, Cernan was unable to reach as planned the new Astronaut Maneuvering Unit (AMU) to attach to his back for greater maneuverability. Its size forced its storage at the rear of the capsule and he lacked the sort of jet gun used by White, or the portable handholds, foot restraints, and waist tethers supplied for future EVAs. Cernan experienced great difficulty controlling his movements, and saw his breath rate double, his heart rate rise to 180 a minute, and the loss of 10 pounds due to his exertions.

The next mission, by Gemini 10, from July 18 to 21, 1966, saw another important American "first," when Michael Collins, using an improved version of Ed White's hand-held jet gun to facilitate his moves, on an almost two-hour EVA was able to replace an instrument package and remove some film from the Agena 8 target. Earlier, Gemini 10 had docked with the Agena and the perigee of the orbit was raised from 99 to 184 miles up, with an apogee of 476 miles. Gemini 11, September 11–15, achieved a "completely successful rendezvous and docking maneuver," and adjusted its orbit from the initial 100 by 175 miles to a perigee of 185 miles and a record apogee of 851 miles above the earth. The series concluded November 11 to 15, with another docking and long space walk from Gemini 12. The latter, by Buzz Aldrin, gave Americans close to 12 hours of EVAs, and Gemini 12 completed 59 orbits between 100 and 168 miles up. It also splashed down in the Atlantic, and its Atlas-Agena-launched Agena target vehicle burned up on re-entry on December 23, 1966.

By then, plans for the next series of ten Apollo missions to meet the deadline of carrying Americans all the way to the moon before the decade was out were well advanced. Michael Collins, who would circle the moon in the command module during the historic July 20, 1969, landing on it by Neil Armstrong and Buzz Aldrin, has also given one of the most dramatic accounts of a Gemini flight, number 10 with John Young, as well as of the views from space. He described days from July 18 to 21, 1966, where

> The view out the window is worth all the months cooped inside a simulator . . . Those aren't counties going by, those are continents; not lakes, but oceans! Look at that, we just passed Hawaii and here comes the California coast, visible all the way from Alaska to Mexico, San Diego to Miami in 9 minutes flat! If I miss something, not to worry, it will be back in 90 minutes . . . the Indian Ocean flashes incredible colors of emerald, jade, and opal . . .

Their altitude made it seem that at some 300 miles a minute, "the ground goes by the window at about the same rate as in an airliner." During the take-off for the first of 48 orbits: "In 1 minute and 20 seconds we . . . accelerated from zero to 1000 mph and have climbed from sea level to 40,000 feet . . . [at] over 5 Gs." The 16 orbits every 24 hours gave a "55 minute 'day,'" and on Collins' first EVA he reported, "It is pitch black," and "My God, the stars are everywhere, even below me. They are somewhat brighter than on earth, but the main difference is that they don't twinkle. . . . The planet Venus also appears absurdly bright, like a 50-watt bulb in the sky. . . . The moon is down below the horizon and the only noticeable light comes from lightning flashes along a row of thunderstorms on earth. [Then] the sun comes up with a fierce burst of piercing white light." After the retrofire, the descent was "like making gliding turns in an airplane except that we are upside down and backward, head down for maximum lift and [to put] the heatshield forward. I can tell that the ablative heatshield is doing its job because we are developing a tail. Tenuous at first, then thicker and more startling, it glows an eerie red and yellow. . . . The Gs taper off now, and at 38,000 feet we let fly our drogue parachute . . . [then] the main chute . . . [before we] plop gently into the Atlantic." Wow!

Flight testing for the trip to the moon had already begun in November 1963, but the first attempt ended in disaster as Apollo 1 exploded in fire during a simulated countdown on January 27, 1967, preparing for the first launch in February. A spark from an exposed electrical wire detonated the pure oxygen being tried in the spacecraft, and all three astronauts, veterans Gus Grissom and Ed White and rookie Roger Chafee, died in agony. The explosive flammability caused by the use of 100 percent oxygen at slightly more than the normal sea-level pressure of 15 pounds per square inch was impossible to control. Future flights would reduce the oxgygen to 60 percent at 5 psi and install escape hatches that could be blown open in less than ten seconds.

Other American astronauts were also killed about that time, but not in the space they were training for. Air Force major Edward Givens died in a car crash near Houston on June 6, and Marine Corps major Clifton Curtiss Williams as his supersonic T-38 went out of control approaching Tallahassee, Florida on October 5, 1967. The crew preparing for Gemini 9, Elliot See and Charles Bassett, died in the crash of another T-38 in a stormy landing at St. Louis on February 28, 1966. And over a year before that, in October 1964, a freak accident to still another T-38 took the life of another untried American astronaut, Ted Freeman. Approaching Houston for landing after a routine training flight, the plane struck a snow goose at 1500 feet and 400 knots. That shattered the plexiglass cockpit canopy, some of which flew into and choked both engines. Freeman was unable to bail out safely and became the first American astronaut to die on duty.

The first death in an actual spaceflight came in the same year of 1967 that saw the Apollo 1 fire, but in the Soviet Union. The first new Soyuz ("Union") 1 crashed in April 1967, killing its lone cosmonaut, Vladimir Komarov. On April 23, the spaceship reached an elliptical orbit, varying between 125 and 139 miles (201–224 kms) up. But fatal problems soon developed. Unlike the American spacecraft using battery power, the Soyuz sought to use solar power, but the left panel jammed and could not be extended into the sun's rays. Then, with insufficient power, the craft's electronic control system failed. Soviet mission control canceled the planned launch and rendezvous with Soyuz 2, and decided to abort the mission of Soyuz 1 after 17 orbits. Although Cosmonaut Komarov somehow miraculously managed re-entry in a ship spinning wildly out of control, its parachute lines tangled and the Soyuz hit the ground near Orenburg in the Urals at 400 mph, exploding in flames.

A previous explosion on a launch pad on October 24, 1960, had killed an observing field marshal and others, but had never been reported. In 1986, the Soviets belatedly reported a launch pad explosion that had killed Cosmonaut Valentin Bondarenko on March 23, 1961, with a flash fire of pure oxygen, strikingly similar to that which consumed the crew of Apollo 1 at Cape Canaveral in January 1967. The Soyuz launch weight was over twice that of the Gemini, at more than 14,000 pounds, though less than that of the Apollos then being constructed by the U.S.

The trauma of that first space death, together with an earlier over-confident slowdown, compounded by the ouster of space enthusiast Nikita Khrushchev in October 1964, caused delays that enabled America to achieve the biggest "first" of all: the landing of humans on the moon.

Russia did in fact send the first unmanned satellites to the moon and beyond. In January 1959, Lunik 1 flew by the earth's satellite, as did the American Pioneer 4 in March. In September, the Soviets crash-landed Lunik 2 there, and shortly afterward Lunik 3 made the first photographs of the moon's hidden side. In 1962, the Kosmos series of satellites began to be launched, and in 1964 the Russians sent Zond ("Probe") 1 toward Venus in April, and Zond 2 toward Mars in November. The first data arriving on earth from such distant missions was reported after Venera 4's entry into the atmosphere of Venus on October 18, 1967, over four months after its launch on June 12. Over a year before, in early 1966, Luna 9 made the first soft landing and sent the first television pictures from the moon. From November 17, 1970, so called Lunokhods began to roam its surface, transmitting data and photographs back to Earth.

By the 1980s, other countries, including China, France, India, and Japan, had launched their own satellites into orbit. But the United States did the most by far and began to surpass Russia in manned space efforts by the mid-1960s with its massive concentration on reaching the moon by the end of the decade. Already on March 3, 1959, NASA had sent Pioneer 4 toward the moon, although it went into solar orbit, as did Pioneer 5 the following year. Ranger, Lunar Orbiter, and Surveyor satellites shortly began increasingly sophisticated photography of the moon. Surveyor 1 sent back 10,000 photos of its surface on June 2, 1966, and then Surveyor 3 was able to soft-land on the moon in April 1967, sending back over 6000 detailed pictures of the lunar surface.

The U.S. also sent satellites beyond the moon, although at first fewer than the Soviets. On August 27, 1962, NASA launched Mariner 2, which flew within 22,000 miles of Venus by December 14. In November 1964, Mariners 3 and 4 were launched, the latter flying within 6100 miles of Mars and sending much-awaited photos back to the earth. By August 5, 1969, Mariner 7 came within 2200 miles of Mars, and Mariner 9 went into orbit around Mars on November 13, 1971, after its launch on May 30.

We shall return to other still more extraordinary probes into inter-planetary space and beyond later, but in the 1960s U.S. efforts concentrated brilliantly on the goal of landing on the moon. It was a nationwide effort, the number of people engaged in space programs going from 50,000 in 1960 to nearly 400,000 people at over 20,000 enterprises at peak in 1965. Reductions set in even before the end of the decade, but NASA itself, which grew from 10,000 workers in 1960 to 36,000 in 1966, still employed some 34,126 people in 1970. They were very much needed because the work was so incredibly complicated and vast. To cope with the tragic explosion of Apollo 1 in January 1967, for example, the Houston spaceflight operations team made some 1341 changes for greater safety, based on over 100,000 pages of documents and transcripts.

Robert Gilruth directed the Houston Manned Space Flight Center, later named the Lyndon Johnson Space Center. Important assistants included Chris Kraft, Gene Krantz, Glynn Lunney, Gerald Griffin, Milt Windler, Rocco Petrone, George Low, Floyd Thompson, and many others with widely varying specialities. Astronauts like Vance D. Brand, Michael Collins, and Jack Lousma offered expert advice and communicated with the astronauts as "Capcom." Deke Slayton served as first Chief of Flight Crew Operations, while Max Faget headed the Space Center's Engineering and Development branch. Homer E. Newell was the first head of the Office of Space Science, coordinating input from universities and other centers. They operated under the overall command, in Washington, of NASA chiefs T. Keith Glennan, James E. Webb, and, after the latter's retirement in the autumn of 1968, Thomas Paine, James C. Fletcher, Richard Truly, Daniel Goldin, and others, with their deputies Robert Crippen, George Mueller, Air Force General Sam Phillips, and many others.

Computers and simulators were of course more important than ever for all their work, and the money and effort put into the space program pioneered many of the new cybernetic breakthroughs of the age. For example, as worked out for the Apollo program, the ability to insert priority items dictated by emergencies ahead of normal sequences, as well as to bypass insoluble problems, saved many a mission. The use of computers from the mid-1950s for the new simulators that evolved out of the old Link trainers was more essential than ever to train for the unknowns of the space age. And the advances in computer technology both enabled and profited from the space age. They were ever more high-speed, the 70-pound Apollo computer for example calculating a cycle of information in 20 milliseconds. Using 40,000 lines of computer code, they did so with unparalleled accuracy and reliability for the speeds, headings, rocket burns, headings, and countless other information. The headings and launch times also had to be synchronized with the "launch windows" necessary to target a satellite or heavenly body according to its position and revolution in space. In a day there may be only one five- or ten- minute launch window for a ship to take off from the earth to join an orbiting space station, depending on its course. On many occasions most dramatically with Apollo 13 and 14—computer experts were called on at all hours of day and night to solve critical problems of the most diverse sort.

After unmanned tests of five new spaceships, Apollo 7 blasted off for the first successful space test of the new moon ship on October 11, 1968. Its three-man crew, headed by Wally Schirra on his third spaceflight, completed 163 orbits 142 to 177 miles up, with rendezvous practice with the discarded third stage and other experiments, before splashing down near Bermuda on October 22. Ironically, this came at the time of the worst year of the Vietnam War, as well as that of the release of the most famous of all space films, Stanley Kubrick and Arthur Clarke's *2001: A Space Odyssey*. It in turn inspired future films as well as TV series like "Lost in Space" and the still-continuing sagas of "Star Trek."

Apollo 7 was launched with a Saturn 1B rocket, but the formidable

Saturn V was ready two months later for Apollo 8, following a first test firing in November 1967 and a second unmanned firing in 1968. By far the most powerful rocket ever built, it was 363 feet tall, or as high as a 36-story building as against the 9-story-high (95 feet) Mercury Atlas that carried John Glenn into orbit in February 1962.

The Saturn V used the first of its three stages to produce 7.5 million pounds of thrust, sending skyward at 7:51 A.M. on December 21, 1968, Apollo 8's initial weight of 6,219,760 pounds. In the first 2.5 minutes, some 4.5 million pounds of propellant were consumed by the five huge engines of the first stage, which, before being jettisoned, pushed the craft to over 6000 mph, or 9000 feet per second. (In space, velocities are measured in feet per second.) The second stage, also with five huge engines, then took over until discarded 100 miles up, also dropping into the Atlantic eleven minutes after lift-off, as had stage one and the needle-nosed escape tower for use if problems developed before orbit. Next, the third stage accelerated the remaining 285,000 pounds into orbit 114 to 116.6 miles up at almost 17,500 mph, or some 25,500 feet per second and over 24 times the speed of sound.

About 10 A.M. on December 21, after some 2 hours, 47 minutes, 37 seconds of flight, on their second orbit of the earth, the crew fired the third stage again for 5.9 minutes, to reach the 23,226 mph, or 35,532 feet per second, necessary to escape the earth's gravity. That is close to 7 miles a second and 50 times the speed of a bullet. At 3 hours and 21 minutes into the mission, with the completion of the final push, called "the translunar injection," the crew ejected the third stage into an orbit that went around the sun.

The remaining 60,000 pounds or so of the mother ship, command and service module, and 35,000 pounds of the readjusted lunar module continued their two-and-a-half-day coast at declining speeds to the moon. The craft slowed to about 2200 mph, some 202,700 miles out and fifty-five and a half hours after lift-off. Then, as the moon's gravity took over 38,900 miles away, Apollo 8 accelerated to 5700 mph before the service module engine fired to slow it to 3700 mph and an initial eliptical orbit of 69.5 by 190 miles above the moon. It was 69 hours and 15 minutes after launch when the main engine fired a precise 247 seconds (4.116 minutes) to enter the moon's orbit, and on the third loop it fired again to achieve the desired nearly circular orbit of 60.7 by 59.7 miles up. If the engine had failed, the greatest safety feature of the Apollo flights, a "free return trajectory," would have allowed the craft to use the moon's gravity to swing around it and begin its return back to earth.

Apollo 8 clearly was one of the most important of all space trips, as it was the first to undertake the hazards of going all the way to the moon. Those hazards included the risk of failure for the over seven million working "systems" of the Saturn V and Apollo spaceship. Even if that risk were judged at only a tenth of one percent, there still was a chance of over 5600 malfunctions! Furthermore, there was the incredible problem of returning to earth, as Commander Frank Borman put it, through a "precise re-entry corridor, a tunnel if you will. If we got below that corridor, the angle was too steep, and if we got above it, the angle was too shallow; it was certain death if we missed the tunnel . . ." The spacecraft would have hit the atmosphere like a rock skipping across water.

Astronaut Michael Collins described the difficulty of that for themselves and the Mission controlers: ". . . hitting a forty-mile entry corridor from 230,000 miles is like trying to split a human hair with a razor blade thrown from a distance of twenty feet." Veterans Al Shepard and Deke Slayton called Apollo 8 "the greatest single gamble in space flight." It was launched over the Christmas season to take advantage of a launch window, and further expanded America's lead over the Soviet Union in the race to the moon. In addition to Borman, fellow Air Force officer William Anders and Navy Lt. Commander James Lovell made up the three-man crew of Apollo 8.

Borman later described the wonders of that flight. A veteran of the Gemini 7 mission, he noted the relative smoothness of the lift-off and spaciousness of the 9-by-13-foot command module— three times the size of his Gemini three years earlier. He used the phrase "a befuddling array" to describe the "24 instruments, 40 'event' indicators, 71 lights, and 566 switches" to be monitored by the crew. These compared to 971 lights, switches and dials on the Boeing 747-200, which were reduced to 365 on the 400 model of the 747.

Midway, Apollo 8 had noted the earth's reduction visually to a size "about as big as the end of my thumb." Like all lunar astronauts, the crew noted the incredible beauty of the mostly blue earth, Anders stating, "We came all this way to explore the moon, and the most important thing is that we discovered the earth." Borman took understandable pride in reporting: "We were the first humans to see the world in its majestic totality." As Edgar Mitchell noted after his nine hours on the moon on Apollo

14, the earth looked like "a sparkling blue-and-white jewel . . . laced with slowly swirling veils of white [clouds] . . . like a small pearl in a thick sea of black mystery."

They made a mid-course correction with the service propulsion system, and fought problems of fever, nausea, and diarrhea, as well as the clouding up of three of the five windows due to moisture deposits forming between the three panes of each window. In lunar orbit, taking about two hours, or a half-hour more than the orbits around the earth because of the lighter pull of gravity, they were finally able to get some rest and six hours of sleep. Given their fatigue and the myriad details to attend to, Borman wondered if space travel confirmed the ancient adage "Flying is hours of boredom punctuated by moments of sheer terror." But as the windows cleared on one of Apollo 8's eleven orbits of the moon, Borman sighted the earth, and called it "the most beautiful, heart-catching sight of my life, one that sent a torrent of nostalgia, of sheer homesickness, surging through me. It was the only thing in space that had any color to it. Everything else was either black or white, but not the earth. It was mostly a soft, peaceful blue, the continents outlined in a pinkish brown. And always the white clouds . . ." Apollo 8's crew noted those wonders and that of being the first men to see the back side of the moon, on one of many television broadcasts, reciting on Christmas Eve moving passages from Genesis.

On the tenth orbit of the moon came the critical firing for almost four minutes of the service module SPS engine, to reach the 5500 mph necessary to begin the journey back to earth. Fortunately, there was no failure and at 1:20 EST Christmas morning they were on the way home. Turning the ship around so that the heat shield would absorb and deflect the up to 5000 degrees Fahrenheit caused by friction for at least three minutes as they entered the earth's atmosphere at 36,194 feet per second or almost 25,000 mph, they then fired some 80 miles above China the explosive device which discarded the service module. Their red-hot glow created an incandescent trail 100 miles long, as noted by a passing American jetliner.

But the astronauts felt no extreme heat, as the ablative heat shields deflected over 90 percent of that back into space. By the time of the shuttles, after 1981, some 30,000 silica-fiber, ceramic tiles were precisely fitted to form improved but similar (previously of nickel-steel and beryllium alloys) heat shields, which partially burned off, while a black boron-silicate glass coating reflected excessive heat so that it never exceeded 350 degrees on the aluminum surfaces and maintained normal temperatures inside the capsule. Borman, for his part, reported feeling as he had with the 17,000 or so mph re-entry of the Gemini 7, that he was in a "neon tube."

The autopilot controlled the inertial navigation system for precisely the right angle of entry. This had to be no less than 5.3 degrees, and no more than 7.7 degrees. If the descent was under 5.3 degrees, the command module would bounce off the earth's atmosphere and go into permanent orbit around the sun. If it was above 7.7 degrees, the friction would incinerate the spaceship. Fortunately, Apollo 8's re-entry was on target, and at 24,000 feet deployed the drogue parachutes and shortly thereafter the main chute. The crew landed in the Pacific about 1000 miles southwest of Hawaii in the early morning of December 27, 1968, only three miles from the waiting aircraft carrier *Yorktown*. In the hour and a half before pickup by helicopter, Borman mused about the irony of becoming seasick, "after flying a half million miles through space."

It remained to perfect the lunar module (LM) itself, which had not yet been attached to an Apollo, and then the techniques for turning it around in flight to enable many necessary maneuvers. It was the first true spaceship in the sense of only for being used in space, looking like a giant bug with its protruding antennae and four spindly legs. It weighed 33,000 pounds, 70 percent of which was fuel, and was in two components, a descent stage to be left behind on the moon and the ascent stage that would rejoin the command and service module circling the moon. Apollo 9, commanded by Jim McDivitt and accompanied by Dave Scott and Rusty Schweickart, successfully demonstrated it with the necessary rendezvous, docking, jettisoning of the lower stage, and other manuevers at up to 113 miles from the mother ship on 151 orbits of the earth from March 3 to 13, 1969. Then Apollo 10, commanded by Tom Stafford from May 18 to 26, again went into orbit around the moon, but also descended the lunar module to less than ten miles above the proposed landing site. The crew was able to control severe tumbling in that descent by using the abort guidance system.

The stage was set for Apollo 11's triumphant landing of two men on the lunar surface. This came on July 20, 1969, a date that will mark the 20th century as much or more even than the dropping of the first atomic bomb on August 6, 1945, to end history's most destructive war. As mission commander Neil Armstrong stepped on the surface of the moon, he stated to a watching world, "That's one small step for man, one giant leap for mankind." Then, after the trip, President Nixon even proclaimed it "the greatest week in the history of the world . . ."

Shortly joining Armstrong to become the second man on the moon was Edwin "Buzz" Aldrin. Circling the moon was fellow Gemini veteran Michael Collins, who later described the dramatic events in his 1974 book, *Carrying the Fire*, and in other works. Armstrong was a former naval pilot with 78 combat missions in the Korean War, and appropriately like the Wright brothers a native of Ohio. He went on to become a civilian test pilot, as earlier mentioned, flying the remarkable X-15. So, too, was Michael Collins, who had been born to a military family in Rome, Italy. He went to West Point, as did Buzz Aldrin. "Buzz" was a nickname derived from his baby sister's attempt to pronounce "brother" in their Montclair, New Jersey home. Aldrin had gone on to do a doctorate at M.I.T. on space rendezvous techniques, and all three men were obliged to, and did work together in perfect harmony.

The momentous journey began at 9:32 EDT on July 16, 1969, as the monster Saturn V roared to life. The final 417-step checklist complete, the first stage's incredible 7.5 million pounds of thrust propelled forward the 6 million pounds in 2.5 minutes to an altitude of 45 miles before being discarded. The five J-2 engines of the second stage then took over until 110 miles up, when the third stage's single engine accelerated the craft to the almost 17,500 mph needed for orbit 114.6 to 116.6 miles above the earth, not quite 12 minutes after launch. After an orbit and a half, less than three hours from launch, the S-4B third-stage engine was again fired for 5.9 minutes to increase the speed to the 24,300 mph necessary to leave the earth's gravity and begin the three-day trip to the moon.

As the craft rotated in the "barbeque mode," to equalize the heat and rays of the sun, only one of four planned mid-course corrections was necessary to come within several hundred miles of the moon almost a quarter million miles away. The service module fired for three seconds 130,000 miles up for the only course correction needed, and at 244,930 miles out again for 6 minutes and 2 seconds, to slow the then 5600 mph to 3700 mph and send the spacecraft into an elliptical orbit of 70 by 195 miles above the moon. On the fourth day from launch, late in the day of July 19, after two such circuits the engine again fired to make a roughly circular orbit of 62 by 75 miles up. About midday on the 20th, the final maneuvers for the descent to the lunar surface began.

Nearly 109 hours into the mission the lunar module (LM), named *Eagle* with Armstrong and Aldrin aboard, separated from the mother ship (command [CM] and service module [SM], or together, the CSM). Called the *Columbia*, it remained under the command of Michael Collins. Descending to about 50,000 feet above the surface of the moon, the LM engine again fired to reduce speed to some 60 mph by 7600 feet about five miles uprange from the landing site in the moon's Sea of Tranquility. The LM was inverted to a face-up position for the final descent. But then with the landing radar and on-board computer in control, an alarm flashed signaling an overload of information. Houston Space Center computer expert Steven Bales and his team determined that the problem would correct itself and need not abort the mission. But given the preoccupation with the alarms, they were four miles off-course as the final maneuvers continued.

Switching to semi-automatic mode, Armstrong then skillfully adjusted the final course to avoid boulders and set down at 4:17:41 EDT on July 20, 1969. There was less than 20 seconds of fuel remaining for the descent engine, and a nervous Houston Space Center reported: "We're breathing again," on hearing Armstrong report: "The *Eagle* has landed."

Canceling the planned four-hour rest period, Armstrong and Aldrin spent over six hours checking the essential systems of the *Eagle* and its ascent engine, as well as preparing to actually go out on the lunar surface. Descending an extended ladder, at 10:56:20 P.M. Armstrong made the momentous first step, and 16 minutes later he was joined by Aldrin. With only one-sixth of the earth's gravity, Armstrong's space suit earth weight of 348 pounds now totaled only 58, which explained the gazelle-like bouncing movements of the two now-famous astronauts. They proceeded to spend up to 2 hours and 31 minutes, at distances up to 200 feet away from the *Eagle*, gathering over 48 pounds of lunar soil and rocks. They planted with some difficulty an American flag and left behind a plaque reading:

HERE MEN FROM THE PLANET EARTH FIRST SET FOOT
UPON THE MOON JULY 1969, A.D.
WE CAME IN PEACE FOR ALL MANKIND.

Most importantly for scientists back on the earth, they deployed a solar wind detector and a type of seismometer to record "moonquakes," which recorded the blast-off of their ascent stage at 1:54 P.M. EDT on July 21. It burned for over seven minutes to achieve the necessary 4128-mph ascent and forward speed to approach *Columbia* three and a half hours later. Another slight burn and they docked, allowing their transfer to the mother ship.

One can imagine the jubilant reunion with Collins, who had just completed ten of the two-hour orbits solo around the moon. They then jettisoned the faithful *Eagle*. Next, the command service module (CSM) fired for the trans-earth injection (TEI) to escape the moon's gravity, which was followed by the ejection of the service module. They repositioned the 11-by-13 foot, 12,570 pound, cone-shaped command module so that its heat shield faced forward, toward the earth. Close to three days later, from 80 or so miles up they made the fiery entry into the earth's atmosphere at over 35,000 feet a second, and then at about 24,000 feet threw off the heat shield and deployed drogue parachutes. At 10,700 feet, pilot chutes pulled out the main parachutes, which reduced the descent speed to 22 mph and less. The capsule splashed into the Pacific about 900 southwest of Hawaii and 13 miles from the waiting aircraft carrier, the *Hornet.*

It was 12:40 P.M. (EDT) on the 24th of July—8 days, 3 hours, 18 minutes, and 35 seconds after their departure. They returned to a world whose mentality had been forever changed by their epochal odyssey.

Five more landings were made on the moon in the next three years. In all, the 12 men of the six Apollos spent about 166 hours on the lunar surface, returning to earth some 2196 samples weighing 841 pounds. Apollo 12, from November 14 to 24, 1969, was distinguished by a landing exactly near, as intended so as to not spray it with moon dust, where the Surveyor 3 satellite had landed two and a half years earlier, in the Ocean of Storms, 960 miles west of Apollo 11's landing site. In 31 hours, 31 minutes on the lunar surface, Pete Conrad and Alan Bean made two EVAs, deploying new scientific instruments and recovering some from Surveyor, before rejoining Dick Gordon in the command module.

Apollo 13, perhaps appropriately called *Odyssey*, never made it to the lunar surface and came close to destruction in space as demonstrated in a popular 1995 movie of that name. On April 11, 1970, when it was

205,000 miles above the earth, after 2 days, 7 hours, and 54 minutes of travel into space, an oxygen tank explosion blew off almost an entire side of its CSM, ripping apart electrical and other systems. Unlike Apollo 12, which automatically recovered from the lightning strike that momentarily cut off all its power, there was no way to recover Apollo 13's essential CSM functions. Yet the crew of Jim Lovell, Jack Swigert, and Fred Haise was able to use the Lunar Module as their lifeboat, "powering down" to hoard enough to stretch the two-day supply of oxygen, fuel, electricity, and water, in order to sustain them for the over three days necessary for their return.

To accomplish that, they used critical computer-based information from Mission Control teams headed by Gene Krantz, Glynn Lunney, John Aaron, Sy Liebergot, Bill Peters, and others, as well as from astronauts like Jack Lousma, John W. Young, and Thomas K. Mattingly. The latter had been bumped from the crew at the last minute, for fear of infection with the German measles going around for which he had no immunity. Recalled to Mission Control, Mattingly was still able to play an all-important role, for his intimate knowledge of the systems and astronauts' requirements made possible solutions to critical problems such as which systems could be shut down to save electricity.

Most important, Apollo 13 also had to alter its trajectory to circle the moon 136 miles up and use that gravity to swing toward earth. Handcrafting an emergency housing of hoses, plastic, paper, socks, and tape to fit lithium hydroxide purifiers to the connections in the lunar module, they were then able to solve the problem of a near-fatal build up of CO_2 from their breathing in a small space with inadequate ventilation. Deprived of most of the spaceship's computers, they used a fix on the earth, moon, and sun to make a final course correction with an untested five-minute use of the lunar module rocket, before jettisoning it. Finally, they were able to return safely on April 17, moments before the exhaustion of their electrical, oxygen, water, and other support systems. The command module's three huge orange-and-white chutes dropped it with remarkable precision only three miles from the waiting carrier *Iwo Jima*, near American Samoa. The heat shields did their job, but without other systems the astronauts suffered temperatures as low as 38 degrees Fahrenheit for three days, describing life in an icebox. It was the closest to space-borne catastrophe an American spaceship ever experienced and the biggest scare since the miraculous return of Gemini 8 four years earlier.

Newsweek called it "the most amazing rescue operation of all time."

The ten-day mission of Apollo 14 after January 31, 1971, reestablished confidence by solving a harrowing docking problem with the lunar module and then spending the longest time yet on the lunar surface. First, American astronaut Alan Shepard and Navy captain Edwin Mitchell spent 9 hours, 17 minutes outside the lunar module near Cone Crater, their prime geological target, in the Fra Mauro region, with a record walk by Shepard of almost 9000 feet, while Stu Roosa circled overhead. The crater was 1100 feet wide with a slope of 400 feet, and given the difficulties of climbing in such terrain, the astronauts could not quite reach the top. But they gathered extensive materials and performed many experiments on "the first flight devoted solely to the scientific exploration of the moon." They had the added insurance of a third oxygen tank and additional spare battery to avoid any Apollo 13-type emergency, and returned safely to earth on February 8.

Then, from July 26 to August 7, 1971, Apollo 15's Dave Scott and Jim Irwin bettered that with a record 66 hours, 55 minutes, near the shore of the moon's Sea of Rains in the mountainous area of the Hadley-Apennines, close to 11,000 feet high. They were outside the LM for 18 hours and 37 minutes, including a trip of over 17 miles in the LRV (lunar rover) at speeds up to 11 mph! Overhead, on August 5, A1 Worden made the first deep-space EVA, transferring film cassettes from the SM to the CM.

Almost nine months later, from April 16 to 27, 1972, Apollo 16 commander John Young and Charles Duke did three EVAs with use of the LRV, for 20 hours, 15 minutes of a total of 71 hours and 2 minutes on the moon, while Ken Mattingly circled in the CM. They were operating 8000 feet higher than the Tranquility base, near the Descartes Crater, and collected 213 pounds of lunar samples as well as deploying more solar wind experiments and conducting magnetometer experiments. The final Apollo, number 17, was also the longest of the series, 12 days and 14 hours, from December 7 to 19, 1972. Veteran Eugene Cernan and the first American scientist to go into space, geologist and future New Mexico Senator Harrison H. "Jack" Schmitt, established new records. These included the longest stay of 74 hours, 59.5 minutes on the moon in the Taurus-Littrow Crater of the Sea of Serenity Basin, with the longest single EVA of 7 hours and 48 minutes, and the longest total EVA time of 22 hours, 5 minutes. While Ron Evans circled overhead, they collected from the Taurus Littrow region the most samples yet—249.3 pounds—and conducted many experiments.

All of the 12 astronauts who landed on the moon described its stark beauty and desolation, as well as the warmer colors of the earth, and realized the most extraordinary moments of their lives. Apollo 14's Edgar Mitchell went further, to later describe his insight with the "Oriental" realization that "I was not separate from the universe. It's a part of me." He conducted secret ESP experiments from the moon to friends back on earth, and went on to found a parapsychology-influenced Institute of Noetic Sciences. The next Apollo flight's Jim Irwin also experienced more than the sensations of extraterrestrial flight. He went through a "born again" experience, and a year later founded the High Flight Ministry. Becoming known as "The Moon Missionary," Irwin devoted his last two decades to preaching, with several trips to search for the remains of Noah's Ark on Mount Ararat in Turkey. His eleven fellow moon-walkers enjoyed successful but more prosaic post-lunar experiences.

17

Satellites, Shuttles and Space Stations

The miracle of exploring the moon was over for the time being, although scientists have been busy for years analyzing the information and materials brought back by the astronauts. Space exploration did not stop, but the emphasis shifted. The United States moved to develop re-usable spaceships, or shuttles, while Russia concentrated on the development of space stations in long-term orbits around the earth, with visits by series of Soyuz cosmonauts. And both countries, joined by many others, launched many satellites for varied communications and scientific research around the globe. The two superpowers also sent probes far out into deeper space, and planned new missions to the moon, Mars, and beyond.

By the end of the 1980s, over 12,000 payloads had been delivered into orbit, with some 7000 trackable space objects still circling the earth in the 1990s, although only a few hundred of those were still functioning. They revolutionized communications—from telephone calls to TV—now with worldwide satellite transmissions, as well as weather prognostication, mapping, and navigation. Space-borne radio signals sending many thousands of bits of information came to be known as "telemetry." Not unnaturally, the governments of the U.S., Russia, China, and other nations used "spy" satellites for military surveillance in ways that would prevent any future "Pearl Harbor"-type attacks. The Europeans concentrated on the launching of commercial satellites with Ariane space rockets from Kourou, in French Guiana. There have been growing problems, however, with space debris, even including the leaking of radioactivity from atomic-powered satellites launched by Russia after 1967 into a frequently used orbit of 600 or so miles up.

More constructively, by the 1990s extremely precise space imaging by radar, microwave, and other techniques was giving the most accurate information yet for archaeological treasures, from Angkor Wat to the Silk Road, the Pyramids, and beyond. For closer-in observations, especially for military intelligence, a series of aircraft were developed. The Russians used, among others, the Myasishchev M-55 spyplane and, as noted in an earlier chapter, the U.S. by the 1960s flew the Lockheed U-2 (later ER-2) and SR-71 to gather photographic intelligence supplementing the space satellite systems. A modification of the Boeing 707, the Airborne Warning and Control System (AWACS), powered by four 21,000-pound thrust turbofan engines, used its "look-down radar" mounted in a rotating rotodome, fixed above the rear fuselage, to give especially detailed information in crisis situations like the 1991 Gulf War.

The sending of satellites high into the atmosphere and beyond accompanied the post-war development of rockets, and then increased exponentially after the launching of the first objects into earth orbit after October 1957. In 1959, the Russians sent the first space probe beyond the earth's gravity with Lunik 1, and the U.S. soon followed, both countries also sending probes into outer space. The Russian Venera 1 flew by Venus in 1961, and Venera 3 impacted it in 1965. Venera 4 made an atmospheric probe of Venus in 1967, and Venera 7 made a first soft landing on such a distant heavenly body on December 15, 1970. Venera 8 was able to send back analyses of soil samples as well as atmospheric conditions, after its soft landing on July 22, 1972. Number 9 sent back pictures from the surface of Venus three years later. The Soviets also made the first fly-by of Mars in 1962, and both a crash and soft landing on the red planet in 1971.

American firsts included the initial pictures of Mars from space by Mariner 4 in 1965, and from its surface by Viking landers in 1976. A Pathfinder satellite is to be launched in December 1996, and land on the Red Planet with a rover to explore its surface on July 4, 1997. Orbiting Astronomical Observatories (OBOs) also began to be launched, after a successful one in December 1968. Then, in 1973, Mariner 10 took close-up pictures of Venus and Mercury, while the year before, Pioneer 10 had sent the first close-up shots of Jupiter and its moons. Pioneer 11 did this for Saturn and its ring in 1973, and Jupiter in December 1974.

Other satellites followed into outer space, using the gravity of outer planets to accelerate to over 100,000 mph. Voyagers 1 and 2, launched August 20 and September 5, 1977, went on to complete a "Grand Tour" of the outer planets. Before continuing into outer space, they sent back over 100,000 pieces and pictures of scientific data. Pioneer 10 became the first spacecraft to leave the solar system at a record speed of over 107,373 mph after flying past Jupiter and Pluto in 1987, some 15 years after its launch. It did so bearing plaques with pictures of Adam- and Eve-like figures and scientific data from the earth for the edification of whoever or whatever might find it awash in the universe. After Voyager 2 flew by Neptune in 1989, it too continued into outer space. But before it did so, it took a picture of the earth as an incoming extraterrestrial spaceship might see it. Astronomer Carl Sagan used that humbling image as the title of his 1994 book, *The Blue Dot.*

The U.S. series "proved to be the most productive interplanetary probes" ever, according to its first chief architect, Wernher von Braun. He praised the extraordinary "astronomical marksmanship"' and value of the reports. Galileo, launched in October 1989, went into orbit around Jupiter six years later, on December 7, 1995, to celebrate the great physicist's first telescopic observations of that largest planet's moons in 1610. On the same day, the 746-pound probe that the 2.5-ton spacecraft had launched in July parachuted into the planet's atmosphere to record 57 minutes of unprecedented detail before it burned up, while Galileo continued to transmit new data. Pioneer 6 was still in space on its thirtieth birthday, December 16, 1995, and distant Pluto was the only planet not yet visited. Other spacecraft were launched to study asteroids and their potentially dangerous trajectories, as well as others to supply electrical power from satellites in the earth's magnetic field linked to the spaceship by long tethers.

The communications satellites have of course been the most followed of all, with their millions of users. Those most efficient for stationary electronic systems have been placed in geosynchronous orbit, 22,300 miles above the equator. By 1995, there were 24 Intelsat communications satellites there and in other orbits. At such a height, the satellite's angular speed matches that of the earth according to sidereal time with an orbit of 23 hours, 54 minutes; and it "appears to remain in the same spot in the sky." From there, it sees "almost one third of the earth's surface," as against the some 1000 miles seen by astronauts about 200 miles up. Already imagined by futurist Arthur C. Clarke in 1945, the first such American satellite, Syncom II, achieved orbit on July 26, 1963, and "was locked into a stationary location near the international date line" on August 19, 1964. In 1965, Intelsat 1 became the first global communications satellite and, after the 1970s, satellites came into use for the new Global Positioning System (GPS). By the 1990s, imaging was refined to the point that people on earth or in flight, using fixes from 4 of 24 satellites in 6 or so different 11,000-mile-high orbits, could fix their positions within 7 meters, or about 21 feet.

As our subject is the history of man flying above the earth, we will mention finally about the satellites only a few references to human efforts with the satellites in space. By the 1980s, the shuttles were releasing numerous ones on each mission, and on occasion retrieving them for repairs. After November 1984, for example, shuttle astronaut Joseph Allen described how he used his rocket backpack (Manned Maneuvering Unit, or MMU) to retrieve, at times "with one hand," a 1200-pound Indonesian satellite in a useless, but weightless, orbit 600 miles up after its launch by a shuttle the previous February. It had been intended for geosynchronous orbit high above the South Pacific, but its own rocket had sputtered out. The following day Dale Gardner made a similar retrieval of a similarly stranded German satellite, also worth millions of dollars. The 300-pound (earth weight) Manned Maneuvering Unit (MMU), with 24 tiny jets propelling nitrogen gas, was first used on a shuttle mission by Mission Specialist Bruce McCandless on February 7, 1984. Its usefulness was demonstrated two months later with the first successful repairs of an important satellite, the Solar Max (Maximum Mission), which had become dysfunctional for its searches of solar phenomena over three years earlier. The crew was able to install a new electronics box in less than an hour as well as make other repairs.

There were many such demonstrations of the perfections of space technology and experience, but the most impressive space rescue so far, with enormous significance for human progress toward the ultimate understanding of the miracles of the universe, was the December 1993 repair of the Hubble telescope, named for the astronomer who demonstrated the expansion of the seemingly infinite universe in the 1920s. The $1.6-billion, 25,000-pound, 42.6-by-14.1-foot scientific package, powered by two 40-foot-long by 8-foot-wide solar panels, was released into an orbit some 381 miles above the earth from the shuttle Discovery on April 25, 1990. It was expected to extend earth-based astronomical observations, obscured by the atmosphere, by at least 10 times. But to great disappointment, it was soon found that defects in its 94.5-inch (2.4- meter) diameter reflecting mirror were distorting some 60 percent of its pictures.

Launched on December 2, 1993, for its 11-day repair mission, the shuttle Endeavor's seven-man crew completed five EVAs and used a 65-foot robot arm to grab and insert the Hubble, its solar panels retracted, into its cargo bay. August 1985 shuttle veteran Richard Covey commanded the mission, while 58-year-old Story Musgrave, who had made the first shuttle EVA in April 1983, headed the repair work. Musgrave, with over 17,000 hours of piloting, including 599 hours in space and 4 on EVAs, as well as parachuting over 460 times, is the "Renaissance man" of the astronauts. A balding ex-Marine with five children, he was born on August 19, 1935, in Boston, and has earned a staggering number of degrees in engineering, mathematics, computing, chemistry, literature, and medicine. He even became a practicing surgeon before joining the astronauts in August 1967.

Most important, of 11 corrections made for the Hubble telescope, the astronauts used some 280 tools and 15,000 pounds of equipment to replace one of the solar panels which had been warped by the extreme temperature differences as the satellite passed from night to day. They also replaced four defective gyroscopes to stop oscillations, installed new cameras, and most critically of all placed ten small new mirrors with warps opposite those of the main mirror to correct its defects as well as a "costar" at the center of the mirror to re-focus its light. They then released Hubble in near-perfect restoration, raising its orbit, which had declined due to atmospheric friction to 330 or so miles up.

The telescope's findings soon electrified the scientific world, with readings of the age of the universe and workings of distant galaxies and heavenly bodies. Many of them also caused bewilderment for cosmologists, such as observations confusing previous data on the age of the universe and the search for its supposedly dominant "dark matter."

The Soviets had earlier demonstrated, as Peter Bond puts it in *Heroes in Space* ". . . the final proof, if further verification was needed, of the value of man in space for the repair and modifiction of all-too-valuable hardware." This came with the repairs of the space station Salyut 7, which had been launched on April 19, 1982. A succession of crews visited it, beginning with that of Soyuz T-5 on May 13, and supplies arrived on May 25; but almost three years later its telemetry ceased. This was six months after the last visitors, and the station remained in decaying orbit. Help was sent with the launch on June 6, 1985 of a new Soyuz, T-13, carrying Vladimir Dzhanibekov and Viktor Savinykh. Three days later, they were able to dock and to re-link the batteries with the solar panels to recharge and begin a series of repairs. By June 14, it was announced that the station was working normally, the cosmonauts beginning a series of experiments, including a five-hour EVA on August 2. A new crew arrived in September 1985, and another the following July, even as the new space station Mir ("Peace"), launched February 20, 1986, readied to receive new series of cosmonauts.

The Soviets had launched the first space station, Salyut ("Salutation") 1 on April 19, 1971, two years before the 85-ton American Skylab 2, which went into orbit from May 25 to June 22, 1973, performing numerous new studies of the earth, moon, and sun. But the 18.9-ton Salyut 1 soon encountered tragedy. The first expected docking by Soyuz 10 later in the month never took place, and then the crew of Soyuz 11 were found dead in their capsule following a seemingly successful re-entry on June 30, 1971, after a record 23 days docked to Salyut 1. It was found that a cabin vent valve had blown open as the command module separated from the rest of the Soyuz during re-entry. The backup crew of Georgi Dobrovolksky, Vladislav Volkov, and Victor Patsayev had had the incredible misfortune to be substituted at the last minute for the sickness-grounded first crew, and died of asphyxiation after they had set a new endurance record and carried out many new experiments.

Before that, following the first death in space of Komarov with the crash of Soyuz 1 on April 24, 1967, the Soviets had resumed successful manned flights in and after August 1968. But they continued to experience difficulties, with new failures of rockets and various experiments. Then, three months after the tragedy of Soyuz 11 and with no reliable means of resupplying the first space station, on October 11, 1971, Salyut 1 was sent to its fiery death over the Pacific after 175 days in orbit. Salyut 2 lasted only three weeks following its launch on April 3, 1973, before tumbling out of control, as did Cosmos 557 after 11 days of orbit in May of that year.

Salyut 3 was launched on June 23, 1974, and a redesigned Soyuz, number 14, joined it for a two-week mission after July 5, raising its orbit to 164 by 171 miles up. But failures in the guidance system of Soyuz 15 prevented its docking in late August. Before long, however, the Soviets far surpassed the new endurance record of 84 days aloft, from November 16 to February 8, 1974, established by the third American Skylab crew of

Jerry Carr, Ed Gibson, and Bill Pogue. The first and second crews to Skylab had flown from May 25 to June 22, and July 28 to September 25, 1973, respectively.

As the Soviets, stung by their loss in the race to the moon, decided to concentrate on studying the effects of long-term weightlessness, four more Salyut space stations were launched from December 26, 1974 to April 19, 1982, with visits by many of the over 30 Soyuz spacecraft sent up by the time of the launching of the new third-generation space station, Mir, on February 20, 1986, less than a month after the blow-up of the *Challenger* space shuttle. Over a dozen crews docked by the mid 1990s with the 20-metric-ton, 110-foot-long Mir, which soon added three new modules with much additional equipment, giving a total ground weight of over 85 tons. The launching into space of such a spaceship, about as big as the earlier American Skylab, became possible for the Russians with the successful testing of the long-delayed but very powerful new Energia rocket after May 15, 1987. Standing 197 feet or 20 stories high, it could lift payloads of over 100 tons.

Already the Soviets had begun flying longer and longer missions. The Salyut 6, launched on September 29, 1977, received the first automatic docking and refueling ever by the cargo ship Progress 1 on January 22, 1978, and then housed crews including those who established new records of 175 and 185 days aloft before its re-entry on July 29, 1982. Salyut 7 crews stayed in orbit for 211 and 237 days, from May 13 to August 27, 1982, and February 8 to April 11, 1984, respectively. Then a new record of an incredible 366 days in orbit some 240 miles up on Mir was established by the crew of Soyuz TM-5, Musa Manarov and Vladimir Titov, a relative of Gherman Titov, the second man to orbit the earth. They descended to earth in another Soyuz, TM-6, on December 22, 1988, 300 or so miles north of the launch site at Baykonur, and not far from usual landing sites near Arkalik, Kazakhstan.

Crews frequently changed from one visting Soyuz to another, and the flight of Titov and Manarov broke by 40 days the 326 days in space of Yuri Romanenko a year earlier. Valery Ryumin spent a total of 360 days in space on two flights of 175 and 185 days to Salyut 6 in 1979 and 1980. Then, a crew including Sergei Krikalev, who two years later would initiate Russian participation on the American space shuttle, was 10 months on Mir until March 1992, even as the Soviet Union broke up and his native city of Leningrad reverted to its previous name, St. Petersburg.

Cosmonaut Valentin Lebedev gave one of the first accounts of such an extended period in orbit, for 211 days from May 13 to December 10, 1982. In his 1983 book *Diary of a Cosmonaut*, he described his bewilderment at the re-entry, as "We are anxious. . . . We're no longer accustomed to life on the ground. Our lives are attuned to this small island in space, and suddenly here we come, back to the Big World."

Still longer Russian missions are planned. Even before a critical docking with Mir and resupply, which prevented its abandonment in September 1994, a new long-duration flight was launched from Baykonur on January 7, 1994. It sent up a crew including Doctor Valery Polyakov for an incredible 14-month voyage of 439 days on the Mir space station, studying weightlessness and other problems.

Such flights have been essential for the planning of the 22-month trip to Mars and beyond. By the time of its breakup in 1992, the Soviet Union had amassed close to 100,000 hours—or over 4000 days—almost 11 years of humans in space! By the mid-1980s the Russians were launching satellites and/or humans into space on average once every four or so days. With escalating problems, understandably launches had to be sharply curtailed, and by mid-1993 personnel working in Russian space programs had declined to 295,000 and the 100-odd cosmonauts were soon reduced by half. Russians continued, however, if at a much reduced rate, to send their own and visiting cosmonauts aloft.

Then, in February 1993, they carried out another newsworthy space event. The Russians used a 65-foot mirror put into space by an unmanned Progress spacecraft to project a weak but highly visible beam of sunlight from 225 miles up onto European countries for about eight minutes in the middle of the night. This was a dramatic demonstration of what could become a widespread use of space, saving unimaginable electricity! The United States created more aesthetic effects the previous year, when in March 1992 a shuttle crew used an electron beam gun 184 miles up to create green and red auroras for several seconds over Australia.

With their successful shuttle missions, the U.S. was rapidly catching up with the former Soviet total time in space. By 1986, Americans had accumulated 40,151 hours, 54 minutes, 41 seconds in space, and the number of shuttle flights more than doubled in the decade following their resumption after September 29, 1988.

Shortly after that, as enabled by the end of the Cold War and the huge financial requirements it involved, there were plans for increased cooperation between space pioneers Russia and the U.S., beginning with the exchange of cosmonauts and astronauts after 1994 and plans for a new international space station by the year 2002. There had already been a preview of U.S.–Russian cooperation in space with the linking of Soyuz 19 and the last Apollo on July 17, 1975.

Fittingly, the two commanders, Tom Stafford for the Apollo and Alexsei Leonov for the Soyuz, enjoyed special backgrounds in their respective space programs. Leonov had made the first EVA trip outside a spacecraft in March 1965, while Stafford was on the Gemini 6 crew completing the world's first space rendezvous with Gemini 7 in December of the same year. He was accompanied by the even more famous space pioneer, Deke Slayton, who made his first space flight after recovery from a heart condition which had kept him grounded since being bumped from the second American orbital flight in May 1962.

The historic meeting of the spaceships came after three years of planning, test flights, and synchronization of systems—which followed an agreement for the Apollo–Soyuz Test Project (ASTP) as it was known, reached by the two superpowers in the detente of 1972. Soyuz 19 blasted off from Baikonur at 3:30 P.M., July 15, 1975, and seven and a half hours later Apollo 18 rose from Cape Canaveral. Maneuvering to about 143 miles (230 kms) up, the Apollo took the active role in inserting the pressure-equalized 10-foot docking module into the Soyuz docking ring over the Atlantic on the craft's respective 36th and 29th orbits of the earth. There followed what has been called the most expensive handshake in history, as Stafford and Slayton remained linked for 47 hours with Leonov and his Soviet co-pilot, Valery Kubasov. The third American, Vance Brand, like Slayton on his first spaceflight, remained behind in the Apollo, which was 11 feet longer and 7 tons heavier than the Soyuz, at 34 feet and 13 tons. Leonov dubbed the Russian of Stafford, born in Weatherford, Oklahoma, in 1930, "Oklahomski," but the two experienced crews were able to work together on planned experiments for almost two days. By agreement, each crew spoke the language of the other country, which they had studied intensively for hundreds of hours. The Soyuz descended finally with a single red-and-white parachute into Kazakhstan on July 21, while the Apollo conducted other experiments before splashing into the Pacific on July 24, 1975.

By now, the U.S. was well on its way to launching the spaceship of the future: the reusable Space Transportation System (STS), known more commonly by the names of the various space shuttles, progressively, Columbia, the ill-fated Challenger, Discovery, Atlantis, and Endeavor. Planning for the rocket-powered airplane began even before the landing on the moon, and went into high gear in the 1970s, using information from previous experiences in space and from the X-series aircraft, especially the X-15, the X-20 Dyna-Soar, and advanced bomber programs. By 1981, over 20,000 people in leading aerospace centers had devised a 100-ton craft which "takes off like a rocket, orbits Earth as a spacecraft, and lands like an airplane," or perhaps one should say, "like a glider."

The Russians also made attempts to develop their own shuttle, and flew various prototypes leading to the November 15, 1988 flight of a Buran, as it was called. They used a new, powerful K-type Energia booster to launch it for two orbits of 3 hours and 44 minutes. But continued concentration on long-duration flights, together with the breakup of the Soviet Union, precluded further progress for the Russian shuttle.

Before lift-off, the American shuttle is attached to two approximately 150-foot high booster rockets and the equally tall but higher up and fatter cylindrical fuel tank. Like some science-fiction cathedral, it is towed as if it were a giant tortoise at 1 mph to the launching site. Once free of its two rockets and the huge tank, the graceful orbiter resembles a stubby delta-winged supersonic airliner. It is designed to carry up to seven persons and is up to 85 feet (25.9 meters) wide and 126 feet (38.4 meters) long. At least 60 feet of that between the cockpit and tail assembly is used for the cargo bay and payloads of up to 18 tons. The Orbiter, with its 10 windows, weighs "only" 150,000 pounds empty, but 100 tons fully loaded with fuel, equipment, and astronauts.

The 15-story-high boosters, filled with 1.1 million pounds of propellant, develop 2.65 million pounds of thrust each. Together with the other engines, they develop some 6,425,000 pounds of thrust, or about as much as the Saturn V used for the Apollo flights, to propel the shuttle to over Mach 4 at about 29 miles up in two minutes or so. The boosters are jettisoned to parachute down for recovery and re-use up to 20 times, as against the up to 100 uses for the shuttles. Then the Orbiter's three main engines take over. Built by Rockwell International, they are the most sophisticated rockets yet, capable of varying power up to 375,000 pounds of thrust each. The propellants are mostly liquid hydrogen and oxygen from the 830-ton main fuel tank, which is disconnected to burn up as the craft nears 17,000 mph. Then the two orbital maneuvering system (OMS) engines on either side of the tail, producing 6000 pounds of thrust each, ignite for the additional speed necessary for orbit. Another 44 smaller thrusters producing from 24 to 870 pounds are used for altitude control and other maneuvers.

Innumerable tests were conducted on the ground, and from 1977 on, five test descents were made from Boeing 747s that later would be used to ferry the craft between California and Florida. The assembly was never tested in space, which led to considerable surprise when veterans John Young and Robert Crippen blasted off for the first manned mission of two days, April 12 to 14, 1981. Flights followed routinely with ever more experimentation and satellite launchings.

On the ninth mission, November 28 to December 8, 1983, the European Space Agency's Spacelab was installed and lifted into orbit to enable the beginning of its sophisticated tests in five major areas of science. The crew, again commanded by John Young, included the first non-American, West German physicist Ulf Merbold. (The Soviets had sent the first non-native into space on March 2, 1978, the Czech Vladimir Remek. He spent over a week on Soyuz 28, and was followed by over a dozen other non-Soviet nationals on Soviet spaceships.) In June 1985, the U.S. was first to launch a tri-national space crew with Arabian Abdul Aziz Al-Saud and Frenchman Patrick Baudry. Americans continued to send increasing numbers of foreign nationals into space, eight of them by 1986.

Although no shuttle flights exceeded 15 days in orbit until after the mid-1990s, the over 67 successful flights by then all demonstrated new techniques and experiments, and saw their unique adventures.

The most catastrophic by far was the explosion of *Challenger* on January 28, 1986. It was the twenty-fifth shuttle to take to the air, and the lift-off seemed normal. But 1 minute and 13 or so seconds later, as the craft rose over 47,000 feet above Cape Canaveral, an explosion killed all seven of the exceptional crew. The unfortunate victims included two traditional astronaut types: commander Francis "Dick" Scobee and pilot Mike Smith. The five other crew members included Ellison Onizuka, a flight-test engineer and the first Asian-American, and Ron McNair, an M.I.T. physicist and the second black American in space. Payload Specialists not under NASA included engineer and satellite designer Gregory Jarvis, and high-school teacher Christa McAuliff, chosen from

11,000 applicants. The final crew member was the second American woman astronaut, Judy Resnik, with a doctorate in electrical engineering.

The high-level, intensive investigation of the calamity discovered that its primary cause was the failure of a joint which linked two segments of one of the boosters. An undetected puff of smoke indicated escaping fire from an O-ring that did not seal, and that exploded the fuel tank a minute later and the entire structure 15 seconds after that. The cold temperature close to freezing, with the intrusion of ice particles, was one factor, and the presidential commission faulted the decision to launch at such a time, as well as numerous other failures of preparation and design. Over 400 changes were made in all sections of the assembly, beginning with the O-rings and joints. Two and a half years after the *Challenger* disaster, on September 29, 1988, the shuttle flights resumed with the launch, thereafter, of at least five or six a year. All have advanced knowledge in many fields from biology to medicine, and geography to meteorology.

The use of more conventional aviation techniques for space travel also has been a spectacular success, pleasing most of all the astronauts themselves. As Michael Collins titled a chapter of his *Lift off: The Story of America's Adventure in Space*, the shuttle meant "wings and wheels at last." But landing a craft still weighing 240,000 pounds at 204 knots (226 mph) with no room for error required all of the great skills and coolness under pressure honed by the commanders' test-pilot careers. After three and a half days of going through the shuttle's five-volume checklist, and then the days in orbit with computer and auto-pilot control during most of their missions, the commanders and pilots of the shuttles then, as detailed by Collins, had to master "three distinctly different flight regimes: hypersonic, supersonic, and subsonic," in order to land safely.

The shuttle pilot must shift from the reaction controls and autopilot used in space to the aerodynamic controls of elevons and rudder, although, as in the latest airliners, orders are transmitted by electric impulses of "fly by wire." As the approach begins, the craft is still falling at a ratio of about four or so feet forward to every one down, "more like a rock than a graceful, gull-like glider," as astronaut Joe Allen put it. His senior colleague Michael Collins stated, "From a pilot's point of view, the trickiest part of the entry is judging the speed and altitude to reach, but not overshoot the runway"—there can be no go-around for the "dead stick" landing. The Orbiter's final descent from about 90,000 feet up in about six minutes, with "a series of dramatic . . . hypersonic turns," reversing banks by up to 90 degrees to dissipate speed "much like a skier controls his or her descent down a slope by making a series of sweeping turns." It descends at an angle of 20 degrees, looping over the runway, until at 1500 feet above Cape Canaveral or Edwards Air Force Base, the stick is pulled back for a 1.5-degree glide path, with the landing gear dropped some 400 feet up. It rolls to a stop in about a mile and a half. Landing in California is done only if forced by weather conditions since all launches are from Cape Canaveral and the shuttle must be piggy-backed there on top of a Boeing 747, at a cost of a million dollars or so.

We have already discussed the incredible success of several shuttle flights in recovering or fixing lost and damaged satellites like the Solar Max in 1984 and the Hubble Telescope in 1993. It remains to mention an aspect or two of life in space and future possibilities.

Undoubtedly, flying in space is indescribable to those who have not done it, since it is rather difficult to imagine over 24 sunrises and sunsets a "day" and floating in weightlessness. Moreover, space medicine to deal with the inevitable problems of travel there has become a whole new science. The worst fears in the early years about the effects of prolonged weightlessness, electro-magnetic waves, particles, and radiation belts proved to be exaggerated, but the concerns were very understandable. First of all, much training on the ground in simulators, centrifuges, and underwater, as well as in aerial configurations to emulate some of the effects, is essential preparation.

In space, even more than on the earth, regular exercising for several hours a day, with bungee cords, treadmills, and exercise machines, was found to be the best way to prevent a decay of muscles, loss of bone calcium, and innumerable other effects of prolonged weightlessness. Those could also include an over-concentration of blood in the upper body, or conversely in the legs, a lowering of blood pressure, loss of blood volume, or accelerated and irregular heart rates. More commonly there were understandable fatigue and inner ear problems, with disorientation, motion sickness, and weight loss or gain.

Improved pressure suits and oxygen supplies and masks helped to solve many of these problems, although they were not always used. There were, of course, the inevitable bouts of colds and other sicknesses of the more common sort, sometimes requiring the substitution of healthy crew members at the last minute, but also on occasion developing in voyage.

Often space travelers were unsteady on their feet and perhaps an inch taller than normal for a few days after their return, given the lack of gravity in weightlessness. Those who landed on the moon were also quarantined for a period to prevent any spread of unknown bacteria, as well as for observation.

Naturally, the space travelers spent many sleepless "nights," especially in the frequent periods of stress. But there were also numerous reports of comfortable periods, with up to eight hours' sleep, as well as of euphoria in the suspension of space and at observation of never-before-seen phenomena. The obvious problems of nausea and the proper mix of oxygen and carbon monoxide were largely overcome after the first days of adaptation to weightlessness, as were those of eating and drinking, where substances flowed freely out of their storage cans. The difficulties of dealing with waste disposal in attachable containers were also controlled, although not very comfortably, as one can imagine.

The most dramatic new possibilities for spaceflight are the projection of a new American-Russian space station and its use not only for new experiments but to launch a manned mission to Mars and beyond.

Preparing for that ideal, in 1994 a Russian, Sergei Krikalev, traveled on a U.S. shuttle flight. On March 16, 1995, the physician Norman E. Thagard, after months of preparation at the Star City space center outside Moscow and the Baykonur Cosmodrome in Kazakhstan, became the first American, the thirteenth non-Russian, and the forty-fourth visitor to the existing close-to-100 ton Russian space station, Mir, which by then had completed over 50,000 revolutions of the earth since its launch on February 20, 1986. He traveled to it for two days on a Soyuz TM for a three-month stay. A new scientific module, Spektr, with 1600 pounds of American scientific equipment, was added to Mir at the same time, complementing the earlier Kvant ("Quantum") and Kristall modules, to form an elaborate space station, resembling some giant space-age Tinker Toy set.

Earlier in 1995, on February 6, the 122-foot-long, 100-ton shuttle Discovery made a rendezvous within 37 feet of the 112-foot-long, 125-ton Mir, to aid in planning for seven actual dockings to be made after June 1995. They would be accomplished by Atlantis, the shuttle especially equipped for docking with Mir. It would station at least four more American astronauts on Mir.

The February 1995 Discovery flight had for the first time as pilot, or number two in command, a woman, Air Force Lt. Colonel Eileen M. Collins. By then, 18 of the 106 or so American astronauts were women, including the backup for Norman Thagard, Bonnie Dunbar, who would join him on Mir in June. The February flight also saw the first EVA performed by a black American, Dr. Bernard Harris.

For his part, the 51-year-old Thagard is another Renaissance man. He was an F-4 pilot in Vietnam, earned a master's degree in electrical engineering, and became a licensed physician. He would use his skills on his fifth spaceflight to complement for the first week aloft on Mir those of the Russian doctor Valery Polyakov, already over a year on Mir after January 7, 1994.

The latter's staggering 437 days in space until March 22, 1995, eclipsed the 366 days that Vladimir G. Titov and Musa Manarov had spent on Mir from December 21, 1987 to December 22, 1988, which included a visit the last autumn by Polyakov and others. Titov then became the second Russian after Sergei Krikalev to fly on a U.S. spaceship, serving as one of the six crew members on the six-day Discovery flight in February 1995. After his record 14-plus months in space, Polyakov had completed over 7000 orbits of the earth. He descended safely to earth in Kazakhstan on March 22, 1995, accompanied by Yelena Kondakova and Aleksandr Viktorenko, and leaving the new crew on Mir of Dr. Thagard, mission commander Vladimir Dezhurov, and flight engineer Gennadi Strekalov.

Adding in his previous ascents, Polyakov had accumulated an astounding 607 days, about 9700 orbits, and some 250 million miles around the earth, topping by far four other cosmonauts with over 300 days in space. For her part, Yelena Kondakova, who had been the first to embrace Thagard on his arrival, spent 169 days in space, the record for a woman, until Shannon Lucid broke it with 188 days in 1996.

The historic trip of six Americans and a Russian on the sixty-ninth flight of a shuttle linked with Thagard and the two Russians on Mir, June 29, 1995. After the launch of Atlantis at 3:32 P.M. EDT on June 27, it approached Mir traveling 17,500 mph 245 miles above Central Asia. It reached a holding position 270 feet below the Russian space station, and then began its final approach, like some celestial ballet between two 100 ton objects, slowing from five inches a second to only one inch a second, with a final rocket push to dock into the bottom of Mir just after 8 A.M. Houston time, June 29.

Then, after almost five days performing 28 different tests of the effects of weightlessness and other experiments, at 6:10 A.M. Central Daylight Time, by happy coincidence on July 4, 1995, Atlantis began its return to earth. Letting go its docking hooks and latches which had secured the pressurized, leak-proof tunnel linking the two spacecraft, giant springs made the initial separation. The shuttle's steering jets then began the maneuvers setting Atlantis on course to land at Cape Canaveral at 10:54 A.M. on July 7.

The six returning Americans included Thagard, who completed a record American stay in orbit of over 115 days, Atlantis commander Navy Captain Robert L. "Hoot" Gibson, Air Force Lt. Colonel Charles J. Precourt, Mission Specialists scientist-engineer Gregory J. Harbaugh, physician Dr. Ellen S. Baker, and biomedical engineer Dr. Bonnie Dunbar. Staying behind for a scheduled ten-week shift on Mir were Commander Anatoly Y. Solovyev, who accompanied the Americans on Atlantis to the linkup, as did flight engineer Nikolai M. Budarin, making his first trip into space. Vladimir Dezhurov and Gennadi Strekalov, who accompanied Thagard to Mir in March, also returned to earth on July 7 on Atlantis.

The second American visit to Mir took place in November 1995. Atlantis blasted off on the 12th to link with Mir 248 miles up, three days later. The highlight of the mission was the installation of a new 15-foot (c. 5 meter) long, 7-foot (c. 2.5 meter) wide docking module, weighing 4.5 tons. Using a 50-foot-long robot arm, the Atlantis crew fixed the docking mechanism to the Krystall module to provide a second and easier entry to Mir for the next five visits scheduled for Atlantis. The shuttle also delivered over a ton of cargo to the long-orbiting Mir, including 715 pounds of scientific equipment, 323 pounds of food, 991 pounds of water, 100 pounds of oxygen and nitrogen, as well as mail and personal items. They would be used awaiting future visits as well as for the two Russians, Yuri Gidzenko, Sergei Avdeev, and one German, Thomas Reiter, who remained on Mir until late February 1996. The five-man Atlantis crew—Cols. Kenneth D. Cameron and Jerry L. Ross, Lt. Cols. James D. Haisell, Jr., and William S. McArthur, Jr., and Canadian Air Force Major Chris A. Hadfield—uncocked with Mir on the 17th and returned safely to Cape Canaveral on November 20, 1995.

The third docking of Atlantis with Mir came after the American spaceship's launch from Cape Canaveral, early on March 22, 1996. It carried new supplies and equipment, and spent five days linked to the Russian space station, from late on March 23rd to the 28th. New experiments designed to advance work for the new space station were carried out, including the first space walk by American astronauts with their spaceship docked to Mir. Biochemist Dr. Shannon Lucid remained on the Russian spaceship until the fourth docking of Atlantis with Mir, scheduled for September 1996. She joined Russian cosmonauts Yuri Onufrienko and Yuri Usachev, who had boarded Mir in February. Commander Col. Kevin Chilton of the Air Force, his colleague, Lt. Col. Richard Searfoss, Army Lt. Col. M. Richard Clifford, physicist Dr. Linda Godwin, and electrical engineer Dr. Ronald Sega returned safely to Cape Canaveral on March 31.

By that point over 600 people—Americans, Russians and a few others—had accumulated something like 38 human years in space on over 100 American and close to that many Russian ascents.

The plans for the new, far bigger space station will borrow much from Russian preparations for Mir II, as well as from the vast American space experience. It will be 361 feet wide, 290 feet long, weigh 460 tons, and house perhaps six astronauts and seven laboratories. The second Mir has been scheduled for launch by 1997, the same year Americans project for the space station they have been thinking of since January 1984. Along with the plans for a mostly Russian-built, U.S.-financed international space station, Alpha, scheduled for launch late in 1997, the European Space Agency, that of Japan, and other countries will also cooperate and plan to send modules to the new sky platform. The first three-person crew is scheduled to go to it in May 1998, and in all up to 70 trips by shuttles and Soyuz spaceships are envisaged to complete its construction and supplies by June 2002.

The U.S. will have paid Russia $650,000,000 through 1997 for the use of Mir and other services, but by the late 1990s, U.S. budgetary restraints, like those in Russia following the breakup of the Soviet Union, have reduced civil service jobs with NASA from 21,060 in 1995 to 17,500, and the number of active astronauts to 88. However, plans and tests have proceeded for a Lockheed Martin "VentureStar," the X-33, which is planned to supercede the shuttle early in the next century. In May 1996, in commemoration of Lindbergh's 1927 flight to Paris, which won the Orteig Prize, an ambitious "X Prize" was announced in St. Louis, "to shape a future of commercial space travel." In other words, some aviation leaders envisage widespread travel in space in the future.

Thus, optimism for a vigorous human future in space continues. The Boeing Company, as one of the prime contractors for a new space station, envisions a fully assembled new space station with a crew of six or more by early in the 21st century. The people aboard the station would be able to use solar panels and new technology to manufacture additional fuel and other necessities for a moon station and/or at least a six-month voyage to Mars, 35 million miles away at its closest. A target date as early as 2003 is set for the launch of a 64-ton Mars expedition vehicle.

From the planned space station, with expansion of the types of relays already carried out to Mir I, the future would be wide open. There would be the possibility of using the new station to assemble materials to start a space colony on the moon, with communications and telescopic equipment of the future, for example, or for sending a spaceship to Mars and beyond. A moon station might mine Helium 3 to accomplish new fusion processes, which could supply energy not only for space voyages but for transmission back to the earth. Various types of manufactures would also be produced, especially for types of alloys, crystals, semiconductors, and pharmaceuticals, which, as proven earlier, are most efficiently produced in a space vacuum. Centrifuges and other techniques are also being experimented with to produce earth-like gravity with the least added weight for the distant voyages of the future. And state-of-the-art computer and software systems continue to be upgraded for all space work. In July 1995, for example, Houston Mission Control began use of a network of 200 computer work stations each able to carry out 120 million operations a second!

Informed thinkers like NASA consultant and renowned physicist Carl Sagan even imagine new breakthroughs enabling speeds of up to the speed of light, with the ability to "colonize the sky." He and other visionaries imagine new technologies of the future as strange to us as present spaceships "might be to our hunter-gatherer ancestors."

The future of aviation and space travel promises to be as interesting as its first 100 years.

18

A Century of Wonder

As we approach the first centenary of powered flight, one can directly ask what other endeavor has ever gone so far in 100 years. That is true not only for the distances—where that is obviously indisputable, given so far a dozen men on the moon with another dozen circling it, the years of humans in orbit around the earth, and the common travel between cities and continents, taking advantage of today's $250 billion aviation industry—it is also true for the wonder of every single flight, in the sense that aviation, defined as the conveyance of people in the air and into space, is indeed a miracle!

The explorations by land and sea after the late 15th century have, to be sure, affected still more people. The earth is home to all of us, but our scientists' full knowledge of its surface was not completed until after the polar and other expeditions to remote spots earlier in the 20th century, often by air and always with the help of vital information from aerial reconnaissance. What people experience when they take to the air, as over a billion a year have been doing since late in the century, therefore can be seen in historical perspective as one of the greatest miracles of all—except, of course, for those of distant space and of birth and life itself. Of course, aviation has been only one part of the many wonders of the scientific and technological revolutions, but it is surely one of the best proofs of those wonders.

To go even a few feet in the air at slower speeds was already astonishing after the first balloon flights in 1783 and the first powered flights of 1903. Today the normal 550 mph or so of the jet airliners and 1000s of mph of supersonic and space travel—not to speak of the distances involved—seem all the more mind-blowing. And the possibilities of flying, not only to wherever humans wish on earth but even into space seem endless.

As astronaut Joseph Allen stated in his 1984 book, *Entering Space*, for example:

Some planners speculate that by early in the twenty-first century, electricity generated in geosynchronous orbit by enormous arrays of solar cells and transmitted to earth could meet most of the United States' annual power needs.

Whether these planners are clairvoyants or dreamers is a question that will have to wait to be answered, of course, but as writer and futurist Arthur C. Clarke has pointed out, humans have always tended to overestimate what can be accomplished in the near future and to underestimate what will be achieved in the longer term. It is not outlandish to imagine that fifty years from now nonpolluting power will be beamed to earth from space, that virtually all earth-based communications will be relayed by orbiting satellites, and that dozens or hundreds of people will live and work in several orbiting villages, devoted to the performance of a variety of proven and successful space tasks.

It also seems reasonable to conjecture that by the middle of the next century, a permanently occupied outpost will be based on the moon, and that minerals mined there will be used in the manufacture of satellites, space stations, and planetary probes. Several year-long manned missions to Mars may have been successfully completed, and plans may be underway for a new generation of explorers . . .

Space, the realm that encompasses the whole universe, is incredibly close at hand. From any point on the earth, space is only about eighty miles away. The earth itself is as much a part of space as is the moon, or meteors, or the Milky Way . . .

Apollo 11 moon orbiter Michael Collins, noting that "most people have always gone where they could go," confirmed such opinions with many more details in his 1990 book, *Mission to Mars: An Astronaut's Vision of Our Future in Space*. In the long term, who can doubt these conjectures?

And on earth those who love to fly, will, with ever new wonders. Senior astronaut Frank Borman joins those giving eloquent expression to that love: "I not only wanted to keep flying. I had to. Flying to me was living, as much a part of me as breathing." After his 1969 trip to Russia, following his first orbiting of the moon and just before the landing there of Armstrong and Aldrin, he also stated what all who love to fly know. At a time of renewed animosity between the United States and the Soviet Union, he reflected on the gift to him of his treasured pilot's wings by the second man to go into orbit around the earth, Gherman Titov, as follows: "No incident on our trip touched me more. There is, indeed, a brother-hood of airmen that no propaganda . . . can destroy. . . . I was an airman among comrades, united by the common experience and love of flight."

Clearly, "flight had become a true and deep religion, and . . . god was the sky itself," best-selling pilot-author Richard Bach has said. As famous Lockheed test pilot Tony LeVier explained why he took his dangerous job beginning with the 1942 testing of the P-38: "I loved to fly, and speed was only part of it. I liked to get away from the earth, and now I could go higher than ever." The man who first broke the sound barrier, Chuck Yeager, described learning to fly about that time as the period of his life that was ". . . the happiest I've ever been. Now that I was a fighter pilot, I couldn't imagine being anything else. . . . Everything about airplanes interested me: how they flew, what each could or couldn't do and why." He described how, later in the war, he reached a new high: "That day was a fighter pilot's dream. In the midst of a wild sky, I knew that dogfight-ing was what I was born to do. It's almost impossible to explain the feel-ing . . . The excitement of those dogfights never diminished. For me, combat remains the ultimate flying experience." When he flew his "sonic boom! The first one by an airplane ever heard on earth," on October 14, 1947, he told how "I sat up there feeling kind of numb, but elated . . ."

Aviation indeed produces wonder, as can be seen in such quotes and many others in this book and elsewhere. All the varieties of ascending above the earth, from balloons and hang-gliding to soaring, powered or spaceflight at greatly different speeds, give their euphoria.

As for "air power," described during its most unrestrained, "total war" phase in Chapter Twelve, one can now surmise, even while knocking on wood, that the medieval theorists may have been correct in predicting this would make many potential wars impractical to pursue. The nations of Western Europe, for example, which had been at each other's throats throughout recorded history until 1945, may never war against each other again, since to do so, during this age of missiles and jet aircraft traveling at supersonic speeds, would, in the words of our previously quoted Italian priest, "cause much disturbance among the civil and political governments of mankind." The major bloodletting that we continue to see in the 1990s, as in Rwanda and Burundi, has been implemented largely with hand-held machetes, or small arms. Those nations capable of putting talented flyers and sophisticated machines into the air have become demonstrably less likely to be attacked by conventional means, though they are sometimes inclined to wield the threat of their air power against lesser nations, as during the recently incessant blood-feud in the mountains of Bosnia. When a vast, Anglo-American-led coalition massed its air power against an aggression by Saddam Hussein's Iraq in 1991, the war ended quickly and in a manner that will presumably discourage future aggressors. In July 1996, Hollywood, presumably for lack of current great power drama, and in order to depict world air forces engaged in total war, invented an alien invasion of earth in the popular film *Independence Day*.

As for the dangers of flying itself, as seen in Chapter Eleven, they are only about a tenth that of driving a car to go the same distance, even if for the time of travel they may be comparable. Where there is motion, naturally, there is risk. Pilots of high-performance aircraft or spaceships are sure the excitement and pleasures far outweigh the risks. Frank Borman stated of his years as a test pilot and astronaut, "I was willing to . . . [risk] my life because the exciting and worthwhile challenges of my job outweighed the dangers." Of the first 73 astronauts selected by NASA, 8 died—3 in the fire on Apollo 1, January 1967, 4 in plane crashes, and 1 in a car crash. Of his 50 test-pilot and astronaut friends, Michael Collins noted in 1988 the deaths of 11 in 25 years—7 in aircraft accidents, 1 in a car crash, 2 of heart attacks, and only 1, Roger Chaffee, in the spacecraft Apollo 1. The 7 victims of the *Challenger* explosion on January 28, 1986, were the first Americans to die in space. At least a half-dozen Soviets also have died in the space effort, some 4 of them on actual flights, and many more of course experienced serious problems and narrow escapes before their safe returns to earth.

Certainly, the astronauts knew they faced the highest risks, as did aircraft carrier and stunt pilots. But, as they stated at times, "I am too busy to be frightened," to cite a variant of a statement by French high-wire artist Philippe Petit after he crossed a tightrope between the two towers of the World Trade Center some 1300 feet above New York on August 7, 1974.

At first, American space experts and astronauts rated the chances of successfully landing on the moon at perhaps 50 percent, and of recovering Apollo 13 at only 10 percent. But with the miraculous return of that crew on April 17, 1970, and the overcoming of other hair-raising dangers, such fears gave way to a more optimistic fatalism. Frank Borman has written, "Most airmen, if they're honest with themselves, believe in fate. . . . They insist that pilots who are killed simply made mistakes . . . that it only happens to someone else." The sight of their home planet, as well as the adventures of space flight and the incredible feeling of weightlessness, more than compensate for the risks of astronauts and cosmonauts. As even Jim Lovell, the commander of the harrowing Apollo 13 flight, could state: "The vast loneliness of the moon up here is awe-inspiring, and it makes you realize just what you have back there on earth. The earth from here is a grand oasis in the big vastness of space."

Poet Archibald Macleish put the universal significance of flight eloquently when the moon trips had just begun, at the time of Apollo 8:

> To see the earth as it truly is, small and blue and beautiful in that eternal silence where it floats, is to see ourselves as riders on the earth together, brothers on the bright loveliness in the eternal cold—brothers who know they are truly brothers.

One of the best expressions of the beauty of more ordinary flight, as well as of that "brotherliness" as demonstrated by her own life, has been written by Le Ly Hayslip to desribe her first trip by air in the war-torn Vietnam of the 1960s. Cited in Chapter One, the following passage is more than worth repeating:

> The flight was much more than a thrilling ride. When we left the ground and banked gently over the ocean, it was as if I was seeing my homeland for the very first time—taking it all in like God in heaven—and I felt my first true sense of peace. The pale sky seemed infinite and I was climbing toward it like a celestial spirit . . .

One of the first astronauts, Walter M. Schirra, speaking of his and future challenges, went further: "We shared a common dream: to test the limits of man's imagination and daring." The U.S. Air Force song is more direct, but also worth quoting in part: "Off we go, into the Wild Blue Yonder, Climbing High, into the Sun . . . Off with one hell of a roar . . ."

Above all, as the commander of the first spaceship to circle the moon, Frank Borman, put it, flying can not only be "sheer fun," but can allow for "freedom from the prosaic" problems of everyday life—as well as give the best means of travel to distant places. The numbers of people doing that are expected to go from the 1.203 billion traveling by air worldwide, with 481 million in the U.S. in 1994, to over one billion in the United States alone and double that elsewhere by the year 2010.

They will be flying new versions of the Boeing 747-400, seating up to 550 passengers: the Boeing 777, with from 250 to over 400 on board, and its rival Airbus 330 and 340. New, bigger models of the Boeing 737 will continue for many more years, in competition with the Airbus 320, the McDonnell Douglas MD-80, 90, and 95, as well as a proposed Asian jetliner. The three-engined DC-10, MD-11, and others are expected shortly to disappear, while new super-jumbos and SSTs take off with ever-increasing travelers between distant cities. For shorter distances, there may well appear "aerocars" to get over traffic jams, and conceivably back-pack jets as well as other science-fiction methods of taking to the air. Hypersonic and enormous military jets will be establishing new records for speed, load, and altitude, even as spaceships travel to literally new worlds.

Such speculations and the impact of the statistics, quotations, and stories related above are clear: Flying is wonderfully unique and uniquely wonderful! Its pleasures should be based not only on imagining the purpose and destination of your flight, but on some awareness of its complexity and wonder, and of all the work, skill, and imagination it took to bring it about. I hope this book has supplied some essentials for the background of those wonders.

Sources

CHAPTER ONE

New York Times, May 26, 1991 / *Le Figaro*, July 21, 1990 / *Air and Space*, June–July and Aug.–Sept., 1995 / *Le Monde*, April 15, 1994 / Bill Gunston, *A Century of Flight* / *New York Times*, Nov. 3, 1988; December 18, 1994 / Curtiss Prendergast, *The First Aviators* / *Aviation History*, Sept. 1995 / Judy Lomax, *Women of the Air* / Henry Serrano Villard, *Contact: The Story of the Early Birds—Man's First Decade of Flight from Kitty Hawk to World War I* / Lawrence Goldstein, *The Flying Machine and Modern Literature* / Cecil Lewis, *Sagittarius Rising* / Lee Kennett, *The First Air War, 1914–1918* / Antoine de Saint-Exupéry, *Airman's Odyssey* / *Treasury of Religious Verse, The*, ed. Donald T. Kauffman / Walter J. Boyne, *The Smithsonian Book of Flight* / Le Ly Hayslip, *When Heaven and Earth Changed Places: A Vietnamese Woman's Journey from War to Peace* / Charles Lindbergh, *The Spirit of St. Louis* / Michael Collins, *Liftoff: The Story of America's Adventure in Space* / *The American Heritage History of Flight*, Alvin W. Josephy, Jr., et al., eds. / Thomas D. Damon, *Introduction to Space: The Science of Space Flight* / Joseph P. Allen and Russell Martin, *Entering Space: An Astronaut's Odyssey* / *Europe's Future in Space* / *New York Times*, Sept. 3, 9, and 13, 1991; Jan. 23, May 15–18, and Aug. 6 and 7, 1992; Sept. 15 and Dec. 9, 1993; Feb. 3, Apr. 14, and June 30, 1994 / Brian Calvert, *Flying Concorde* / Jim Webb, *Fly the Wing*, Ames / Jack Broughton, *Going Downtown: The War Against Hanoi and Washington* / Robert J. Serling, *Legend and Legacy: The Story of Boeing and Its People* / Neil D. Van Sickle, *Modern Airmanship* / Robert N. Buck, *Weather Flying* / *La Météo de A à Z*, Paris, 1988 / *La Météorologie*, Paris, 1986 / Bill Yenne, *The History of the U.S. Air Force* / Jerry Scuts, *Northrop F 5/F 20* / Air & Space museum brochure, Dec. 1994 / Lindsay Peacock, *F/A 18 Hornet* / *Mirage III, Mirage 2000* / *Flying*, June 1995 / Paris interview with Air France Commandant Pierre Chanoine / Philip Birtles and Allan Burney, *Concorde* / Pierre Chanoine, "Où en est notre super Concorde?", *Concorde Info*, Summer 1991 / T. Gwynn-Jones, *Wings Across the Pacific* / Hiroshi Seo, *Boeing 747: The 747 Story* / Robert Redding and Bill Yenne, *Boeing: Plane Maker to the World* / Leik Myrabo and Dan Ing, *The Future of Flight* / Ivan Rendall, *Reaching For the Skies* / *Aviation: The Pioneer Years*, Ben Mackworth-Praed, ed. / *Air and Space*, Oct.–Nov. 1991 / *New York Times*, Aug. 13 and 14; Dec. 4, 1993

CHAPTER TWO

Clive Hart, *Images of Flight* / Psalms 55: 6 / *The American Heritage History of Flight*, Alvin W. Josephy, Jr., et al., eds. / Clive Hart, *The Dream of Flight: Aeronautics from Classical Times to the Renaissance* / C.H. Gibbs-Smith, *A History of Flying* / C.H. Gibbs-Smith, *Aviation: An Historical Survey from Its Origins to the End of World War II* / Edmond Petit, *Nouvelle Histoire Mondiale de l'Aviation* / Edmond Petit, *Histoire de l'Aviation* / Peter Haining, *The Compleat Birdman* / *Encyclopedia Britannica*, Vol. 8 (1957 edition) / Arthur Waley, *Li Po* / J.C. Cooper, *Chinese Alchemy: The Taoist Quest for Immortality* / *History Today*, June 1993 / Exhibit, Metropolitan Museum of Art, June 1994 / Catalogue (statue), Metropolitan Museum of Art, Munsey Fund, 1936 / *New York Times*, April 24, 1988 / Paul O'Neil, *Barnstormers and Speed Kings* / Walter J. Boyne, *The Smithsonian Book of Flight* / C.H. Gibbs-Smith, *Flight Through the Ages* / Gary Dorsey, *The Fullness of Wings* / *Encyclopedia Britannica*, Vol. 10 (1957 edition) / Donald Dale Jackson, *The Aeronauts* / Daniel Boorsin, *The Creators* / Michael J.H. Taylor, *History of Fligh* / *Aviation: The Pioneer Years*, Ben Mackworth-Praed, ed. / Michelin Guide Vert: *Bourgogne* / *Encyclopedia Britannica*, Vol. 20 (1957 edition) / Alvise Zorzi, *Venice: The Golden Age* / Joseph Needham, *Science and Civilization in China*, Vol. 4 (Part 3) / Berthold Laufer, *The Pre-History of Aviation* / Frank Ching, *Ancestors: 900 Years of a Chinese Family* / Joseph Campbell with Bill Moyers, *The Power of Myth* / Marco Polo, *The Travels* / Genesis 28: 12 / *The Travels of Sir John Mandeville* / Sir Robert Saundby, *Early Aviation* / U.S. Air Force Museum / Mark R. Chartrand and Ron Miller, *Golden Guide: Exploring Space* / Richard P. Hallion, *Test Pilots: The Frontiersmen of Flight* / Michelin Guide Vert: *Provence*

CHAPTER THREE

Peter Haining, *The Compleat Birdman* / Clive Hart, *The Dream of Flight: Aeronautics from Classical Times to the Renaissance* / Brian P. Levack, *The Witch Hunt in Early Modern Europe* / Clive Hart, *Images of Flight* / Robert Strayer, *The Making of the Modern World* / *Aviation: The Pioneer Years*, Ben Mackworth-Praed, ed. / *Time*, February 14, 1977 / C.H. Gibbs-Smith, *Aviation: An Historical Survey from Its Origins to the End of World War II* / *The American Heritage History of Flight*, Alvin W. Josephy, Jr., et al., eds. / Michael J.H. Taylor, *History of Flight* / C.H. Gibbs-Smith, *A History of Flying* / C.H. Gibbs-Smith, *Flight Through the Ages* / Edmond Petit, *Nouvelle Histoire Mondiale de l'Aviation* / *Great Issues in Western Civilization*, Vol. 1, Brian Tierney et al., eds. / Lawrence Goldstein, *The Flying Machine and Modern Literature* / Richard P. Hallion, *Test Pilots: The Frontiersmen of Flight* / William H. McNeil, *A History of the Human Community* / *Men in the Air*, Brandt Aymar, ed. / Marjorie Hope Nicolson, *Voyages to the Moon* / Roger D. Launius, *NASA: A History of the U.S. Civil Space Program* / Simon Schama, *Citizens: A Chronicle of the French Revolution*

CHAPTER FOUR

Donald Dale Jackson, *The Aeronauts* / Walter J. Boyne, *The Smithsonian Book of Flight* / C.H. Gibbs-Smith, *Flight Through the Ages* / C.H. Gibbs-Smith, *A History of Flying* / C.H. Gibbs-Smith, *Aviation: An Historical Survey from Its Origins to the End of World War II* / Edmond Petit, *Nouvelle Histoire Mondiale de l'Aviation* / Richard P. Hallion, *Test Pilots: The Frontiersmen of Flight* / Michael J.H. Taylor, *History of Flight* / *Air and Space*, Feb.–March 1989 / *The American Heritage History of Flight*, Alvin W. Josephy, Jr., et al., eds. / *Aviation: The Pioneer Years*, Ben Mackworth-Praed, ed. / Robert Saundby, *Early Aviation* / Peter Haining, *The Compleat Birdman* / *L'Aérophile*, No. 6 (1902) / U.S. Air Force Museum / William Péne du Bois, *The Twenty-One Balloons* / Michael J.H. Taylor and and David Mondey, *Spies in the Sky* / Lee Kennett, *A History of Strategic Bombing* / Mark R. Chartrand and Ron Miller, *Golden Guide: Exploring Space*

CHAPTER FIVE

C.H. Gibbs-Smith, *Flight Through the Ages* / C.H. Gibbs-Smith, *Aviation: An Historical Survey from Its Origins to the End of World War II* / Richard P. Hallion, *Test Pilots: The Frontiersmen of Flight* / Lawrence Goldstein, *The Flying Machine and Modern Literature* / Edmond Petit, *Nouvelle Histoire Mondiale de l'Aviation* / Peter Haining, *The Compleat Birdman* / Michael J.H. Taylor, *History of Flight* / Donald Dale Jackson, *The Aeronauts* / Tom D. Crouch, *The Bishop's Boys: A Life of Wilbur and Orville Wright* / C.H. Gibbs-Smith, *A History of Flying* / U.S. Air Force Museum / *Aviation: The Pioneer Years*, Ben Mackworth-Praed, ed. / Charles Dollfus, *Les Avions* / Frank Howard and Bill Gunston, *The Conquest of the Air* / Michael S. Sherry, *The Rise of American Air Power: The Creation of Armageddon* / George Sand, *Oeuvres Complètes* / Michael Paris, "Fear of Flying: The Fiction of War, 1886–1916," *History Today*, June 1993 / Nadar (Gustave-Félix Tournachon), *Le Droit au Vol* / R. Lestienne, *Les Fils du Temps* (1990) / *Encyclopedia Britannica*, Vol. 2 (1957 edition) / Thomas Damon, *Introduction to Space: The Science of Spaceflight* / Michael Collins, *Liftoff: The Story of America's Adventure in Space* / *Histoire*, March 1995 / Mark R. Chartrand and Ron Miller, *Golden Guide: Exploring Space* / John Noble Wilford, *We Reach the Moon* / Owen S. Lieberg, *The First Air Race: The International Competition at Rheims, 1909* / Fred Howard, *Wilbur and Orville: A Biography of the Wright Brothers* / Martin S. Caiden, *Test Pilots: Riding the Dragon* / Lee Kennett, *The First Air War, 1914–1918* / Lee Kennett, *A History of Strategic Bombing* / Musée de l'Air, Le Bourget / Henry Serrano Villard: *Contact: The Story of the Early Birds—Man's First Decade of Flight from Kitty Hawk to World War I* / Pierre Lissarague, *Clément Ader: Inventeur d'Avions* / Christopher Chant, *Histoire de l'Aviation* / Jacques Noetinger, in *Concorde Info*, Winter 1990 / *Le Monde*, October 14, 15, 1990 / *Science et l'Avenir*, August 1990 / *New York Times*, Oct. 9, 1988; Nov. 15, 1989 / Seattle Air and Space Museum/ Musée de l'Air, Le Bourget / Walter J. Boyne, *The Smithsonian Book of Flight*

CHAPTER SIX

C.H. Gibbs-Smith, Aviation: *An Historical Survey from Its Origins to the End of World War II* / Edmond Petit, *Nouvelle Histoire Mondiale de l'Aviation* / C.H. Gibbs-Smith, *A History of Flying* / Richard P. Hallion, *Test Pilots: The Frontiersmen of Flight* / Owen S. Lieberg, *The First Air Race: The International Competition at Rheims, 1909* / Tom D. Crouch, *The Bishop's Boys: A Life of Wilbur and Orville Wright* / Fred Howard, *Wilbur and Orville: A Biography of the Wright Brothers* / C.H. Gibbs-Smith, *Flight Through the Ages* / Lawrence Goldstein, *The Flying Machine and Modern Literature* / Robert Saundby, *Early Aviation* / Curtiss Prendergast, *The First Aviators* / *Aviation History*, March 1996 / Rick Young, "The Wright Brothers' Glider," *Aerospace: An Exhibition of Flight*, Science Museum of Virginia, 1990 / Harry Combs, with Martin Caidin, *Kill Devil Hill: Discovering the Secret of the Wright Brothers* / Peter Haining, *The Compleat Birdman* / Michael J.H. Taylor, *History of Flight* / Pierre Lissarague, *Clément Ader: Inventeur d'Avions* / Orville Wright, *How We Made the First Flight*, 1913; repr., 1988 / Henry Serrano Villard, *Contact: The Story of the Early Birds—Man's First Decade of Flight from Kitty Hawk to World War I* / Flyer, Man Will Never Fly Memorial Society (Richmond, Va.), Nov.–Dec. 1990 / Samuel Elliott Morrison, *The Oxford History of the American People* / *New York Times*, July 2, 1991

CHAPTER SEVEN

Walter J. Boyne, *The Smithsonian Book of Flight* / Curtiss Prendergast, *The First Aviators* / Henry Serrano Villard, *Contact: The Story of the Early Birds—Man's First Decade of Flight from Kitty Hawk to World War I* / Fred Howard, *Wilbur and Orville: A Biography of the Wright Brothers* / Tom D. Crouch, *The Bishop's Boys: A Life of Wilbur and Orville Wright* / Richard P. Hallion, *Test Pilots: The Frontiersmen of Flight* / Les Cahiers de Science et Vie: Naissance de l'Aviation* / C. H. Gibbs-Smith, *Flight Through the Ages* / Joseph J. Corn, *The Winged Gospel: America's Romance with Aviation, 1900–1950* / Frank Howard and Bill Gunston, *The Conquest of the Air* / Christopher Chant, *Histoire de l'Aviation* / Bill Gunston, *A Century of Flight* / *The Lore of Flight*, John W.R. Taylor, et al., eds. / Pierre Lissarague, *Clément Ader: Inventeur de l'Aviation* / Robert Wohl, in *Air and Space*, Apr.–May 1996 / Edmond Petit, *Nouvelle Histoire Mondiale de l'Aviation* / *Aviation: The Pioneer Years*, Ben Mackworth-Praed, ed. / Owen S. Lieberg, *The First Air Race: The International Competition at Rheims, 1909* / Oral histories of Gabriel Voisin and Maurice Farman, Columbia University (1960) / Donald Dale Jackson, *The Aeronauts* / *Le Monde*, July 25, 1989 / Lee Kennett, *The First Air War, 1914–1918* / *Air and Space*, Apr.–May 1996 / *Aviation History*, Sept. 1995 and Jan. 1996 / Paul O'Neil, *Barnstormers and Speed Kings* / Wayne Biddle, *Barons of the Sky: From Early Flight to Strategic Warfare—The Story of the American Aerospace Industry* / Michael S. Sherry, *The Rise of American Air Power: The Creation of Armageddon* / Ezra Bowen, *Knights of the Air* / Eugene Emme, *The Impact of Air Power: National Security and World Politics* / Sterling Seagrave, *Soldiers of Fortune* / *Air and Space*, Aug.–Sept. 1989 / Terry

Gwynn-Jones, *Wings Across the Pacific* / *The American Heritage History of Flight*, Alvin W. Josephy, Jr., et al., eds. / Eileen Lebow, *Cal Rodgers and the Vin Fiz: The First Trans-Continental Flight* / Edmond Petit, *La Vie Quotidienne dans l'Aviation en France au Début du Vingtième Siècle, 1900–1935* / Michael J.H. Taylor and David Mondey, *Spies in the Sky* / Ivan Rendall, *Reaching For the Skies*

CHAPTER EIGHT

Henry Serrano Villard, *Contact: The Story of the Early Birds—Man's First Decade of Flight from Kitty Hawk to World War I* / Terry Gwynn-Jones, *Wings Across the Pacific* / C.H. Gibbs-Smith, *Flight Through the Ages* / Fred Howard, *Wilbur and Orville: A Biography of the Wright Brothers* / Lawrence Goldstein, *The Flying Machine and Modern Literature* / *Aviation: The Pioneer Years*, Ben Mackworth-Praed, ed. / Eugene Emme, *The Impact of Air Power: National Security and World Politics* / Lee Kennett, *The First Air War, 1914–1918* / Guide Michelin Vert: *Paris* / Michael S. Sherry, *The Rise of American Air Power: The Creation of Armageddon* / Mark Clodfelter, *The Limits of Air Power: The American Bombing of North Vietnam* / Edmond Petit, *Nouvelle Histoire Mondiale de l'Aviation* / Ezra Bowen, *Knights of the Air* / Peter Kilduff, *Richthofen: Beyond the Legend of the Red Baron* / C.H. Gibbs-Smith, *A History of Flying* / *Air and Space*, Oct.–Nov. 1991 / Frank Howard and Bill Gunston, *The Conquest of the Air* / Christopher Chant *Histoire de l'Aviation* / Michael J.H. Taylor, *History of Flight* / Richard P. Hallion, *Test Pilots: The Frontiersmen of Flight* / Walter J. Boyne, *The Smithsonian Book of Flight* / Bill Yenne, *The History of the U.S. Air Force* / *The American Heritage History of Flight*, Alvin W. Josephy, et al., eds. / Roger E. Bilstein, *Flight in America, 1900–1983: From the Wrights to the Astronauts* / Paul O'Neil, *Barnstormers and Speed Kings* / Matthew Cooper, *The German Air Force, 1933–45: An Anatomy of Failure* / *France-Amérique*, Nov. 9, 1991 / "NOVA" (television), Jan. 5, 1993 / *Encyclopedia Britannica*, Vol. 15 (1957 edition) / *Aviation History*, May 1995 / Brig. General William Mitchell, *Memoires of World War I: From Start to Finish of Our Greatest War* / Claude W. Sykes, *French War Birds* / Thomas G. Foxworth, *The Speed Seekers* / Michael Collins, *Liftoff: The Story of America's Adventure in Space* / David Jefferis, *Supersonic Flight* / David Nevin, *The Pathfinders* / Hy Steirman and Glenn D. Kittler, *The First Transatlantic Flight, 1919* / Frank T. Courtney, *The Eighth Sea* / *New York Times*, Sept. 4, 1988 / Oliver Stewart, *First Flights* / Ronald Jackson, *China Clipper* / Richard Sanders Allen, *Revolution in the Sky: Those Fabulous Lockheeds and the Pilots Who Flew Them* / *Aviation History*, Nov. 1995 / Bill Gunston, *A Century of Flight* / Donald Dale Jackson, *Flying the Mail* / *Aviation History*, March 1996 / *Le Monde*, Feb. 28–29, 1988 / *Icare*, Nos. 124 and 126 / Raymond Danel, *L'Aéropostale, 1927–1933* / Georges Clerc, *L'Aéropostale* / Emmanuel Chadeau, *Latécoere*

CHAPTER NINE

David Nevin, *The Pathfinders* / Ted Gilman, *Lindbergh: The Flight* / Walter S. Ross,

The Last Hero: Charles A. Lindbergh / *Aviation: The Pioneer Years*, Ben Mackworth-Praed, ed. / Edmond Petit, *Nouvelle Histoire Mondiale de l'Aviation* / Roger E. Bilstein, *Flight in America, 1900–1983: From the Wrights to the Astronauts* / Christopher Chant, *Histoire de l'Aviation* / Richard P. Hallion, *Test Pilots: The Frontiersmen of Flight* / Joseph J. Corn, *The Winged Gospel: America's Romance with Aviation, 1900–1950* / Walter J. Boyne, *The Smithsonian Book of Flight* / Lawrence Goldstein, *The Flying Machine and Modern Literature* / *The American Heritage History of Flight*, Alvin W. Josephy, Jr., et al., eds. / Charles A. Lindbergh, *The Spirit of St. Louis* / Joyce Milton, *Loss of Eden: A Biography of Charles and Anne Morrow Lindbergh* / Leonard Moseley, *Lindbergh: A Biography* / Michael S. Sherry, *The Rise of American Air Power: The Creation of Armageddon* / Bill Gunston, *A Century of Flight* / Richard Sanders Allen, *Revolution in the Sky: Those Fabulous Lockheeds and the Pilots Who Flew Them* / Michael J.H. Taylor, *History of Flight* / Maurice Bellonte, *Le Premier Paris–New York* / Paul O'Neil, *Barnstormers and Speed Kings* / Don Dwiggins, *The Barnstormers: Flying Daredevils of the Roaring 1920s* / Martin S. Caidin, *Test Pilots: Riding the Dragon* / Henry Serrano Villard, *Contact: The Story of the Early Birds—Man's First Decade of Flight from Kitty Hawk to World War I* / Curtiss Prendergast, *The First Aviators* / Sterling Seagrave, *Soldiers of Fortune* / Henry M. Holden with Captain Lori Griffith, *Ladybirds: The Untold Story of Women Pilots in America* / Frank T. Courtney, *The Eighth Sea* / Judy Lomax, *Women of the Air* / Martin S. Caidin, *Barnstorming* / *Air and Space*, Oct.–Nov. 1992 / Thomas G. Foxworth, *The Speed Seekers* / *Aviation History*, July 1995 / *Air and Space*, Dec. 1995 / Terry Gwynn-Jones, *Wings Across the Pacific* / Frank Chichester, *Ride the Wind* / Nancy T. Galloway, *Lost in the Clouds* (forthcoming)

CHAPTER TEN

Amelia Earhart, *Last Flight* / Judy Lomax, *Women of the Air* / Roger E. Bilstein, *Flight in America, 1900–1983: From the Wrights to the Astronauts* / *The American Heritage History of Flight*, Alvin W. Josephy, Jr., et al., eds. / Christopher Chant, *Histoire de l'Aviation* / David Nevin, *The Pathfinders* / Mary S. Lovell, *The Sound of Wings: The Life of Amelia Earhart* / Doris L. Rich, *Amelia Earhart: A Biography* / Susan Ware, *Still Missing: Amelia Earhart and the Search for Modern Feminism* / Randall Brink, *Lost Star: The Search for Amelia Earhart* / *New York Times*, March 17, 1992; Feb. 15, 1994 / *Air and Space*, Aug.–Sept. 1992 / Terry Gwynn-Jones, *Wings Across the Pacific* / Richard Sanders Allen, *Revolution in the Sky: Those Fabulous Lockheeds and the Pilots Who Flew Them* / Henry M. Holden with Captain Lori Griffith, *Ladybirds: The Untold Story of Women Pilots in America* / Valerie Moolman, *Women Aloft* / Captain X and Reynolds Dodson, *The Unfriendly Skies: Revelations of a Deregulated Airline Pilot* / Anthony Sampson, *Empires of the Sky: The Politics, Contests and Cartels of World Airlines* / *New York Times*, March 7 and Aug. 31, 1989; Aug. 6, 1991 / *Richmond Times Dispatch*, Nov. 26, 1989 / Marianne Verges, *On Silver Wings* / C.H. Gibbs-Smith, *Flight Through the Ages* / Anne Noggle, *A Dance with Death: Soviet*

Airwomen in World War II / Beryl Markham, *West with the Night* / Jacqueline Cochran, *Jackie Cochran: An Autobiography* / Edmond Petit, *Nouvelle Histoire Mondiale de l'Aviation* / Michael J.H. Taylor, *History of Flight* / *New York Times*, Aug. 23, 1987; May 1 and Aug. 24, 1993 / Joseph J. Corn, *The Winged Gospel: America's Romance with Aviation, 1900–1950* / Gore Vidal, *At Home* / *New York Times*, June 8, 1994 / *Air and Space*, Dec. 1995 / *Aviation History*, Jan. 1996 / Henri Mignet, *The Flying Flea: How to Build and Fly It* / Robert J. Serling, *Legend and Legacy: The Story of Boeing and Its People* / Walter J. Boyne, *The Smithsonian Book of Flight* / Frank T. Courtney, *The Eighth Sea* / Martin S. Caidin, *Barnstorming* / Bill Gunston, *A Century of Flight* / Anthony W. LeVier, with John Guenther, *Pilot* / Paul O'Neil, *Barnstormers and Speed Kings* / *Aviation: The Pioneer Years*, Ben Mackworth-Praed, ed. / Richard P. Hallion, *Test Pilots: The Frontiersmen of Flight* / Wayne Biddle, *Barons of the Sky: From Early Flight to Strategic Warfare—The Story of the American Aerospace Industry* / T.A. Heppenheimer, *Turbulent Skies: The History of Commercial Aviation* / Frank Howard and Bill Gunston, *The Conquest of the Air* / Lee Kennett, *The First Air War, 1914–1918* / Thomas G. Foxworth, *The Speed Seekers* / Martin S. Caidin, *Test Pilots: Riding the Dragon* / Ivan Rendall, *Reaching For the Skies* / James H. Doolittle, with Carroll V. Glines, *I Could Never Be So Lucky Again: An Autobiography* / Ronald Jackson, *China Clipper* / Robert L. Gandt, *China Clipper: The Age of the Great Flying Boats*

CHAPTER ELEVEN

Captain X and Reynolds Dodson, *Unfriendly Skies: Revelations of a Deregulated Airline Pilot* / Anthony Sampson, *Empires of the Sky: The Politics, Contests and Cartels of World Airlines* / Donald J. Clausing, *The Aviator's Guide to Modern Navigation* / *New York Times*, Dec. 22, 1988; Aug. 31 and Sept. 3, 1989; Jan. 19 and Aug. 6, 1991; Sept. 25 and Nov. 2, 1993; Oct. 29, 1995; Jan. 31, 1996 / *Le Monde*, Dec. 12, 1993 / John Allen Paulos, *Innumeracy: Mathematical Illiteracy and Its Consequences* / Milovan S. Brenlove, *The Air Traffic System* / *U.S. News and World Report*, June 26, 1995 / *Time*, May 16, 1988; Jan. 20, March 13, 27, and Sept. 25, 1989; Sept. 19, 1994 / *New York Times*, May 11 and Aug. 13, 1993; Jan. 1, Apr. 27, May 22, Oct. 16, and Dec. 1, 18, 1994; Oct. 15 and 16, 1995 / *Le Monde*, March 13, 19, and Apr. 13, 1989; Feb. 15, 1991 / *Flying*, July 1989 / "Les 'Bouchons' du Ciel," Air France (brochure) Aug. 1993 / Michael S. Sherry, *The Rise of American Air Power: The Creation of Armageddon* / James P. Harrison, "History's Heaviest Bombing," in *The Vietnamese War: Vietnamese and American Perspectives*, Jayne Werner and Luu Doan Huynh, eds. / Sterling Seagrave, *Soldiers of Fortune* / *The American Heritage History of Flight*, Alvin W. Josephy, Jr., et al., eds. / Ivan Rendall, *Reaching For the Skies* / Edmond Petit, *Nouvelle Histoire Mondiale de l'Aviation* / *New York Times*, May 12, 1994 / Charles R. Bond and Terry Anderson, *A Flying Tiger's Diary* / Robert Lee Scott, *Flying Tiger: Chennault of China* / Walter J. Boyne, *The Smithsonian Book of Flight* / Roger E. Bilstein, *Flight in America, 1900–1983: From the Wrights to the Astronauts* / Lloyd E. Eastman, *The Nationalist Era in China, 1927–1949* / Barbara W. Tuchman, *Stilwell and the American Experience in China, 1911–45* / Bill Yenne, *The History of the U.S. Air Force* / Clark G. Reynolds, *The Carrier War* / Edward Jablonski, *America in the Air War* / Anthony W. LeVier, with John Guenther, *Pilot* / Duane P. Schultz, *A Maverick War: Chennault and the Flying Tigers* / Daniel Ford, *Flying Tigers: Claire Chennault and the American Volunteer Group* / John Toland, *Flying Tigers* / *Air and Space*, June–July 1993; Apr.–May 1994 / Otha C. Spencer, *Flying the Hump: Memories of an Air War* / Lt. General William Tunner, *Over the Hump* / John B. Lundstrom, *The First Team and the Guadalcanal Campaign: Naval Fighter Combat from August to November, 1942* / T.A. Heppenheimer, *Turbulent Skies: The History of Commercial Aviation* / Wayne Biddle, *Barons of the Sky: From Early Flight to Strategic Warfare—The History of the American Aerospace Industry*

CHAPTER TWELVE

National Geographic, Dec. 1991 / *Air and Space*, Dec.–Jan. 1992–93 ???? / Edward Jablonski, *America in the Air War* / Clark G. Reynolds, *The Carrier War* / Paul Kennedy, *The Rise and Fall of the Great Powers* / Henry C. Clausen and Bruce Lee, *Pearl Harbor: Final Judgment* / Ted Lawson, with Bob Considine, *Thirty Seconds Over Tokyo* / *The American Heritage History of Flight*, Alvin W. Josephy, Jr., et al., eds. / *New York Times*, Apr. 16, 1992 / James H. Doolittle, with Carroll V. Glines, *I Could Never Be So Lucky Again* / Carroll V. Glines, *The Doolittle Raid: America's Daring First Strike Against Japan* / Duane P. Schultz, *The Doolittle Raid* / Roger E. Bilstein, *Flight in America, 1900–1983: From the Wrights to the Astronauts* / Bill Gunston, *A Century of Flight* / Michael J.H. Taylor, *Great Moments in Aviation* / John Keegan, *The Second World War* / Samuel Hynes, *Flights of Passage: Reflections of a World War II Aviator* / John K. Fairbank, Edwin O. Reischauer and Albert M. Craig, *East Asia: Tradition and Transformation* / Michael J.H. Taylor, *History of Flight* / Frank Howard and Bill Gunston, The Conquest of the Air / Walter J. Boyne, *The Smithsonian Book of Flight* / *Time*, Aug. 7, 1995 / *U.S. News and World Report*, July 31, 1995 / *New York Times*, Aug. 6 and 9, 1995 / Gordon W. Prange, *Target Tokyo: The Story of the Sorge Spy Ring* / R.R. Palmer and Joel Colton, *A History of the Modern World* / James H. Doolittle in Smithsonian pamphlet (1992) for American Air Museum / Robert Denny, *Aces: A Novel of World War II* / Harry H. Crosby, *A Wing and a Prayer: The "Bloody 100th" Bomb Group of the U.S. Eighth Air Force in Action Over Europe in World War II* / Michael S. Sherry, *The Rise of American Air Power: The Creation of Armageddon* / Peter Townsend, *Duel of Eagles* / Matthew Cooper, *The German Air Force, 1933–45: An Anatomy of Failure* / Harold Faber, *Luftwaffe: A History* / Peter Fritzsche, *A Nation of Fliers: German Aviation and the Popular Imagination* / E. Beck, *Under the Bombs: The German Home Front, 1942–45* / Janusz Piekalkiewicz, *The Air War, 1939–45* / Wayne Biddle, *Barons of the Sky: From Early Flight to Strategic Warfare—The Story of the American Aerospace Industry* / Edmond Petit, *Nouvelle Histoire Mondiale de l'Aviation* / Maurice Harvey, *The Allied Bomber War, 1939–1945* / *New York Times*, Jan. 25, 1995 / W. Raymond Wood, *Or Go Down in Flame: A Navigator's Death Over Schweinfurt* / *Private Pilot*, Apr. 1996 / Robert Lee Scott, *Flying Tiger: Chennault of China* / Ivan Rendall, *Reaching For the Skies* / Francis Gabreski, *Gabby: A Fighter Pilot's Life* / James H. Howard, *Roar of the Tiger* / T. Coffey, *Hap: The Story of the U.S. Air Force and the Man Who Built It* / *Time*, Aug. 28, 1995 / *New York Times*, Aug. 20 and 21, 1995 / Robert Lee Sherrod, *The History of Marine Corps Aviation in World War II* / T.A. Heppenheimer, *Turbulent Skies: The History of Commercial Aviation*

CHAPTER THIRTEEN

T.A. Heppenheimer, *Turbulent Skies: The History of Commercial Aviation* / R.E.G. Davies, *Airlines of the U.S. Since 1914* / Anthony Sampson, *Empires of the Sky: The Politics, Contests and Cartels of World Airlines* / John Newhouse, *The Sporty Game* / *New York Times*, Feb. 5, 1992; Feb. 18, May 12, and Dec. 18, 1994; July 16, 1995 / *Air and Space*, Oct. 1994; Oct.–Nov. 1995 / *Le Monde*, Jan. 12, 1993 / *Le Figaro*, Apr. 28, 1995 / *Time*, July 20, 1987; Feb. 5, 1990 / C.H. Gibbs-Smith, *Flight Through the Ages* / C.H. Gibbs-Smith, *A History of Flying* / Roger E. Bilstein, *Flight in America, 1900–1983: From the Wrights to the Astronauts* / *The American Heritage History of Flight*, Alvin W. Josephy, Jr., et al., eds. / Captain X and Reynolds Dodson, *Unfriendly Skies: Revelations of a Deregulated Airline Pilot* / *Asia Pacific Observor* (East–West Center), July 1994 / *Aviation and Aerospace Almanac* (McGraw-Hill), 1996 / *The Lore of Flight*, John W.R. Taylor, et al., eds. / *Aviation: The Complete Book of Aircraft and Flight*, David Mondey, ed. / Donald J. Clausing, *The Aviator's Guide to Modern Navigation* / Roger D. Launius, *NASA: A History of the U.S. Civil Space Program* / Bill Gunston, *A Century of Flight* / *FAA Statistical Handbook of Aviation*, 1990 / Richard P. Hallion, *Test Pilots: The Frontiersmen of Flight* / Robert N. Buck, *Weather Flying* / Ivan Rendall, *Reaching For the Skies* / Christopher Chant, *Histoire de l'Aviation* / Wayne Biddle, *Barons of the Sky: From Early Flight to Strategic Warfare—The Story of America's Aerospace Industry* / Ezra Bowen, *Knights of the Air* / Michael J.H. Taylor, *History of Flight* / *International Directory of Company Histories* / Michael J.H. Taylor, *Great Moments in Aviation* / Frank Howard and Bill Gunston, *The Conquest of the Air* / *New York Times*, March 16, 1996 / *Private Pilot*, Apr. 1996 / *Aviation History*, Nov. 1995 / Walter J. Boyne, *The Smithsonian Book of Flight* / Michael Collins, *Liftoff: The Story of America's Adventure in Space* / J.W.R. Taylor and Kenneth Munson, *History of Aviation* / *Aviation: The Pioneer Years*, Ben Mackworth-Praed, ed. / *Air and Space*, Apr. 1994 / Joseph J. Corn, *The Winged Gospel: America's Romance with Aviation, 1900–1950* / Ronald Jackson, *China Clipper* / *Frequent Flyer*, Feb. 1992 / *Air and Space*, Aug.–Sept. 1994 / *New York Times*, Oct. 17 and Dec. 3, 1994 / Frank Borman, with Robert J. Serling, *Countdown: An Autobiography* / Edmond Petit, *Nouvelle Histoire Mondiale de l'Aviation* / Edmond Petit, *Histoire de l'Aviation* / *Richmond Times Dispatch*, June 17 and Nov. 26, 1989 / *New York Times*, March 20, 1988; Aug. 31, 1989; Sept. 1, 1991; Jan. 26 and Dec. 12, 1993; Oct 17 and 23, 1994 / *Time*, Oct. 10, 1989; Jan. 7, 1991; Nov. 23, 1992 / *U.S. News and World Report*, Oct. 17, 1994 / *Le Monde*, Dec. 28, 1993 / Henry Holden and Captain Lori Griffith, *Ladybirds: The Untold Story of Women Pilots in America* / Robert J. Serling, *Legend and Legacy: The Story of Boeing and Its People* / *Time*, May 9, 1994 / Robert Redding and Bill Yenne, *Boeing: Planemaker to the World* / Michael J.H. Taylor, *Boeing* / Jeana Yeager and Dick Rutan, with Phil Patton, *Voyager*

CHAPTER FOURTEEN

Michael Collins, *Liftoff: The Story of America's Adventure in Space* / Robert J. Serling, *Legend and Legacy: The Story of Boeing and Its People* / Roger E. Bilstein, *Flight in America, 1900–1983: From the Wrights to the Astronauts* / Bill Gunston, *A Century of Flight* / *The Lore of Flight*, John W.R. Taylor, et al., eds. / Michael J.H. Taylor, *History of Flight* / Richard P. Hallion, *Test Pilots: The Frontiersmen of Flight* / Bill Yenne, *The History of the U.S. Air Force* / *New York Times*, July 2, 1993 / *Air and Space*, Oct.–Nov. 1992 / Bryce Walker, *Fighting Jets* / Robert L. Shaw, *Fighter Combat: Tactics and Maneuvering* / General Chuck Yeager and Leo Janos, *Yeager: An Autobiography* / Benson Hamlin, *Flight Testing Conventional and Jet Propelled Airplanes* / Martin S. Caidin, *Test Pilots: Riding the Dragon* / *Air and Space*, Dec.–Jan. 1990–91 / *The American Heritage History of Flight* / Ivan Rendall, *Reaching For the Skies* / Michael J.H. Taylor, *Great Moments in Aviation* / Neil D. Van Sickle, *Modern Airmanship* / Tom Wolfe, *The Right Stuff* / T.A. Heppenheimer: *Turbulent Skies: The History of Commercial Aviation* / David Jefferis, *The Jet Age: From the Jet to Swing-wing Bombers* / *New York Times*, Dec. 18, 1994 / Anthony Sampson, *Empires of the Sky: The Politics, Contests and Cartels* of *World Airlines* / *Illustrated History of Aircraft*, Brendan Gallagher, ed. / *New York Times*, May 23 and June 5, 1994 / Jack Broughton, *Going Downtown: The War Against Hanoi and Washington* / Walter J. Boyne, *The Smithsonian Book of Flight* / Edmond Petit, *Nouvelle Histoire Mondiale de l'Aviation* / Frank Howard and Bill Gunston, *The Conquest of the Air* / Jim Webb, *Fly the Wing* / D.P. Davies, *Handling the Big Jets* / Robert Redding and Bill Yenne, *Boeing: Planemaker to the World* / C.H. Gibbs-Smith, *Flight Through the Ages* / *Aviation: The Complete History of Aircraft and Flight*, David Mondey, ed. / *New York Times*, Aug. 29, 1990 / *The Vietnam War: Vietnamese and American Perspectives*, Jayne Werner and Luu Doan Huynh, eds. / *New York Times*, March 11, 1992 / *Time*, Nov. 23, 1992 / *New York Times*, March 27 and Apr. 30, 1988; Nov. 6, 1990 / *Time*, May 9, 1988 / *Air and Space*, Feb.–March 1994

CHAPTER FIFTEEN

Pierre Muller, *Airbus: L'Ambition Européen* / *Le Monde*, Oct. 5, 1991 / *Time*, May 11, 1987 / *France-Amérique*, Jan. 16, 1993 / *New York Times*, Nov. 2, 1987; Sept. 8, 1990; Feb. 24 and Apr. 2, 1992; Feb. 3, 24, and March 4, 1993 / Bill Gunston, *Harrier* / Mike Rogers, *VTOL Military Research Aircraft* / *Air and Space*, Apr.–May 1994 / *U.S. News and World Report*, Apr. 11, 1994; Jan. 16, 1995 / *New York Times*,

Oct. 16 and Dec. 19, 1990; Nov. 10, 1991; Sept. 14 and Dec. 3, 1992; May 8, June 30, and Dec. 7, 1993; Sept. 6, 1994; July 11, 1995 / *Le Monde*, June 4, 1995 / *France-Amérique*, June 24, 1995 / *Air and Space*, Dec.–Jan. 1989–1990 / Alan Shepard and Deke Slayton, *Moon Shot: The Inside Story of America's Race to the Moon* / *U.S. News and World Report*, Feb. 28, 1994 / *Air and Space*, Aug.–Sept. 1988; Aug.–Sept. 1989; Oct.–Nov. 1993 / *Flying*, June 1995 / *Time*, Sept. 12, 1988; Sept. 30, 1991 / Michael J.H. Taylor, *Jet Warplanes: The 21st Century* / Milton O. Thompson, *At the Edge of Space: The X-15 Flight Program* / *New York Times*, June 19 and Aug. 7, 1995 / *Encyclopedia Britannica*, Vol. 4 (1993 edition) / Bill Siuru and John D. Busick, *Future Flight: The Next Generation of Aircraft Technology* / Leik Myrabo and Dean Ing, *The Future of Flight* / Paul F. Crickmore, *SR-71 Blackbird: Lockheed's Mach 3 Hot Shot* / Lindsay Peacock, *B-1B Bomber* / Nick Kotz, *Wild Blue Yonder: Money, Politics and the B-1 Bomber* / *Air and Space*, Apr.–May 1991; June–July 1993; Oct.–Nov. 1994 and Dec.–Jan. 1994–95 / *Time*, March 18 and May 6, 1991 / *New York Times*, May 10, 1987 / *Le Monde*, March 8, 1990 / A. Scott Crossfield, *Always Another Dawn: The Story of a Rocket Test Pilot*

CHAPTER SIXTEEN

Michael Collins, *Liftoff: The Story of America's Adventure in Space* / Frank Borman, with Robert J. Serling, *Countdown: An Autobiography* / Milton O. Thompson, *At the Edge of Space: The X-15 Flight Program* / *Air and Space*, June–July 1994 / Michael Collins, *Carrying the Fire* / Alan Shepard and Deke Slayton, *Moon Shot: The Inside Story of America's Race to the Moon* / Jim Lovell and Jeffrey Kluger, *Apollo 13* / John Noble Wilford, *We Reach the Moon* / Peter Bond, *Heroes in Space: From Gagarin to Challenger* / David Baker, *The History of Manned Space Flight* / Joseph P. Allen and Russell Martin, *Entering Space: An Astronaut's Odyssey* / Thomas D. Damon, *Introduction to Space: The Science of Space Flight* / Valentin Lebedev, *Diary of a Cosmonaut: 211 Days in Space* / Dennis Newkirk, *Soviet Manned Space Flight* / Michael Cassutt, *Who's Who in Space* / Tom Wolfe, *The Right Stuff* / Roger D. Launius, *NASA: A History of the U.S. Civil Space Program* / Wernher Von Braun and Frederick I. Orway III, *History of Rocketry and Space Travel* / Mike Gray, *Angle of Attack: Harrison Storms and the Race to the Moon* / Michael Collins, *Mission to Mars: An Astronaut's Vision of Our Future in Space* / *Air and Space*, Feb.–March 1993 / *New York Times*, May 9 and Sept. 29, 1992 / *Aviation: The Complete Book of Aircraft and Flight*, David Mondey, ed. John W.R. Taylor and Kenneth Munson, *History of Aviation* / Neil Armstrong, Michael Collins, and Edwin "Buzz" Aldrin, *First on the Moon* / Andrew Chaikin, *A Man on the Moon: The Voyages of the Apollo Astronauts* / *Air and Space*, Apr.–May 1993; Aug.–Sept. 1994

CHAPTER SEVENTEEN

Michael J.H. Taylor, *History of Flight* / Mark R. Chartrand and Ron Miller: *Golden Guide: Exploring Space* / *Richmond Times Dispatch*, June 24, 1995 / *Time*, Jan. 2,

1989 / *Air and Space,* June–July 1989; Apr.–May, June–July, Aug.–Sept., and Oct.–Nov. 1994 / *New York Times,* July 17 and 20, 1994 / *U.S. News and World Report,* July 11, 1994 / *Le Figaro,* July 22, 1989; Aug. 10, 1993 / *Le Monde,* July 20, 1989 / Edwin "Buzz" Aldrin and Malcolm McConnell, *Men from Earth* / Douglas Mackinnon and Joseph Baldanza, *Footprints: The 12 Men Who Walked on the Moon Reflect on their Flights, Their Lives and the Future* / Michael J.H. Taylor, *Great Moments in Aviation* / Robert J. Serling, *Legend and Legacy: The Story of Boeing and Its People* / *Newsweek,* July 3, 1995 / *New York Times,* Nov. 28 and Dec. 2–14 1993; Feb. 7, Sept. 24, and Dec. 8, 1995 / *Time,* Apr. 16 and July 9, 1990; Nov. 29 and Dec. 13, 1993; Dec. 11, 1995 / *Europe's Future in Space* / Richard P. Hallion, *Test Pilots: The Frontiersmen of Flight* / *Aviation Week and Space Technology,* Aug. 16, 1993 / *New York Times,* July 11, 1995 / *Time,* Oct. 10, 1988 / Associated Press, March 16, 1995, on Valery Polyakov / *Washington Post,* March 23 and June 28, 1995 / *New York Times,* Jan. 15, Feb. 1–12, March 15–24, May 18, June 29–July 8, July 11, 16, Nov. 10 and 13–19, 1995; Jan. 28, 1996 / Carl Sagan, *Pale Blue Dot*

CHAPTER EIGHTEEN

Joseph P. Allen and Russell Martin, *Entering Space: An Astronaut's Journey* / Michael Collins, *Mission to Mars: An Astronaut's Vision of Our Future in Space* / Roger D. Launius, *NASA: A History of the U.S. Civil Space Program* / Frank Borman, with Robert J. Serling, *Countdown: An Autobiography* / Richard Bach, *A Gift of Wings* / Anthony W. LeVier, with John Guenther, *Pilot* / General Chuck Yeager and Leo Janos, *Yeager: An Autobiography* / Alan Shepard and Deke Slayton, *Moon Shot: The Inside Story of America's Race to the Moon* / Walter M. Schirra, Jr., *Schirra's Space* / Le Ly Hayslip, *When Heaven and Earth Changed Places: A Vietnamese Woman's Journey from War to Peace* / Michael Collins, *Liftoff: The Story of America's Adventure in Space* / Andrew Chaikin, *A Man on the Moon: The Voyages of the Apollo Astronauts* / Philippe Petit, *Traité du Funambulisme*

Bibliography

Bibliographies

Pisano, Dominick A., and C.S. Lewis, eds. *Air and Space History: An Anno tated Bibliography*. New York: Garland, 1988.

Smith, Myron, ed. *The Airlines Bibliography: The Salem College Guide to Sources on Commercial Aviation*. West Cornwall, CT: Locust Hill, 1986.

Chronologies

Baker, David. *Flight and Flying: A Chronology*. New York: Facts on File, 1994.

Chronicle of Aviation. Liberty, MO: J.L. International, 1992.

Taylor, Michael J.H., and David Mondey. *Milestones of Flight*. London: Jane's, 1983.

References

The Airlines Industry: United States Encyclopedia. 1992.

Airman's Information Manual/Federal Aviation Regulations (AIM/FAR). Blue Ridge Summit, PA: Tab Books, 1986.

Air Transport Association of America: Facts and Figures. Washington, DC, 1937 on.

Encyclopedia of Aviation. New York: Scribners, 1977.

FAA Statistical Handbook of Aviation. Washington, DC, 1989.

Gunston, Bill. *Jane's Aerospace Dictionary*. London, 1980.

Hubin, W.N. *The Science of Flight: Pilot Oriented Aeronautics*. Ames: Iowa State University Press, 1992.

International Directory of Company Histories. Chicago: St. James, 1990.

Jane's All the World's Aircraft. London, annual.

Jane's Encyclopedia of Aviation. Danbury, CT: Grolier, 1980.

Jane's International Aerospace Directory. London, annual.

Lampf, Richard, ed. *Aviation and Aerospace Almanac.* New York: McGraw-Hill, 1995.

McGraw-Hill Aviation and Aerospace Almanac, 1996. New York, 1996.

Mondey, David, ed. *The International Encyclopedia of Aviation.* New York: Crown, 1977.

Naissance de l'Aviation, in *Les Cahiers de Science et Vie.* Paris, 1991.

Simpson, R.W. *Airlife's General Aviation: A Guide to Post-War General Aviation Manufacturers and Their Aircraft.* United Kingdom, 1995.

Van Sickle, Neil. *Modern Airmanship.* New York: Van Nostrand Reinhold, 1971. (Fourth Edition used for this book; in 1995, Tab Books published the Seventh Edition.)

Periodicals

Air and Space. Washington, DC: Smithsonian Institution Press.

Air Force Magazine. Arlington, VA.

Air Force Times. Springfield, VA.

Air International. Stamford, England.

Air Review. London: Air League.

Aircraft Owner's and Pilot's Association (AOPA). Frederick, MD.

Airline Pilot Magazine. Arlington, VA.

Airliners: The World's Airline Magazine. Castro Valley, CA.

Aviation History. Leesburg, VA: Cowles History Group.

Aviation Magazine International. Paris: Editions Larivière.

Aviation Week and Space Technology. New York: McGraw-Hill.

Le Fanatique de l'Aviation. Paris:15 Quai de l'Oise.

Flight. Mount Morris, IL.

Flying. Greenwich, CT.

Icare: Revue de l'Aviation Française. Paris. Syndicat National des Pilotes.

Northeast Weekend Flyers. Great Barrington, MA.

Pégase. Le Bourget, Paris: Musée de l'Air.

Private Pilot. Irvine, Calif.: Fancy, 1965 on.

U.S. Aviation. Winter Haven, FL.

Books

Aldrin, Edwin "Buzz," and Malcolm McConnell. *Men from Earth.* New York: Random House, 1973.

Allen, Joseph P., and Russell Martin. *Entering Space: An Astronaut's Odyssey.* New York: Stewart, Tabori and Chang, 1985.

Allen, Richard Sanders. *Revolution in the Sky: Those Fabulous Lockheeds and the Pilots Who Flew Them.* Brattleboro, VT: Stephen Greene, 1967.

Anderson, John D. (tr.), *Introduction to Flight.* New York: McGraw-Hill, 1989.

The Army Air Forces in World War II, 7 vols. Washington, DC: Office of Air Force History, 1983.

Armstrong, Neil, Michael Collins, and Edwin "Buzz" Aldrin. *First on the Moon.* New York: Criterion, 1970.

Aymar, Brandt, ed. *Men in the Air.* New York: Crown, 1990.

Bach, Richard. *Stranger to the Ground.* New York: Harper & Row, 1963.

———. *A Gift of Wings.* New York: Bantam, 1974.

Baker, David. *The History of Manned Space Flight.* New York: Crown, 1981.

Bellonte, Maurice. *Le Premier Paris–New York.* Paris: Carlo Descamps, 1977.

Biddle, Wayne. *Barons of the Sky: From Early Flight to Strategic Warfare—The Story of the American Aerospace Industry.* New York: Henry Holt, 1991.

Bilstein, Roger E. *Flight Patterns: Trends in Aeronautical Development in the United States.* Athens: University of Georgia, 1983.

———. *Flight in America, 1900 1983: From the Wrights to the Astronauts.* Baltimore: Johns Hopkins, 1984, 1994.

Birtles, Philip. *Concorde.* London: Ian Allan, 1984.

Bond, Charles R., and Terry Anderson. *A Flying Tiger's Diary.* College Station, University of Texas A&M, 1984.

Bond, Peter. *Heroes in Space: From Gagarin to Challenger.* New York: B. Blackwell, 1987.

Borman, Frank, with Robert J. Serling. *Countdown: An Autobiography.* New York: Morrow, 1988.

Bowen, Ezra. *Knights of the Air.* Alexandria, VA: Time-Life, 1980.

Boyne, Walter J. *The Leading Edge.* New York: Stewart, Tabori, and Chang, 1986.

———. *The Smithsonian Book of Flight.* Washington, DC: Smithsonian Institution, 1987.

——— *Siver Wings; A History of the United States Air Force.* New York, Simon and Schuster, 1993

Boyne, Walter J., and Donald S. Lopez. *The Jet Age: Forty Years of Jet Aviation.* Washington, DC: Smithsonian Institution, 1979.

Brenlove, Milovan S. *The Air Traffic System.* Ames: Iowa State University, 1987.

Brink, Randall. *Lost Star: The Search for Amelia Earhart.* New York: Norton, 1994.

Broughton, Jack. *Going Downtown: The War Against Hanoi and Washington.* New York: Orion, 1988.

Buck, Robert N. *Weather Flying.* New York: Macmillan, 1988.

Caidin, Martin S. *Barnstorming.* New York: Bantam, 1965, 1991.

———. *Ragwings and Heavy Iron: The Agony and the Ecstasy of Flying History's Greatest Warbirds.* Boston: Houghton Mifflin, 1984.

———. *Test Pilots: Riding the Dragon.* New York: Bantam, 1992.

Calvert, Brian. *Flying Concorde.* Shrewsbury, UK: Airlife, 1981, 1989.

Captain X and Reynolds Dodson. *Unfriendly Skies: Revelations of a Deregulated Airline Pilot.* New York: Doubleday, 1989.

Carson, Annette. *Flight Fantastic.* Newbury Park, CA: Haynes, 1986.

Carteret, J. Grand. *La Conquête de l'Air Vue par l'Image.*N.p.: Librairie des Annales, 1910.

Cassutt, Michael, ed. *Who's Who in Space.* New York: Macmillan, 1993.

Ceruzzi, Paul. E. *Beyond the Limits: Flight Enters the Computer Age.* Cambridge: M.I.T. University, 1989.

Chaban, Emmanuel. *Latécoere.* Paris: Orban, 1990.

Chaikin, Andrew. *A Man on the Moon: The Voyages of the Apollo Astronauts.* New York: Viking, 1994.

Chant, Christophe. *Histoire de l'Aviation.* Paris: Editions Atlas, 1979.

Chant, Christopher and John Batchelor. *Aviation: An Illustrated History.* London: Graham Beehag Books. 1994

Chartrand, Mark R., and Ron Miller. *Golden Guide: Exploring Space.* New York: Golden Guide, 1991.

Chichester, Frank. *Ride the Wind.* New York: Paragon, 1989.

Choi, Jin Tai. *Aviation Terrorism.* New York: St. Martin's, 1994.

Christy, Joe, and LeRoy Cook. *American Aviation: An Illustrated History.* Blue Ridge Summit, PA: Tab, 1987, 1993.

Clancy, Tom. *Fighter Wing: A Guided Tour of an Air Force Combat Wing.* New York: Berkley, 1995.

Clark, Allan. *Aces High: The War in the Air Over the Western Front, 1914–1918.* New York: Putnam and Sons, 1973.

Clausing, Donald J. *The Aviator's Guide to Modern Navigation.* Blue Ridge Summit, PA: Tab, 1987.

Clodfelter, Mark. *The Limits of Air Power: The American Bombing of North Vietnam.* New York: Free Press, 1989.

Cochran, Jacqueline, and Mary Ann Brinley. *Jackie Cochran: An Auto-*

biography. New York: Bantam, 1987.

Coffey, Thomas M. *Hap: The Story of the U.S. Air Force and the Man Who Built It*. New York: Viking, 1982.

Collier, Basil. *A History of Air Power*. New York: Macmillan, 1974.

Collins, Michael. *Carrying the Fire*. New York: Farrar, Straus & Giroux, 1974.

———. *Liftoff: The Story of America's Adventure in Space*. New York: Grove, 1988.

———. *Mission to Mars: An Astronaut's Vision of Our Future in Space*. New York: Grove, 1990.

Collins, Richard L. *Flying IFR*. Charlottesville, VA: Thomasson-Grant, 1993.

Combs, Harry, with Martin Caidin. *Kill Devil Hill: Discovering the Secret of the Wright Brothers*. Boston: Houghton Mifflin, 1979.

Cooper, Matthew. *The German Air Force, 1933–45: An Anatomy of Failure*. London: Jane's, 1981.

Corn, Joseph. *The Winged Gospel: America's Romance with Aviation, 1900–1950*. New York: Oxford University Press, 1983.

Courtney, Frank T. *The Eighth Sea*. New York: Doubleday, 1972.

Crosby, Harry H. *A Wing and a Prayer: The "Bloody 100th" Bomb Group of the U.S. Eighth Air Force in Action Over Europe in World War II*. New York: HarperCollins, 1993

Crossfield, A. Scott. *Always Another Dawn: The Story of a Rocket Test Pilot*. Cleveland: World, 1960.

Crouch, Tom D. *The Bishop's Boys; A Life of Wilbur and Orville Wright*. New York: Norton, 1989

Crickmore, Paul F. *SR-71 Blackbird: Lockheed's Mach 3 Hot Shot*. London: Osprey, 1987.

Dahl, Raul. *Going Solo*. New York: Jonathan Cape, 1986.

Damon, Thomas D. *Introduction to Space: The Science of Space Flight*. Malabar, FL: Orbit, 1989.

Davies, D.P. *Handling the Big Jets*. London: Norman Brothers, 1967.

Davies, R.E.G. *The World's Airlines*. New York: Oxford University Press, 1964.

———. *Airlines of the U.S. Since 1914*. Washington, DC: Smithsonian Institution, 1972.

Denny, Robert. *Aces: A Novel of World War II*. New York: Donald Fine, 1990.

Doolittle, James H., and Carroll Glines. *I Could Never Be So Lucky Again: An Autobiography*. New York: Bantam, 1991.

Dorr, Robert. *Air War: Hanoi*. London: Blandford, 1988.

————. *Air War: South Vietnam*. London: Arms & Armour, 1990.

Dorr, Robert, and Warren Thompson. *The Korean Air War*. Osceola, WI: Motorbooks, 1994.

Dorsey, Gary. *The Fullness of Wings: The Making of a New Daedalus*. New York, 1990.

Douhet, Giulio. *Command of the Air*. New York: Coward-McCann, 1921, 1942.

Du Bois, William Pene. *Balloons*. New York: Viking, 1948, 1975.

Dupre, Flint. *Hap Arnold: Architect of American Air Power*. New York: Macmillan, 1972.

Dwiggins, Don. *The Barnstormers: Flying Daredevils of the Roaring 1920s*. Blue Ridge Sumit, PA: Tab, 1981.

Earhart, Amelia. *Last Flight*. New York: Orion, 1937, 1988.

Emme, Eugene. *The Impact of Air Power: National Security and World Politics*. Princeton, NJ: Van Nostrand, 1959.

————, ed. *Two Hundred Years of Flight in America: A Bicentennial Survey*. San Diego: Univelt, 1977.

Ethell, Jeffrey. *Frontiers of Flight*. New York: Orion, 1992.

————, *Wings of War: Fighting World War II in the Air*. Annapolis, MD. Naval Institute Press. 1994

Ethel, Jeffrey and Don Downie. *Flying the Hump*. Osceola, WI: Motorbooks, 1996

Europe's Future in Space. London: Royal Institute of International Afairs, 1988.

Faber, Harold. *Luftwaffe: A History*. New York: Times Books, 1977.

Faure, C. Marin. *Flying a Seaplane*. Blue Ridge Summit, PA: Tab, 1996.

Ford, Daniel. *Flying Tigers: Claire Chennault and the American Volunteer Group*. Washington, DC: Smithsonian Institution, 1991.

Foxworth, Thomas G. *The Speed Seekers*. New York: Doubleday, 1974.

Francillon, René. *Vietnam: The War in the Air*. New York: Arch Cape, 1987.

Frey, J.J. *How To Fly Floats*. College Point, NY: EDO Corporation, 1995

Fritzsche, Peter. *A Nation of Fliers: German Aviation and the Popular Imagination*. Cambridge, MA: Harvard University, 1992.

Gabreski, Francis. *Gabby: A Fighter Pilot's Life*. Oil City, PA: Orion, 1991.

Gallagher, Brendan, ed. *Illustrated History of Aircraft*. London: Octopus, 1977.

Gandt, Robert L. *China Clipper: The Age of the Great Flying Boats*. Annapolis, MD: Naval Institute, 1991.

————. *Sky Gods: The Fall of Pan Am*. New York: Morrow, 1995.

Gann, Ernest K. *Blaze of Noon.* New York: Henry Holt, 1946.

———. *The Aviator.* New York: Arbor House, 1974.

Gibbs-Smith, C.H. *A History of Flying.* New York: Praeger, 1954.

———. *Aviation: An Historical Survey from Its Origins to the End of World War II.* London: Her Majesty's Stationery Office, 1970, 1985.

———. *Flight Through the Ages.* New York: Crowell, 1974.

Gilman, Ted. *Lindbergh: The Flight.* Vernon Hills, IL: Heather Ridge, 1986.

Glines, Carroll V. *The Doolittle Raid: America's Daring First Strike Against Japan.* New York: Orion, 1988.

———. *Air Mail.* Blue Ridge Summit, PA: Tab Books, 1990.

———. *Roscoe Turner.* Washington, DC: Smithsonian Institution, 1995.

Goldstein, Lawrence. *The Flying Machine and Modern Literature.* Bloomington: Indiana University, 1986.

Gray, Mike. *Angle of Attack: Harrison Storms and the Race to the Moon.* New York: Norton, 1992.

Greard, André. *Le Métier de Pilot de Ligne.* Paris: Editions France-Empire, 1979.

Greenaway, Peter. *Flying Out of This World.* Chicago: University of Chicago, 1994.

Greenwood, James R. *Stunt Flying for the Movies.* Blue Ridge Summit, PA: Tab, 1982.

Groves, Clinton A. *Jetliners: The World's Great Jetliners, 1950s and Today.* Osceola, WI: Motorbooks, 1993.

Gunston, Bill. *Harrier.* New York: Arco, 1984.

———. *A Century of Flight.* New York: Gallery, 1988.

Gwynn-Jones, Terry. *Wings Across the Pacific.* New York: Orion, 1991.

Haining, Peter. *The Compleat Birdman.* New York: St. Martin's, 1976.

Hallion, Richard P. *Test Pilots: The Frontiersmen of Flight.* Washington, DC: Smithsonian Institution, 1988.

Hamlin, Benson. *Flight Testing Conventional and Jet Propelled Airplanes.* New York, 1946.

Hamlen, Joseph. *Flight Fever.* Garden City, NY: Doubleday, 1971.

Hardy, M.J. *Boeing.* London: Jane's, 1982.

Hart, Clive. *The Dream of Flight: Aeronautics from Classical Times to the Renaissance.* London: Faber and Faber, 1972.

———. *Images of Flight.* Berkeley: University of California, 1988.

Harvey, Frank. *Air War Vietnam.* New York: Bantam, 1967.

Harvey, Maurice. *The Allied Bomber War.* New York: Sarpedon, 1993.

Heppenheimer, T.A. *Turbulent Skies: The History of Commercial Aviation.*

New York: John Wiley & Sons, 1995.

Higham, Robin. *Air Power: A Concise History*. New York: St. Martin's, 1972.

Higham, Robin, and Carol Williams, eds. *Flying Combat Aircraft of the United States Air Force*, 3 vols. Manhattan, KS: Sunflower University, 1978 and on.

Holden, Henry M., with Captain Lori Griffith. *Ladybirds: The Untold Story of Women Pilots in America*. Mt. Freedom, NJ: Black Hawk, 1991.

Howard, Frank, and Bill Gunston. *The Conquest of the Air*. New York: Random House, 1972.

Howard, Fred. *Wilbur and Orville: A Biography of the Wright Brothers*. New York: Ballantine, 1987.

Hoyt, Edwin P. *The Airmen: The Story of American Fliers in World War II*. New York: McGraw-Hill, 1990.

Huntington, Roger. *The Thompson Trophy Races*. Osceola, WI: Motorbooks, 1989.

Hynes, Samuel. *Flights of Passage: Reflections of a World War II Aviator*. New York: Pocket Books, 1988.

Irving, Clide. *Wide Body: The Triumph of the 747*. New York: Morrow, 1993.

Jablonski, Edward. *America in the Air War*. Alexandria, VA: Time-Life, 1982.

Jackson, Donald Dale. *The Aeronauts*. Alexandria, VA: Time-Life, 1981.

———. *Flying the Mail*. Alexandria, VA: Time-Life, 1982.

Jackson, Ronald. *China Clipper*. New York: Everest, 1980.

Jefferis, David. T*he Jet Age: From the Jet to Swing-wing Bombers*. New York: Franklin Watts, 1988.

———. *Supersonic Flight*. New York: Franklin Watts, 1988.

Jensen, Claus. *No Downlink: A Dramatic Narrative About the Challenger Accident and Our Time*. New York: Farrar, Straus and Giroux, 1996.

Josephy, Alvin W., Jr., et al., eds. *The American Heritage History of Flight*. New York: American Heritage, 1962.

Karman, Theodor Von. *Aerodynamics*. New York: McGraw-Hill, 1963.

———. *The Wind and Beyond*. Boston: Little, Brown, 1967.

Kennett, Lee. *A History of Strategic Bombing*. New York: Scribners, 1982.

———. *The First Air War, 1914–1918*. New York: Free Press, 1991.

Kermode, A.C. *Mechanics of Flight*. London: Pitman, 1972.

Kershner, William R. *The Flight Instructor's Manual*. Ames: Iowa State University, 1974, 1981, 1993.

Kilduff, Peter. *Richthofen: Beyond the Legend of the Red Baron*. New York: John Wiley & Sons, 1994.

Killen, John. *A History of the Luftwaffe*. Garden City, NY: Doubleday, 1968.

Krause, S.S. *Aircrfat Safety: Accidents Investigations, Analyses and Applications.* Blue Ridge Summit, PA: Tab, 1996.

Lanbright, W. Henry. *Powering Apollo: James E. Webb of NASA.* Baltimore: Johns Hopkins University, 1995.

Langwiesche, Wolfgang. *Stick and Rudder: An Explanation of the Art of Flying.* Blue Ridge Summit, PA: Tab, 1944, 1972.

Launius, Roger D. *NASA: A History of the U.S. Civil Space Program.* Malabar, FL: Krieger, 1994.

Lawson, Ted, with Bob Considine. *Thirty Seconds Over Tokyo.* New York: Random House, 1943.

Lebedev, Valentin. *Diary of a Cosmonaut: 211 Days in Space.* New York: Bantam, 1983, 1990.

Lebow, Eileen. *Cal Rodgers and the Vin Fiz: The First Trans-Continental Flight.* Washington, DC: Smithsonian Institution, 1989.

LeMay, General Curtis *Mission with LeMay: My Story.* New York: Doubleday, 1965.

LeVier, Anthony W., with John L. Guenther. *Pilot.* New York: Harper & Brothers, 1954.

Lewis, Cecil. *Sagittarius Rising.* New York: Harcourt Brace, 1936.

Lieberg, Owen S. *The First Air Race: The International Competition at Rheims, 1909.* New York: Doubleday, 1974.

Lindbergh, Anne Morrow. *North to the Orient.* New York: Harcourt Brace, 1935.

———. *Listen to the Wind.* New York: Harcourt Brace, 1938.

Lindbergh, Charles A. *We.* New York: Putnam, 1927.

———. *The Spirit of St. Louis.* New York: Harcourt Brace Jovanovich, 1953, 1978.

Lissarague, Pierre. *Clément Ader: Inventeur d'Avions.* Paris: Editions Privat, 1990.

Littauer, Raphael, and Norman Uphoff, eds. *The Air War in Indochina.* Boston: Beacon, 1972.

Lopez, Donald S. *Aviation: A Smithsonian Guide.* New York: Macmillan, 1995.

Lovell, Jim, and Jeffrey Kruger. *Apollo 13* (earlier titled *Lost Moon: The Perilous Voyage of Apollo 13*; Boston, Houghton Mifflin, 1994.). New York: Pocket Books, 1995.

Lovell, Mary S. *The Sound of Wings: The Life of Amelia Earhart.* New York: Harper & Row, 1963.

Lomax, Judy. *Women of the Air.* New York: Ballantine, 1986.

Lundstrom, John B. *The First Team and the Guadalcanal Campaign: Naval Fighter Combat from August to November, 1942*. Annapolis, MD: Naval Institute, 1993.

Mackinnon, Douglas, and Joseph Baldanza. *Footprints: The 12 Men Who Walked on the Moon Reflect on Their Flights, Their Lives and the Future*. Washington, DC: Acropolis, 1989.

Mackworth-Praed, Ben, ed. *Aviation: The Pioneer Years*. London: Studio Editions, 1990.

Markham, Beryl. *West with the Night*. San Francisco: North Point, 1983.

Markowski, Michael A. *Ultralight Flight: The Pilot's Handbook of Ultralight Knowledge*. Hummelstown, PA: Ultralight, 1982.

Matricardi, Paolo. *A Concise History of Aviation*. New York: Crescent, 1985 (translation of *Storia dell' Aviazione*).

Middleton, Drew, et al., eds. *Air War Vietnam*. New York: Bobbs-Merrill, 1978.

Mignet, Henri. *The Flying Flea: How to Build and Fly It*. London and Vista, CA: Aeolus, 1988 (translation of *Le Sport de l'Amateur*, Paris, 1934).

Milton, Joyce. *Loss of Eden: A Biography of Charles and Anne Morrow Lindbergh*. New York: HarperCollins, 1993.

Mitchell, Brig. General William. *Memoires of World War I: From Start to Finish of Our Greatest War*. New York: Random House, 1960.

Momyer, William. *Air Power in Three Wars*. New York: Arno, 1988.

Mondey, David, ed. *Aviation: The Complete Book of Aircraft and Flight*. London: Octopus, 1980.

Moolman, Valerie. *Women Aloft*. Alexandria, VA: Time-Life, 1981.

Morrow, John H., Jr. *The Great War In the Air: Military Aviation From 1909 to 1921*. Washington, DC Smithsonian Books. 1993

Moseley, Leonard. *Lindbergh: A Biography*. New York: Doubleday, 1976.

Muller, Pierre. *Airbus: L'Ambition Européen*. Paris: L'Harmattan, 1989.

Murray, Charles. *Apollo: The Race to the Moon*. New York: Simon & Schuster, 1989.

Myrabo, Leik, and Dean Ing. *The Future of Flight*. New York: Baen, 1985.

Nadar (Gustave-Félix Tournachon). *Le Droit au Vol*. Paris, 1865.

Nader, Ralph, and Wesley J. Smith. *Collision Cruise: The Truth About Airline Safety*. Blue Ridge Summit, PA: Tab, 1994.

Nevin, David. *The Pathfinders*. Alexandria, VA: Time-Life, 1980.

Newhouse, John. *The Sporty Game*. New York: Knopf, 1982.

Newkirk, Dennis. *Soviet Manned Space Flight*. Houston: Gulf, 1990.

Noggle, Anne. *A Dance with Death: Soviet Airwomen in World War II*.

College Station: Texas A&M, 1994.

Nolan, Michael S. *Fundamentals of Air Traffic Control.* Belmont, CA: Wadsworth, 1994.

Oberg, James E. *Red Star in Orbit.* New York: Random House, 1981.

———. *Mission to Mars: Plans and Concepts for the First Manned Landing.* Harrisburg, PA: Stackpole, 1982.

———. *The New Race for Space.* Harrisburg, PA: Stackpole, 1984.

O'Dell, Bob. *Aerobatics Today.* New York: St. Martin's, 1980, 1984.

O'Neil, Paul. *Barnstormers and Speed Kings.* Alexandria, VA: Time-Life, 1981.

O'Neil, Ralph. *A Dream of Eagles.* Boston: Houghton Mifflin, 1973.

Orlebar, Christopher. *The Concorde Story.* London: Temple, 1986, 1995.

Ott, James, and Raymond E. Neidl. *Airline Odyssey: The Airline Industry's Turbulent Flight into the Future.* New York: McGraw-Hill, 1995.

Owen, Kenneth. *Concorde.* London: Jane's, 1982.

Padfield, H. Randall. *Learning to Fly Helicopters.* Blue Ridge Summit, PA: Tab, 1992.

Paulos, John Allen. *Innumercay; Mathematical Illiteracy and Its Consequences.* New York. Hill and Wang, 1988.

Perret, Geoffrey. *Winged Victory: The Army Air Forces in World War II.* New York: Random House, 1993

Peterson, Barbara, and James Glab. *Rapid Descent: The Shake-out in the Airlines.* New York: Simon & Schuster, 1994.

Petit, Edmond. *La Vie Quotidienne dans l'Aviation en France au Début du Vingtième Siècle, 1900–1935.* Paris, 1977.

———. *Nouvelle Histoire Mondiale de l'Aviation.* Paris: Albin Michel, 1987.

Petzinger, Thomas, Jr. *Hard Landing: How the Epic Contest for Power and Profits Plunged the Airlines into Chaos.* New York: Random House, 1995.

Piekalkiewicz, Janusz. *The Air War: 1939–45.* Harrisburg, PA: Blandford, 1985.

Post, Wiley, and Harold Gatty. *Around the World in Eight Days: The Flight of the Winnie Mae.* New York: Orion, 1989.

Prendergast, Curtis. *The First Aviators.* Alexandria, VA: Time-Life, 1981.

Rae, John B. *Climb to Greatness: The American Aircraft Industry.* Cambridge: M.I.T., 1968.

Redding, Robert, and Bill Yenne. *Boeing: Planemaker to the World.* New York: Crescent, 1983.

Reiss, Bob. *Frequent Flyer: One Plane, One Passenger, and the Spectacular Feat of Commuter Flight.* New York: Simon & Schuster, 1994.

Rendall, Ivan. *Reaching For the Skies*. London: BBC Books, 1988.

Reynolds, Clark G. *The Carrier War*. Alexandria, VA: Time-Life, 1982.

Rich, Ben, and Leo Tamoz. *Skunk Works: A Personal Memoir of My Years at Lockheed*. Boston: Little, Brown, 1994.

Rich, Doris L. *Amelia Earhart: A Biography*. Washington, DC: Smithsonian Institution, 1989.

Ride, Sally. *To Space and Back*. New York: Lothrop, Lee & Shepherd, 1986.

Rogers, Mike. *VTOL Military Research Aircraft*. New York: Orion, 1989.

Ross, Walter. *The Last Hero: Charles A. Lindbergh*. New York: Harper & Row, 1964.

Sagan, Carl. *Pale Blue Dot*. New York: Random House, 1994.

Saint-Exupéry, Antoine de. *Airman's Odyssey*. New York: Harcourt Brace Jovanovich, 1984.

Sampson, Anthony. *Empires of the Sky: The Politics, Contests and Cartels of World Airlines*. New York: Random House, 1984.

Saundby, Robert. *Early Aviation*. New York: American Heritage, 1971.

Schaffer, Ronald. *Wings of Judgment: American Bombing in World War II*. New York: Oxford University Press, 1985.

Schiff, Stacy. *St. Exupéry: A Biography*. New York: Knopf, 1994.

Schirra, Walter M., Jr. *Schirra's Space*. Boston: Quinlan Press, 1988.

Schultz, D.P. *A Maverick War: Chennault and the Flying Tigers*. New York: St. Martin's, 1987.

———. *The Doolittle Raid*. New York: St. Martin's, 1988.

Scott, Robert Lee. *God Is My Co-Pilot*. New York. Scribners Compony. 1943 (1989)

———. *Flying Tiger: Chennault of China*. Westport, CT: Greenwood, 1959, 1973.

———. *The Day I Owned the Sky*. New York: Bantam, 1988.

Seagrave, Sterling. *Soldiers of Fortune*. Alexandria, Va.: Time-Life, 1981.

Seo, Hiroshi. *The 747 Story*. London: Jane's, 1984.

Serling, Robert J. *Eagle: The Story of American Airlines*. New York: St. Martin's, 1985.

———. *Legend and Legacy: The Story of Boeing and Its People*. New York, 1992.

Shaw, Robert L. *Fighter Combat: Tactics and Maneuvering*. Annapolis, MD: Naval Institute, 1985.

Shepard, Alan, and Deke Slayton. *Moon Shot: The Inside Story of America's Race to the Moon*. Atlanta: Turner, 1994.

Sherrod, Robert Lee. *The History of Marine Corps Aviation in World War II*.

San Rafael, CA: Presidio, 1980.

Sherry, Michael S. *The Rise of American Air Power: The Creation of Armageddon.* New Haven, CT: Yale University, 1987.

Sikorsky, Igor. *The Story of the Winged S.* New York: Dodd, Mead, 1938, 1967.

Siuru, Bill, and John D. Busick. *Future Flight: The Next Generation of Aircraft Technology.* Blue Ridge Summit, PA: Tab, 1987.

Skinner, Michael. *Red Flag: Combat Training in Today's Air Force.* New York: Berkeley, 1984.

Smith, Henry Ladd. *Airways: The History of Commercial Aviation.* Washington, DC: Smithsonian Institution, 1942, 1991.

Solberg, Carl. *Conquest of the Sky: A History of Commercial Aviation.*

Spencer, Otha C. *Flying the Hump: Memories an Air War.* College Station: Texas A&M, 1992.

Steirman, Hy, and Glenn D. Kittler. *The First Transatlantic Flight, 1919.* New York: Harper & Row, 1961.

Stever, H.G. *Flight.* Alexandria, VA: Time-Life, 1965.

Stewart, Stanley. *Flying the Big Jets.* Shrewsbury, UK: Airlife, 3rd ed. 1992.

Stokesbury, James. *A Short History of Air Power.* New York: Morrow, 1986.

Sweetman, Bill. *Advanced Fighter Technology.* Shrewsbury, UK: Airlife, 1988.

Sykes, Claud W. *French War Birds.* Vista, CA: Aeolus, 1987.

Taylor, Barry. *Pan Am's Ocean Clippers.* Blue Ridge Summit, PA: Tab, 1991.

Taylor, David P. *Handling the Big Jets.* Red Hill, Surrey, UK: Brabazon House, 1967.

Taylor, John W.R., ed. *The Lore of Flight.* Hong Kong: Octopus, 1970, 1986.

Taylor, John W.R., and Kenneth Munson. *History of Aviation.* London: New English Library, 1972.

Taylor, Michael J.H. *Boeing.* Guildford, Surrey, UK: 1982.

———. *Great Moments in Aviation.* New York: Mallard, 1989.

———. *History of Flight.* New York: Crescent, 1990.

Taylor, Michael J.H., and David Mondey. *Spies in the Sky.* New York: Scribners, 1973.

Tessendorf, K.C. *Barnstormers and Daredevils.* New York: Atheneum, 1988.

Thompson, Milton O. *At the Edge of Space: The X-15 Flight Program.* Washington, DC: Smithsonian Institution, 1992.

Thyraud, Jacques, and Pierre Favre. *Histoire des Hommes Volants.* Paris: Albin Michel, 1977.

Tiburzi, Bonnie. *Take Off: The Story of America's First Woman Pilot for a Major Airline.* New York: Crown, 1984.

Toland, John. *Flying Tigers.* New York: Random House, 1963.

Townsend, Peter. *Duel of Eagles.* New York: Random House, 1963.

Trotti, John. *Marine Air: First to Fight.* New York: Berkeley Books, 1985.

Tunner, William. *Over the Hump.* Washington, DC: Office of Air Force History, 1965, 1985.

Van Mises, Richard. *Theory of Flight.* New Brunswick, NJ: Rutgers University, 1945 (Dover, 1959).

Vaughan, Diane. *The Challenger Launch Decision: Risky Technology, Culture and Deviance at NASA.* Chicago: University of Chicago, 1996.

Verges, Marianne. *On Silver Wings.* New York: Ballantine, 1991.

Verne, Jules. *De la Terre à la Lune.* Paris, 1865.

Villard, Henry Serrano. *Contact: The Story of the Early Birds—Man's First Decade of Flight from Kitty Hawk to World War I.* Washington, DC: Smithsonian Institution, 1987.

Vines, Mike. *Wind in the Wires: The Golden Era of Flight, 1909–1939.* Osceola, WI: Motorbooks, 1995.

Von Braun, Wernher, and Frederick I. Orway III. *History of Rocketry and Space Travel.* New York: Crowell, 1967.

Walker, Bryce S. *Fighting Jets.* Alexandria, VA: Time-Life, 1983.

Ware, Susan. *Still Missing: Amelia Earhart and the Searach for Modern Feminism.* New York: Norton, 1993.

Webb, Jim. *Fly the Wing.* Ames: Iowa State University, 1990.

Wilford, John Noble. *We Reach the Moon.* New York: Bantam, 1969.

Wohl, Robert. *A Passion for Wings: Aviation and the Western Imagination, 1908–1918.* New Haven, CT: Yale University, 1994.

Wolfe, Tom. *The Right Stuff.* New York: Farrar, Straus and Giroux, 1979.

Wood, W. Raymond. *Or Go Down in Flame: A Navigator's Death Over Schweinfurt.* New York: Sarpedon, 1994.

Wright, Orville (FAA, Michael E. Wayda, ed.). *How We Made the First Flight.*

Yeager, General Chuck, and Leo Janos. *Yeager: An Autobiography.* New York: Bantam, 1985.

Yeager, Jeana, and Dick Rutan, with Phil Patton. *Voyager.* New York: Harper & Row, 1987.

Yenne, Bill. *The History of the U.S. Air Force.* New York: Exeter, 1984.

Index